Networking:
A Beginner's Guide,
Fifth Edition

BRUCE **HALLBERG**

New York Chicago San Francisco
Lisbon London Madrid Mexico City Milan
New Delhi San Juan Seoul Singapore Sydney Toronto

The McGraw·Hill Companies

Cataloging-in-Publication Data is on file with the Library of Congress

McGraw-Hill books are available at special quantity discounts to use as premiums and sales promotions, or for use in corporate training programs. To contact a representative, please e-mail us at bulksales@mcgraw-hill.com.

Networking: A Beginner's Guide, Fifth Edition

1234567890   DOC DOC   019

ISBN   978-0-07-163355-0
MHID   0-07-163355-3

Sponsoring Editor Jane K. Brownlow	**Technical Editor** Bruno Whittle	**Production Supervisor** Jean Bodeaux
Editorial Supervisor Patty Mon	**Copy Editor** Marilyn Smith	**Composition** Glyph International
Project Manager Ekta Dixit, Glyph International	**Proofreader** Carol Shields	**Illustration** Glyph International
Acquisitions Coordinator Joya Anthony	**Indexer** Robert Swanson	**Art Director, Cover** Jeff Weeks

For my daughters, Vivian and Maxine,
of whom I am extraordinarily proud.

About the Author

Bruce Hallberg has been involved in information technology (IT) for more than 25 years and has consulted for Fortune 1000 firms on the implementation of management information and networking systems. He is the best-selling author of more than 20 books.

About the Technical Editor

Bruno Whittle has administered voice and data networks for almost 10 years. He was delighted at the opportunity to be part of a rewarding experience of sharing this knowledge with the many people who are interested in learning more about networking. Bruno is currently an IT systems consultant, and most recently was the IT Systems Manager at Genelabs Technologies, Inc. in Redwood City, California. He is immensely dedicated to continued learning, but he ensures that his wife Reena and his pride and joys—Sonali, Shane, and Stanley—are always his first priority.

Contents

Part I

Networking Ins and Outs

Part II

Hands-on Knowledge

Acknowledgments

Jane Brownlow was the Sponsoring Editor for this book, which means that she ran the overall show. I have known Jane for over 10 years now, and I continue to be delighted to work with her. Also, Jane, thank you for cutting me some slack on the schedule!

Joya Anthony was the Acquisitions Coordinator for the book. This is a really tough job, and is essentially the project manager for the book. It involves keeping all of the parts of the book moving forward, knowing where all the chapters are at any given time, and occasionally politely reminding authors (ahem) that they need to get cracking on getting some work done and turned in.

The Technical Editor for this fifth edition was Bruno Whittle. Technical editors read the entire book as its being written, and ensure that it is technically accurate. When there are steps involved, they repeat them to ensure that you, the reader, can also successfully duplicate them. I have worked with Bruno for more than 15 years. He is a remarkable individual and helped improve this book in important ways.

Introduction

have run into many people over the years who have gained good—even impressive—working knowledge of PCs, operating systems, applications, and common problems and solutions. Many of these people are wizards with desktop computers. However, quite a few of them have been unable to make the transition into working with networks; they have had trouble gaining the requisite knowledge to conceptualize, understand, install, administer, and troubleshoot networks. In many cases, this inability limits their career growth, because most companies believe networking experience is fundamental to holding higher-level information technology (IT) positions. And, in fact, networking experience *is* very important.

Certainly, networks can be complicated beasts. To add to the difficulty, most companies are not willing to let people unskilled with networks experiment and learn about them using the company's production network! This leaves the networking beginner in the difficult position of having to learn about networks in the following ways:

- Reading an endless number of books and articles
- Attending classes
- Building small experimental networks at home, using cobbled-together and/or borrowed parts and software

This book is designed for people who understand computers and the rudiments of computer science, but who want to begin an education about networks and networking. I assume you understand and are comfortable with the following topics:

- How bits and bytes work

- The notion of binary, octal, decimal, and hexadecimal notation

- How basic PC hardware works, and how to install and replace PC peripheral components

- Two or three desktop operating systems in detail, such as Windows, Macintosh, Linux or UNIX, and maybe even DOS (or the Windows command prompt)

- Detailed knowledge of a wide variety of application software

The purpose of this book is both to educate and familiarize. The first part of the book discusses basic networking technology and hardware. Its goal is to help you understand the fundamental components of networking, so you can build a conceptual framework into which you can fit knowledge that is more detailed in your chosen area of expertise. The second part of the book is concerned with familiarizing you with two important network operating systems: Windows Server 2008 and Fedora Linux. In the second part, you learn the basics of setting up and administering these network operating systems.

This book is meant to be a springboard from which you can start pursuing more detailed knowledge in the areas that interest you. Following are some ideas about areas that you may wish to continue exploring, depending on your career goals:

- **Small-to-medium network administrator**   If you plan on building and administering networks with 200 or fewer users, you should extend your knowledge by studying the network operating systems you intend to use, server hardware, client PC administration, and network management. You may find more detailed knowledge of network hardware, like routers, bridges, gateways, switches, and the like to be useful, but these may not be an important focus for you.

- **Large network administrator**   If you plan on working with networks with more than 200 users, then you need to pursue detailed knowledge about TCP/IP addressing and routing and network hardware, including routers, bridges, gateways, switches, and firewalls. Also, in large networks, administrators tend to specialize in certain areas, so you should consider several areas of particular specialization, such as e-mail servers like Lotus Notes or Microsoft Exchange, or database servers like Oracle or SQL Server.

- **Internet administrator**   Many people these days are pursuing specialization in Internet-based technologies. Depending on the area you want to work in, you should learn more about web and FTP servers, HTTP and other application-level Internet protocols, CGI and other web scripting technologies, HTML design, and SMTP mail connections. You may also want to become an expert in TCP/IP and all its related protocols, addressing rules, and routing techniques.

■ **End-user support**   If your primary job is supporting end users, perhaps with application or client computer support, you may still benefit from a deeper understanding of networking. Client computer applications usually interact with the network, and understanding networks will undoubtedly help you be more effective.

If you are working toward getting a job in the field of networking, I suggest that you find job postings on the Internet and carefully study the job requirements. This can be a useful technique to direct your studies appropriately. When you do this, you will notice that for their most important jobs, most employers ask for people who are certified by Microsoft, Cisco, Novell, or other companies.

You should seriously consider pursuing an appropriate certification. While certifications can never replace experience, they are one way that a person can demonstrate a needed level of knowledge and expertise in a particular area. This difference may be key in getting the best possible job offers and in being able to gain more experience. Often, an appropriate certification can be worth several years' experience in terms of compensation and job responsibilities, so it is an investment in yourself that will usually pay for itself over a fairly short period of time.

Part I

Networking Ins and Outs

Chapter 1

The Business of Networking

This book is a soup-to-nuts beginner's guide to networking. Before delving into the bits and bytes of networking, which are covered in the rest of the book, you should start by understanding the whys and wherefores of networking.

This chapter discusses networking from a business perspective. You'll learn about the benefits that networking brings a company and the different types of networking jobs available. You'll also discover how networks are supported from the business perspective, and how you can begin a career in networking. Finally, you'll learn about the Sarbanes-Oxley Act of 2002 and how its requirements affect networking professionals.

Understanding Networking: The Corporate Perspective

To be truly effective in the field of networking, you need to start by understanding networking from the corporate perspective. Why are networks important to companies? What do they accomplish for the company? How can networking professionals more clearly meet the needs of the company with the networks that they build and maintain? It's important to realize that there are no single correct answers to these questions. Every company will have different needs and expectations with regard to their network. What is important is that you learn the relevant questions to ask about networking for your company and arrive at the best possible answers to those questions for your particular company. Doing so will ensure that the company's network best meets its needs.

What Does the Company Need?

There are many possible reasons that a company might need or benefit from a network. In order to understand your particular company, you should start by exploring the following questions. You may need to ask a variety of different people in the company their perspective on these questions. Some of the managers that you may need to interview include the chief executive officer or owner, the chief financial officer, and the heads of the various key departments within the company, such as manufacturing, sales and marketing, accounting, purchasing and materials, retail operations, and so forth. The range of managers that you interview will depend on the type of business in which the company is engaged.

It's important that you first start by understanding the business itself and the business-oriented perspectives of these different individuals and the people in their departments. Consider the following questions for each of these key areas of the organization:

- What is their function for the company?
- How do their objectives tie into the company objectives?
- What are the key goals for their function in the coming year? How about in the coming five years?
- What do they see as the chief challenges to overcome in achieving their objectives?

■ How might information technology (IT) play a role in supporting their objectives?

■ What sorts of automation do they think might help them accomplish their objectives?

■ How is the work in their area accomplished? For instance, do most of the employees do mechanical work, like on a production line, or are most of them so-called "knowledge workers" who generate documents, analyze information, and so forth?

■ What are the key inputs for the functional area, in terms of information or materials, and what are the key outputs for the functional area? What processes convert the inputs into the outputs?

Your objective in asking these questions, and others that may occur to you, is to get a good understanding of each functional area: what it does and how it does it, as well as what it wants to be able to do in the future. With this knowledge, you can then start to analyze the impact that the network—or improvements to the existing network— might have in those various areas.

Beginning from a business perspective is absolutely essential. Networks are not built and improved "just because." Instead, any particular network or network upgrade needs to be driven by the needs of the business. Justifications for networks or improvements to existing networks should clearly show how they are necessary to the proper functioning of the business, or how they will play an important role in the company achieving its objectives, consistent with the cost and effort involved.

How Will the Network Benefit the Company?

After getting a good understanding of the company, its objectives, and how it accomplishes its work, you can then analyze different ideas that you may have for the network, and how those ideas will benefit some or all parts of the business. In doing so, you need to consider at least the following areas:

■ Are there any areas in which the lack of a network, or some failing of the existing network, is inhibiting the company from realizing its goals or accomplishing its work? For example, if an existing network is undersized and this causes people to waste too much time on routine tasks (such as saving or sending files, or compiling programs), what improvements might address those shortcomings? Or maybe the network and its servers are unreliable, and so people are frequently losing their work or are unproductive while problems are addressed.

■ Are there capabilities that you could add to the network that would provide benefits to the business? For example, if many people in the company are constantly sending faxes (for instance, salespeople sending price quotations to customers), would adding a network-based fax system produce significant productivity benefits? What about other network-based applications? (Chapter 3 lists some common network features that you may want to review to help in answering this question.)

- What other automation plans exist that will require the support of the network? For example, say you're the network administrator in a company. What new applications or features will be added to the network that you need to support? Is the company planning on installing some kind of videoconferencing system, for instance? If so, do you know what changes you will need to make to the network to support the system?

- What needs to be done to the network simply to maintain it? In most companies, file space requirements grow rapidly, even if the business itself isn't expanding. How much additional storage space does the network need to keep going forward? How many additional servers and other components will be needed to keep the network working smoothly?

Obviously, a list such as the preceding one can't be exhaustive. The important point is that you need to approach the job of networking first from the perspective of the company and its needs. Within that framework, use your creativity, knowledge, experience, and business and technical acumen to propose and execute a plan for the network. The remainder of this book discusses the information you need to start learning about this important part of any company's infrastructure.

Understanding Networking Jobs

If you're planning on entering the field of networking (and this book is designed as a good start for that), it's important to have some understanding of the various networking jobs that you're likely to encounter and what they typically require. Of course, actual job requirements will vary widely between companies and for different established networks. Also, companies may have different entry-level opportunities through which you can enter a networking career. That said, the following descriptions are broad overviews of some key jobs.

Network Administrator

Network administrators are responsible for the operations of a network or, in larger companies, for the operations of key parts of the network. In a smaller company that has only one network administrator, duties include the following:

- Creating, maintaining, and removing user accounts
- Ensuring that necessary backups are made on a regular basis
- Managing the "keys" to the network, such as the administrative accounts and their passwords
- Managing network security policies
- Adding new networking equipment, such as servers, routers, hubs, and switches, and managing that equipment

- Monitoring the network, its hardware, and its software for potential problems and for utilization levels for planning network upgrades

- Troubleshooting network problems

Network administrators may also be called system administrators, LAN administrators, and other variations on that theme.

Typically, you should have several years' experience performing network-related duties with a similar network for this job. Certifications such as the Microsoft Certified Systems Engineer (MCSE), Microsoft Certified Systems Administrator (MCSA), or one of the appropriate CompTIA certifications can reduce the amount of experience that an employer will require. Employers usually consider these certifications important, because they clearly establish that a candidate meets minimum requirements for the networking system in question.

TIP   The Computing Technology Industry Association (CompTIA) offers a number of different vendor-neutral certifications that can help you enter the field of networking. You can learn more about them at http://certification.comptia.org/.

Network Engineer

Network engineers are more deeply involved in the bits and bytes of a network. They are expected to be expert in the network operating systems with which they work, especially in the network's key hardware, such as its hubs, routers, switches, and so forth. Network engineers are also usually the troubleshooters of last resort, who are brought in to diagnose and fix the most vexing problems that surpass the ability of the network administrator to resolve.

Aside from often holding a degree in electrical engineering or computer science, network engineers typically have at least five years' experience running and trouble-shooting complex networks. Also, network engineers typically carry certifications from networking equipment companies, such as Cisco's well-regarded certification program.

TIP   Learn more about Cisco's certification programs at http://www.cisco.com.

Network Architect/Designer

Network architects (sometimes also called network designers) usually work for companies that sell and support networks or for organizations with large networks that are constantly changing and expanding. Essentially, network architects design networks. They need to combine important qualities to be successful. They must know the business requirements that the network needs to meet and have a thorough understanding of all of the networking products available, as well as how those products interact. Network architects are also important when growing a sophisticated network and helping to ensure that new additions to the network don't cause problems elsewhere in the network.

Other Network-Related Jobs

There are a wide variety of other network-related jobs, including some that do not involve working directly with the network, such as the job of database administrator. Organizations employ e-mail administrators, webmasters, web designers, network support technicians, and so on. In fact, a dizzying number of different jobs are available in the networking field.

If you've chosen to enter the field of networking, it would make sense to spend time browsing job ads for the various networking jobs and to get a sense of what these different types of jobs require. Once you find one that reflects your interests, you can then analyze what additional skills, classes, or certifications you may need to enter one of those jobs. Many opportunities are available. The important thing is to get started and pursue your objectives.

Sarbanes-Oxley Act of 2002

You may be wondering what a law that was passed by the U.S. Congress has to do with the field of networking, and why it's discussed in this book. The reason is that this law has an important impact on the networks of all public companies, and so it's important for you to understand what all the fuss is about.

The Sarbanes-Oxley Act of 2002 (usually referred to as SOX, pronounced "socks") was an act sponsored by Senator Sarbanes and Representative Oxley in response to the many cases of corporate wrongdoing that preceded it, such as Enron, Global Crossing, Arthur Andersen, Tyco, and others. The act makes sweeping changes to a number of areas of corporate governance and accounting. One change in particular is likely to impact most networking professionals, especially those involved in day-to-day network operations, such as network administrators.

Section 404 of the act places new requirements on public companies to annually assess their system of internal controls, and on their outside auditors to examine the company's internal controls and to attest to the effectiveness of the company's internal controls over the company's use and reporting of financial information. This may sound like a requirement that pertains only to accounting departments, and in fact, it mostly does. However, accounting internal controls rely heavily on network system controls—in particular, those system controls that impact important systems the company uses for managing and reporting financial information.

Generally, outside auditors classify company systems as being either within the scope of their audit ("in scope") or outside the scope of their audit. Systems that are in scope include the company's accounting system, payroll system, stock administration system, materials management system, shipping system, billing system, banking system, and so forth. The computers and all related hardware and software that perform those functions, or host, or run the software that performs those functions are also in scope. Additionally, other network operations that support those systems may also be in scope, such as the network-wide password settings, backup and restore procedures, new and terminated user account management, and so forth.

Accordingly, network administrators for publicly traded companies will need to work closely with their accounting departments to comply with the SOX 404 requirements on an ongoing basis. Doing so will include activities such as the following:

- Documentation of all user account creation, maintenance, and deactivation activities, including appropriate sign-offs for new, changed, and terminated users of in-scope systems

- Creation of a change-control system for any system that the company modifies from time to time, such as an accounting system for which the company uses custom-developed reports or processing programs

- Documentation of the security settings of the network

- Documentation of the security settings and user account and password management of the in-scope systems

- Documentation of routine maintenance activities for in-scope systems

- Collaboration with the accounting staff and the auditors to prove that all of the controls that are in place are being followed, without exceptions

- Creation and maintenance of systems (even manual procedural systems) to detect unauthorized changes to any in-scope systems

Obviously, a book about networking cannot fully address all of the factors involved in Sarbanes-Oxley compliance. You should, however, have a general idea of what it is and what is involved. The accounting professionals charged with this important requirement will have more detailed information about the exact steps required for your company.

Chapter Summary

Many people I've met who work in some area of information technology, such as networking, don't consider the business reasons for the network when they go about their day-to-day jobs or when they propose improvements to the network. This certainly isn't limited to the field of networking; many people who work in any area of a company sometimes forget that the reason their function exists is to support the objectives of the company in which they work. The most successful employees of any company keep firmly in mind why they do what they do, before they consider how best to do it. Some of the suggestions in this chapter should help you to approach managing and improving a network successfully, by keeping in mind the benefits the network brings to the company. Once you know what the company needs, you can then propose the best solutions to solve problems that arise or make appropriate improvements to the network.

This chapter also discussed several broad areas you might consider pursuing in the field of networking. Demand for trained, capable networking people is extremely high, salaries are top-notch, and people working in the networking field have jobs that are—more than most—fun, stimulating, and rewarding in many ways.

Finally, you learned a little about the Sarbanes-Oxley Act of 2002 and how it impacts networking professionals.

The next chapter starts exploring the technical details of networking by briefly discussing some basic computer science concepts that you need to understand. If you already know about different numbering systems and about how data rates are measured, you can probably skip the next chapter and move on to the networking topics that follow, although be warned that you need a strong grasp of how binary numbers work to understand some of the discussion surrounding network protocols in Chapter 8.

Chapter 2

Laying the Foundation

Y ou don't need to have a Ph.D. in computer science to be an effective networking person, but you do need to understand some rudiments of the subject. This chapter discusses basic computer terminology and knowledge that you should possess to make the information in the rest of the book more useful and understandable.

If you've been working with computers for a while, and especially if you have training or experience as a computer programmer, you might not need to read this chapter in detail. However, it is a good idea to at least skim it, to make sure that you understand these subjects thoroughly.

Bits, Nibbles, and Bytes

Most people know that computers, at their most fundamental level, work entirely using only 1s and 0s for numbers. Each of these numbers (whether it is a 0 or 1) is called a *bit*, which is short for *binary digit*. String eight bits together, and you have a byte; string about 1,000 bits together, and you have a *kilobit*; or you can string about 1,000 bytes together for a *kilobyte*. A rarely used unit is composed of four bits strung together, called a *nibble*. Remember this for when you play *Jeopardy*!

Understanding Binary Numbers

Before you learn about binary numbers, it's useful to recall a few things about the numbering system that people use on a daily basis. This is called the *decimal numbering system* or, alternatively, the *base-10 numbering system*. The decimal numbering system is built using ten different symbols, each of which represents a quantity from zero to nine. Therefore, ten possible digits can be used: 0 through 9. (The base-10 numbering system gets its name from the fact that only ten digits are possible in the system.)

An important part of any numbering system is the use of *positions* in which the numerical symbols can be placed. Each position confers a different quantity to the number being represented in that position. Therefore, the number 10 in the decimal system represents the quantity ten. There is a 1 in the *tens position* and a 0 in the *ones position*. This can also be represented as (1×10) + (0×1). Now consider the number 541. This number uses the *hundreds position* as well as the tens and ones positions. It can be represented as (5×100) + (4×10) + (1×1). In English, you could state this number as five hundred plus forty plus one.

Every written number has a *least-significant digit* and a *most-significant digit*. The least-significant digit is the one farthest to the right, and the most-significant digit is the one farthest to the left. For binary numbers, people also talk about the least- and most-significant bits, but it's the same idea.

So far, this section has simply reviewed basic number knowledge that you learned in grade school. What grade school probably didn't cover is the fact that basing a numbering system on ten is completely arbitrary; there is no mathematical reason to favor a base-10 system over any other. You can create numbering systems for any base you like. You can have a base-3 numbering system, a base-11 numbering system, and so on. Humans have come to favor the base-10 system, probably because we have ten fingers and thus tend to think in tens. Computers, on the other hand, have only two digits with which they can work—1 and 0—so they need to use a different numbering system. The natural numbering system for a computer to use would therefore be the base-2 numbering system, and, in fact, that's what they do use. This system is called the *binary numbering system*. Computers use only 1s and 0s at their most basic level because they understand only two states: on and off. In the binary numbering system, a 1 represents on, and a 0 represents off.

Recall that in the decimal numbering system, the position of each number is important. It is the same in the binary numbering system, except that each position doesn't correspond to powers of 10, but instead to powers of 2. Here are the values of the lowest eight positions used in the binary numbering system:

| 128 | 64 | 32 | 16 | 8 | 4 | 2 | 1 |

So, suppose that you encounter the following binary number:

| 1 | 0 | 1 | 0 | 1 | 1 | 0 | 1 |

You would follow the same steps that you use to understand a decimal numbering system number. In this example, the binary number represents $128 + 32 + 8 + 4 + 1$, or 173 in the decimal system. You can also write (or calculate) this number as follows:

$$(128 \times 1) + (64 \times 0) + (32 \times 1) + (16 \times 0) + (8 \times 1) + (4 \times 1) + (2 \times 0) + (1 \times 1)$$

So, two main things separate the decimal numbering system from the binary numbering system:

- The binary system uses only 1s and 0s to represent every value.
- The value of numerals in the different positions varies.

You might be wondering how you can tell whether you're reading a binary number or a decimal number. For instance, if you're reading a book about computers and you see the number 10101, how do you know whether it's supposed to represent ten thousand one hundred and one or twenty-one? There are several ways that you can tell:

- Usually, binary numbers are shown with at least eight positions (a full byte), even if the leading digits are 0s.
- If you're looking at a bunch of numbers and see only 1s and 0s, it's a pretty good bet that they are binary numbers.
- Binary numbers don't use the decimal point to represent fractional values, so 10100.01 should be assumed to be a decimal system number.

- ■ Decimal numbers should use commas as you were taught in school. So, the number 10,100 should be read as ten thousand one hundred, whereas the number 10100 should be read as the binary number for the quantity twenty.

- ■ Sometimes people put the letter *b* at the end of a binary number, although this convention isn't widely followed.

Put all these things together, plus a little common sense, and you'll usually have no doubt whether you're reading a binary or decimal value.

Other Important Numbering Systems

Two other important numbering systems that you encounter in the world of networking are octal and hexadecimal. Hexadecimal is far more prevalent than octal, but you should understand both.

The octal number system is also called the base-8 numbering system. In this scheme, each position in a number can hold only the numerals 0 to 7. The number 010 in the octal numbering system corresponds to 8 in the decimal numbering system. Octal numbers can be indicated with a leading zero, a leading percent symbol (%), or a trailing capital letter *O*.

The hexadecimal numbering system is fairly common in networking, and is often used to represent network addresses, memory addresses, and the like. The hexadecimal system (also called the base-16 numbering system) can use 16 different symbols in each of its positions. Since we have written numerals for only 0 to 9, the hexadecimal system uses the letters *A* through *F* to represent the extra symbols.

How to Quickly Convert Hexadecimal, Decimal, Octal, and Binary Numbers

The Calculator application that comes with all versions of Windows allows you to convert values quickly between hexadecimal, decimal, octal, and binary. With the calculator open, place it into Scientific mode (open the View menu and choose Scientific). This mode reveals a lot of advanced features in the calculator. In the upper-left area of the calculator, you can now see four option buttons labeled Hex, Dec, Oct, and Bin. These correspond to the hexadecimal, decimal, octal, and binary numbering systems. Just choose which system you want to use to enter a number, and then click any of the other options to convert the number instantly.

For instance, suppose that you click the Bin option button and enter the number 110100100110111010. If you then click the Dec button, the calculator reveals that the number you just entered is 215,482 in the decimal system. If you click the Hex button, you find that the binary number that you entered is 349BA in the hexadecimal numbering system. And if you click the Oct button, you discover that the number is 644672 in the octal numbering system. You can also go in the other direction: Click the Dec button, enter some number, and then click the other option buttons to see how the number looks in those other numbering systems.

Hexadecimal numbers are usually preceded with a leading zero followed by the letter x, and then the hexadecimal number. The letter x can be either lowercase or uppercase, so both 0x11AB and 0X11AB are correct. Hexadecimal numbers may also be shown with a trailing letter h, which can be lowercase or uppercase. Rarely, they may be preceded with the dollar sign ($), as in $11AB. Often, you can easily recognize hexadecimal numbers simply by the fact that they include some letters (A to F). For hexadecimal numbers, A equals 10 in the decimal system, B equals 11, C equals 12, D equals 13, E equals 14, and F equals 15.

You can determine the decimal value for a hexadecimal value manually using the same method as shown earlier in this chapter for decimal and binary numbers. The hexadecimal position values for the first four digits are as follows:

4096   256   16   1

So, the number 0x11AB can be converted to decimal with the formula $(1 \times 4096) + (1 \times 256) + (10 \times 16) + (11 \times 1)$, or 4,523 in decimal.

Basic Terminology to Describe Networking Speeds

The business of networking is almost entirely about moving data from one point to another. Accordingly, one of the most important things that you need to understand about any network connection is how much data it can carry. Broadly, this capacity is called *bandwidth*, which is measured by the amount of data that a connection can carry in a given period of time.

The most basic measurement of bandwidth is *bits per second*, abbreviated as *bps*. Bandwidth is how many bits the connection can carry within a second. More commonly used are various multiples of this measurement, including thousands of bits per second (Kbps), millions of bits per second (Mbps), or billions of bits per second (Gbps).

 TIP Remember that bits per second is not bytes per second. To arrive at the bytes per second when you know the bits per second (approximately), divide the bps number by 8. In this book, bits per second units are written with a lowercase letter *b* and bytes per second units with an uppercase *B*. For example, 56 Kbps is 56 thousand bits per second, and 56 KBps is 56 thousand bytes per second.

A closely related measurement that you will also see bandied about is *hertz*, which is the number of cycles being carried per second. Hertz is abbreviated as *Hz*. Just as with *bps*, it is the multiples of hertz that are talked about the most, including thousands of hertz (KHz, or kilohertz) and millions of mertz (MHz, or megahertz). For example, a microprocessor running at 100 MHz is running at 100 million cycles per second. The electricity in the United States runs at 60 Hz; in Europe, the speed is 50 Hz.

Hertz and bits per second are essentially the same and are sometimes intermixed. For example, thin Ethernet cable is said to run at 10 MHz and also to carry 10 Mbps of bandwidth.

Chapter Summary

This book would double in size if I tried to explain every networking term every time it was used. To keep it at a reasonable length (and readable), I assume that you understand the basic concepts presented in this chapter, as well as the information found in the glossary near the end of the book. Most people leave glossaries unread until they come across a term they don't know. In this case, I recommend that you spend a few minutes reviewing this book's glossary before you read the following chapters, to make sure that you are familiar with the terms that are used. *Node, host, broadband, baseband, workstation, client*, and *server* are some examples of terms that the rest of the book assumes that you understand. The glossary defines these terms and many others.

In the next chapter, you learn about the basic types of networks, as well as an important conceptual model of networking that you will frequently encounter when working with networks: the Open Systems Interconnection (OSI) model. The OSI model is used in virtually every aspect of networking, and it provides a framework for how networks operate.

Chapter 3

Understanding Networking

There are *a lot* of aspects to networking, and this tends to make the subject seem more complex than it really is. This chapter discusses some basic and key networking concepts. If you're new to networking, getting a good understanding of the subjects in this chapter will enable you to build a mental framework into which you can fit more detailed knowledge as it is presented in the remainder of this book. In addition, the rest of this book assumes you're comfortable with all the concepts presented in this chapter.

Knowing Network Relationship Types

The term *network relationships* refers to how one computer makes use of another computer's resources over the network. Two fundamental types of network relationships exist: peer-to-peer and client/server. These two types of network relationships define the logical structure of a network. To understand them better, you might compare them to different business management philosophies. A *peer-to-peer network* is much like a company with a decentralized management philosophy, where decisions are made locally and resources are managed according to the most immediate needs. A *client/server network* is more like a company that uses centralized management, where decisions are made in a central location by a relatively small group of people. Circumstances exist where both peer-to-peer and client/server relationships are appropriate, and many networks incorporate aspects of both types.

Both peer-to-peer and client/server networks require certain network *layers*. Both types require a physical network connection between the computers, use of the same network protocols, and so forth. In these respects, the two types of network relationships are the same. The difference comes in whether you spread the shared network resources around to all the computers on the network or use centralized network servers.

 NOTE   The mechanics of how a network actually functions are broken down into layers. The concept of layers and what goes into each layer are described later in this chapter, in the "Understanding the OSI Networking Model" section.

Peer-to-Peer Network Relationships

In a peer-to-peer network relationship, the computers on the network communicate with each other as equals. Each computer is responsible for making its own resources available to other computers on the network. These resources might be files, directories, application programs, devices (such as printers, modems, or fax cards), or any combination of these items. Each computer is also responsible for setting up and maintaining its own security for those resources. Additionally, each computer

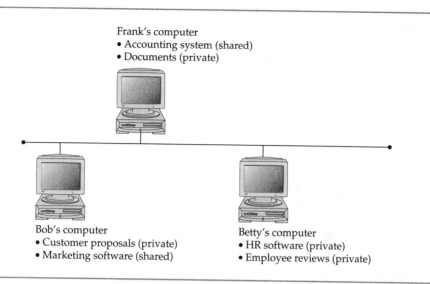

Figure 3-1.   A peer-to-peer network with resources spread across computers

is responsible for accessing the network resources it needs from other peer-to-peer computers, knowing where those resources are located in the network, and handling the security required to access them. Figure 3-1 illustrates how this works.

NOTE   Even in a pure peer-to-peer network, using a dedicated computer for certain frequently accessed resources is possible. For example, you might host the application and data files for an accounting system on a single workstation, and not use that computer for typical workstation tasks, such as word processing, so that all of the computer's performance is available for the accounting system. The computer is still working in a peer-to-peer fashion; it's just used for a single purpose.

Client/Server Network Relationships

In a client/server network relationship, a distinction exists between the computers that make available network resources (the *servers*) and the computers that use the resources (the *clients*, or *workstations*). A pure client/server network is one in which *all* available network resources—such as files, directories, applications, and shared devices—are centrally managed and hosted, and then are accessed by the client computers. None of the client computers share their resources with other client computers or with the servers. Instead, the client computers are pure consumers of these shared network resources.

NOTE   Don't confuse client/server networks with client/server database systems. While the two mean essentially the same thing (conceptually), a client/server database is one where the processing of the database application is divided between the database server and the database clients. The server is responsible for responding to data requests from the clients and supplying them with the appropriate data, while the clients are responsible for formatting, displaying, and printing that data for the user. For instance, Windows Server 2008 is a client/server network operating system, while Oracle's database or Microsoft's SQL Server are client/server database systems.

The server computers in a client/server network are responsible for making available and managing appropriate shared resources, and for administering the security of those resources. Figure 3-2 shows how resources would be located in such a network.

Comparing Peer-to-Peer and Client/Server Networks

As mentioned earlier, most networks have aspects of both peer-to-peer and client/server relationships. Before deciding on setting up a network using one or both types of relationships, you should examine their pros and cons and determine how each meets the needs of your company. Consider the following advantages and disadvantages of using each type.

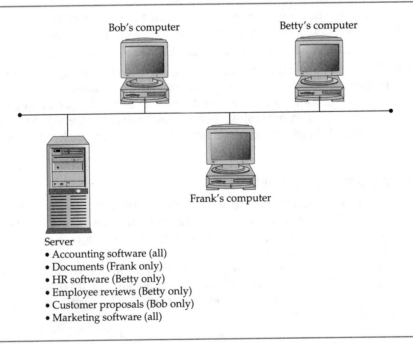

Figure 3-2.   A client/server network keeps resources centralized

Pros for Peer-to-Peer Networks

Peer-to-peer networks offer a number of advantages, particularly for smaller firms, as follows:

- **Use less expensive computer hardware**   Peer-to-peer networks are the least hardware-intensive. In a pure peer-to-peer network, the resources are distributed over many computers, so there is no need for a high-end server computer. The impact on each workstation is usually (but not always) relatively minor.

- **Easy to administer**   Peer-to-peer networks are, overall, easiest to set up and administer, provided that there aren't too many computers within the peer-to-peer network. Because each machine performs its own administration—usually for certain limited resources—the effort of administering the network is widely distributed among many different people.

- **No network operating system required**   Peer-to-peer networks do not require a network operating system (NOS). You can build a peer-to-peer network using Windows XP or Vista on all the workstations, or all Macintosh computers for that matter. These client operating systems include all the features necessary for peer-to-peer networking. Similarly, you can do this with all UNIX-or Linux-based computers (although this is much more complicated to set up and maintain, because UNIX and Linux are very powerful and complex).

- **More built-in redundancy**   If you have a small network, with 10 to 20 workstations each storing some important data, and one fails, you still have most of your shared resources available. A peer-to-peer network design can offer more redundancy than a client/server network because fewer single points of failure can affect the entire network and everyone who uses it.

Cons for Peer-to-Peer Networks

There are also various drawbacks to peer-to-peer networks, particularly for larger networks or for networks that have more complex or sophisticated requirements. The disadvantages include the following:

- **Might impact user's performance**   If some workstations have frequently used resources on them, the use of these resources across the network might adversely affect the person using the hosting workstation.

- **Not very secure**   Peer-to-peer networks are not nearly as secure as client/ server networks because you cannot guarantee that all of the users will appropriately administer their machines. In fact, in a network of any size (say, more than ten people), you can expect that at least a few people will not follow good administration practices on their own machines. Moreover, the most common desktop operating systems used for peer-to-peer networking, like Windows XP or the Macintosh, are not designed to be secure network operating systems.

- **Difficult to back up**   Reliably backing up all the data scattered over many workstations is difficult, and it is not wise to delegate this job to the user of each machine. Experience shows that leaving this vital task up to users means it will not get done.

- **Hard to maintain version control**   In a peer-to-peer network, with files potentially stored on a number of different machines, it can become extremely difficult to manage different document versions.

Pros for Client/Server Networks

Client/server networks offer the opportunity for centralized administration, using equipment suited to managing and offering each resource. Client/server networks are the type commonly used for networks larger than about ten users, and there are quite a few good reasons for this, as follows:

- **Very secure**   A client/server network's security comes from several things. First, because the shared resources are located in a centralized area, they can be administered at that point. Managing a number of resources is much easier if those resources are all located on one or two server computers, as opposed to needing to administer resources across tens or hundreds of computers. Second, usually the servers are physically in a secure location, such as a lockable server room. Physical security is an important aspect of network security, and it cannot be achieved with a peer-to-peer network. Third, the operating systems on which client/server networks run are designed to be secure. Provided that good security and administration practices are in place, the servers cannot be easily "hacked."

- **Better performance**   While dedicated server computers are more expensive than standard computer workstations, they also offer considerably better performance, and they are optimized to handle the needs of many users simultaneously.

- **Centralized backup**   Backing up a company's critical data is much easier when it is located on a centralized server. Often, such backup jobs can be run overnight when the server is not being used and the data is static. Aside from being easier, centralized backups are also much faster than decentralized backups.

- **Very reliable**   While it is true that more built-in redundancy exists with a peer-to-peer network, a good client/server network can be more reliable overall. Dedicated servers often have much more built-in redundancy than standard workstations. They can handle the failure of a disk drive, power supply, or processor and continue to operate until the failed component can be replaced. Also, because a dedicated server has only one relatively simple job to do, its complexity is reduced and its reliability increased. Contrast this with a peer-to-peer network, where actions on the part of the users can drastically reduce each workstation's reliability. For example, needing to restart a PC or a Macintosh every so often is not uncommon, whereas dedicated servers often run for months without requiring a restart or crashing.

Cons for Client/Server Networks

Client/server networks have some drawbacks, particularly for companies that don't have their own in-house network administration or that want to minimize the expense of the network as much as possible. The following are the disadvantages of client/ server networks:

- **Require professional administration**   Client/server networks usually need some level of professional administration, even if they are small. Knowing the ins and outs of a network operating system is important, and requires experience and training. You can hire a network administrator, or you can use a company that provides professional network administration services.

- **More hardware-intensive**   In addition to the client computers, you also need a server computer, usually a pretty "beefy" computer with a lot of memory and disk space. Plus, you need a network operating system and an appropriate number of client licenses, which can add at least several thousand dollars to the cost of the server. For large networks, these requirements add tens of thousands of dollars.

In a nutshell, choose a peer-to-peer network for smaller networks with fewer than 10 to 15 users, and choose a client/server network for anything larger. Because most networks are built on a client/server concept, this book generally assumes such a network.

Learning Network Features

Now that you know the two basic ways computers on a network can interact with each other, let's look at the types of tasks you can do with a network. The following sections discuss common network features and capabilities.

File Sharing

Originally, file sharing was the primary reason to have a network. In fact, small and midsize companies in the mid-1980s usually installed networks just so they could perform this function. Often, this was driven by the need to computerize their accounting systems. Of course, once the networks were in place, sharing other types of files became easier as well.

File sharing typically involves word processing files, spreadsheets, and other files to which many people needed regular access. It requires a shared directory or disk drive that many users can access over the network, along with the underlying programming logic needed to make sure that more than one person doesn't make changes to a file at the same time (called *file locking*). The reason you don't want multiple people making changes to a file at the same time is that they might both be making *conflicting* changes simultaneously, without realizing it. Most software programs don't have the ability to allow multiple changes to a single file at the same time and to resolve problems that might arise.

NOTE Most database programs do allow multiple users to access a database simultaneously. Often, this is done using a technique called *row locking*, which restricts changes to any given record to only one user at a time.

Network operating systems that perform file sharing also administer the security for the shared files. This security can control, with a fine level of detail, who has access to which files and what kinds of access they have. For example, some users might have permission to view only certain shared files, while others have permission to edit or even delete certain shared files.

Printer Sharing

A close runner-up in importance to file sharing is printer sharing. While it is true that laser printers are currently so inexpensive that you can afford to put one in every office if you wish, sharing laser printers among the users on the network is still more economical overall.

Printer sharing enables you to reduce the number of printers you need and also to offer much higher-quality printers. Newer digital copiers that can handle large print jobs at more than 80 pages per minute and provide special printing features can cost more than $20,000. Sharing such printers among many users makes sense.

Printer sharing can be done in several ways. The most common way is to use *print queues* on a server. A printer queue holds print jobs until any currently running print jobs are finished, and then automatically sends the waiting jobs to the printer. Using a print queue is efficient for the workstations because they can quickly print to the print queue and don't need to wait for the printer itself to process any waiting print jobs.

Another way to share printers on a network is to let each workstation access the printer directly (most printers can be configured so they are connected to the network just like a network workstation). In this case, usually each workstation must wait its turn if many workstations are vying for the printer.

Networked printers that use printer queues have a *print server* that handles the job of sending each print job to the printer in turn. The print server function can be filled in a number of ways:

- By a file server that is connected either directly or across the network to the printer.

- By a computer connected to the network, with the printer connected to that computer. The computer runs special print server software to perform this job.

- Through the use of a built-in print server on a printer's network interface card (NIC), which contains the hardware necessary to act as a print server. For example, many laser printers offer an option to include a NIC in the printer. This is far less expensive than dedicating a stand-alone computer to the job.

- Through the use of a dedicated network print server, which is a box about the size of a deck of cards that connects to the printer's parallel or USB port (or even a wireless 802.11 protocol connection) on one end and the network on the other end. Dedicated print servers also contain the hardware necessary to act as print servers. This can be a good option when you need to share a printer that does not contain the necessary networking connections.

Application Services

Just as you can share files on a network, you can often also share applications. For example, if you have the proper type of software license, you can have a shared copy of some applications stored on the network server. When a workstation wants to run the program, it loads the files from the network into its own memory, just as it would from a local disk drive, and runs the program normally. Keeping applications centralized reduces the amount of disk space needed on each workstation and makes it easier to administer the application. (For instance, with some applications, you need to upgrade only the network copy; with others, you also must perform a brief installation for each client.)

Another application service you can host on the network is a shared installation point for applications. Instead of needing to load a CD-ROM onto each workstation to install an application, you can usually copy the contents of the CD-ROM to a folder on a server, and then have the installation program run from that folder for each workstation. This makes installing the applications much faster and more convenient.

CAUTION   Make sure any applications you host on a network server are licensed appropriately. Most software licenses do *not* let you run an application on multiple computers. Even if you need only one actual copy of the application to set up the files on the server, you still must have a license for every user. Different applications have different fine print regarding licensing—some require one license per user, some require one license per computer, some allow your network users to use a copy at home freely, and so forth. Make sure to carefully read the license agreements for your business software and adhere to their terms and conditions.

E-mail

An extremely valuable and important network resource these days is e-mail. Not only can it be helpful for communications within a company, but it is also a preferred vehicle to communicate with people outside a company.

E-mail systems are roughly divided into two different types: file-based and client/server. A file-based e-mail system is one that consists of a set of files kept in a shared location on a server. The server doesn't actually do anything beyond providing access to the files. Connections required from a file-based e-mail system and the outside (say, to the Internet) are usually accomplished with a stand-alone computer—called a *gateway server*—that handles the e-mail interface between the two systems, by using gateway software that is part of the file-based e-mail system.

In a client/server e-mail system, an e-mail server contains the messages and handles all the e-mail interconnections, both within and outside the company. Client/ server e-mail systems, such as Microsoft Exchange and Lotus Notes, are more secure and far more powerful than their file-based counterparts. They often offer additional features that enable you to use the e-mail system to automate different internal business processes, such as invoicing and purchasing.

For smaller companies (with fewer that 25 employees), e-mail is just as important, but an e-mail server or dedicated e-mail system is usually overkill and too costly to purchase and maintain. These companies can use other strategies that do not require running their own internal e-mail system (file-based or client/server), such as the following:

- Install a shared connection to the Internet that all of their computers can access, and then set up e-mail accounts either through their Internet service provider (ISP) or a free e-mail service, such as Yahoo! Mail or Google's Gmail.

- Run Microsoft Windows Small Business Server 2008, which includes a limited version of Exchange Server, along with other server-based applications that are packaged together to make them more economical for smaller companies.

- Use mailboxes from a service provider that runs a high-end e-mail system (and handes administration and backups). Companies usually pay a monthly fee for the number of mailboxes used.

Remote Access

Another important service for most networks is remote access to the network's resources. Users use this feature to access their files and e-mail when they're traveling or working from a remote location, such as a hotel or their home. Remote access systems come in many different flavors. The following are some of the methods used to provide remote access:

- Set up a simple remote access service (RAS) connection on a Windows server, which can range from using a single modem to a bank of modems.

- Use a dedicated remote access system, which handles many simultaneous connections and usually includes many computers, each on its own stand-alone card.

- Employ a workstation on the network and have users dial in using a remote control program like Symantec's pcAnywhere or Citrix's GoToMyPC.

- Set up a virtual private network (VPN) connection to the Internet, through which users can access resources on the company network in a secure fashion.

- Install Windows Terminal Services (on a Windows server) or Citrix XenDesktop, which allow a single server to host multiple client sessions, each appearing to the end user as a stand-alone computer.

To choose the most suitable remote access solution, you'll need to consider what the users need to do remotely, the number of users (both in total and at any given time), and how much you want to spend. See Chapter 10 for more information about remote access.

Wide Area Networks

You should think of a wide area network (WAN) as a sort of "metanetwork." A WAN is simply multiple local area networks (LANs) connected together. This can be accomplished in many different ways, depending on how often the LANs need to be connected to one another, how much data capacity (bandwidth) is required, and how great the distance is between the LANs. Solutions include full-time leased telephone lines that can carry 56 Kbps of data, dedicated DS1 (T-1) lines carrying 1.544 Mbps, DS3 lines carrying 44.736 Mbps, and other forms (like private satellites) carrying even higher bandwidths. You can also create a WAN using VPNs over the Internet. Although this method usually offers inconsistent bandwidth, it's often the least expensive.

WANs are created when the users of one LAN need frequent access to the resources on another LAN. For instance, a company's enterprise resource planning (ERP) system might be running at the company's headquarters, but the warehouse location needs access to it to use its inventory and shipping functions.

As a general rule, if you can design and build a system that doesn't require a WAN, you're usually better off, because WAN links are often expensive to maintain. However, the geographic and management structure of a particular company can dictate the use of a WAN.

Internet and Intranet

The Internet has become vital to the productivity of most businesses, and handling Internet connectivity on a network is often an important network service. Many different types of services are available over the Internet, including e-mail, the Web, and Usenet newsgroups.

DEFINE-IT! xAN

A myriad of terms refer to what are essentially wide area networks, all with variations on the *x*AN acronym scheme. Some examples include metropolitan area network (MAN), distance area network (DAN), campus area network (CAN), and even—I'm not making this up—personal area network (PAN), which was an IBM demonstration technology where two people shaking hands could exchange data through electrical signals carried on the surface of their skin. All of these different names, and others that I haven't listed here, are a bit silly. I suggest you just stick with the two core terms: LAN and WAN.

An Internet connection for a network consists of a telecommunications network connection to an ISP, using a physical connection such as a leased DSL line, an ISDN line, or a fractional or full DS1 (T-1) connection. This line comes into the building and connects to a box called a channel service unit/data service unit (CSU/DSU), which converts the data from the form carried by the local telephone company to one usable on the LAN. The CSU/DSU is connected to a router that routes data packets between the local network and the Internet. (Sometimes both the CSU/DSU and the router are built into the same device.) Internet security is provided either by filtering the packets going through the router or, more commonly, by adding a firewall system. A firewall system runs on a computer (or has a computer built into it, if it's an appliance device) and helps you secure your network against various threats.

An *intranet*, as its name suggests, is an internally focused network that mimics the Internet itself. For example, a company might deploy an intranet that hosts a web server, which stores documents such as employee handbooks, purchasing forms, and other information that the company publishes for internal use. Intranets can also host other Internet-type services, such as FTP servers or Usenet servers, or these services can be provided by other tools that offer the same functionality. Intranets usually are not accessible from outside the LAN (although they can be) and are just a much smaller version of the Internet that a company maintains for its own use.

Understanding the technologies, services, and features of the Internet is complex. You can learn much more about some of the hardware that makes the Internet work in Chapter 6.

Network Security

Any time you share important and confidential information on a network, you need to carefully consider the security of those resources. Users and management must help set the level of security required for the network and the different information it stores, and they need to participate in deciding who has access to which resources.

Network security is provided by a combination of factors, including features of the network operating system, the physical cabling plant, the network connection to other networks, the features of the client workstations, the actions of the users, the security policies of management, and how well the security features are implemented and administered. All these factors form a chain, and any single weak link in the chain can cause it to fail. Security failures can have severe consequences, so network security is usually an extremely important part of any network. For a more detailed discussion of network security, see Chapter 11.

Understanding the OSI Networking Model

The Open Systems Interconnection (OSI) model defines all the methods and protocols needed to connect one computer to any other over a network. It is a conceptual model, used most often in network design and in engineering network solutions. Generally, real-world networks conform to the OSI model, although differences exist between the theory and actual practice in most networks. Still, the OSI model offers an excellent way to understand and visualize how computers network to each other, and it is required knowledge for anyone active in the field of networking. Just about all employers expect networking professionals to be knowledgeable about the OSI model, and it comes up on most networking certification tests. This might be a very dry topic, but it's important to learn!

The OSI model defines a basic framework for how modern networks operate. It separates the methods and protocols needed for a network connection into seven different layers. Each higher layer relies on services provided by a lower layer. If you were to think about a desktop computer in this way, its hardware would be the lowest layer, and the operating system drivers—the next-higher layer—would rely on the lowest layer to do their job. The operating system itself, the next-higher layer, would rely on both of the lower layers working properly. This continues all the way up to the point at which an application presents data to you on the computer screen. Figure 3-3 shows the seven layers of the OSI model.

 NOTE The OSI model is sometimes called the *seven-layer model*. It was developed by the International Standards Organization (ISO) in 1983 and is documented as Standard 7498.

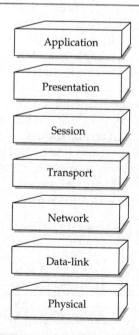

Figure 3-3.   The seven layers of the OSI model

For a complete network connection, data flows from the top layer on one computer, down through all the lower layers, across the wire, and back up the seven layers on the other computer. The following sections discuss each layer, making comparisons to real networking systems as appropriate.

Physical Layer

The bottom layer, layer 1, is called the *physical layer*. It defines the properties of the physical medium used to make a network connection. The physical layer specifications result in a physical medium—a network cable—that can transmit a stream of bits between nodes on the physical network. The physical connection can be either point-to-point (between two points) or multipoint (between many points, such as from one point to many others), and it can consist of either *half-duplex* (one direction at a time) or *full-duplex* (both directions simultaneously) transmissions. Moreover, the bits can be transmitted either in series or in parallel. (Most networks use a serial stream of bits, but the OSI model allows for both serial and parallel transmission.) The specification for the physical layer also defines the cable used, the voltages carried on the cable, the timing of the electrical signals, the distance that can be run, and so on. A NIC, for example, is part of the physical layer.

Data-Link Layer

The *data-link layer*, layer 2, defines standards that assign meaning to the bits carried by the physical layer. It establishes a reliable protocol through the physical layer so the network layer (layer 3) can transmit its data. The data-link layer typically includes error detection and correction to ensure a reliable data stream. The data elements carried by the data-link layer are called *frames*. Examples of frame types include X.25 and 802.*x* (802.*x* includes both Ethernet and Token Ring networks).

The data-link layer is usually subdivided into two sublayers, called the *logical link control* (LLC) and *media access control* (MAC) sublayers. If used, the LLC sublayer performs tasks such as call setup and termination (the OSI model can be applied to telecommunications networks as well as LANs) and data transfer. The MAC sublayer handles frame assembly and disassembly, error detection and correction, and addressing. The two most common MAC protocols are 802.3 Ethernet and 802.5 Token Ring. Other MAC protocols include 802.12 100Base-VBG, 802.11 Wireless, and 802.7 Broadband.

On most systems, the software drivers for the NIC perform the work done at the data-link layer.

Network Layer

The *network layer*, layer 3, is where a lot of action goes on for most networks. The network layer defines how data *packets* get from one point to another on a network and what goes into each packet. The network layer uses different packet protocols, such as Internet Protocol (IP) and Internet Protocol Exchange (IPX). These packet protocols include source and destination routing information. The routing information in each packet informs the network where to send the packet to reach its destination and tells the receiving computer from where the packet originated.

The network layer is most important when the network connection passes through one or more *routers*, which are hardware devices that examine each packet and, from their source and destination addresses, send the packets to their proper destination. Over a complex network, such as the Internet, a packet might go through ten or more routers before it reaches its destination. On a LAN, a packet might not go through any routers to get to its destination, or it might go through one or more.

Note that breaking the network layer (also known as the *packet layer*) into a separate layer from the physical and data-link layers means the protocols defined in this layer can be carried over any variations of the lower layers. So, to put this into real-world terms, an IP packet can be sent over an Ethernet network, a Token Ring network, or even a serial cable that connects two computers. The same holds true for an IPX packet: If both computers can handle IPX, and they share the lower-level layers (whatever they might be) in common, then the network connection can be made.

Transport Layer

The *transport layer*, layer 4, manages the flow of information from one network node to another. It ensures that the packets are decoded in the proper sequence and that all packets are received. It also identifies each computer or node on a network uniquely.

The various networking systems (such as Microsoft's, or Novell's) implement the transport layer differently. In fact, the transport layer is the first layer where differences between network operating systems occur.

Examples of transport layer protocols include Transmission Control Protocol (TCP) and Sequenced Packet Exchange (SPX), which are used in concert with IP and IPX, respectively.

Session Layer

The *session layer*, layer 5, defines the connection from a user computer to a network server, or from a peer computer on a network to another peer computer. These virtual connections are referred to as *sessions*. They include negotiation between the client and host (or peer and peer) on matters of flow control, transaction processing, transfer of user information, and authentication to the network. They are called *sessions* because they set up connections that persist for some period of time.

Presentation Layer

The *presentation layer*, layer 6, takes the data supplied by the lower-level layers and transforms it so it can be presented to the system (as opposed to presenting the data to the user, which is handled outside the OSI model). The functions that take place at the presentation layer can include data compression and decompression, as well as data encryption and decryption.

Application Layer

The *application layer*, layer 7, controls how the operating system and its applications interact with the network. The applications you use, such as Microsoft Word or Lotus 1-2-3, are not a part of the application layer, but they certainly benefit from the work that goes on there. An example of software at the application layer is the network client software you use, such as the Windows Client for Microsoft Networks, or the Windows Client for Novell Networks. It also controls how the operating system and applications interact with those clients.

Understanding How Data Travels Through the OSI Layers

As mentioned earlier in this section, data flows from an application program or the operating system, and then goes down through the protocols and devices that make up the seven layers of the OSI model, one by one, until the data arrives at the physical layer and is transmitted over the network connection. The computer at the receiving end reverses this process: The data comes in at the physical layer, travels up through all the layers until it emerges from the application layer, and is made use of by the operating system and any application programs.

At each stage of the OSI model, the data is "wrapped" with new control information related to the work done at that particular layer, leaving the previous layers' information intact and wrapped within the new control information. This control information is different for each layer, but it includes *headers, trailers, preambles*, and *postambles*.

For example, when data goes into the networking software and components making up the OSI model, it starts at the application layer and includes an application header and application data (the actual data being sent). Next, at the presentation layer, a presentation header is wrapped around the data, and it is passed to the component at the session layer, where a session header is wrapped around all of the data, and so on, until it reaches the physical layer. At the receiving computer, this process is reversed, with each layer unwrapping its appropriate control information, performing whatever work is indicated by that control information and passing the data on to the next higher layer. It all sounds rather complex, but it works very well in practice.

Learning About Network Hardware Components

This chapter is really about understanding networks, with a "view from 30,000 feet." An overview of the hardware that enables networks to operate completes this discussion. Understanding the general types of devices you typically encounter in a network is important, not only for planning a network, but also for troubleshooting and maintenance.

Servers

A *server* is any computer that performs network functions for other computers. These functions fall into several categories, including the following:

- File and print servers, which provide file sharing and services to share network-based printers.

- Application servers, which provide specific application services to an application. An example is a server that runs a database that a distributed application uses.

- E-mail servers, which provide e-mail storage and interconnection services to client computers.

- Networking servers, which can provide a host of different network services. Examples of these services include the automatic assignment of TCP/IP addresses (DHCP servers), routing of packets from one network to another (routing servers), encryption/decryption and other security services, and VPN access.

- Internet servers, which provide Web, Usenet News (NNTP), and Internet e-mail services.

- Remote access servers, which provide access to a local network for remote users.

As noted earlier, servers typically run some sort of network operating system, such as Windows Server 2008, Linux, or UNIX. Depending on the operating system chosen, the functions previously listed might all be performed on one server or distributed to many servers. Also, not all networks need all the services previously listed.

NOTE   Server computers can be nearly any type of computer, but today they are usually high-end Intel-based PCs. You might also see certain types of servers that use a different platform. For instance, many dedicated web servers run on UNIX-based computers, such as those from Sun Microsystems, IBM, Hewlett-Packard, and other vendors.

A number of features distinguish a true server-class computer from a more pedestrian client computer, including the following:

- Built-in redundancy with multiple power supplies and fans (for instance) to keep the server running if something breaks.

- Special high-performance designs for disk subsystems, memory, and network subsystems to optimize the movement of data to and from the server, the network, and the client computers.

- Special monitoring software and hardware that keeps a close watch on the health of the server, warning of failures before they occur. For example, most servers have temperature monitors; if the temperature starts getting too high, a warning is issued so the problem can be resolved before it causes failure of any of the hardware components in the server.

You can learn more about servers in Chapter 13.

Hubs, Routers, and Switches

Hubs, routers, and switches are the most commonly seen "pure" networking hardware. (They're pure in the sense that they exist only for networking and for no other purpose.) Many people refer to this class of equipment as *internetworking devices*. These are the devices to which all the cables of the network are connected. They pass the data along at the physical, data-link, or network layer of the OSI model.

A *hub*, sometimes called a *concentrator*, is a device that connects a number of network cables coming from client computers to a network. Hubs come in many different sizes, supporting from as few as 2 computers up to 60 or more computers. (The most common hub size supports 24 network connections.) All the network connections on a hub share a single *collision domain*, which is a fancy way of saying all the connections to a hub "talk" over a single logical wire and are subject to interference from other computers connected to the same hub.

A *switch* is wired very similarly to a hub and actually looks just like a hub. However, on a switch, all of the network connections are on their own collision domain. The switch makes each network connection a private one. Often, switches are connected to one or more backbone switches, which usually run at a much higher speed than the individual switches. If hubs are used (and they're becoming rare because switches are inexpensive), often the hubs will be connected to a single switch that will serve as a backbone. Figure 3-4 shows a typical switch and hub wiring arrangement.

A *router* routes data packets from one network to another. The two networks connect to the router using their own wiring type and connection type. For example, a router that connects a 10Base-T network to an ISDN telephone line has two connections: one leading to the 10Base-T network and one leading to the ISDN line provided by the phone company. Routers also usually have an additional connection that a terminal can be connected to; this connection is just used to program and maintain the router.

Hubs, routers, and switches are discussed in more detail—along with other networking hardware—in Chapter 6.

Cabling and Cable Plants

Many types of network cable exist, but you need to be concerned with only a few of the more common ones. The most common network cable for LANs is Category 5 (called *Cat-5* for short) twisted-pair cable. This cable carries the network signal to each point through eight wires (four twisted pairs). Cat-5 cable is used to support 100Base-T and 1000Base-T Ethernet networks.

NOTE   The twisting of each pair in the cable jacket reduces the chances of the cable picking up electrical interference.

You will also occasionally see a lower-grade cable used called Category 3 (*Cat-3*) cable. This is similar to Cat-5 cable, but has half as many wires running through it and

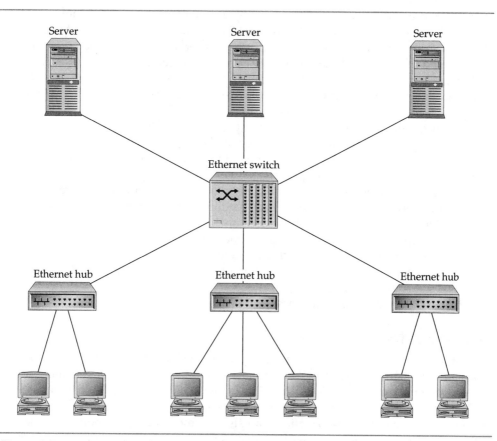

Figure 3-4.   Using switches and hubs in concert

uses smaller connectors (although they're still the modular phone-style connectors). Cat-3 cable is used for older 10Base-T networks. While existing Cat-3 cable is usually serviceable, it is rare to see it in use today.

> **NOTE**   It is possible to run a Cat-3 network connection over Cat-5 cable. Because of this, many companies installed the higher-grade cable, even if they didn't immediately need it, because the cost of rewiring an entire building is very high.

Cat-5 cable has been improved and is now called *Cat-5E cable*. Also, an even newer standard called *Cat-6* has been approved. Both Cat-5E and Cat-6 are essentially the same as Cat-5, but they meet higher-quality specifications to handle faster network speeds. They are both also backward-compatible with the prior network types. In other words, you can run a 100Base-T network over Cat-6 cable, even though only Cat-5 is required.

Coaxial cable (called *coax*) is not currently used for new cable installations, but you might still come across it in older buildings. Coax cable has a center core of copper (called the *conductor*) surrounded by a plastic wrapper, which is wrapped with braided metal, called the *shield*, and then finally, an outer plastic coating. For instance, the cable that you use to connect a television to a cable TV network is a type of coax cable (the same coax is used for cable modems, by the way). Most coax cable used for networks is a type called RG-58, which is used for 10Base-2 (Thin Ethernet) networks. Another is RG-56, used for ARCnet networks. The different types of coax cable refer to the specifications of the cable, which determine whether a particular network type can make use of the cable. You cannot mix different types of coax cable in a single network, and you must use the correct type for the network you are building.

The term *cable plant* refers to the entire installation of all your network cable. It includes not only the cable run throughout a building, but also the connectors, wall plates, patch panels, and so forth. It's extremely important that a new installation of a cable plant be performed by a qualified contractor trained to install that type of cable. Cable may appear simple, but it is actually quite complicated, and its installation is also complex. Moreover, if problems develop in a cable plant, they can be expensive to resolve. It's best to get it right the first time!

Chapter 4 provides more information about network cabling.

Workstation Hardware

Any computer on a network that is used by people is usually referred to as a *network workstation*. Sometimes such workstations are also called *network clients*. Usually, a network client is an Intel-based PC running some version of Windows, which has a NIC and network client software installed, allowing the workstation to participate on the network. Network workstations can also be any other type of computer that includes the necessary network hardware and software, such as an Apple Macintosh or some form of UNIX-based computer.

 TIP   Don't confuse *network workstations* (a generic term) with workstation-class computers. Workstation-class computers are higher-end desktop computers used for computer-aided design, engineering, and graphics work.

Chapter Summary

This chapter introduced a number of important networking concepts. You learned about how computers on a network relate to one another, how the different parts of a network connection are logically broken down in the OSI network model, and how this model is useful in understanding networks. You also learned about a number of basic network features and resources.

The following chapters cover these subjects in more detail, starting with the next chapter, which discusses the often-misunderstood world of network wiring.

Chapter 4

Understanding Network Cabling

If you were to compare a computer network to the human body, the network cabling system would be the nerves that make up the physical manifestation of the nervous system. The network cabling system is what actually carries all the data from one point to another and determines how the network works. How a network is cabled is of supreme importance to how the network functions, how fast it functions, how reliable the network will be as a whole, and how easy it will be to expand and change the network.

With any new network, your first task after assessing the needs for the network is to determine how the network should be wired; all the other components of the network are then built on that foundation. This is much like the OSI seven-layer model you learned about in Chapter 3, in that the network cabling makes up layer 1 (the physical layer), and all the upper networking layers rely on it.

Many people think that network cabling is relatively simple. After all, what could be simpler than running a wire between two points? However, as you will see, the topic of network cabling encompasses more than meets the eye, and it's an extremely important area to get right. If you make mistakes selecting or installing network cable, your network will likely be unreliable and may perform poorly. Because of the labor costs involved in wiring a network, the best time to address any potential problems in this area is well *before* they occur.

Understanding Cable Topologies

The word *topology* basically means *shape,* and the term *network topology* refers to the shape of a network—how all of the nodes (points) of a network are wired together. Networks may be wired in several different topologies, and the choice of a topology is often your most important decision when you plan a network. The topologies have different costs (both to install and maintain), levels of performance, and levels of reliability.

DEFINE-IT! Network Segment

The term *network segment* can mean somewhat different things depending on the topology of the network, but the concept is simplest to understand when thinking about a bus network, and is essentially the same for any topology. A *segment* is a single length of cable to which all the nodes in that segment are connected. In truth, a segment is not a single continuous length of cable, because it is broken at each computer connection point with a connector that lets the node connect to the network cable, but the cable is *electrically* one single cable.

In any given segment, all the network traffic is "seen" by all the nodes on that segment. You need to take this into account when planning how many nodes you will connect to any given segment. If you have 20 computers, all fully using that segment at the same time, each computer will achieve only approximately one-twentieth of the available maximum bandwidth. This is simplified; you will learn more about how this works later in this chapter and in following chapters.

The main topologies in use today are bus, star, and ring. These topologies are described in this section.

Bus Topology

A *bus topology,* more completely called a *common bus multipoint topology,* is a network where, basically, a single network cable is used from one end of the network to the other, with different network devices (called *nodes*) connected to the cable at different locations. Figure 4-1 illustrates a simple bus topology network.

Different types of bus networks have different specifications, which include the following factors:

- How many nodes can be in a single segment
- How many segments can be used through the use of repeaters
- How close nodes can be to each other
- The total length of a segment
- Which coaxial cable type is required
- How the ends of the bus must be terminated

Bus topology networks use coaxial cable, described later in this chapter. Each end of each segment of the network has a special cable terminator on it, without which the network will not function. Some bus topology networks, such as Thin Ethernet (10Base-2) use BNC connectors to tie all the individual pieces of cable together. Each computer is connected to the network through the use of a BNC *T-connector* (called that because it's shaped like the letter *T*), which allows the network to continue its bus and lets the computer connect to it. Figure 4-2 shows several different BNC connectors.

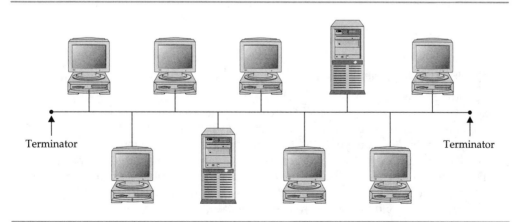

Figure 4-1.   A simple bus topology network

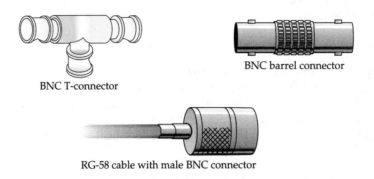

BNC T-connector

BNC barrel connector

RG-58 cable with male BNC connector

Figure 4-2.   BNC connectors used in a coax-based bus topology network

Bus network topologies are by far the least expensive to install because they use much less cable than the other two topologies and, accordingly, use less material and need less installation labor.

But bus networks have some big drawbacks. Because all the subcables that make up the segment and run from node to node must be connected at all times, and because a failure in any part of the segment will cause the entire segment to fail, bus networks are prone to trouble. And even more important, that trouble can take a long time to track down, because you must work your way through all the cable connections until you find the one causing the problem. Often, the source of the problem isn't visually apparent, so you need to use various techniques and equipment to find it (as discussed in the "Troubleshooting Coaxial Networks" section later in this chapter).

Because of the tendency of bus networks to be unreliable, new network wiring installations do not use bus topologies, although many older networks still do.

DEFINE-IT! BNC Connectors

Depending on whom you ask, BNC stands for Bayonet Nut Connector, British Naval Connector, or Bayonet Neill-Concelman (with the latter two words standing for its inventors, Mr. Paul Neill of Bell Labs and Carl Concelman of Amphenol Corporation). BNC is a bayonet-style connector that quickly attaches and detaches with a quarter turn. A variety of different parts—T-connectors, barrel connectors, elbow connectors, cable ends that splice onto appropriate cable, and so forth—use BNC connectors, so you can achieve nearly any type of connection needed. The BNC connector is extremely easy to use and makes a secure connection.

By far, the most prevalent bus network used in the past (and in limited existence today) is one called 10Base-2 Ethernet, or more commonly, Thin Ethernet. This network type has the following characteristics:

- Has a rated maximum speed of 10 Mbps
- Uses RG-58/AU or RG-58/CU coaxial cable and BNC connectors
- Requires a 50-ohm terminating connector at each end of each segment to function
- Can handle a maximum of 30 nodes per segment
- Can be run up to a maximum segment length of 185 meters (607 feet)
- Can use extended segments through the use of repeaters
- Requires each node to be at least 0.5 meter (1.5 feet) of cable distance from any other node

If repeaters are used, you can connect a maximum of three segments together, and each segment may have up to 30 nodes (with the repeater counting as a node). You can also have two additional segments (a total of five) if those extra two segments are used for distance only and do not have any nodes on them. An entire repeated segment must never exceed a total of 925 meters (3,035 feet). Remember the 5-4-3 rule: five segments, four repeaters, three populated segments.

NOTE Repeaters are hardware devices that electrically boost the signal on a cable so it can be extended further; they do not route any of the data. In fact, a repeater is "ignorant" of any of the data it carries. Repeaters are inexpensive and reliable. However, remember that extending a cable with a repeater means that all the network traffic on one side of the repeater is echoed to the cable on the other side of the repeater, regardless of whether that traffic needs to go on that other cable. Repeaters are discussed in more detail in Chapter 6.

Star Topology

A *star topology* is one in which a central unit, called a *hub* or *concentrator,* hosts a set of network cables that radiate out to each node on the network. Technically, the hub is referred to as a multistation access unit (MAU), but that particular terminology tends to be used with only Token Ring networks, which use a logical ring topology (see the following section). Each hub usually hosts about 24 nodes, although hubs range in size from 2 nodes up to 96 nodes. Regardless of the hub size, you can connect multiple hubs together to grow the network in any way that makes sense. See Chapter 6 for more on connecting hubs together in different configurations. Figure 4-3 shows a simple star topology network.

All the network traffic used on any of the network connections to the hub is echoed to all the other connected nodes on that particular hub. Because of this, all the bandwidth of any single node's connection is shared with all other node's connections. For example, if one of the nodes connected to the hub is using half the available bandwidth, all the

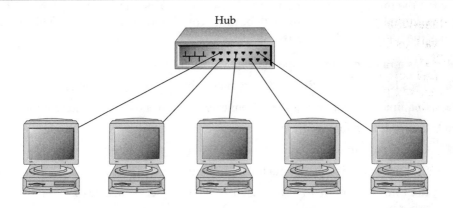

Figure 4-3. A star topology network

other nodes must contend with that use for their own. In other words, if you're using a network type with a capacity of 100 Mbps, that's the total amount of bandwidth available to all of the nodes connected to the hub.

> **NOTE** Networks that are physically wired in a star topology are logically either a bus or a ring. This means that, despite what the network looks like, it still "behaves" as either a bus or a ring. Ethernet networks wired in a star fashion are logically a bus. Token Ring networks wired in a star fashion are logically a ring.

Star topology networks can use one of several forms of Ethernet. The most common is 100Base-T Ethernet, which provides 100 Mbps of bandwidth. Quite a few older networks use 10Base-T Ethernet, which provides 10 Mbps of bandwidth. A newer standard called Gigabit Ethernet (1000Base-T) offers 1 Gbps of bandwidth. Most recently, a standard called 10 Gigabit Ethernet (or alternately 10GBase-X), which can run at 10 Gbps over fiber-optic cable, has been approved.

10Base-T requires a type of twisted-pair cable called Category 3 (Cat-3) cable. 100Base-T requires Category 5 (Cat-5) cable. 10Base-T can also use Cat-5, but 100Base-T cannot use Cat-3. These days, you should always use the most recent Cat-5 cable—called Cat-5E—even if it's intended for only a 10Base-T network. (Cat-5 cable provides eight wires—four twisted pairs—and so can carry two connections in each cable if desired.) If cost is not an issue, consider even moving up to Cat-6.

10Base-T networks share the following wiring characteristics:

■ Require four actual wires (two twisted pairs in a single sheath); can be either unshielded twisted-pair or shielded twisted-pair

■ Can be run on either Cat-3 or Cat-5 cable

■ Are limited to a length of 100 meters (328 feet) for each node connection

10Base-What?

The various Ethernet standards referred to as, for instance, 10Base-2, 10Base-T, 100Base-T, and so on contain in their name all you need to know about what they do. The first portion—the number—can be 10, 100, or 1000, and this number indicates the data rate (in Mbps) that the standard carries. The word *Base* means the network is *baseband* rather than *broadband*. (A baseband connection carries only one signal at a given instant; a broadband connection carries multiple signals at any time.) The terminating letter or number indicates what sort of cable is used: *T* for twisted pair, 2 for thin coaxial, 5 for thick coaxial, and *F* or *X* usually indicating fiber-optic cable. Here's a quick reference guide to the different standards commonly seen:

10Base-2	10 Mbps, coaxial (RG-58) cable
10Base-5	10 Mbps, coaxial (RG-8) cable
10Base-T	10 Mbps, twisted-pair (two pairs, Cat-3 or higher) cable
100Base-T	100 Mbps, twisted-pair (two pairs, Cat-5) cable; a variant called 100 Base-T4 designates four pairs
100Base-TX	100 Mbps, twisted-pair (two pairs, Cat-5) cable
100Base-FX	100 Mbps, fiber-optic cable
1000Base-T	1 Gbps, twisted-pair (four pairs, Cat-5) cable
10GBase-X	10 Gbps, fiber-optic cable

- Are not limited in the number of nodes in a single logical segment
- Use RJ-45 connectors for all connections (this type of connector is similar to a modular telephone connector, but the RJ-45 is larger)

100Base-T networks are similar to 10Base-T networks and have these characteristics:

- Require four actual wires (two twisted pairs in a single sheath)
- Must use Cat-5 cable or better
- Are limited to a length of 100 meters (328 feet) for each node connection
- Are not limited in the number of nodes in a single logical segment
- Use RJ-45 connectors for all connections

1000Base-T networks are notable in that they can run over existing Cat-5 cable, but at ten times the speed of 100Base-T networks. Running over Cat-5 cable is a significant advantage for 1000Base-T, because over 75 percent of installed network cabling today is Cat-5, and rewiring an entire building for a new networking standard is an extremely expensive proposition. 1000Base-T over Cat-5 networks have these characteristics:

■ Require eight actual wires (four twisted pairs in a single sheath)

■ Must use Cat-5 cable or better

■ Are limited to a length of 100 meters (328 feet) for each node connection

■ Are not limited in the number of nodes in a single logical segment

■ Use RJ-45 connectors for all connections

Compared to bus networks, star topology networks are more expensive. Much more actual wire is required, the labor to install that wire is much greater, and an additional cost exists for the needed hubs. To offset these costs, however, star topologies are far more reliable than bus topologies. With a star topology, if any single network connection goes bad (is cut or damaged in some way), only that one connection is affected. While it is true that hubs echo all the network signals for the connected nodes to all other nodes on the hub, they also have the capability to *partition*, or cut off, any misbehaving node connections automatically—one bad apple won't spoil the whole bunch. In addition, because each cable is run directly from the hub to the node, it is extremely easy to troubleshoot; you don't need to go traipsing over an entire building trying to find the problem.

Ring Topology

A ring topology is actually not a physical arrangement of a network cable, as you might guess. Instead, rings are a logical arrangement; the actual cables are wired in a star, with each node connected on its own cable to the MAU. However, electrically, the network behaves like a ring, where the network signals travel around the ring to each node in turn. Figure 4-4 shows a sample ring topology network.

Ring topology LANs are based on Token Ring instead of Ethernet. Some may also run Fiber Distributed Data Interface (FDDI)—a 100 Mbps fiber-optic network—instead of copper-based cable. Rings are also used for some larger telecommunications networks like Synchronous Optical Network (SONET), as well as in storage area networks and some other applications.

DEFINE-IT! Physical Versus Logical

You'll often hear the terms *physical* and *logical* bandied about when discussing networks. These terms are used for quite a few different things. *Physical*, used in the context of networking, means the actual, physical thing—what you can see and feel. *Logical* means how something works, despite its appearance. For example, a Token Ring network is physically wired in a star; each cable radiates out from the MAU to each node. Logically, though, it's a ring in which the signals travel from node to node in a circular fashion. The fact that the signals physically travel from the node to the MAU and back to the next node is usually unimportant when thinking about the logical circular arrangement of the Token Ring network.

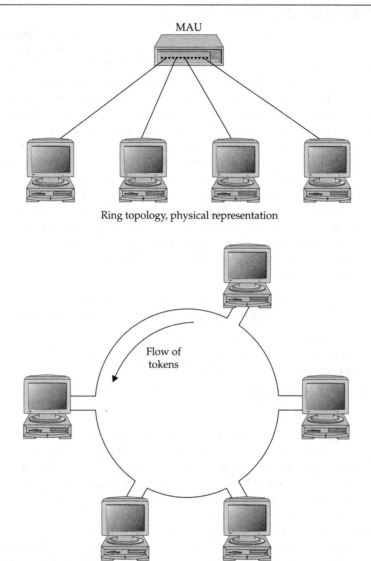

Ring topology, physical representation

Ring topology, electrical representation

Figure 4-4.   A sample ring topology network

Comparing Rings to Stars and Buses

To compare rings to stars and buses, you first need to understand the basic concept of how Ethernet networks work. Ethernet networks manage all the needed signals on the network using a technique called CSMA/CD, which stands for Carrier Sense Multiple Access with Collision Detection. CSMA/CD allows each node on a segment to transmit data whenever it likes. If two nodes try to transmit at the same time, they each detect this occurrence with their collision detection, and then both nodes wait a random amount of time (counted in milliseconds) to retry their transmissions.

Considering how data packets flow on a network using CSMA/CD, you might think that it could quickly become a confusing mess, with data and collision retries causing more collisions. And you would probably think the potential exists for the network to reach a saturation point where virtually nothing gets transmitted because of excessive collisions. You would be right. For 10Base-T networks, this point occurs somewhere around 3.5 Mbps (about one-third of the 10 Mbps theoretical maximum that one node could achieve sending a stream of data to one other node). However, the reality is that excessive collisions don't pose much of a problem on most networks these days for three reasons:

- Most network traffic is bursty, and network nodes rarely consume all the bandwidth on a particular network for any significant length of time.

- Even on a network where excessive collisions are hampering performance, breaking the network segment into smaller pieces and reducing the chances of collisions proportionately is relatively easy.

- Currently, most networks use switches instead of hubs. Switches prevent data from colliding between their ports.

Ultimately, CSMA/CD does the job, and Ethernet is the predominant network standard in the world because it works so well in practice and is so flexible.

Token Ring networks operate on a different principle than CSMA/CD. Token Ring networks manage their bandwidth with a technique called *token passing*. Electrically, a data entity called a *token* circulates around the logical network ring. The token has two states: free and busy. When a node wants to transmit some data, it waits until the token coming into it is in a free state, and then the node marks the token as busy. Next, after adding to the token packet the data to be sent and the destination address, the node sends the packet on to the next node. The next node, finding the token set to its busy state, examines the destination address and passes the token on unchanged toward the destination. Once the destination node receives the token, it gets its data, marks the token as free, and sends it along to the next workstation. If the token somehow becomes "lost," then a workstation generates a new, free token automatically after a set period of time passes.

The beauty of Token Ring networks is that they behave predictably as the bandwidth needs of the nodes increase. Also, Token Ring networks are never bogged down by collisions, which are impossible in such a network. However, these benefits of Token Ring networks are offset somewhat by the greater overhead and processing needs to handle the tokens. Overall, Token Ring networks perform about as fast as Ethernet networks with similar bandwidth.

IBM invented the Token Ring network technology in the late 1960s, and the first Token Ring networks started appearing in 1986. While quite a few Token Ring LANs are installed (running at either 4 Mbps or 16 Mbps), you tend to see them predominantly in companies that have a strong IBM relationship and, perhaps, also use an IBM mainframe or minicomputer.

If you're designing a new LAN, generally your best bet is to use Ethernet in a star topology. You'll find network equipment for this choice is readily available and inexpensive. Many qualified installers are available for 100Base-T or 1000Base-T. (There is little sense in installing 10Base-T these days; in fact, the equipment is no longer available.) As noted earlier, for new networks, you should install Cat-5E cable at a minimum, even if you're initially going to use 100Base-T, so that you have a ready upgrade path to the faster standards.

Use Token Ring if some external need is driving this choice, such as connectivity to an old IBM mainframe that doesn't support Ethernet.

Demystifying Network Cabling

Network cabling can be incredibly confusing. Not only are there many different types of network cables—all with their own names and properties—but often you can select different types of cables for a single type of network. For example, Ethernet networks can use an astonishing number of cables, ranging from coaxial cable, to unshielded or shielded twisted-pair cable, to fiber-optic cable. To design or support any given network, you need to know your cable choices and how to maintain the particular type of cable you select.

The focus in this section is to demystify cabling systems for you. It covers the most common types of network cable—the kinds that you'll find in 99 percent of the networks in existence and that you'll use for 99 percent of any new networks. When appropriate, I will make passing reference to other cable types so that you know what they are, but you should focus your attention on only a few ubiquitous cable types—primarily the ones discussed here.

Overview of Basic Cable Types

The most common network cable types are unshielded twisted-pair (UTP) and coaxial, followed by shielded twisted-pair (STP) and fiber optic. UTP is by far the most common type in use today.

UTP cable consists of two or more pairs of plastic-insulated conductors inside a cable sheath (made from either vinyl or Teflon). For each pair, the two conductors are twisted within the cable, helping the cable resist outside electrical interference. Rigid standards exist for how this cable is made, including the proper distance between each twist of the pair. Figure 4-5 shows an example of UTP cable.

Figure 4-5.   UTP cable

STP is similar to UTP, but STP has a braided metal shield surrounding the twisted pairs to further reduce the chance of interference from electrical sources outside the cable.

Coaxial cable consists of a central copper conductor wrapped in a plastic insulation material, which is surrounded by a braided wire shield and, finally, wrapped in a plastic cable sheath. (The coaxial cable used for televisions is similar in design.) Two main types are used for networks: Thin Ethernet (10Base-2), which uses RG-58/AU or RG-58/CU cable, and Thick Ethernet (10Base-5), which uses—you guessed it—a much thicker coaxial cable called RG-8. Figure 4-6 shows an example of coaxial cable.

Fiber-optic cable uses a glass strand and carries the data signals as light instead of electricity. It used to be that fiber-optic cable was required for higher-speed networks, but this is changing, and often UTP or STP can be used instead. This is good news, as fiber-optic cable is extremely expensive to purchase, install, and maintain. However, fiber-optic cable can do one thing that copper cables cannot: span extremely long distances. Fiber-optic cable can easily reach two miles at 100 Mbps. For this reason, fiber-optic cable is often used to connect together buildings in a campus-like setting. But other than when you need to span very long distances, you should avoid fiber-optic cable.

Twisted-Pair Cabling: The King of Network Cables

For a number of years, virtually all new networks have been built using some form of twisted-pair cabling. Usually, Cat-5 grade twisted-pair cable is used, although you may see some old networks in which Cat-3–grade cable is installed. UTP is used instead of STP in almost all cases, because it's less expensive, easier to install and maintain, and

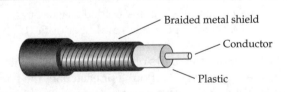

Figure 4-6.   Coaxial cable

not much affected by electrical interference (even without the shield). Both Ethernet and Token Ring networks use twisted-pair cabling. Note that different Ethernet types require different cables, and some higher-speed standards require STP.

When a new twisted-pair network is installed, a number of wiring components form the complete run from the workstation to the hub. As shown in Figure 4-7, the cabling starts at the hub, where a patch cable (usually 6 to 10 feet long, or 2 to 3 meters) connects a port on the hub to a patch panel, using RJ-45 connectors on each end. On the other side of the patch panel, the twisted-pair cable is hard-wired to the patch panel connection, and then runs continuously to a wall jack (in an office, for instance) to which it is also hard-wired. The wall jack contains an RJ-45 connector on its other side, to which another patch cable connects, and then connects to the computer's network interface card (NIC). The distance from the connector on the hub to the connector on the computer's NIC cannot exceed 100 meters (328 feet) of cable length.

Anywhere twisted-pair cabling isn't hard-wired, it uses RJ-45 modular connectors. These are just like the modular connectors you see on telephones, but they are larger and can accommodate up to eight wires. 10Base-T and 100Base-T use four of those wires (two pairs: one for transmit and one for receive). 1000Base-T uses eight of those wires.

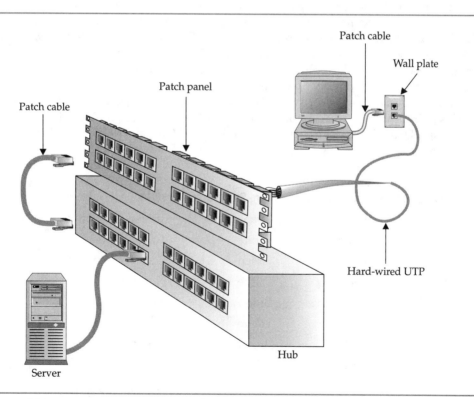

Figure 4-7. A typical twisted-pair network wiring arrangement

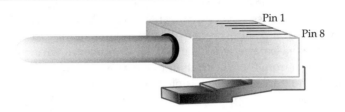

Figure 4-8. An RJ-45 connector

The eight wires in the RJ-45 connector are numbered from one to eight. If you were to hold the connector in your left hand, with the pins in the connector facing up and pointed forward, pin 1 of the connector is the one farthest away from you (see Figure 4-8). Table 4-1 shows both the colors of standard Cat-5 cable that should be wired to each pin and the 10/100Base-T assignments.

DCE and DTE Wiring

Most communications and network devices, including those designed to use RJ-45 connectors, are either *data communications equipment* (DCE) or *data terminal equipment* (DTE). If you have DTE on one end, you need DCE on the other end. In a way, they're just like screws and nuts. Two screws don't go directly together, and neither do two nuts. The same principle applies here: DCE devices can't talk directly to other DCE devices, nor can DTE devices talk directly to DTE devices.

The RJ-45 jack on a hub or switch is DCE, while the RJ-45 jack on a computer's NIC is DTE. Note that you cannot communicate between DCE and DCE devices or between DTE and DTE devices using a standard twisted-pair/RJ-45 cable that has been

Pin Number	Wire Base Color	Wire Stripe Color	10/100Base-T Use
1	White	Orange	Transmit negative
2	Orange	White	Transmit positive
3	White	Green	Receive negative
4	Blue	White	Not used
5	White	Blue	Not used
6	Green	White	Receive positive
7	White	Brown	Not used
8	Brown	White	Not used

Table 4-1. 10/100Base-T Wire Assignments for RJ-45 Connectors

Cable End 1			Cable End 2		
Pin	Wire Base Color	Wire Stripe Color	Pin	Wire Base Color	Wire Stripe Color
1	White	Orange	1	White	Green
2	Orange	White	2	Green	White
3	White	Green	3	White	Orange
6	Green	White	6	Orange	White

Table 4-2. Twisted-Pair/RJ-45 Crossover Cable Wiring

wired as described in Table 4-1. For instance, you cannot use a standard twisted-pair patch cable to connect directly from a network server to a workstation, or between two workstations, because those are all DTE devices. Instead, you must purchase or prepare a *crossover cable* for this connection. For 10/100Base-T networks, Table 4-2 shows the wiring needed for a crossover cable.

TIP You can easily purchase all the tools and parts needed to make twisted-pair/RJ-45 cables, and you should do so if you manage a network of any appreciable size (more than 50 workstations). Knowing how to use these tools and parts to make patch cables or to replace a failed cable is invaluable. This way, you can quickly make cables of any length you need. However, even though you should be able to do this, and it can get you out of a jam quickly, you're better off purchasing premade twisted-pair/RJ-45 cables to use with your network. Professionally made cables are more reliable and should give you fewer problems than the ones that you make yourself. Make your own cables when you're in a pinch.

What's All This About Cable Categories?

Twisted-pair network cables are rated in terms of their capability to carry network traffic. These ratings are defined by the Electronic Industries Alliance (EIA) and the Telecommunications Industry Association (TIA) and are referred to as Levels 1 and 2 and Categories 3, 4, 5, and 6. The different category levels are simply called Cat-3 through Cat-6. Table 4-3 shows the rated performance for each of these levels.

To achieve a particular performance rating in practice, you not only need cable certified to that performance level, but you must observe other requirements, including using connectors and patch cables that also meet that level of performance. For example, for a Cat-5 installation, you must have Cat-5 cable, connectors, patch panels, and patch cables. The entire circuit, from where the client computer connects to the hub connection at the other end, needs to be tested and certified to the performance level you need to achieve.

Level or Category	Rated Performance
Level 1	Not performance rated
Level 2	1 Mbps
Category 3	10 Mbps
Category 4	16 Mbps
Category 5	100 Mbps to 1 Gbps
Category 6	>1 Gbps

Table 4-3.   Twisted-Pair Performance Designations

Coaxial Cable

Many older networks (those built prior to circa 1992) still have coaxial cable installed. Most of this coaxial cable is the thin variety, which is RG-58, and is used with Thin Ethernet. A few may also use the thicker RG-8 cable for Thick Ethernet, but this is rare.

Thin Ethernet cabling is wired in a bus arrangement, where each network segment starts with a terminator that connects to the end of the cable, runs to each node in turn, and ends with another terminator on the other end. The terminators contain special 50-ohm resistors, and the network cable will not work unless both are installed.

All the connectors in a Thin Ethernet system are BNC connectors, a quick-release bayonet-style connector, both reliable and easy to use. BNC connectors come in a variety of different styles to enable you to make just about any network connection you need along the bus. T-connectors have two female BNC connectors on each side of the crossbar of the *T* and a male BNC connector at the end of the shaft of the *T*. The two female connectors are used for the RG-58 cable coming into and out of a node, while the male connector attaches to a female BNC connector on the node's Ethernet card. Barrel connectors have two female connectors that are used to connect two Thin Ethernet wires together. Barrel connectors are also available in different shapes, including an elbow bend and a U-shaped bend, but usually the simple straight barrel connector is used. Figure 4-2, earlier in the chapter, shows the various parts of a Thin Ethernet BNC cable system.

Coaxial cable has a central *conductor,* which can be either a solid, single copper wire or a stranded set of wires. A white plastic material surrounds the central conductor, which is surrounded by a metal foil and then a braided wire *shield*. The shield is finally wrapped in a plastic cable sheath.

CAUTION   Cable types must not be mixed in any coaxial network. If the network uses, say, RG-58A/U, then that is what you must always use—not any other coaxial cable. Not mixing RG-58A/U and RG-58/U is also a good idea because they have ever-so-slightly different signaling characteristics. (A/U cable uses a stranded center conductor, while /U—sometimes called C/U—uses a solid center conductor.)

Plenum Versus Nonplenum Cable

In a building, the area between the ceiling of the rooms and the roof of the building is called the *plenum space*. Most buildings use ducts (big, flexible hoses) to provide conditioned air to the rooms in the building, and they use the open plenum space for air returned from the rooms. Typically, the air returned from the rooms is partially reused by the air conditioning units to save energy because it's already cooled or heated as appropriate. Occasionally, a building uses ducts for the return air, but the standard for office space is simply to use the plenum space.

Why is this discussion of office building air handling important in a chapter about cables? Because to run network cable through the ceiling of a building that uses the plenum for return air, you must either install the cable inside special piping, called *conduit piping* (which is extremely expensive), or use plenum-grade cable. The difference between nonplenum cable and plenum cable is that the plastics used in plenum cable do not give off toxic fumes in case of a fire. Because most office buildings reuse the air in the plenum space, the last thing you would want to happen is to have the cables redistributing toxic fumes if a fire broke out somewhere in the building's roof or plenum space. A fire in a very small area could cause the fumes from the burning cable to be distributed to a very large area of the building because of how these ventilation systems work—most definitely a Bad Thing.

Make sure to check with your cabling contractor for details about the municipality in which you are installing network cable, but virtually all local codes in the United States require either conduit or plenum-grade cable for buildings with plenum air returns. It's important for the cable installer to be able to handle any required wall penetrations that cross one-hour, fire-rated corridors or building fire zones. Those wall penetrations must be properly sealed to maintain the building's fire ratings.

Learning to make coaxial cables with BNC connectors is fairly easy, but you need two special tools to make the job easy. First, you need a wire stripper that will cut the various parts of the cable to the right length. Many good strippers can do this for you automatically; check with your cable supplier to order one. You also need a crimper that both can crimp the central BNC pin onto the central conductor of the cable and crimp the metal sleeve that holds the entire connector onto the wire. Again, you can buy special crimpers that can easily do both jobs. The best crimpers use a ratcheting mechanism to make it easier to exert the proper amount of force for a solid, reliable connection.

Installing and Maintaining Network Cabling

Not only is the selection of a type of network cabling important, but the cabling must be installed correctly. A cable plant installation should include all of the following:

■ Proper cable and connectors for the type of network, including documentation of the components selected and used. (This is so that people adding to the network in the future can make sure to match these selections.)

■ Complete labeling of all parts of the network, which should include the wall plates, cables, patch panel ports, patch cables, and hub port assignments. This is important for troubleshooting.

■ An as-built drawing of the building showing all the cabling routes and locations.

■ A certification report showing that all the installed cables operate properly using a special network cable test device.

CAUTION   For bus-type networks, users should be made aware that they should not touch the coaxial cable for any reason whatsoever. The coaxial cable will cause all other nodes in the segment to fail if the cable is separated. Make sure that facilities personnel also know this.

Making sure that a new cable plant installation is properly installed and well documented will save you time over the long run. The network will be more reliable and much easier to maintain and repair.

Choosing a Cabling Contractor

When building a new network, choosing a cabling contractor is extremely important. A contractor who does high-quality, well-documented work is desirable and, unfortunately, hard to find. Make sure that the contractor you choose has a lot of experience installing networks like the one you're installing. In addition, assess the following issues as part of your selection:

■ How will the contractor document the cable plant? What are the contractor's standards, and do you think those documentation standards meet your needs? (Remember that no such thing exists as too much documentation for cable plants.)

■ Will the contractor provide a set of as-built drawings showing how the cables were installed in the building?

■ How does the contractor install the cable to avoid electrical interference sources in the ceiling and walls?

■ Does the contractor recommend a wiring solution that combines telecommunication wiring with data wiring? Generally, keeping these two cable plants separate is best. They have different requirements and respond differently to various building conditions. What works fine for telephones may not work for network cable, and vice versa.

- Has the contractor done any local installations that you can visit and view?

- Does the contractor also provide speedy postinstallation support for new wiring drops? This is important, as many wiring contractors who specialize in new construction wiring are not good about returning to do the occasional single drop for new node locations. Ask for references regarding this important information.

- What equipment does the contractor use to certify the cable plant? What certification documentation will the contractor provide upon completion?

- Does the contractor also provide postinstallation troubleshooting services?

Make sure to spend time finding the best local cable contractors available to you and compare them carefully. You may want to contact other companies like yours, or computer user group members in your area to seek recommendations and learn about their experiences with contractors. Try not to rely on only the references provided by the contractor; even firms that do sloppy work can usually put together a few good references.

TIP   For a large cabling job, make sure to negotiate an appropriate payment schedule. You should aim for something along the lines of 30 percent on inception; 50 percent on completion; and 20 percent on delivery of as-built drawings, certification reports, and any other final deliverables. Make sure to keep no less than 15 percent for these final deliverables to ensure that the cable contractor provides them expediently. Contractors are notorious for dragging their feet on things like this after the wiring itself is done, so you need to make sure you have a way to motivate them to get everything done.

Solving Cable Problems

Cable problems can be extremely hard to diagnose and repair. Many cable problems are intermittent or result in reduced network bandwidth for the affected nodes. Tracking down the source of the problem can be difficult. At times, you may not even be aware that there *is* a problem with the cables!

Problems with network cabling typically exhibit themselves in the following ways:

- Abnormally slow network performance, particularly if one node is much slower than other, similar nodes (for star networks) or if all nodes on one segment have slower network performance than nodes on other segments (for bus networks)

- Sporadic disconnections from the network

- Complete loss of network connectivity, which can also be an intermittent problem

Troubleshooting Star Networks

Star networks are the easiest to troubleshoot. Because each node is on its own network cable leading to the hub, you can often quickly isolate the problem to several lengths of cable.

If you're having trouble with a node on a star topology network, first determine if something is wrong with the computer or the cabling. Move the computer to a different location in the building and see if the same problems occur. If they do, then it's a sure bet the problem is in the computer, such as a failing NIC.

If the computer has normal network performance in a different location, try replacing the patch cable leading from the node to the wall. These cables can often become slightly damaged as furniture or computers are moved around.

Next, in the wiring closet, you can try connecting the patch panel from the node's location to a different port on the hub using a different patch cable. While wiring closet patch panels are less likely to fail, because they aren't moved around much, they can still have poor connections or wiring that can become problematic over time.

Finally, if you have eliminated all other factors, consider replacing the cable leading from the wiring closet to the node's location. At this point, having a qualified network cabling contractor to assist you can be extremely helpful. The contractor has equipment to test the cable in the wall and to determine if it's bad before pulling a replacement cable through the building. For troubleshooting help, you should expect to pay around $150 for a contractor to come out and test a length of cable. If the contractor must pull a new cable all the way to the location, you'll also need to pay for labor and materials for that work.

Troubleshooting Coaxial Networks

Coaxial networks can be difficult to troubleshoot because many nodes share a single segment of the network. Usually, a problem in one part of the segment affects all nodes on the segment similarly.

By far, the most common problem on coaxial networks is loss of network connectivity for all the nodes in a segment. Someone disconnecting the network cable so it is not a continuous run invariably causes this loss. Find out who is moving to another office, rearranging an office, painting an office, or performing other work of this type is in the building. The chances are excellent the problem is there. If this fails, then the troubleshooting job becomes much more difficult.

To track down cable breaks that aren't obvious, you can try using a coaxial cable scanner. These are hand-held instruments that can be attached to a coaxial network cable to detect how far along the cable shorts or breaks are occurring. Keep attaching the cable scanner to the network cable in different locations until you can track down the problem.

Another approach is to test with an extra terminator for the network. Disconnect the cable in a particular location and attach the terminator. See if the computers on the new, smaller segment can log in to a server. (A server must be available in the same segment; otherwise, you can use the PING command, if you're using the TCP/IP protocol on your computers, and try to ping another workstation in the complete segment.) If they can log in, then you know the problem is further on along the cable. Move to a new location, attach the extra terminator, and try again. Eventually, you will find two nearby locations where the terminator will allow the network to work in one spot but not in the next spot. You should find the cable problem somewhere between those two node locations. This approach requires patience, but it works fine in a pinch.

More troublesome still on coaxial networks is a problem that is causing poor network performance, but not causing any nodes to actually disconnect from the network. Such problems are often intermittent and not easy to find with a cable scanner. When you have this type of problem, your best approach is to come up with a test that can quickly tell you how fast the nodes are communicating with the network. For example, you can time how long it takes to copy a particular file from the server. Next, use a terminator to close off a large part of the segment and perform the test again. Keep moving the terminator and retrying the test until you discover which part of the cable slows down network performance on the segment. Then either replace all those portions or narrow your search further. This type of problem is usually caused by a poor connection in one of the male cable-end BNC connectors, although a flaky T-connector or barrel connector can also be the culprit. It's usually fastest—providing you narrow the problem to a small enough area—to simply replace all the cable and connectors in that location.

Having a second person help you troubleshoot coaxial cable problems makes the job much easier. One person remains in a fixed location at one end of the segment with a test computer, and the other person moves from location to location with a terminator. While the mobile troubleshooter maps out parts of the segment with the terminator, the stationary person can quickly test to see if any individual parts of the segment prove to be a source of the problem (communicating via a cell phone or portable radio).

TIP   Before going to the trouble of pulling a new section of cable through the wall or replacing various cables and connectors, try simply running an extra cable from one location to another, such as out the door of one room, down the hallway, and into the room of another. Then test to see if this "mapping out" of the suspect portion of the segment fixes the problem. If it does, go ahead and have a new cable run in the walls. If the problem is still there, you need to look further before replacing cable and connectors.

As a general rule, troubleshooting cable problems requires a careful, step-by-step approach and patience. For coaxial cable systems, troubleshooting is made more difficult because a lot of network users are breathing down your neck while you're trying to concentrate and find the problem. You're lucky if you can find a coaxial network problem and solve it within an hour. Some problems may take several hours (or more) to resolve.

Chapter Summary

In this chapter, you learned about network cable systems. It covered the major topologies in which networks are wired, how CSMA/CD and token passing work, what types of cables are commonly used, and how they should be installed. You also learned some tips about selecting cabling contractors and troubleshooting network cable problems.

The next chapter expands on this discussion by focusing on creating small office or home office networks. As part of that discussion, you will also learn about wireless networking.

Chapter 5

Home Networking

Although this book focuses on business networking, small office and home office (SOHO) networking is growing in importance, and no introduction to networking would be complete without at least of brief discussion of this topic. This chapter provides an overview of how multiple computers in a home can be networked together.

Benefits from Home Networking

Many of the benefits that businesses receive from having a network also apply to homes that have multiple computers, as follows:

- **Printer sharing**   Printers can be shared. For example, some homes may have both color inkjet and black-and-white laser printers. By sharing these printers through a home network, each person can use the most appropriate printer for any particular print job.

- **Connection sharing**   A high-speed Internet connection can be shared. Most localities now have various high-speed Internet connections available in them, including DSL and cable networks. Both types can be configured to support multiple computers in a home. However, in order to take advantage of such connections, the computers must already be networked within the home.

- **File sharing**   Files can be shared, and available disk space on different computers can be used more effectively. What if a particular computer starts to run out of storage space? With a home network, all the computers in the home can use the available space on all of the other computers. This way, you don't need to spend money on a replacement computer or additional hard disk drive. Files can easily be moved from one computer to another, and then simply accessed over the network from any of the networked computers.

- **Easier backups**   Backup devices can be shared. With a home network, critical files from all of the computers can be backed up over the network to a common tape drive, or a CD or DVD burner. Alternatively, critical files from each system can be copied onto one of the other systems as a form of backup (provided the computers have enough free space for the backup files).

- **Easier access to resources**   If you install a wireless home network, you will be able to more conveniently access the Internet and other home network resources from a notebook computer in any room of the house, or even from immediately outside the house.

I'm sure you can see how these benefits would be helpful for homes with more than one computer. So, what is the best way to select and install a home network?

Choosing a Home Network Technology

Due to the growth in interest in home networking, many manufacturers offer special home networking hardware and software. Additionally, in many cases, a home network can take advantage of traditional networking hardware and software. This section provides an overview of the various home networking options.

Standard Network Hardware

In the past, it wasn't viable for home networks to use networking equipment designed for businesses, because business network equipment was too expensive and was designed to support only larger networks. A 24-port Ethernet hub would definitely be overkill for a home with two or three computers!

These days, business network equipment is available in all shapes and sizes, and low-end solutions designed for business use will often work quite nicely in most homes. Small Ethernet hubs or switches that can economically support two to four computers are readily available for around $50 to $75.

If you consider all the components that you would need for a small network, you'll find that you really don't require all that much:

- **Central hub or switch**   You can install this hub in a convenient location, such as where the home's telephone wiring is located, or in a garage, closet, attic, or basement. You will need an available power outlet for the hub in whatever location you select.

- **Network interface card**   Each computer needs a network interface card (NIC) that supports the type of network that you are installing. Most modern computers come with built-in 10/100/1000Base-T Ethernet cards. If your computer doesn't have one of these cards, it's usually easy and inexpensive to purchase and install a standard NIC. The cost for a good Ethernet NIC is around $50 to $100. Also, there are good Ethernet interfaces that can connect to a computer's USB port, and these are similarly inexpensive and work well.

- **Cabling**   You will need to be able to cable the network. This could be the hardest part of network setup, depending on the actual location of the computers and the ease with which you can run network cable to each location. If you aren't comfortable running the cable yourself, a good electrician or telephone wiring technician should be able to do the job for you. The cost of professional wiring is about $100 to $150 per network cable run, and this price should include all connectors, cable, and extras (such as wall plates and jacks).

- **Operating system**   The operating system on most home computers—usually Windows XP or Vista, but possibly Windows 9X or Windows Me—is perfectly capable of handling all of the networking duties that you'll need for a home network. If you configure the operating systems for a peer-to-peer network, you'll be able to share printers and files through the system's built-in networking software. No additional software is needed.

All of these components are available separately, just as you would purchase them for a business. You can also purchase home networking kits, which include all of the components that you need, along with instructions for setting up the home network.

 TIP   Look for recent reviews of products for home networking and use those reviews to help you decide which product meets your needs. Many computer magazines have up-to-date product reviews, including reviews of home-oriented products. Check your local library or the magazine rack at your local bookstore.

Phoneline and Powerline Networking Options

A point made in the preceding section bears repeating: The hardest part of installing a home network is the wiring. Most people aren't qualified to install network cabling, nor do they want to start making holes in their walls and trying to figure out how to route cabling through their house (or under their house). Many companies have come out with alternative network options that eliminate the need for installing network cabling, including phoneline and powerline networks.

Phoneline Networks

It's possible to use a home's existing telephone wiring to provide a network connection between computers in a home. This option becomes attractive if there are telephone connections near each computer. Intel, 3Com, D-Link, and other companies offer phoneline network kits for the home.

A resource available on the Internet for phoneline networking is http://www .homepna.org.

Powerline Networks

Some companies offer hardware that lets you network computers through a home's existing power wiring. The network equipment transmits its information through the power wiring, and all that's needed is to plug a special adapter into an available outlet near each computer.

Be aware that powerline networks are subject to electrical noise from various types of equipment in the home. (One reviewer, in fact, had his powerline network crash every time his refrigerator's compressor came on.) However, if this approach makes sense in your home, give it a try. Just be sure to save your receipts and ensure you can return the equipment if it doesn't work in your home.

You can learn more about powerline networking at http://www.homeplug.com.

Wireless Networking

By far, the most popular home networking option is to use wireless connections. Quite a number of companies—including NETGEAR, D-Link, and Linksys—offer wireless home networking equipment.

When using the latest technology, wireless networks run at a pretty fast clip. They start at 11 Mbps (more than adequate for home use), and many variants go up to 54 Mbps. However, different factors in your home may limit the wireless network's speed or functionality. For example, an appliance may be the source of electrical interference, or something in the walls might limit the signal strength between rooms or floors. Make sure that you can return or exchange the equipment if it doesn't work properly in your home.

Wireless Standards

Three basic wireless standards are in wide use: 802.11b, 802.11a, and 802.11g. It's counterintuitive, but in this particular case, 802.11a is a more advanced and faster standard than 802.11b. 802.11g is essentially an upgrade to 802.11b and uses the same frequencies to transmit data.

The 802.11g standard is presently leading the market, and many good and relatively inexpensive solutions use this standard. You can even purchase units that combine an 802.11g wireless access point (WAP), which is sort of like a wireless hub, with a router intended to share a home's high-bandwidth Internet connection among multiple computers. The nice thing about such combination units is that you don't need to pay more for Internet service for multiple computers, since the router makes it appear as if only one computer were on the connection.

NOTE A new wireless Ethernet standard called 802.11n is starting to emerge. It promises higher speeds and potentially better range than the existing standards. This is still a draft standard, expected to be finalized around the end of 2009. Products that use the draft standard are currently available, but if there are changes to the draft 802.11n standard in its final release, these products may not work properly with devices based on the final version.

Wireless Network Caveats

Before you install a wireless network, you should be aware of the following:

■ The predominant standards operate at different data speeds. 802.11b operates at 11 Mbps; 802.11g and 802.11a both operate at up to 54 Mbps.

■ The particulars of the home and other installed equipment may interfere with a wireless network. This is most pronounced with 802.11b and 802.11g, which operate at 2.4 GHz—the same frequency as many portable telephones and also near the frequency where microwave ovens operate. For example, when I set up an 802.11b network at my home several years ago, I kept getting dropped connections, and I couldn't use my portable phone anywhere near the wireless network connections because it caused audible interference. 802.11a operates at 5 GHz, which may be less subject to interference in a home that has interference in the 802.11b/g frequency.

- A wireless network potentially exposes you to security risks. People with wirelenss network cards installed in their notebook computers can cruise around looking for free connections. More likely is that your neighbors may be able to "hitch a free ride" on your Internet connection through your home network if you don't secure it when you install it (this is more common than you might think).

- This area is continuing to evolve very rapidly, and a solution purchased today may not be compatible with equivalent hardware available in a couple of years.

Chapter Summary

In this chapter, you learned a little about the rapidly changing field of home networking. In many cases, you can build a home network using inexpensive, off-the-shelf parts designed for small business networks. The main problem with this approach is cabling the house, although if all of the computers are in one room, this won't be too difficult. For more complicated setups, or to have more flexibility, consider using alternative networking technologies.

NOTE   For more on setting up a home network, see *Home Networking Survival Guide* by David Strom (McGraw-Hill/Professional, 2001).

Generally, most people should first investigate using wireless home networking equipment. This equipment works well in many homes, is inexpensive, and is well supported for this purpose. In certain cases, it may be appropriate to use standard wired networking equipment or even phoneline or powerline networking equipment. As always, assess your needs carefully and make sure that you can exchange or return any home network equipment if it doesn't work properly in your home.

Chapter 6

Understanding Network Hardware

If network wiring constitutes the nervous system of a network, then the devices discussed in this chapter represent the various organs. These network devices— repeaters, routers, hubs, and such—are responsible for moving data from one network cable to another. Each device has different properties and uses. A good network design uses the correct device for each of the various jobs the network must fulfill.

In this chapter, you learn about essential networking hardware, including the following:

- Repeaters
- Hubs and concentrators
- Switches
- Bridges
- Routers
- Gateways
- Firewalls
- Short-haul modems for short interbuilding connections

It is essential that you understand these basic components that go into building a network, as well as the job each performs.

Directing Network Traffic

The critical test of any network design is its capability to direct network traffic from one node to another node. You must connect the network's various devices in a configuration that enables the network to pass signals among the devices as efficiently as possible, taking into account the type of network and the different connectivity requirements for the network. The following are the basic connection devices:

- **Repeaters** These extend the distance that network traffic can travel over a particular type of network media.
- **Hubs (concentrators)** These devices are used to connect nodes to one another when you use a star topology, such as 100Base-T.
- **Bridges** These are basically intelligent repeaters that direct traffic from one segment to another only when the traffic is destined for the other segment.
- **Routers** These can intelligently route network traffic in a variety of important ways.
- **Switches** These form fast point-to-point connections for all the devices connected to them. Connections from one port on a switch to another port are made on an as-needed basis and are not broadcast to ports that aren't involved in the traffic. By limiting the connections made, switches help eliminate traffic collisions caused by noncommunicating segments.

Putting together all the necessary pieces in the proper way is the art of network design. Chapter 15 discusses important aspects of assembling these devices so they work together optimally, but first you need to know what they are and what they can do. The following sections discuss these essential network devices.

Repeaters

A *repeater* is a device that extends the distance of a particular network run. It takes a weak network signal in on one side, boosts the signal, and then sends it out its other side. You most often see repeaters on Thin Ethernet networks, but they are available for virtually any network connection. For instance, if you need to run a 100Base-T Cat-5 cable longer than 100 meters (328 feet), a repeater enables you to double that distance.

Repeaters operate at the physical layer of the OSI networking model. They do not have the intelligence to understand the signals they are transmitting. Repeaters merely amplify the signal coming in either side and repeat it through their other side. (Remember that they also amplify any noise on the cable!) Repeaters are used to connect only the same type of media, such as 10Base-2 Thin Ethernet to 10Base-2 Thin Ethernet, or Token Ring twisted-pair to Token Ring twisted-pair. In practice, repeaters are usually used with 10Base-2 networks (Thin Ethernet), which are discussed in Chapter 4.

Repeaters do have a small amount of intelligence that can be useful. They can separate one of their connections from the other when there is a problem. For example, consider two segments of Thin Ethernet that are connected using a repeater. If one of those segments is broken, the repeater allows the good segment to continue working within itself. Users on the good segment will be unable to connect to resources on the broken segment, but they can still use the good segment without trouble. (But remember that this capability does you little good if your servers are on the broken segment and your workstations are on the good segment!) Figure 6–1 shows a network extension using repeaters.

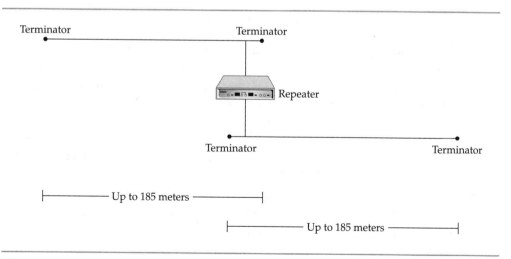

Figure 6-1. Using repeaters to extend network length (10Base-2 Thin Ethernet shown)

Hubs and Concentrators

Intelligent LAN concentrators—usually just called *concentrators* or, even more simply, *hubs*—are used to connect network nodes to network backbones. Nodes are connected to hubs in a physical star fashion (cables fan out from the hub to each node), whether they are used for a star topology or a ring topology network (these topologies are discussed in Chapter 4). A simple network might consist of just a hub or two; smaller networks usually don't require a network backbone.

Hubs are available for virtually any network media type, with the higher-end units using replaceable modules to support multiple media types. For example, you can purchase a high-end hub chassis that can house both Ethernet and Token Ring modules.

You can purchase hubs in a variety of sizes, ranging from those that support only 2 workstations to those that support more than 100 workstations. Many network designers use stackable hubs, which usually support 24 node connections each. These hubs are often used in concert with switches, which are discussed in the next section.

Hubs have two important properties:

- Hubs echo all data from each port to all the other ports on the hub. Although hubs are wired in a star fashion, they actually perform electrically (logically) more like a bus topology segment in this respect. Because of this echoing, no filtering or logic occurs to prevent collisions between packets being transmitted by any of the connected nodes.

- Hubs can automatically partition (in this context, *cut off*) a problematic node from the other nodes—in effect, shutting down that node. Such partitioning occurs if a cable short is detected, if the hub port is receiving excessive packets that are flooding the network, or if some other serious problem is detected for a given port on the hub. Automatic partitioning keeps one malfunctioning connection from causing problems for all of the other connections.

Hubs are becoming much more sophisticated. They often have a number of advanced built-in features, including the following:

- Built-in management, where the hub can be centrally managed over the network, using SNMP or other network management protocols and software.

- Autosensing of different connection speeds. For example, Ethernet hubs that can automatically detect and run each node at either 10 Mbps (10Base-T) or 100 Mbps (100Base-T) are common.

- High-speed uplinks that connect the hub to a backbone. These usually operate at ten times the basic speed of the hub. (For example, for a 100 Mbps hub, the uplink ports might run at 1 Gbps.)

- Built-in bridging and routing functions, which make it unnecessary to use separate devices to perform bridging and routing.

- Built-in switching, where nodes on the hub can be switched instead of shared.

When ordering a hub, it's important to know how many nodes you want to connect, how much bandwidth each requires, and what type of network backbone is being used. Backbones can be anything from shared 10 Mbps Thin Ethernet, to 100 Mbps 100Base-TX, to higher-speed backbones. Your choice of a backbone technology depends on the total amount of bandwidth that you need and the various other network design criteria that you must meet.

Each hub is a separate *collision domain*, or an area of the network in which collisions can occur. Connecting all hubs together in some fashion generally results in a larger collision domain, encompassing all the hubs. The exception to this rule is a configuration where all the separate hubs are connected to a switch (see the next section), which keeps each hub in its own collision domain. Figure 6–2 shows an example of a network using hubs.

Switches

Switches, as their name implies, can switch connections from one port to another, and they can do so rapidly. They are connection-oriented and dynamically switch among their various ports to create these connections. Think of a train yard, with many trains coming in on some tracks and leaving on other tracks. The yard manager orders the

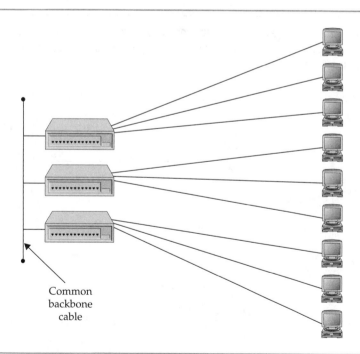

Common
backbone
cable

Figure 6-2. A typical hub arrangement

track "switches" to take place so the trains can get to their destination. A network switch is much like the yard manager, except that the switch directs packets rather than trains and uses Ethernet cabling rather than train tracks to transport its cargo.

NOTE   Switches are a lot like bridges, except that they have many ports and otherwise look like hubs. You might think of a switch as a bridge with multiple ports.

Because switches form one-to-one connections between any two ports, all the ports coming into a switch are not part of a single collision domain. In this sense, the switch acts as a sort of super bridge (bridges are discussed in the next section).

Switches are often used to connect a number of hubs to a much faster backbone. For example, suppose that you have 10 hubs, each with 24 workstation nodes connected. If you simply connect all the hubs together on a common backbone, all 240 workstations would share a single collision domain, which could hurt performance quite a bit. Instead, a much better approach is to install a 12-port switch and connect each hub to one of the ports on the switch. For instance, it is common to use 100Base-T Ethernet for workstation connections, but 1000Base-T (or some other faster network connection) for the backbone. This allows all the traffic being generated by each of the 10 hubs to continue to run at about a 100 Mbps connection speed to the servers, even though all the hubs are sharing the backbone. Figure 6–3 illustrates this approach.

NOTE   Switches often are used simply to connect two given ports (such as traffic from port 5 to port 21, for instance), but they are also intelligent enough to echo certain types of broadcast packets to all ports simultaneously.

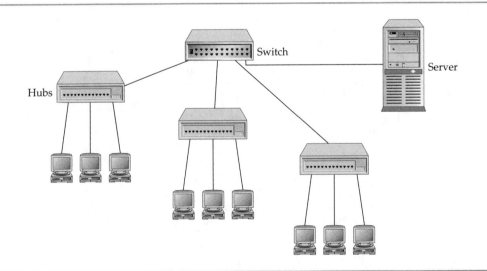

Figure 6-3.   A network built using hubs and switches

Is It Better to Use Fewer Large Switches or More Small Switches?

Larger switches that can host hundreds of connections within a single chassis are generally more powerful than their smaller 24-port siblings, and they tend to have more built-in redundancy, such as redundant power supplies in the unit and so forth. However, sometimes it's easier and less expensive to build a network using smaller 24-port switches. You can simply purchase an extra 24-port unit as a hot-swap backup (a backup unit that can be quickly swapped in to take the place of a failed unit) that you can manually implement at a moment's notice. The only real disadvantage to this approach is that the redundancy is not automatic. If one 24-port switch fails, you'll need to move its connections to the backup switch. In contrast, a larger unit can switch to redundant features automatically. As always, consider such trade-offs carefully for your particular company and its needs.

Switches have become inexpensive and are blazingly fast. For local area network (LAN) connections, switches make more sense than hubs, partly because of their cost and their relative simplicity. In fact, purchasing bridges has become difficult, as switches now dominate the market.

Additionally, most new networks eschew hubs in favor of a 100 percent–switched approach. In fact, it's virtually impossible to purchase hubs any longer, because manufacturers typically offer only switches. (You may still be able to purchase very small hubs, with four to eight ports, but even in these small applications, switches are preferable and not much more expensive.)

It's important that you understand the difference between hubs and switches, because you may still encounter hubs installed in existing networks. For new networks, you will use switches exclusively. Doing so dramatically reduces the opportunity for network packet collisions, which are more likely in a hub arrangement.

Bridges

Bridges are, in a nutshell, more intelligent versions of repeaters. Bridges can connect two network segments together, but they have the intelligence to pass traffic from one segment to another *only when that traffic is destined for the other segment*. Bridges are used to segment networks into smaller pieces. Some bridges can span different networking systems and media, such as from coaxial Thin Ethernet to twisted-pair Token Ring.

As you might recall, repeaters operate at the physical layer (layer 1) of the OSI networking model. Bridges operate one layer higher, at the data-link layer (layer 2). Bridges examine the media access control (MAC) address of each packet they encounter to determine whether they should forward the packet to the other network. Bridges contain address information about all the parts of your network, through either a static routing table that you program or a dynamic, learning-tree system that discovers all the devices and addresses on the network automatically.

NOTE   Because they operate below the network layer at which protocols such as TCP/IP and IPX/SPX are defined, bridges don't care about the network protocols they're carrying. They care only about the information required to operate at the data-link layer. This means that whether or not data is carried over the bridge depends on its MAC address.

You should use bridges only on smaller networks, or in cases where you would otherwise use a repeater, but would benefit from keeping traffic on one segment from being transmitted on the other segment unnecessarily. Often, routers or switches offer solutions that perform better and create fewer problems, so examine these other options before choosing a bridge.

Routers

Just as bridges are basically more intelligent repeaters, routers are more intelligent bridges. *Routers* operate at the network layer (layer 3) of the OSI model, and they are far more intelligent than bridges in sending incoming packets off to their destination. Because routers operate at the network layer, a connection across a router requires only that the higher layers use the same protocols. The router can translate from any of the protocols at layers 1 through 3 to any other protocols at layers 1 through 3 (provided the router has been configured and designed to do so). Routers can connect both similar and dissimilar networks. They are often used for wide area network (WAN) links.

Routers actually become a node on a network, and they have their own network address. Other nodes send packets to the router, which then examines the contents of the packets and forwards them appropriately. For this reason, routers often have fast microprocessors—usually of the reduced instruction set computer (RISC) type—and memory built into them to perform this job. Routers can also determine the shortest route to a destination and use it. They can perform other tricks to maximize network bandwidth and dynamically adjust to changing problems or traffic patterns on a network.

NOTE   To learn about the networks to which they're connected, and what they should do to route various types of packets properly, routers use a process called *discovery*. During the discovery process, the router carefully "listens" to traffic on its ports and also sends out advertisement packets letting other devices know of the router's presence.

Routers form the backbone of the Internet. When you use the TRACERT command to trace the route from a node to a destination, most of the addresses that appear for the hops are actually different routers, each one forwarding the packet to the next until it reaches its destination.

NOTE   Routers can route only protocols that are routable. AppleTalk, NetBIOS, and NetBEUI are examples of protocols that are not routable, while TCP/IP and IPX/SPX are routable.

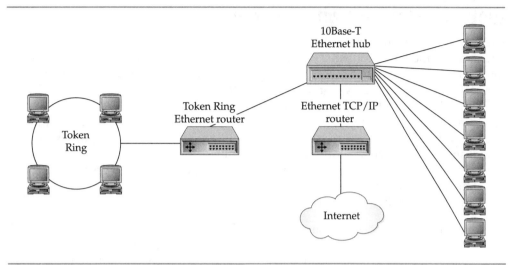

Figure 6-4. A network using routers

Routers must be programmed to function correctly. They need to have the addresses assigned to each of their ports, and various network protocol settings must be configured. Routers are usually programmed in one of two ways:

- Most routers include an RS-232C port. You can connect a terminal or PC with terminal emulation software to this port and program the router in text mode.

- Most routers have network-based software that enables you to program the router, often using graphical tools or a simple web interface.

The method you use depends on the router and your security needs. (You might want to disable network-based router programming so that unauthorized users cannot change the router's configuration.) Figure 6-4 shows an example of a network that uses routers.

Gateways

Gateways are application-specific interfaces that link all seven layers of the OSI model when they are dissimilar at any or all levels. For instance, if you need to connect a network that uses one of the OSI networking models to one using IBM's Systems Network Architecture (SNA) model, use a gateway. Gateways can also translate from Ethernet to Token Ring, although simpler solutions than gateways exist if you need such a translation. Because gateways must translate so much, they tend to be slower than other solutions, particularly under heavy loads.

The primary use for gateways today is for handling e-mail. POP3 and SMTP are two examples of protocols that are handled by gateways. Most e-mail systems that can connect to disparate systems either use a computer set up as a gateway for that chore or let the e-mail server handle the gateway chores itself.

Protecting a Network with Firewalls

Firewalls are hardware devices that enforce your network security policies. Firewalls often are installed with routers. For instance, firewalls are sometimes installed with routers to create internetwork connections. In most routers designed for small office/ home office use, a firewall is part of the router itself. Equipment for larger networks still keeps these duties in separate pieces of equipment, however.

A firewall is a hardware device (which can be a computer set up for the task that runs firewall software or a dedicated firewall device that contains a computer within it) that sits between two networks and enforces network security policies. Generally, firewalls sit between a company LAN and the Internet, but they can also be used between LANs or WANs.

There are basically two different types of firewalls:

- A *network-based firewall* operates at the network level (layer 3) and usually implements a technique called packet filtering, where packets between networks are compared against a set of rules programmed into the firewall before the packets are allowed to cross the boundary between the two networks. Packet-filtering rules can allow or deny packets based on source or destination address, or based on TCP/IP port.

- An *application-based firewall* usually acts in a proxy role between the two networks, such that no network traffic passes directly between the two networks. Instead, the firewall (usually called a proxy firewall) acts as a proxy for the users of one network to interact with services on the other network. This proxy interaction is usually done using a technique called network address translation (NAT), where the network addresses on the internal network are not directly exposed to the external network. In the application-based model, the proxy firewall takes care of translating the addresses so that the connections can take place.

NOTE Firewalls do not provide a network security panacea. The best firewall in the world won't protect your network from other security threats, such as some discussed in Chapter 11. However, they are an important part of network security, particularly for LANs connected to the Internet.

Firewalls come in all shapes and sizes, and range in cost from as little as a few hundred dollars to thousands of dollars. In fact, these days, you can even find small personal firewalls for home use that cost less than $200 for hardware-based devices, or around $40 for firewall software that can be installed on a home computer.

Different firewall devices have various features, and might encompass both network-based and application-based techniques to protect the network. Firewalls also usually serve as an audit point for the traffic between the two networks, using logging and reporting tools to help the administrator detect and deal with inappropriate network traffic.

Firewalls are discussed in the context of network security in Chapter 11.

Connecting RS-232 Devices with Short-Haul Modems

While some might not consider a short-haul modem to be a true network device, it is a device that your network might require to provide point-to-point connectivity between a workstation or terminal and another device. Short-haul modems (sometimes called *line drivers*) enable you to connect two distant RS-232C devices to one another. Standard RS-232C cables are limited in distance to 15 to 30 meters (50 to 100 feet). Short-haul modems allow the same connection to run as far as 5 miles using simple telephone-grade twisted-pair cabling.

Short-haul modems can often be perfect solutions when a computer needs terminal access to a remote device. For example, a user might need to access a terminal on a PBX telephone system, which uses an RS-232C port. You have two options to provide this remote access:

■   Install regular modems on each end and use a telephone connection to connect from the workstation to the PBX.

■   Use two short-haul modems and run a twisted-pair cable between the two points.

Depending on how frequently access is needed and how distant the device is, either approach can be good. Generally, short-haul modems are preferred when the two devices often or always need to be connected, and running a twisted-pair wire between the locations is not prohibitively expensive or difficult. Short-haul modems are fairly inexpensive, at about $100 each.

In most short-haul modem systems, two pairs of wire connect each short-haul modem, although one-pair variants exist. With the two-pair variety, one pair is used to transmit data and the other to receive data. Most short-haul modems are full duplex, allowing transmission to take place in both directions simultaneously.

To hook up two devices using short-haul modems, you use a standard RS-232C cable to connect each device to its short-haul modem. Then you wire the twisted-pair wire to the short-haul modem, using the instructions that come with the modem. Finally, most short-haul modems require external power, so you need to plug them into a power outlet. Figure 6-5 shows an example of a short-haul modem connection.

TIP   If you frequently do RS-232C interfacing, you should invest in a device called a *breakout box*. This is a small device that has two RS-232C connectors on each end. In the box, each of the RS-232C pin signals is represented with a light-emitting diode (LED). Special patch posts and switches in the breakout box enable you to reconfigure the RS-232C connection on the fly. Breakout boxes can be invaluable for achieving RS-232C communications between two devices that aren't communicating. They can show what is actually happening with the signals and enable you to try different cable configurations dynamically. Once you use the breakout box to figure out how to make the devices communicate, a permanent cable can then be made to those specifications.

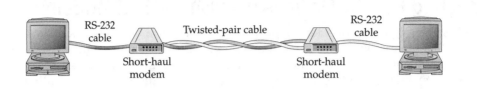

Figure 6-5.   Short-haul modem connection

Chapter Summary

In this chapter, you learned about the key pieces of hardware that make up most networks. It is important for you to be familiar with the capabilities of all these types of network hardware, which should form the basis of any network design or performance-tuning efforts. Be aware that you need to know about other types of network hardware as well. Additional important network hardware is discussed in later chapters. In particular, you should also know about remote access hardware, hardware that supports WAN links, and certain network functions that are carried out on different types of network servers.

Chapter 7 discusses the different technologies used to connect networks to other networks, usually over large distances. WAN connections are used to connect to the Internet and also to form part-time or full-time connections between LANs, such as from one company location to another.

Chapter 7

Making WAN Connections

Many companies have multiple locations that need to share network resources. For example, maybe the company's accounting system runs at the headquarters building where the accounting and MIS staff are located, but the warehouse across town still needs access to the accounting system for inventory picking tickets, data entry, and other order fulfillment and inventory tasks. Or, perhaps the company uses a groupware system such as Lotus Notes that requires regular updates of information and messages from one site to another. In the real world, the situation can become even more complex. Some companies have offices all around the globe, and each office has different requirements both to access and update data in other locations.

All of these are situations in which a *wide area network* (WAN) can be useful. Certainly, in a pinch, multiple offices can exchange data by using Federal Express and identical tape machines, CD-R discs, external USB hard disks, or other media. Sure, it's possible to simply send the data back and forth like this (assuming the application supports exchanging data in this fashion), but such an arrangement has some drawbacks—the biggest one being that it is pretty slow.

There are many ways to connect local area networks (LANs) in one location to LANs in another location, and making such connections is the subject of this chapter. But before looking into the different WAN technologies, you should assess your networking requirements. Because of the cost and the time required to implement and maintain a WAN, you usually do not want to install one unless it's the only way to meet your needs.

Determining WAN Needs

WAN links are almost always fairly expensive to maintain. Bandwidth needs increase over time; and these upgrades are costly. Also, WAN links are generally much more prone to trouble than LANs, because many additional possible points of failure exist. For these reasons, it's important to assess the need for a WAN carefully, and then study the different options available, their costs, and the trade-offs involved.

Costs can vary wildly between different technologies, speeds, and other factors (including your location), so you need to rely heavily on cost and availability data from local providers for your own WAN analysis. Plus, prices and availability change almost every week, so make sure to get current data from your local providers before committing to a particular WAN technology.

TIP   Often, the need for a WAN can be satisfied using a technology called virtual private networks (VPNs). A VPN is a private network created through a public network, typically the Internet. A VPN is called "private" because all of the packets between two points are encrypted, so even though the packets are transmitted over a public network, their information remains secure. And because VPNs use the Internet, they're usually much cheaper than dedicated WAN links, and they often can make use of existing Internet connections for two (or more) locations. VPNs are discussed in detail in Chapter 10.

Analyzing Requirements

A company's first WAN is usually driven by a particular application, such as an accounting system. Then once the WAN is operational, the company begins to use the WAN for other applications.

If you fail to take into account all the uses that the company might have for the WAN, you could find that you've invested a lot of money in a solution that doesn't meet all of your needs. Here are some questions to help you determine the requirements for your company's WAN:

- What are the locations that will participate in the WAN and what kind of WAN services are available to them? A sales office in Tahiti, for instance, is unlikely to be able to purchase the latest *x*DSL line.

- How much data needs to be transferred from each site to each other site, and in what time frame?

- How quickly does the data need to be transferred?

- Does the data transfer need to be synchronous or can it be asynchronous? For example, a warehouse clerk who is entering records directly into an accounting system located at another site requires a synchronous (real-time) connection, while a restaurant that needs to upload sales data to its headquarters at some time each night needs only an asynchronous connection.

- When do the data transfers need to be accomplished? Do they need to occur 24 hours a day, 7 days a week? Or do they need to occur once every 30 minutes, or follow some other schedule?

- What are the budget constraints, and what are the costs of the different available alternatives?

Once you have the answers to these questions, you can determine whether you need a switched or dedicated link, and if it should be public or private. These issues are discussed in the following sections.

Switched or Dedicated?

A *switched* WAN link is one that is not active all the time. For instance, a dial-up modem connection or an ISDN connection from one location to another is a switched connection. These are connections that are formed only when you need them, and you usually pay for the time the connection is open, rather than the amount of data you're able to transmit over the connection. Figure 7-1 is an example of a switched WAN link.

Switched links can be either connection-based or packet-based. A *connection-based switched link* forms a connection as needed and makes a fixed amount of bandwidth available over that link. A *packet-based switched link* sends data packets into a network cloud in which they can follow a number of paths to their destination, and then emerge from the cloud. Packet-switched networks can be more reliable because the data can take many different paths, but you are not guaranteed that each packet will arrive in

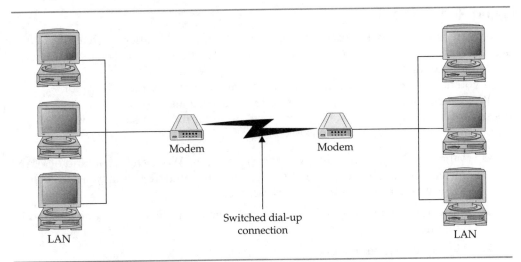

Figure 7-1. A switched WAN link

a certain amount of time. A connection-based switched link just gives you one "pipe" from your source to your destination, but you can control what goes into the pipe and how long it will take to get to its destination.

A *dedicated* WAN link is one that is always up and running. Examples of dedicated WAN connections are DS1 (T-1) lines, *x*DSL lines, and leased telephone lines. You use a dedicated connection when you need the connection to be up all the time or when the overall economics show that such a connection is cheaper than a switched link. Figure 7-2 illustrates a dedicated WAN link.

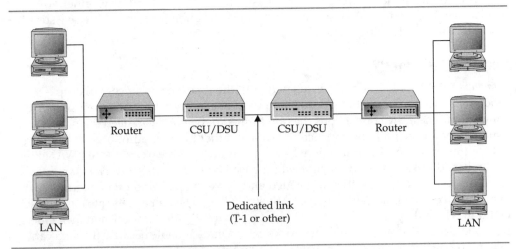

Figure 7-2. A dedicated WAN link

Private or Public?

A *private network* is one that is exclusive to a particular company. No other company's data is sent over the private network. The advantages are that the data is secure, you can control how the network is used, and you can predict how much bandwidth you have available. A *public network* (or *external network*), such as the Internet, is a network through which many companies' data passes. Public networks are less secure than private networks, but the advantages are that public networks are less expensive to use and you don't need to maintain the external network yourself.

Use a public network under the following conditions:

- You don't care if data occasionally takes longer to reach its destination or if the delay between sites is relatively unpredictable.

- You want the lowest cost network connection possible.

- The data does not need to be secure or you have the ability to make it secure over the public network. (Technologies such as virtual private networks or some types of data encryption can provide such security.)

Use a private network under these conditions:

- Data security is of utmost concern.

- You have a large, experienced staff to set up and maintain the public network.

- Cost is unimportant relative to the benefits that the network brings.

- You need full, reliable control over the network's bandwidth use.

Comparing WAN Connection Types

Now that you understand some basics of WAN links, the remainder of this chapter provides an overview of the available WAN technologies, ranging from telephone connections to very high-speed, high-bandwidth connections.

Plain Old Telephone Service (POTS)

Plain old telephone service (POTS) is the telephone service everyone knows. While it does not technically qualify as a WAN connection (at least as most people think of WANs), POTS can still serve to link two or more sites together for certain low-bandwidth needs. Although it is among the slowest methods of establishing a network connection, POTS is ubiquitous and easily used throughout the world.

POTS is carried over one set of twisted-pair wires (in other words, just two wires). In some cases, two sets of twisted-pair wires are used, but only the two main wires carry the telephone signal and ring signals. The other two wires are used for other features, such as backlighting a keypad on a phone or providing a message-waiting light with some PBX systems. POTS connections currently use RJ-11 telephone jacks, which simply snap into place.

The maximum theoretical speed of basic analog POTS is 33.6 Kbps. Many factors can decrease this speed; chief among them is line quality. Telephone lines with static typically do not connect at the top speed of 33.6 Kbps, and they might lose their connections unexpectedly, lose data being transmitted, or pause for excessive periods of time as bursts of static inhibit the ability to transfer data.

When you are using POTS to establish a network connection, having matched modems at both ends is optimal. Matched modems from the same manufacturer more easily negotiate the highest possible data transmission rates and often can support "step-down" modes, which automatically use a slower speed when line noise unexpectedly becomes a problem.

POTS transmits analog signals, not digital ones. The data sent between systems is converted from digital data to analog data using a modem. The word *modem* is actually an acronym based on the device's function—modulator/demodulator. At each end of the connection, the sending system's modem modulates the digital data into an analog signal and sends the signal over the telephone line as a series of audible sounds. At the receiving end, the modem demodulates the audible analog signal back into digital data for use with the computer.

With much higher speed Internet connections being ubiquitous these days, POTS is not often used for transmitting data, except in extremely rare cases. However, given its heavy past use, and the remote chance that you might run into a system using a POTS connection for some type of data transmission, you should be familiar with it.

Integrated Services Digital Network (ISDN)

ISDN stands for Integrated Services Digital Network. It is a high-speed digital communications network based on existing telephone services. Although it has existed for more than ten years, because of extensive upgrades required at telephone company central offices (COs), it has not become widely available until recently. Even now, it is usually available only in larger metropolitan areas. ISDN has not been as widely adopted as was once hoped. It has been eclipsed by *x*DSL and other connection types.

ISDN comes in two basic forms: the Basic Rate Interface (BRI) and the Primary Rate Interface (PRI). The ISDN-BRI connection is made up of three channels. Two channels are called *bearer channels* and carry data at speeds of 64 Kbps per channel. Bearer channels can also carry voice calls—that is, spoken telephone calls. (Each bearer channel can carry one voice call at a time.) The third channel, called a *data channel*, carries call setup information and other overhead communications necessary to manage the two bearer channels. The data channel carries 16 Kbps of data. Bearer channels are abbreviated as *B-channels*; the data channel is abbreviated as a *D-channel*. Thus, an ISDN-BRI connection is often called a 2B+D connection, which reflects the number and the type of channels it contains.

An ISDN-PRI connection is made up of 24 B-channels and one D-channel. A PRI connection can carry a total of 1.544 Mbps—the same amount as a T-1 line.

NOTE Different flavors of PRI configurations are available in different parts of the world. The configuration named 24B+D is common, and you might also see variations such as 22 B-channels with a 64 Kbps D-channel, 24 56 Kbps B-channels, or even 30 standard B-channels (totaling 1.92 Mbps).

ISDN connections are usually formed as needed—they are switched. For a WAN link, you use on-demand ISDN routers at each end, which can "dial up" the other router when data is pending. Because ISDN has extremely fast call setup times, ISDN connections are formed much more quickly than POTS connections—usually in less than a second.

 NOTE Although many systems can also use the Internet for videoconferencing, most firms rely on ISDN as the mainstay connection type for these types of calls. If you are setting up a videoconferencing system, you should plan on installing at least two BRI connections (three is better) and purchase a videoconferencing system that supports at least 256 Kbps of bandwidth. Videoconferencing calls over a single BRI (128 Kbps) are fairly poor quality, two BRIs (256 Kbps) are much better, and three BRI (384 Kbps) connections are very good. Note also that both ends of a call need to support the same speed and number of BRIs.

ISDN pricing changes occur regularly. ISDN prices also vary considerably in different parts of the country. Getting full pricing information from your own regional Bell operating company (RBOC) before choosing ISDN is important. Then, using your projected usage data, you should be able to calculate the cost to use ISDN. Generally, the installation of an ISDN-BRI line, assuming no wiring changes are necessary, costs about $150. Some RBOCs might waive the installation charge if you sign an agreement to keep the ISDN line for one to two years.

Monthly ISDN usage charges and long-distance ISDN call charges are similar to POTS charges. But remember that connecting with two B-channels is equivalent to making two separate calls, and whatever charge exists for a single call will double when you use both B-channels.

Digital Subscriber Line (DSL)

The digital subscriber line (DSL) connection type has become widely available. A number of different flavors of DSL exist. Each of these types begins with a different initial or combination of initials, which is why DSL is often called *x*DSL. The available flavors include the following:

- **ADSL** Asymmetric DSL (ADSL) allows for up to 8 Mbps of data to be received and up to 1 Mbps of data to be sent. However, many RBOCs offer only up to 1.5 Mbps to be received (which is called the *downstream* direction) and 256 Kbps to be sent (called the *upstream* direction), and distance from the RBOC's local CO (the place where the RBOC equipment is located) might affect the speeds available at any particular location. At further distances, connections might be available only at much slower speeds (although in all cases, ADSL is still faster than POTS connections using a modem).

- **HDSL**   High-speed DSL (HDSL) allows from 768 Kbps to 2.048 Mbps connections between two sites. HDSL is symmetric, meaning that the available upstream bandwidth and downstream bandwidth are the same.

- **RADSL**   Rate-adaptive DSL (RADSL) allows for 600 Kbps to 12 Mbps of data to be received and 128 Kbps to 1 Mbps of data to be sent. RADSL is asymmetric.

- **SDSL**   Symmetric DSL (SDSL) allows bidirectional rates varying from 160 Kbps to 2.048 Mbps.

- **VDSL**   Very-high-speed DSL (VDSL) allows up to approximately 52 Mbps of bandwidth. VDSL can be either symmetric or asymmetric.

- **IDSL**   ISDN-based DSL (IDSL) speed is about the same as ISDN. IDSL is used for data almost exclusively, because it's an always-on connection to a single destination (as discussed earlier, ISDN can be used to place calls to other ISDN connections).

A lot of interest surrounds *x*DSL, particularly ADSL. The cost per megabyte of data transmitted is far less than POTS and is even considerably less expensive than ISDN. Presently, *x*DSL is available in most cities in the United States.

In this section, you learn about how *x*DSL works and about when you might be able to implement its high-bandwidth capabilities. This discussion focuses on ADSL because it is the most prevalent and the least expensive. For WAN links, however, you should consider SDSL if your WAN data needs are similar in both the downstream and upstream directions.

How *x*DSL Works

The twisted-pair copper wire that carries POTS is capable of carrying signals with up to a 1 MHz spread of frequencies. However, POTS uses only 8 KHz of that potential frequency bandwidth. The RBOC's CO switch contains a card that interfaces with the analog signal that the twisted-pair wire sends to the phone company's digital network. This interface card allows only 4 KHz of signaling frequencies in each direction, even though the wire itself is capable of carrying a far broader frequency range. This limitation exists for standard telephone service because 4 KHz provides reasonable clarity for voice communications, and much of the telephone system is designed around those types of circuits.

*x*DSL works by opening up that 1 MHz maximum capability through the use of new *x*DSL interface cards, which the RBOCs install in their CO switch in place of the cards used for voice lines. The distance from the computer equipment to the CO switch limits the data rate, however. Most *x*DSL implementations function optimally at up to 3,600 meters (12,000 feet, or about 2 miles). In particular, the 8 Mbps downstream and 1 Mbps upstream data rates of ADSL are possible only within the 3600-meter distance to the CO. Longer distances are possible, but not at that full possible data rate. For instance, running an ADSL connection at 5,500 meters (18,000 feet)—the distance at which 95 percent of telephone locations exist in relation to their CO switch—degrades the performance to about 1.5 Mbps (at best) in the downstream direction. Only an estimated 50 percent of U.S. locations are within 3,600 meters of an RBOC CO switch.

The good news is that some newer implementations of *x*DSL might be able to overcome the distance limitation. Also, there are extender devices (essentially repeaters) that the RBOCs can install to let them offer DSL connections to more remote rural areas.

ADSL

As mentioned, ADSL can support up to 8 Mbps of receive data (also called *downstream* data) and up to 1 Mbps of send data (also called *upstream* data). In addition to the data channel, ADSL carves out an 8 KHz channel for POTS, which can coexist with the ADSL data channels.

Specific implementations of ADSL vary in their data rates. Some of the slower implementations function at only 1.5 Mbps downstream and 256 Kbps upstream. In some cases, this speed might even decrease to 384 Kbps downstream and 64 Kbps upstream.

T-1/T-3 (DS1/DS3) Connections

More than 40 years ago, Bell Laboratories developed a hierarchy of systems that can carry digital voice signals. At the lowest level in this hierarchy is a *DS0 connection* (DS stands for Digital Signal), which carries 64 Kbps of bandwidth. A *DS1* connection aggregates 24 DS0 channels and can carry up to 1.544 Mbps when all channels are in use. The next-common level is called a *DS3*, which carries 672 DS0 channels, for an aggregate total of 44.736 Mbps.

The DS1 connection is commonly called a *T-1 connection*, which actually refers to the system of repeaters that can carry the DS1 traffic over a four-wire twisted-pair connection.

Why Asymmetric DSL?

Many data access needs are asymmetrical. In other words, at any given time, a system often needs to receive more data than it needs to send, or vice versa. Most remote access connections, particularly Internet connections, are asymmetrical. The emphasis is on being able to receive data rapidly, rather than on sending data rapidly.

Because of this, ADSL is the most popular among the *x*DSL implementations, simply because it offers more benefits within the same amount of total frequency bandwidth. Many applications will work far better with the data rate being faster downstream than upstream.

Some *x*DSL implementations are symmetric, such as SDSL and HDSL. These connection types are more suited to uses where the exchange of data is roughly equal in both directions, such as two remote LANs that are connected to one another.

Surprisingly, DS1 requires only two twisted-pairs, not fiber-optic cable or anything exotic. (For details on how much data can be carried over simple telephone wire, see the preceding section on DSL.)

DS1 connections are commonly used as digital connections between a company's PBX and a point of presence (POP) for a long-distance telephone carrier. They are also commonly used to connect LANs to the Internet. A DS1 connection can handle up to 24 voice calls or as many as 24 data connections simultaneously. Or, using a multiplexer and a DS1, you can form one big 1.544 Mbps connection.

A popular technology called *fractional T-1* also exists, where a full DS1 is installed, but only the number of channels you pay for are turned on and available for use. Fractional T-1 is great because you can buy just the bandwidth you need, and increasing the bandwidth (up to the maximum for a DS1) is just a phone call (and some more money!) away.

NOTE DS0, DS1, and DS3 WAN connections use frame-relay signaling technology on the RBOC's side of the connection. Understanding the ins and outs of frame relay isn't especially important, although you should be aware that when you install a DS*x* connection to the Internet for your LAN, you are really using frame-relay services.

At your end of a DS1 connection are two key pieces of equipment: a CSU/DSU that converts the DS1 signals into network signals, and a router that directs data between the DS1 and the LAN.

Asynchronous Transfer Mode (ATM)

Asynchronous Transfer Mode, commonly called just ATM, is a very high-speed technology for transmitting data between locations. ATM is a multiplexed, cell-based networking technology that collects data into entities called *cells* and then transmits the cells over the ATM network connection.

ATM networks can carry both voice and data. ATM is very fast, with speeds ranging from 155 Mbps to 622 Mbps, and in some cases can go as high as 10 Gbps. Usually, ATM is used only by relatively large companies that need ATM's speed for their WAN links, or by companies that need to send enormous amounts of data through a network connection, such as a lot of video data.

X.25

X.25 connections have been available for a long time, but they are not typically used for WAN connections because of the overhead involved. Also, the trade-off between price and bandwidth is not competitive with other solutions. Some older networks might still have X.25 connections in place, however, and they were commonly used in Europe.

X.25 is a packet-switched WAN connection, in which data travels through an X.25 cloud, which works similarly to the Internet but uses a private/public X.25 network. X.25 connections are typically relatively slow (56 Kbps), but might be faster.

The U.S. military originally developed and designed X.25 to make military voice traffic available even after a nuclear strike. As you might guess from this design objective, X.25 is an extremely reliable, secure protocol for transmitting data. All frames (similar to packets) sent over X.25 networks are completely verified from one end of the connection to the other.

Chapter Summary

In this chapter, you learned about concepts and technologies relating to WANs, including different types of links and different types of connections, as well as how to specify a particular type of WAN technology for a given application. While the number of choices may make this area confusing, it becomes easier when you break the problem down into smaller chunks. Basically, make sure you do a careful and thorough job of identifying your WAN needs, and then work with various WAN providers in your area to analyze how their solutions may meet your needs.

The next chapter moves into network protocols, like TCP/IP and IPX/SPX. You learn how these network protocols work, how their packets are constructed, and various characteristics of each type of network protocol. You also learn about some of the other common protocols, particularly those associated with TCP/IP, such as SMTP, HTTP, and WINS.

Chapter 8

Understanding
Networking Protocols

A network *protocol* is a set of rules that data communications over a network follow to complete various network transactions. For example, TCP/IP defines a set of rules used to send data from one node on a network to another node. SMTP is a set of rules and standards used to transfer e-mail and attachments from one node to another. DHCP is a set of rules and standards used to allocate IP addresses dynamically for a network, so they do not need to be set manually for each workstation.

Many protocols are used in networking. In fact, in a sense, almost *every* activity on a network follows a protocol of one sort or another. Some protocols function at a low level in the OSI network model, others operate at a high level, and some operate in between.

In this chapter, you learn about the essential networking protocols used to transmit and receive data across a network.

Understanding TCP/IP and UDP

As its name suggests, TCP/IP is actually two protocols used in concert with one another. The Internet Protocol (IP) defines how network data is addressed from a source to a destination and in what sequence the data should be reassembled at the other end. IP operates at the network layer in the OSI model. The Transmission Control Protocol (TCP) operates one layer higher than IP, at the transport layer. TCP manages connections between computers. TCP messages are carried (encapsulated) in IP datagrams.

The User Datagram Protocol (UDP) serves the same role as TCP but offers fewer features. Both TCP and UDP packets are carried within IP packets, but the only reliability feature that UDP supports is the resending of any packets not received at the destination. (UDP is called a *connectionless* protocol.) The chief advantage to UDP is that it is much faster for trivial network communications, such as sending a web page

DEFINE-IT! Datagrams, Frames, and Packets

A *packet* is any collection of data sent over a network, and the term is usually used generically to refer to units of data sent at any layer of the OSI model. For instance, people talk about *IP packets*, even though technically the correct term is *IP datagrams*. In this book, *packet* is used generically. The persnickety definition of packet applies only to messages sent at the top layer of the OSI model, the application layer.

Network layer units of data, such as those carried by IP, are called *datagrams*. Units of data carried at the data-link layer (layer 1) are called *frames*.

All of these terms to refer to a collection of data that is transmitted as a single unit.

to a client computer. Because UDP doesn't offer many error-checking or error-handling features, it should be used only when it isn't that important if data occasionally gets mangled between points and needs to be resent, or when an application program provides its own extensive error-checking and error-handling functions.

TCP and UDP Ports

Both TCP and UDP support the concept of *ports,* or application-specific addresses, to which packets are directed on any given receiving machine. For example, most web servers run on a server machine and receive requests through port 80. When a machine receives any packets that are intended for the web server (such as a request to serve up a web page), the requesting machine directs those packets to that port number. When you request a web page from a web server, your computer sends the request to the web server computer and specifies that its request should go to port 80, which is where HTTP requests are directed.

Hundreds of different ports have standardized uses. Defining your own ports on a server for specific applications is easy. A text file called SERVICES defines the ports on a computer. An example of a portion of a Windows SERVICES file follows. (Only selected entries are shown due to space constraints; the following is not a complete SERVICES file, but it illustrates what the file contains.)

```
# Copyright (c) 1993-1999 Microsoft Corp.
#
# This file contains port numbers for well-known
# services as defined by
# RFC 1700 (Assigned Numbers).
#
# Format:
#
# <service name>port number></protocol> [aliases ...] [# <comments>]
#
echo            7/tcp
echo            7/udp
discard         9/tcp sink null
discard         9/udp sink null
systat          11/tcp          users #Active users
daytime         13/tcp
daytime         13/udp
chargen         19/tcp          ttytst source      #Character generator
chargen         19/udp          ttytst source      #Character generator
ftp-data        20/tcp              #FTP, data
ftp             21/tcp              #FTP. control
telnet          23/tcp
smtp            25/tcp          mail  #SMTP
time            37/tcp          timserver
time            37/udp          timserver
```

```
tftp          69/udp              #Trivial File Transfer
gopher        70/tcp
finger        79/tcp
http          80/tcp      www www-http        #World Wide Web
kerberos-sec      88/tcp      krb5  #Kerberos
kerberos-sec      88/udp      krb5  #Kerberos
rtelnet       107/tcp             #Remote Telnet Service
pop2          109/tcp     postoffice #POP-V2
pop3          110/tcp             #POP v3-
nntp          119/tcp     usenet      #NNTP
ntp           123/udp             #Network Time Protocol
snmp          161/udp             #SNMP
snmptrap      162/udp     snmp-trap    #SNMP trap
print-srv     170/tcp             #Network PostScript
irc           194/tcp             #Relay Chat Prot
ipx           213/udp             #IPX over IP
ldap          389/tcp             #Lightweight DAP
https         443/tcp     MCom
https         443/udp     MCom
who           513/udp     whod
cmd           514/tcp     shell
syslog        514/udp
printer       515/tcp     spooler
router        520/udp     route routed
netnews       532/tcp     readnews
uucp          540/tcp     uucpd
wins          1512/tcp            #Windows Name Service
```

As you can see, most of the Internet services that you might be familiar with actually work through the use of TCP and/or UDP ports, such as HTTP for the Web, SMTP for e-mail, NNTP for Usenet, and so forth. The use of ports ensures that network communications intended for a particular purpose are not confused with others that might also be arriving at the same machine.

Ports allow the receiving machine to direct arriving data appropriately. An example is a server that hosts web pages and also receives and processes e-mail. Packets arriving at port 80 will be sent to the web-serving software, while those that arrive at port 25 will go to the e-mail software. Other services on the machine, such as Telnet and FTP, can also function concurrently through this mechanism.

IP Packets and IP Addressing

IP packets include addresses that uniquely define every computer connected to the Internet (see Figure 8-1). These addresses are used to route packets from a sending node to a receiving node. Because all the routers on the Internet know the network addresses to which they are connected, they can accurately forward packets destined for a remote network.

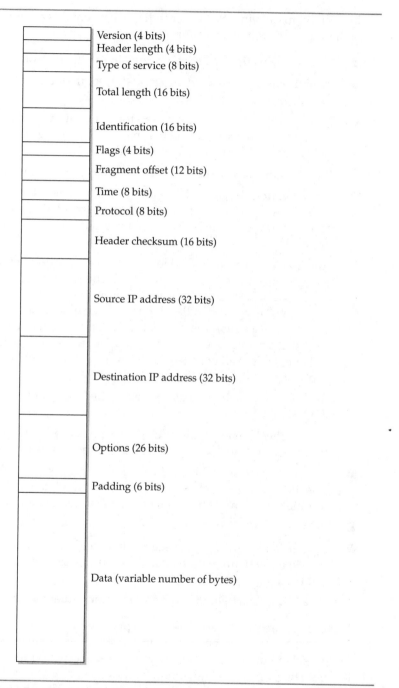

Figure 8-1.   A schematic showing the layout of an IP packet

In addition to carrying its data, each IP packet contains a number of fields, which are organized in the following order:

- **Version**   This field indicates the version of the IP protocol being used.

- **Header length**   This field indicates the length of the header information before the data begins in the packet.

- **Type of service**   This field is used for different purposes by different vendors. It can be used for features such as requesting high-priority routing, requesting highest possible reliability, and so forth.

- **Total length**   This field indicates the total length of the packet.

- **Identification, flags, and fragment offset**   These three fields are used to reassemble an IP packet that was disassembled at some point during transmission. They include all the information necessary for the correct reassembly of the packet at the receiving end.

- **Time to live**   This field (called "Time" in Figure 8-1) defines how many network hops the packet can traverse before it is declared dead and the routers stop forwarding it to other routers. This number is set when the packet is sent, and each router that handles the packet decrements the value by one. When the number reaches zero, the packet is dead and is no longer transmitted. If there is a routing configuration error on the path to the destination that causes the packet to go into an endless loop between routers, this is the feature that will stop it after a period of time.

- **Protocol**   This field indicates whether the IP packet is contained within a TCP or a UDP packet.

- **Header checksum**   The header checksum is used to help ensure that none of the packet's header data (the fields discussed in this list) is damaged.

- **Source IP address**   This field contains the address of the sending computer. It is needed in case a packet must be retransmitted, to tell the receiving node (or, in some cases, a router) from which node to request a retransmission.

- **Destination IP address**   This field contains the address of the receiving node.

- **Options and padding**   These final two fields of the header of the IP packet are used to request any required specific routing instructions or to specify the time that the packet was sent.

- **Data**   The final field of an IP packet is the actual data being sent.

IP addresses are 32 bits long, allowing for a theoretical maximum number of addresses of 2^{32}, or about 4.3 billion addresses. To make them easier to work with and to help route them more efficiently, they are broken up into four *octets*, which are each 1 byte long. Thus, in decimal notation, IP addresses are expressed as *xxx.xxx.xxx.xxx*, where each *xxx* represents a base-10 number from 0 to 255. The numbers 0, 127, and 255 are usually reserved for special purposes, so they are typically unavailable for

Help! We're Almost Out of Addresses!

The current implementation of IP, called IP version 4 (IPv4), is approaching the point where running out of addresses is becoming a real possibility. In 1994, a proposal was issued to address this limitation. Called IP Next Generation (IPng, now IP version 6, or IPv6), the new version of IP takes care of the addressing limitation by bumping up the address length from 32 bits to 128 bits. This allows 3.4×10^{38} (34 followed by 37 zeros, or around 340 trillion, trillion, trillion) unique addresses, which should leave plenty of room for all anticipated Internet addresses, even allowing for refrigerators, toasters, and cars to have their own IP addresses!

assignment to nodes. The remaining 253 unique addresses are available for assignment in each octet.

Addresses on the Internet are guaranteed to be unique through the use of an address registration service, presently administered by the Internet Corporation for Assigned Names and Numbers (ICANN). Actual registrations of domain names and addresses are handled through one of many *registrars*, which include companies such as InterNIC, Network Solutions, and many others. ICANN is the overall authority.

ICANN assigns three major classes of addresses, called Class A, B, and C, as follows:

- For a Class A address, ICANN assigns the owner a number in the first octet. The owner is then free to use all possible valid combinations in the remaining three octets. For example, a Class A address might be 57.*xxx.xxx.xxx*. Class A addresses enable the owner to address up to around 16.5 million unique nodes.

- Class B addresses define the first two octets, leaving the remaining two open for the address's owner to use. For instance, 223.55.*xxx.xxx* would be a valid Class B address assignment. Class B addresses enable the holder to have about 65,000 unique nodes.

- Class C follows this progression, defining the first three octets and leaving only the last octet available for the Class C owner to assign. The owner can assign up to 255 unique addresses.

An Internet service provider (ISP) might own either a Class A or a Class B address, and then can handle a number of Class C addresses within its own address structure. Changing ISPs, even for a company that has a valid Class C address, means changing the company's address from a Class C address available through the first ISP to a Class C address available from the new ISP.

As mentioned earlier, the addresses 0, 127, and 255 are reserved. Usually, address 0—as in 123.65.101.0—refers to the network itself, and the router that connects the network to other networks handles this address. The address 127 is a special *loopback address* that can be used for certain kinds of testing. The address 255 refers to all computers on the network, so a broadcast message to address 223.65.101.255 would go to all addresses within 223.65.101.*xxx*.

IP addresses are made up of two main components. The first, or leftmost, is the *network ID*, also called the *netid*. The other is the *host ID*, usually referred to as *hostid*. The netid identifies the network, while the hostid identifies each node on that network. (In IP parlance, every node is called a *host*, regardless of whether it's a server, client computer, printer, or whatever.) For a Class C address, for instance, the netid is set in the first three octets, and the hostids use the fourth octet. For a Class B address, the first two octets are the netid, and the final two octets are hostids. These address parts are important for subnetting, as described next.

IP Subnetting

Suppose that a company has three networks in three different buildings, all connected by a 64 Kbps ISDN link. Each network has about 25 nodes. Each building has its own set of servers and printers for the workers in that building. The ISDN link between the networks is for the occasional need to transmit information between buildings, such as e-mail messages or accounting transactions. How should the company assign IP addresses in this situation?

The company could request a single Class C set of addresses, and then assign those addresses across the three networks in some fashion. This seems like a simple solution, but it's actually a poor idea for a couple of reasons. Typically, a lot of network traffic is sent to each hostid within a single netid. The slow ISDN link between the buildings would become a tremendous bottleneck in this situation, and the entire network would function very poorly.

Another idea is to use separate Class C addresses (netids) for each building. This is a relatively simple solution, and it would work just fine, except that the ISP might not be able to assign three separate Class C addresses. Also, it would be terribly wasteful of the available pool of IP addresses. In this situation, each building would be wasting more than 200 addresses for no good reason.

What if there were a way to divide a Class C address so that each building could have its own *virtual* netid? Such a solution is what subnetting is all about. *Subnetting* allows you to subdivide a *hostid* range (usually that of a Class C address, but such subnetting can also be done with Class A or B addresses) across two or more networks. Subnetting is done through the use of subnet masks, which are discussed in the next section.

NOTE   To understand subnetting, you first need to understand the binary representation of IP addresses. For a quick overview of how binary numbers work, see Chapter 2.

Subnet Masks

If you look at a computer's IP configuration, you'll see that the computer always has both an IP address (such as 205.143.60.109) and a *subnet mask* (such as 255.255.255.0). The subnet mask defines which part of the computer's IP address is the netid and which part is the hostid. To see this clearly, you need to represent the addresses in binary form:

```
Computer IP Address (Dec):      205       143       60        109
Computer IP Address (Bin):      11001101  10001111  00111100  01101101
Subnet mask (Dec):              255       255       255       0
Subnet mask (Bin):              11111111  11111111  11111111  00000000
```

The netid of an address, defined by the subnet mask, is whatever portion of the address has a binary 1 set in the corresponding subnet mask. In the preceding example, the netid is the full first three octets (the first 24 bits), and the hostid is the last octet (the last 8 bits). Now you can see why 255 (decimal) is used so frequently in subnet masks: 255 corresponds to having all bits set to 1 in an 8-bit number.

NOTE   Subnet masks should always use contiguous 1s, starting from the left and working to the right. The hostid portion should contain all contiguous 0s, working backward from the right to the left. While it is theoretically possible to build subnet masks that have interspersed 1s and 0s, it is never done in practice because it would quickly become too complicated to manage properly and because there's no real reason to do so. Also, the portion of the hostid that is subnet-masked cannot consist of all 0s or all 1s. While certain implementations of IP do allow all 0s, such a configuration is not part of the accepted standard IP rules, and thus using such a hostid is risky because some devices on the network might not understand it.

Let's now return to the example of the company with three buildings. What if the company could divide a single Class C address so that each building could use its own portion, and the routers connecting the buildings would understand which transmissions should be forwarded to the other buildings and which ones should not be? Such a configuration is where subnet masks are useful.

A subnet mask allows you to "borrow" some bits from your hostids and then use those bits to create new netids. For the example, you would need to borrow three bits from the Class C address (the fourth octet) and use that address to create four separate netids. Examine how this configuration would work in binary format:

```
Subnet mask (Bin):        11111111  11111111  11111111  11100000
Bldg. 1 IP addresses:     11001101  10001111  00111100  100xxxxx
Bldg. 2 IP addresses:     11001101  10001111  00111100  011xxxx
Bldg. 3 IP addresses:     11001101  10001111  00111100  101xxxxx
Subnet mask (Dec):        255       255       255       224
Bldg. 1 IP addresses:     205       143       60        129 - 158
Bldg. 2 IP addresses:     205       143       60        97 - 126
Bldg. 3 IP addresses:     205       143       60        161 - 190
```

Using this configuration, the company can create up to 6 netids, and each building can be provided with 30 available hostid addresses. By using subnetting to designate each separate netid, the company can program the routers to send packets between networks only when the packets are supposed to be routed.

Binary Mask	Decimal Equivalent	Number of Subnets	Number of Hostids per Subnet
00000000	0	1	254
10000000	128	2	126
11000000	192	4	62
11100000	224	8	30
11110000	240	16	14
11111000	248	32	6
11111100	252	64	2
11111110	254	N/A	N/A
11111111	255	N/A	N/A

Table 8-1. Most Common Subnet Masks

Because subnet masks are usually created using contiguous bits for the mask itself, only nine subnet masks are commonly used, as shown in Table 8-1.

In Table 8-1, some configurations are marked as N/A, for not applicable. These subnet masks would result in no available addresses, because of the rule that the subnet portion of the netid cannot be all 0s or all 1s. For example, consider the subnet mask of 224, which uses three hostid bits for the subnetid. In theory, this configuration should result in eight subnets. However, the subnets represented by 000 and 111 are not valid. Likewise, 128 is not a valid subnet mask because that one bit would always be either a 1 or a 0.

TIP   If you need to implement subnets, you should initially work through the project with an experienced network engineer, who can help you avoid pitfalls (which were not explicitly described in the preceding section). You might also want to learn more about TCP/IP through resources devoted to detailed coverage of the concepts introduced here.

Understanding Other Internet Protocols

Quite a few other protocols used on the Internet either rely on or make use of TCP/IP. In this section, you learn about these different protocols.

Domain Name System (DNS)

If you had only IP address numbers to address computers over the Internet, trying to keep track of them and using their correct addresses might make you a little crazy. To go to the web site for Google, for example, you would need to remember to type the address http://209.85.171.100. To solve this problem, a system called the Domain Name System (DNS) was developed.

DNS enables people to register domain names with ICANN and then use them to access a particular node over the Internet. Therefore, DNS is the service that allows you to open a web browser and type http://www.google.com to connect to a particular computer over the Internet. In this case, google.com is the full domain name.

NOTE   Domain names are given out on a first-come, first-served basis. However, ICANN gives preference to a holder of a valid registered trademark if a conflict develops. ICANN, upon being presented with valid trademark information and notice of the domain name that infringes on that trademark, goes through a process to assess the truth of the claim and, if necessary, takes a domain name away from its present holder and transfers the name to its rightful owner.

Domains are organized in a tree arrangement, like a directory tree on a disk drive. The top level defines different *domain types,* called *top-level domain names* (TLDs). The most common is the .com domain type, usually used with for-profit commercial entities. The following are other common domain types:

- .edu for educational institutions
- .gov for governmental entities
- .mil for military entities
- .net for Internet-related entities
- .org for nonprofit entities
- *.xx* for different countries, such as .it for Italy and .de for Germany (Deutschland)

NOTE   In recent years, a number of other TLDs have been added to the system, such as .biz, .info, and .name. You can find a complete list of the TLDs at http://www.icann.org.

Within a domain name, entities are free to add other names before the beginning of the domain name, and these usually refer to a particular host or server, or sometimes to a particular type of service for that domain. For example, if you had the domain bedrock.gov, you would be free to create additional names, such as quarry.bedrock.gov and flintstone.bedrock.gov.

As a matter of standards, the first portion of a domain name preceding the actual domain name indicates what type of service is being connected. For instance, www .bedrock.gov would be used for a World Wide Web server for the domain bedrock.gov and ftp.bedrock.gov would be used for an FTP server. The standards for service types within the domain name are usually followed, but not always. The owners of domain names are free to invent their own service types that meet their particular needs. For example, some domain name holders refer to their e-mail servers as smtp.domain.org; others might prefer to use mail.domain.org.

Domain names are resolved to IP addresses through the use of *domain name servers* (DNS servers), which are servers that accept the typed domain name, perform a database query, and then return the actual address that should be used for that domain name. Generally, each ISP maintains its own DNS servers (and many companies and organizations maintain their own DNS servers as well). Any changes are propagated throughout all the Internet's DNS servers within about an hour.

NOTE Changes to DNS entries used to take up to several days to propagate throughout the Internet, but updates to the system now allow changes to propagate much more quickly—often within minutes of the change being posted.

Dynamic Host Configuration Protocol (DHCP)

In the early days of TCP/IP-based networks, administrators defined each node's address in a text file or dialog box. From then on, the address was fixed unless someone changed it. The problem was that administrators occasionally would mistakenly put conflicting addresses into other nodes on the network, causing a network's version of pandemonium. To resolve this problem and to make it easier to assign TCP/IP addresses, a service called Dynamic Host Configuration Protocol (DHCP) was invented.

DHCP services run on a DHCP server, where they control a range of IP addresses called a *scope*. When nodes connect to the network, they contact the DHCP server to get an assigned address that they can use. Addresses from a DHCP server are said to be *leased* to the client that uses them, meaning they remain assigned to a particular node for a set period of time before they expire and become available for another node to use. Often, lease periods are for just a few days, but network administrators can set any time period they want.

You should not use DHCP for nodes that provide network services, particularly for servers that provide services over the Internet. This is because changing a TCP/IP address would make reliably connecting to those computers impossible. Instead, use DHCP to support client workstations that do not need to host services for other nodes.

DEFINE-IT! Host

You might think a *host* is a server, and in some networking contexts, you would be right. However, in the jargon of Internet names and addresses, every computer that has an IP address is called a *host*, thus the name, Dynamic Host Configuration Protocol. Remembering that every computer is called a host is particularly important in the UNIX and Linux worlds, where the term is much more common than in the Windows or Macintosh worlds.

Hypertext Transfer Protocol (HTTP)

The World Wide Web is made up of documents that use a formatting language called Hypertext Markup Language (HTML). These documents are composed of text to be displayed, graphic images, formatting commands, and hyperlinks to other documents located somewhere on the Web. HTML documents are displayed most often using web browsers, such as Mozilla Firefox or Microsoft Internet Explorer.

A protocol called Hypertext Transfer Protocol (HTTP) controls the transactions between a web client and a web server. HTTP is an application-layer protocol. The HTTP protocol transparently makes use of DNS and other Internet protocols to form connections between the web client and the web server, so the user is aware of only the web site's domain name and the name of the document itself.

HTTP is fundamentally an insecure protocol. Text-based information is sent "in the clear" between the client and the server. To address the need for secure web networking, alternatives are available, such as HTTP Secure (HTTPS) and Secure Sockets Layer (SSL).

Requests from a web client to a web server are connection-oriented, but they are not persistent. Once the client receives the contents of an HTML page, the connection is no longer active. Clicking a hyperlink in the HTML document reactivates the link, either to the original server (if that is where the hyperlink points) or to another server somewhere else.

File Transfer Protocol (FTP)

The acronym FTP stands for two things: File Transfer Protocol and File Transfer Program (which makes use of the File Transfer Protocol). It's sort of like, "it's a dessert topping *and* a floor polish," (from the *Saturday Night Live* TV show). Because FTP (the program) makes use of FTP (the protocol), it can become confusing to know which is being discussed. This section discusses the protocol. (When I'm referring to the program, I'll say so.)

FTP is an application-layer protocol used to send and receive files between an FTP client and an FTP server. Usually, this is done with the FTP program or another program that can also use the protocol (many are available). FTP transfers can be either text-based or binary-based, and they can handle files of any size.

When you connect to an FTP server to transfer a file, you log in to the FTP server using a valid username and password. However, some sites are set up to allow *anonymous FTP*, where you enter the username *anonymous* and then enter your e-mail address as the password. For example, Microsoft maintains an FTP site you can use to download updates to its products, located at ftp.microsoft.com, which allows anonymous FTP.

To use the FTP program, on most platforms you type the command **ftp** followed by the address to which you want to connect. So, to use the Microsoft example, you would type **ftp.microsoft.com**, press ENTER, and then log in. Then you can use all of the FTP commands—PUT, GET, MGET, and so forth. Most FTP program implementations have online help to assist you with the various commands. Type **?** or HELP to access this feature.

TIP   Recent versions of Windows also support FTP connections using Internet Explorer. Just open Internet Explorer and instead of entering an http:// address in the address bar, type an address preceded by ftp://. For example, to connect to Microsoft's FTP server, you would use the address ftp://ftp.microsoft.com. This trick also works in most other current web browsers, such as Mozilla Firefox. Note that for FTP sites that require a login, the browser must support logging in. In Internet Explorer, a Logon As option is available on the File menu after you browse to an FTP site.

Network News Transfer Protocol (NNTP)

Usenet (NetNews) is a set of discussion groups devoted to an extremely wide variety of topics. There are well over 100,000 such such groups in existence. Usenet conversations are posted to Usenet servers, which then echo their messages to all other Usenet servers around the world. A posted message can travel to all the Usenet servers in a matter of hours, and then be available to users accessing any particular Usenet server.

Usenet discussion groups are loosely organized into the branches of a tree. The following are some of the main branches:

- Alt, for discussions about alternative lifestyles and other miscellaneous topics
- Comp, for computer-oriented discussions
- Gov, for government-oriented discussions
- Rec, devoted to recreational topics
- Sci, for science-based discussions

Usenet groups can either be public, which are echoed to other Usenet servers, or private, which are usually hosted by a particular organization and require the user to enter appropriate login credentials before reading and posting messages.

The NNTP protocol is what makes Usenet possible. It allows for a connection between a Usenet reader (also called a *news reader*) and a Usenet server. It also provides for message formatting, so messages can be text-based or can also contain binary attachments. Binary attachments in Usenet postings are usually encoded using Multipurpose Internet Message Encoding (MIME), which is also used for most e-mail attachments. Some older systems use different methods to encode attachments, including one method called UUEncode/UUDecode and, on the Macintosh, a method called BinHex.

Telnet

Telnet defines a protocol that allows a remote terminal session to be established with an Internet host, so remote users have access similar to using a terminal connected directly to the host computer. Using Telnet, users can control the remote host, performing tasks such as managing files, running applications, or even (with appropriate permissions) administering the remote system. Telnet is a session-layer protocol in the OSI model.

For Telnet to work, Telnet software must be running on both the server and client computer. You run the program Telnet on a client computer and run the program Telnetd on the server computer to allow the connection. Telnet is specific to the TCP protocol and typically runs on port 23 (although it can run on any port that has been enabled on the server system). Once users connect using Telnet, they must log in to the remote system using the same credentials they would use if they were working from a directly connected terminal.

Simple Mail Transfer Protocol (SMTP)

E-mail had a somewhat rocky start on the Internet, with early e-mail programs sharing few standards with other e-mail programs, particularly in the handling of attached binary data. The good news is that the situation is now resolved, and all current e-mail software supports all the widely accepted standards.

The Simple Mail Transfer Protocol (SMTP) is used to send and receive e-mail messages from one e-mail server to another. The SMTP protocol defines a dialog between a sending system and a receiving system.

An SMTP dialog starts when a sending system connects to port 25 of a receiving system. After the connection is established, the sending system sends a HELO command, followed by its address. The receiving system acknowledges the HELO command along with its own address. The dialog then continues, with the sending system issuing a command indicating that the system wants to send a message and identifying the recipient for whom the message is intended. If the receiving system knows of the recipient, it acknowledges the request, and then the sending system transmits the body of the message along with any attachments. Finally, the connection between the two systems is terminated once the receiving system acknowledges that it has received the entire message. Figure 8-2 illustrates this process.

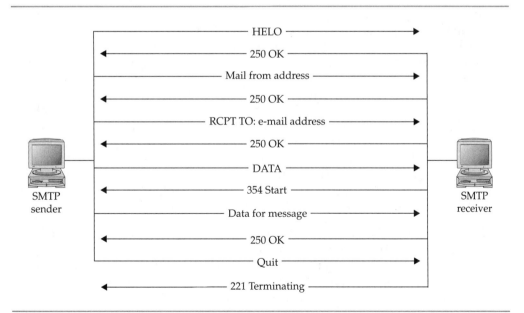

Figure 8-2.   Part of an SMTP dialog between systems

> *TIP*   Details on SMTP can be found in RFC 821 (http://www.faqs.org/rfcs/rfc821.html).

Voice over IP (VoIP)

An important emerging set of IP protocols concerns the transmission of voice and facsimile information over IP-based networks, called *Voice over IP*, or *VoIP* for short (pronounced "voyp"). VoIP is a protocol that allows analog voice data—for telephone calls—to be digitized and then encapsulated into IP packets and transmitted over a network. VoIP can be used to carry voice telephone calls over any IP network, such as a company's local area network (LAN) or wide area network (WAN), or the Internet.

Sending voice data over IP networks has some very attractive possible payoffs. One is more efficient use of available connections.

Consider a large company with two main offices. At any given time, hundreds of voice conversations might be occurring between those two offices. Each traditional voice connection consumes one DS0 line, capable of carrying up to 56 Kbps of data if the line were used digitally. Each conversation does not use all of the available bandwidth on the line. Part of this is because most conversations have a lot of silent spaces—time between words or sentences, time where one party stops speaking and the other starts, and so forth. Plus, most conversations, were they encoded digitally, could be significantly compressed. Add all of this up, and each voice conversation is likely to use only one-third to one-half of the available bandwidth on a single DS0 circuit.

If you were able to carry all of these voice conversations digitally, much less bandwidth would be required. Instead of 100 DS0 lines for 100 conversations, for example, the same conversations might use up only 25 to 33 DS0 lines if they were digitally packaged. Many companies can save a significant amount of money by using VoIP.

Another advantage of VoIP is that the connections are packet-oriented. When the user places a call, a single connection is formed between the caller and the receiver. This connection is static for the duration of the call. If the conversation were digitized and sent over a packet-oriented network, however, many possible paths would be available for each packet, and much more redundancy would be automatically available. For instance, if some portion of the network between the two points went down, the packets could still arrive at their destination through an alternate route, just as data packets do over the Internet. Also, available circuits would be used more efficiently, allowing more calls to be routed within a particular geographic area.

VoIP also has some disadvantages that you need to consider:

- **No guaranteed delivery**   VoIP does not guarantee delivery of IP packets over the Internet. For a digital transmission of data, this is no big deal; if a packet isn't confirmed as being received, it is simply retransmitted. For a real-time voice conversation, the loss of packets directly inhibits the conversation, and you can't go back in time to retransmit missing packets.

■ **Out-of-sequence packets**   Not only can IP packets simply fail to arrive at their destination on occasion, but sometimes they arrive out of sequence due to other Internet traffic and other reasons. This is fine for transmitting things such as files, because the packets can be reassembled on the other end in the proper sequence once they are all received. For a real-time application such as voice, however, having packets arrive out of sequence results in a hopelessly jumbled, and thus useless, transmission.

■ **QoS not widely implemented**   Real-time uses of the Internet, such as VoIP or multimedia streaming and time-sensitive transmissions, should be given priority over transmissions that are not particularly time-sensitive, such as the transmission of an e-mail message. Fortunately, IP has a quality of service (QoS) field that enables the user to prioritize traffic for such reasons. However, QoS is not widely implemented in all parts of the Internet.

VoIP is a hot, emerging technology that is virtually certain to become an important part of the Internet and most companies' networks. However, there is still much work to be done toward actually implementing this technology widely and solving the problems outlined in this section. In other words, if you're learning about networking, you should be aware of VoIP—what it is and what it does—although the technology is still relatively early on the adoption curve.

 NOTE   There are a number of companies offering VoIP services for residential customers, including AT&T, Vonage, Verizon, and Time Warner Cable. These companies provide packages that allow virtually unlimited calling over an existing high-bandwidth Internet connection for as little as $30 additional per month. They often package the necessary VoIP hardware with a subscription agreement.

Comparing Important Proprietary Protocols

While Microsoft-based, Novell-based, and Apple-based networks can work with TCP/IP and all the previously discussed protocols, each type of network got its start supporting proprietary protocols unique to the company, and each of these protocols can still be found in current networks. All these companies have embraced TCP/IP and support it fully, both for servers and for network clients.

Microsoft and Novell networks (as of Windows NT 4 and Novell NetWare 5) can be easily deployed using only TCP/IP. In theory, you could do the same thing with an Apple-based network, but you would lose a good deal of the Macintosh's network functionality if you did so. Because of this, an Apple-based network should support both AppleTalk (Apple's proprietary protocol) and TCP/IP.

Novell networks originally used the Internetwork Packet Exchange/Sequenced Packet Exchange (IPX/SPX) protocols. These are not the same as TCP/IP, but they are comparable. IPX is analogous to IP, and SPX is analogous to TCP.

Microsoft networks were originally based on an IBM-developed protocol called Network Basic Input/Output System (NetBIOS). NetBIOS is a relatively high-level protocol that, in essence, extends the functionality of DOS to a network. Microsoft also used IBM's NetBIOS Extended User Interface (NetBEUI), an enhancement to NetBIOS.

Apple Macintosh computer networks originally supported only AppleTalk. The protocol was designed expressly for the purpose of sharing Apple LaserWriter printers within small workgroups using a low-bandwidth (230 Kbps originally) network media called LocalTalk. Over time, Apple extended AppleTalk somewhat to enable file sharing and other network functions. However, AppleTalk is still an extremely inefficient network protocol that, even over Ethernet (called EtherTalk in Apple's implementation), works slowly.

Novell's IPX/SPX

Novell's IPX protocol was originally a derivative of the Xerox Network Systems (XNS) architecture and closely resembles it. While IPX can be used on any of the popular network media (Ethernet, Token Ring, and so forth), it was originally designed for Ethernet networks and works best with that media. In fact, the IPX protocol depends on Ethernet MAC addresses for part of its own addresses. IPX addresses are dynamic and are automatically negotiated with the server at login, rather than being statically set, as is the case with TCP/IP without DHCP services.

An IPX network address is composed of both a 32-bit network address and a 48-bit node address. In addition, another 16 bits are used for a connection ID, which allows up to 65,000 unique connections between a client and a server. The address design of IPX theoretically allows for about 281 trillion nodes on each of 16 million networks.

IPX was originally designed only for LANs, but it has been enhanced to support WAN connections. While typically considered a "chatty" protocol that requires a lot of send/acknowledgment transactions, IPX has been enhanced with burst-mode capabilities, which increase the size of packets destined for a WAN and decrease the number of back-and-forth communications required. IPX can be routed, but only if the network includes an IPX-capable router.

NetBIOS and NetBEUI

IBM originally developed NetBIOS and NetBEUI to support small networks. Microsoft adopted the protocols as part of LAN Manager, a network operating system built on top of early versions of the OS/2 operating system.

Neither protocol is routable, so each is suitable only for small LANs that do not rely on routers between different LAN segments. However, NetBIOS can be encapsulated within TCP/IP packets on Windows networks using a service called NetBIOS over TCP/IP (abbreviated as NBT).

Microsoft LANs (prior to Windows 2000) rely on a NetBIOS service called NetBIOS Names to identify each workstation uniquely. In a simple NetBIOS implementation, names are registered with all workstations through a broadcast message. If no computer has already registered a particular name, the name registration succeeds. In a more complex Windows–based network that also uses TCP/IP, however, the NetBIOS names resolve to TCP/IP addresses through the use of Windows Internet Name Service (WINS). The names can also be resolved using static name definition entries contained in a file called LMHOSTS (for LAN Manager HOSTS).

Because some networking applications still use NetBIOS Names, either WINS or LMHOSTS allows such applications to continue to function in a TCP/IP-only network. As far as the application is concerned, it is still working with NetBIOS, while TCP/IP performs the actual work in the background.

AppleTalk

AppleTalk has been extended into AppleTalk Phase 2, which now allows routing of AppleTalk packets (assuming an AppleTalk Phase 2-capable router). The Phase 2 variant can run over Ethernet, Token Ring, or Apple's LocalTalk media. Under Ethernet, AppleTalk uses a variant of the 802.2 frame type called Ethernet Subnetwork Access Point (SNAP).

AppleTalk has an important history for Apple Macintosh networking, but Apple now fully supports and recommends TCP/IP for its computers.

Chapter Summary

This chapter is built on the knowledge you gained in earlier chapters, delving into various important protocols involved in virtually all networks, including the Internet. You learned primarily about the TCP/IP protocol, which has essentially displaced older protocols such as IPX/SPX and NetBIOS/NetBEUI (although these older protocols are still used). You also learned about some specific application-layer Internet protocols, such as SMTP, DHCP, and HTTP. These are all vital protocols to understand for any networking professional.

It would be nice if the protocols discussed in this chapter were all you had to contend with, but, unfortunately, many more protocols exist. Some are specific to certain functions, such as remote access to a network, and are discussed in appropriate chapters within this book. Others are still being developed and are not a factor now, but may be in the near future. You will certainly want to stay up-to-date with emerging protocols that may become important to networking.

The next chapter is about directory services, which make complex networks easier to use and administer.

Chapter 9

Exploring Directory Services

In the early days of local area networks (LANs), finding server resources was simple. Most organizations started with just a file server and a print server or two, so knowing which files, printers, and other services were in which locations on the LAN was easy.

These days, the situation is considerably more complex. Even relatively small organizations might have multiple servers, all performing different jobs—storing different sets of files and providing different Internet or intranet services, such as e-mail servers, web hosting, database servers, network services, and so forth.

Directory services work to bring organization to this far-flung network clutter. In this chapter, you learn about what directory services do and how they work. You also learn about the directory services in use today and those slated for use in the near future. With directory services becoming more and more central to the administration of networks, learning this information becomes an increasingly important part of designing, deploying, and managing networks.

What Is a Directory Service?

In most networks, you optimize the function of different services by hosting them on different computers. Doing so makes sense. Putting all your services on one computer is a bit like placing all your eggs in one basket—if you drop the basket, you'll break all your eggs. Moreover, you can achieve optimal performance, more reliability, and higher security by segregating network services in various ways.

Most networks have quite a few services that need to be provided, and often these services run on different servers. Even a relatively simple network now offers the following services:

- File storage and sharing
- Printer sharing
- E-mail services
- Web hosting, both for the Internet and an intranet
- Database server services
- Specific application servers
- Internet connectivity
- Dial-in and dial-out services
- Fax services
- Domain Name System (DNS) service, Windows Internet Naming Service (WINS), and Dynamic Host Configuration Protocol (DHCP) services
- Centralized virus-detection services
- Backup and restore services

This is only a short list. Larger organizations have multiple servers sharing in each of these functions—with different services available through different means in each building or location—and might have additional services beyond those listed here.

All this complexity can quickly make a network chaotic to manage. If each one of the individual servers required separate administration (with, for instance, separate lists of users, passwords, groups, printers, network configurations, and so on), the job would become virtually impossible in no time.

Directory services were invented to bring organization to networks. Basically, directory services work just like a phone book. Instead of using a name to look up an address and phone number in a phone book, you query the directory service for a service name (such as the name of a network folder or a printer), and the directory service tells you where the service is located. You can also query directory services by property. For instance, if you query the directory service for all items that are "printers," it can return a complete list, no matter where the printers are located in the organization. Even better, directory services enable you to browse all the resources on a network easily, in one unified list organized in a tree structure.

One important advantage of directory services is that they eliminate the need to manage duplicates of anything on the network because the directory is automatically shared among all of the servers. For example, you don't need to maintain separate user lists on each server. Instead, you manage a single set of user accounts that exists in the directory service and then assign them various permissions to particular resources on any of the servers. Other resources work the same way and become centrally managed in the directory service. Not only does this mean that you have only one collection of objects to manage, but also that users have a much simpler network experience. From the users' perspective, they have only one network account with one password, and they don't need to worry about where resources are located or keep track of multiple passwords for different network services or servers.

NOTE In this chapter, the term *network resource* refers to any discrete resource on a network, such as a user account, security group definition, e-mail distribution list, storage volume, folder, or file. The term *directory* refers to the directory that a directory service uses, rather than a directory on a hard disk.

To provide redundancy, directory services usually run on multiple servers in an organization, with each of the servers having a complete copy of the entire directory service database. Because a directory service becomes central to the functioning of a network, this approach lets the network as a whole continue to operate if any single server with directory services on it crashes. Servers that do not actually host a copy of the directory still make use of it by communicating with the directory servers. For instance, if a user tries to open a file hosted on a server that doesn't actually host the directory service, the server will automatically query the directory service on another server to authenticate the user's access request. To the user, this happens behind the scenes.

You should know about five important directory services: Novell eDirectory, Microsoft's Windows NT domains, Microsoft's Active Directory, X.500 Directory Access Protocol, and Lightweight Directory Access Protocol. These are described later in this chapter.

Forests, Roots, Trees, and Leaves

One thing common to all directory services is a tree-based organization (with the tree usually depicted upside-down with the root at the top), somewhat similar to the organization of directories on a hard disk. A *forest* is a collection of trees managed collectively. At the top of each directory tree is the *root* entry, which contains other entries. These other entries can be containers or leaves. A *container object* is one that contains other objects, which can also include more containers and leaves. A *leaf object* represents an actual resource on the network, such as a workstation, printer, shared directory, file, or user account. Leaf objects cannot contain other objects. Figure 9-1 shows a typical directory tree.

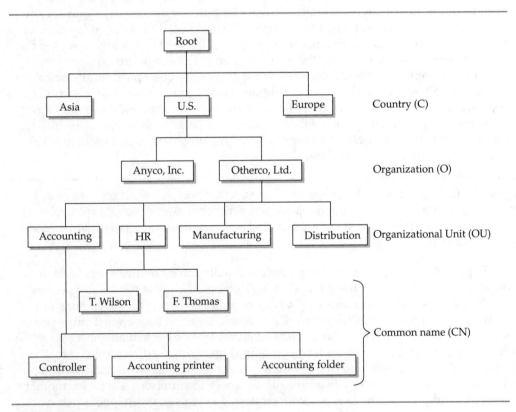

Figure 9-1.   A typical directory tree

All the objects in a directory tree have *attributes* (sometimes called *properties*), which vary depending on the type of object to which the attribute is attached. For example, a *printer leaf object* might contain attributes that describe the printer, who can administer the printer, what the printer's name is on the network, and so forth. A *user account leaf object* might contain attributes that include the full name of the user account, its password, and resources that the user can access. The details of what attributes attach to what leaf or container objects vary among all the directory services, although they generally use similar attributes.

Department of Redundancy Department

Keeping directory services running is essential for any network that relies on them. Because they contain all details about accounts, resources, and security, the absence of directory services means the network won't work—at all! Since the directory services become so important to a network, you must protect them with some degree of redundancy. As mentioned earlier, keeping duplicate copies of the directory on multiple servers provides the necessary redundancy. This is done using one of two approaches:

- In the *primary/backup model*, a single primary database contains the primary (or "real") directory on one server, while other servers hold one or more backup copies. If the primary copy stops working for some reason, the backups can continue to provide directory services to the network without the user even knowing that the primary copy isn't available. Windows NT domains use a primary/backup approach.

- In the *multimaster model*, multiple directory servers exist, but they are all peers to one another. If one goes down, the other peers continue to operate normally. The advantage of the multimaster model is that each directory server can fully participate in doing the work of the directory service. Active Directory (in Windows 2000 Server and later) uses the multimaster approach.

Directory servers—whether they use the primary/backup or multimaster approach—must keep in sync with changes on the network. The separate databases are kept synchronized through a process called *replication*, in which changes to any of the individual directory databases are transparently updated to all the other directory service databases.

A potential problem exists with any replication process, though: If two changes are made to the same leaf object on two different directory servers and the changes are different, what does the system do when the changes "collide" during replication? The various directory services handle this problem in slightly different ways. In the case of Novell eDirectory, the timestamps of the changes drive which of two conflicting changes will win. (Because of this, servers running eDirectory must carefully keep their time synchronized; this synchronization is also handled during replication.) Microsoft's Active Directory doesn't use timestamps, but instead uses sequence numbers in a clever scheme that avoids the potential problems of a timestamp approach. (Even though eDirectory servers synchronize their time, their time can still become out of sync between synchronizations.)

Some directory services also allow a concept called *partitioning*, in which different directory servers keep different parts of the entire directory tree. In this case, a controlling directory server usually manages the entire tree (called the *global catalog* in Active Directory), and then other directory servers can manage smaller pieces of the total tree. Partitioning is important for networks with multiple LANs connected by a wide area network (WAN). In such cases, you want to host a partition that relates to a particular LAN locally, yet still allow access to the entire tree for resources accessed over the WAN. Each LAN hosts its own partition, but can still access the total tree when needed. You arrange the partitions (and set the scheduled replication times) to make the best use of the WAN's performance, which usually is slower than that of a LAN.

Learning About Specific Directory Services

Quite a few different directory services are available. Choosing one usually goes hand in hand with choosing a main network operating system, although this isn't always the case. Both eDirectory and Active Directory can handle non-Novell and non-Microsoft servers, respectively. Consequently, even a network that currently uses mostly Windows servers might still rely on eDirectory for directory services through the use of Novell's eDirectory for Windows product. Using a single directory service with different network operating systems often happens because an organization starts out favoring a particular network operating system and then later finds itself forced to support additional ones, but the organization still wants to maintain a coherent, single directory service to manage the network operating systems.

The following are the main directory services:

■ *Novell eDirectory* (previously called Novell Directory Services, or NDS) is the network directory service that has been available for the longest time. eDirectory runs on NetWare 4.*x* and later servers, and is also available for other server operating systems (such as Solaris, Linux, and Windows), enabling you to use eDirectory as a single directory service for managing a multivendor network.

■ *Windows NT domains* (introduced with Windows NT 4) are not actually complete directory services, but they provide some of the features and advantages of directory services.

■ *Microsoft's Active Directory* debuted with the Windows 2000 Server line of products. This is a true directory service, and it brings the full features of a directory service to a network predominantly built using Windows servers.

■ *X.500 Directory Access Protocol* (DAP) is an international standard directory service that is full of features. However, X.500 provides so many features that its overhead makes deploying and managing it prohibitive. Consequently, X.500 is in an interesting position: it is an important standard, yet, paradoxically, it is not actually used.

■ The *Lightweight Directory Access Protocol* (LDAP) was developed by a consortium of vendors as a subset of X.500 to offer an alternative with less complexity than X.500. LDAP is in wide use for e-mail directories and is suitable for other directory service tasks. The most recent versions of eDirectory and Active Directory are compatible with LDAP.

These are the predominant directory services that you will encounter, although others exist. For instance, a number of companies offer different software that provides LDAP-compliant directory services on different platforms.

eDirectory

Novell eDirectory has been available since 1993, introduced as NDS as part of NetWare 4.*x*. This product was a real boon and was rapidly implemented in Novell networks, particularly in larger organizations that had many NetWare servers and desperately needed its capabilities. eDirectory is a reliable, robust directory service that has continued to evolve since its introduction. Version 8.8 is now available, and it incorporates the latest directory service features.

eDirectory uses a primary/backup approach to directory servers and also allows partitioning of the tree. In addition to running on Novell network operating systems, eDirectory is also available for Windows, Solaris, AIX, and Linux systems. The product's compatibility with such a variety of systems makes it a good choice for managing all these platforms under a single directory structure.

You manage the eDirectory tree from a client computer logged in to the network with administrative privileges. You can use a graphical tool designed to manage the tree, such as Novell Identity Manager, or other tools that mimic the look and feel of the operating system on which they run and that are also available from Novell.

The eDirectory tree contains a number of different object types. The standard directory service types—countries, organizations, and organizational units—are included. The system also has objects to represent NetWare security groups, NetWare servers, and NetWare server volumes. eDirectory can manage more than a billion objects in a tree.

Windows NT Domains

The Windows NT domain model breaks an organization into chunks called *domains*, all of which are part of an organization. The domains are usually organized geographically, which helps minimize domain-to-domain communication requirements across WAN links, although you're free to organize domains as you wish. Each domain is controlled by a *primary domain controller* (PDC), which might have one or more *backup domain controllers* (BDCs) to kick in if the PDC fails.

All changes within the domain are made to the PDC, which then replicates those changes to any BDCs. BDCs are read-only, except for valid updates received from the PDC. In case of a PDC failure, BDCs automatically continue authenticating users. To make administrative changes to a domain that suffers PDC failure, any of the BDCs can be *promoted* to PDC. Once the PDC is ready to come back online, the promoted BDC can be *demoted* back to BDC status.

Windows NT domains can be organized into one of four domain models.

■ **Single domain** In this model, only one domain contains all network resources.

■ **Master domain** The master model usually puts users at the top-level domain and then places network resources, such as shared folders or printers, in lower-level domains (called *resource domains*). In this model, the resource domains trust the master domain.

■ **Multiple master domain** This is a slight variation on the master domain model, in which users might exist in multiple master domains, all of which trust one another, and in which resources are located in resource domains, all of which trust all the master domains.

■ **Complete trust** This variation of the single-domain model spreads users and resources across all domains, which all trust each other.

You choose an appropriate domain model depending on the physical layout of the network, the number of users to be served, and other factors. (If you're planning a domain model, you should review the white papers on Microsoft's web site for details on planning large domains, because the process can be complex.)

Explicit trust relationships must be maintained between domains using the master or multiple master domain model and must be managed on each domain separately. Maintaining these relationships is one of the biggest difficulties in the Windows NT domain structure approach, at least for larger organizations. If you have 100 domains, you must manage the 99 possible trust relationships for each domain, for a total of 9,900 trust relationships. For smaller numbers of domains (for example, less than 10 domains), management of the trust relationships is less of a problem, although it can still cause difficulties.

Active Directory

Windows NT domains work relatively well for smaller networks, but they can become difficult to manage for larger networks. Moreover, the system is not nearly as comprehensive as, for example, eDirectory. Microsoft recognized this problem and developed a directory service called Active Directory, which is a comprehensive directory service that runs on Windows 2000 Server and later. Active Directory is fully compatible with LDAP (versions 2 and 3) and also with the Domain Name System (DNS) used on the Internet.

Active Directory uses a peer approach to domain controllers; all domain controllers are full participants at all times. As mentioned earlier in this chapter, this arrangement is called *multimaster* because there are many "master" domain controllers but no backup controllers.

Active Directory is built on a structure that allows "trees of trees," which is called a *forest*. Each tree is its own domain and has its own domain controllers. Within a domain, separate organizational units are allowed to make administration easier and more logical.

Trees are then aggregated into a larger forest structure. According to Microsoft, Active Directory can handle millions of objects through this approach.

Active Directory does not require the management of trust relationships, except when connected to Windows NT 4.*x* servers that are not using Active Directory. Otherwise, all domains within a tree have automatic trust relationships.

X.500

The X.500 standard was developed jointly by the International Telecommunications Union (ITU) and the International Standards Organization (ISO). The standard defines a directory service that can be used for the entire Internet. Because of its broad applicability, the X.500 specification is too complex for most organizations to implement. Also, because of its design, it is intended to publish specific organizational directory entries across the Internet, which is something most companies would not want to do. Just the same, the X.500 standard is extremely important, and most directory services mimic or incorporate parts of it in some fashion.

The X.500 directory tree starts with a root, just like the other directory trees, and then breaks down into country (C), organization (O), organizational unit (OU), and common name (CN) fields. To specify an X.500 address fully, you provide five fields, as in the following:

```
CN=user name, OU=department, OU=division, O=organization, C=country
```

For example, you might configure the fields as follows:

```
CN=Bruce Hallberg, OU=Networking Books, OU=Computer Books, O=McGraw-Hill,
C=USA
```

LDAP

To address the complexity problems involved with full X.500 DAP, a consortium of companies came up with a subset of X.500, called LDAP. LDAP's advocates claim that it provides 90 percent of the power of X.500, but at only 10 percent of the processing cost. LDAP runs over TCP/IP and uses a client/server model. Its organization is much the same as that of X.500, but with fewer fields and fewer functions.

LDAP is covered predominantly by RFC 1777 (for version 2) and RFC 2251 (for version 3). (Some other RFCs also describe aspects of LDAP.) The LDAP standard describes not only the layout and fields within an LDAP directory, but also the methods to be used when a person logs in to a server that uses LDAP, or queries or updates the LDAP directory information on an LDAP server. (Because directory services might fulfill many simultaneous authentications, run simultaneous queries, and accept simultaneous updates, it is important that these methods be clearly defined to avoid collisions and other potentially corrupting uses of the directory by client applications and administrative tools.)

NOTE   Many of the standards on the Internet are controlled by documents called Request for Comments (RFCs). These are documents that describe a proposed standard and are submitted to the Internet Engineering Task Force group. You can read more about this group, as well as peruse any of the networking RFCs you see mentioned in this book (or elsewhere) from the group's home page at http://www.ietf.org.

An LDAP tree starts with a root, which then contains entries. Each entry can have one or more *attributes*. Each of these attributes has both a *type* and *values* associated with it. One example is the CN ("common name"), which contains at least two attributes: FirstName and Surname. All attributes in LDAP use the text string data type. Entries are organized into a tree and managed geographically and then within each organization.

The following four basic models describe the LDAP protocol:

- **Information model**   This model defines the structure of the data stored in the directory. It describes a number of aspects of the directory, including the schema, classes, attributes, attribute syntax, and entries. The directory's *schema* is the template for the directory and its entries. *Classes* are categories to which all entries are attached. *Attributes* are items of data that describe the classes, such as CN and OU. The *syntax* for the attributes specifies exactly how attributes are named and stored, and what sort of data they are allowed to contain (such as numbers, string text, dates and times, and so forth). Finally, *entries* are distinct pieces of data; like objects, that can be either a container or a leaf.

NOTE   Microsoft uses nomenclature to describe LDAP that differs from the terms defined in the RFCs. Most notably, Microsoft calls an *entry* an *object*, and calls an *attribute* a *property*. These names refer to the same things, and you should be aware of this when reading the RFCs or other documents about LDAP and comparing the information to that found in documents from Microsoft.

- **Naming model**   This model describes how to reference and organize the data. It defines the names that serve as primary keys for entries in the directory: *distinguished names* (DNs), which are full names of entries, as well as *relative distinguished names* (RDNs), which are components of DNs. Each component of the DN—such as the CD, OU, or O entries—is an RDN. The following is an example of an LDAP DN:

```
CN=Bruce Hallberg, OU=Networking Books, OU=Computer Books,
O=McGraw-Hill, C=USA.
```

- **Functional model**   This model describes how to work with the data. It defines how LDAP accomplishes three types of operations: authentication, interrogation, and updates. *Authentication* is the process by which users prove their identity to the directory. *Interrogation* is the process by which the information in the directory is queried. *Updates* are operations that post changes to the directory.

- **Security model** This model defines how to keep the data in the directory secure. For most implementations of LDAP, a security protocol called Simple Authentication and Security Layer (SASL) is used. RFC 2222 describes SASL.

One nice feature of LDAP is that an organization can build a global directory structure using a feature called *referral*, where LDAP directory queries that are managed by a different LDAP server are transparently routed to that server. Because each LDAP server knows its parent LDAP server and its child servers, any user anywhere in the network can access the entire LDAP tree. In fact, the users won't even know they are accessing different servers in different locales.

Chapter Summary

In this chapter, you learned about both the importance of directory services and the factors driving that importance. You also learned how directory services work, what they accomplish, and those common features found in almost all directory services. Finally, the most important directory services were each reviewed, including Novell's eDirectory, Microsoft's domain service, and Active Directory service.

The next chapter continues the discussions about essential network technologies and services by teaching you about remote access services, in which far-flung users can access LANs from anywhere in the world. Implementing a good remote access system that everyone is happy with is one of the most difficult things to do—especially for large organizations with many different needs—so a variety of approaches are discussed.

Chapter 10

Connections from Afar: Remote Network Access

In the preceding chapters, you learned about networking systems together through a local area network (LAN) and through a wide area network (WAN), and about the technologies that go into both types of networks. You also need to know about another important type of network connection: remote access to a network. With today's travel-happy corporate cultures, and with companies needing to support such things as working from home and small remote offices, remote access has become more important than ever. Unfortunately, it's also one of the most difficult parts of a network to get right, as you will see in this chapter.

One of the big problems with remote access is that it can seem as though all the remote users have different requirements, the various solutions address different needs, and none of those solutions takes care of *all* the needs. Finding solid solutions that meet those needs is usually nontrivial and requires a fair amount of time and effort. This chapter describes how you might analyze your company's needs and then discusses the remote access technologies that can provide a solution (or solutions) for your network.

Determining Remote Access Needs

Every company has a different mix of remote users, and their specific needs may vary from company to company. Moreover, even when needs are identical, the solutions you employ might change based on other criteria. For instance, you might handle access to an accounting system from a remote location differently, depending on whether it's a client/server or a monolithic application.

Understanding Application Implications for Remote Access

Client/server applications consist of processes (programs) that run on both the server side and the client side, and work in concert. For example, a database server performs queries for the client, and then transmits to the client only the results of that query. The client's job is just to display the results and maybe format them for printing.

A monolithic application, on the other hand, performs all of its work on one computer, typically the client computer. The server for a monolithic application serves up only the files needed for the application to run and the data files that the application manipulates.

Generally, client/server applications require much less bandwidth to work at acceptable speeds than monolithic applications. A slow network connection might be adequate for a client/server application, such as an accounting system, whereas that connection would be totally inadequate for that same application designed to be monolithic.

What Types of Remote Users Do You Need to Support?

Users who require remote access generally fall into one of the following four categories:

- Broad traveler
- Narrow traveler
- Remote office user
- Remote office group

Each category of remote user has different needs, and different technologies and remote access solutions are often required to satisfy these needs completely. Your first step in finding a remote access solution is to determine which categories of remote users *you* must support. So, let's look at each of these remote access user categories.

The *broad traveler* is the most common type of remote access user. This is someone who normally is based in an office that has LAN access, but also travels on business. Travel takes this person to virtually any place in the world, so the traveler must contend with different telephone systems, long-distance carriers, and other geographic challenges (see Figure 10-1). Often, this type of user mostly needs e-mail access, with occasional access to stored or e-mailed files. The user might normally use a desktop computer on the LAN but have a laptop computer for traveling, might use a single laptop both on the LAN and when traveling, might check out laptop computers from a shared pool when travel needs arise, or might even rent a laptop computer for an occasional travel need. These different approaches further complicate providing services to the broad traveler.

The *narrow traveler* is someone who travels to relatively few locations, such as from corporate headquarters to the company's manufacturing plants or distribution centers.

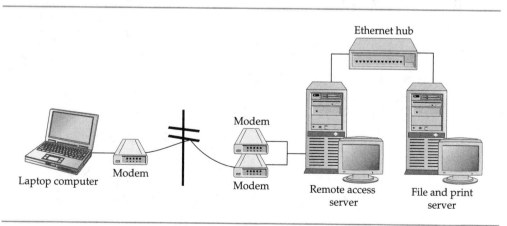

Figure 10-1.   A typical remote access session

Since you can predict the sites from which the user might need to access data, local support may be available to help. For instance, you might have a way for the user to log in to the distribution center's LAN and access e-mail and files at the headquarters location through an existing WAN link, as shown in Figure 10-2. This type of user needs e-mail, file access, and possibly access to a centralized application, such as an accounting system.

The *remote office user* is in a single location and needs access to the corporate LAN for e-mail and possibly for application access (see Figure 10-3). This person usually does not need file access, except to send files through the e-mail system, because this person maintains local file storage. This user is in a single location, so you can pursue certain high-speed links that are not feasible for the travelers. A person telecommuting from home would fall into the category of remote office user.

Sometimes a small group (two to five people) stationed in a remote location needs certain services from the corporate LAN. These services are not cost-effective for this group to have locally, yet these users have a small local LAN for printer and file sharing, as illustrated in Figure 10-4. These users fall into the *remote office group* category, which needs a combination of services. Partly they are like any user of a remote LAN, and partly they are like a remote office user. They usually require a mixture of both types of solutions for proper support.

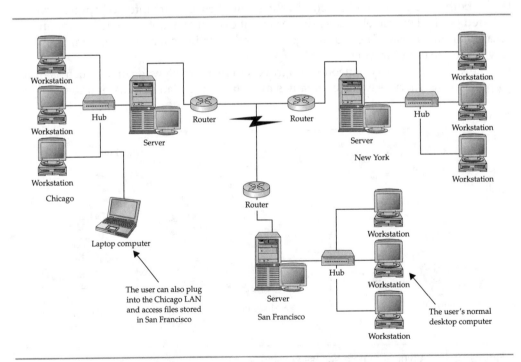

Figure 10-2.   A WAN used by a "narrow traveler"

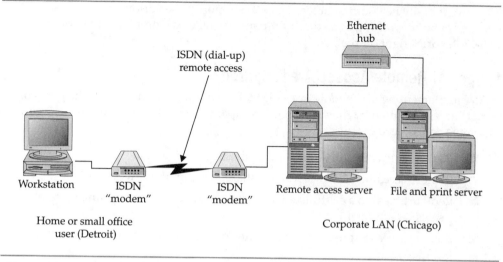

Figure 10-3.   A remote office user's network setup

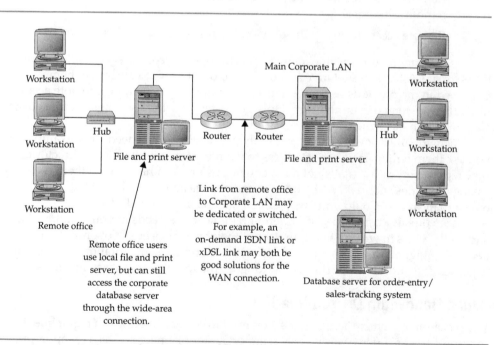

Figure 10-4.   Supporting a small remote office that requires LAN access

You generally need different strategies to support these various types of users. Of course, if you're working in a small company, you likely won't have to support all these categories right off the bat.

What Types of Remote Access Are Required?

Before implementing any remote access system, you must define clearly the types of remote access required by the users in the company. The following are some examples of remote access needs:

- Easy remote access to e-mail and to files stored in e-mail

- Remote access to stored private or shared files on the LAN

- Remote access to a centralized application, such as an accounting system or a sales order system

- Remote access to groupware programs or custom applications

- Internet access

- Intranet/extranet access, including any hosted web-based applications on those systems

- Remote access to any of the previous features from a fixed location, such as a remote sales office

- Remote access to any of the previous features from anywhere in the world

To understand your specific remote access support needs, interview all the potential users (or at least a representative subset) and find out how to categorize them, as described in the previous section. Chances are that you must support remote access through more than one mechanism. How you categorize the users and their needs will suggest which mechanisms make sense.

When you interview the users, carefully probe all possible needs. For example, if you ask them if they need remote access to the files stored in their LAN directories and they reply, "not really," that's not an adequate answer. You need to pin them down by asking questions such as, "Will you *ever* need remote access to files? What if you had only e-mail access? Could your assistant e-mail you any needed files?"

Once you have come up with different remote access needs in your company, try to survey the users in writing to inquire about their specific needs. Not only should you get less ambiguous answers, but you also get important documentation to justify the expenses and effort in acquiring and setting up the remote access systems needed.

How Much Bandwidth Do You Need?

When examining remote access needs, you need to estimate bandwidth requirements and tolerances for the different users. This is important for planning and also for appropriately setting user expectations. For example, if salespeople want minute-to-minute access to a sales-tracking system and also frequently want to download 10MB file packages to use for quotations, you must explain the limitations of modem speeds and telephone or cellular wireless connections to reduce these users' expectations. Or you can find different solutions that are consistent with the amount of bandwidth you can offer.

You can estimate a particular application program's bandwidth requirements by actually measuring the amount of bandwidth that application uses. On the LAN, you can monitor the amount of data being sent to a particular node that uses the application in the way it would be used remotely. You can measure the data in a number of ways. For a Windows PC, you can run System Monitor or Performance Monitor on the client and look at the network traffic that the PC is consuming (see Figure 10-5). You can also measure the volume of data from the server. For a Windows server, you can use Performance Monitor to measure bytes transmitted to and from the client. For a Novell server, you can use the console Monitor application and watch the amount of data being sent and received by the client's server connection.

If the bandwidth requirements of an application are simply too great to handle over the type of remote connection that you have available (such as a 33.6 Kbps modem connection), you need to explore other alternatives. These include using a remote control solution (discussed later in this chapter) or using the application in a different way. For example, you might load the application onto the remote computer rather than use it across the LAN. Also, perhaps the user does not need the data to be updated so frequently, and you can set up a procedure whereby the user receives weekly data updates on a CD-R disc or an overnight download.

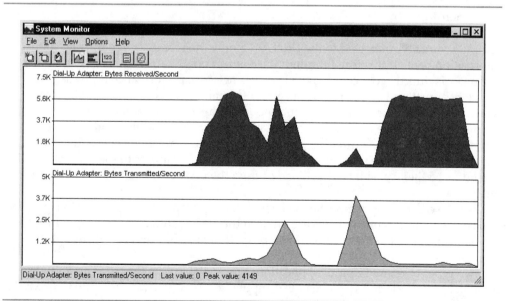

Figure 10-5.   Using Windows System Monitor to look at the bandwidth that an application is using

The ways that you can satisfy remote access needs are virtually limitless. However, the key is to assess those needs carefully and to work creatively, given your available or proposed remote access technology.

Learning Remote Access Technologies

A variety of different ways exist to accomplish remote access connections for users. Sometimes these different technologies are appropriate for some users but not for others. Sometimes the choices you have are restricted by how the remote user needs to access the data. For example, a remote user at a single location can fairly easily set up a high-speed link to the corporate LAN, while a traveling remote user might be limited to using modems and dial-up telephone connections in some places in the world.

The following sections discuss different techniques and technologies, along with the pros and cons of each. The ones you implement depend on the needs you've identified, your budget, and the existing infrastructure of your network.

Remote Node Versus Remote Control

Remote users can connect to a network in two basic ways: remote node and remote control. A *remote node connection* is one in which the remote computer becomes a node on the network. Data flows between the remote node and the network much as it would for a LAN-connected user, albeit usually at much slower rates. When you connect to an Internet service provider (ISP) to access the Internet, you are using a remote node connection.

A *remote control connection* is one in which a remote user takes control of another computer directly connected to the LAN, with only the screen, keyboard, and mouse information being transmitted through the connection. Because the remote control computer is directly connected to the LAN, its network performance is just as fast as that of any other LAN workstation. The information actually transmitted—the screen information, keyboard data, and mouse data—usually doesn't require much bandwidth. (One exception to this rule is a highly graphical application, such as a computer-aided drafting drawing program.) Remote control connections also have ways to transfer files back and forth from the remote computer to the controlled computer, so files can still be downloaded from the LAN to the remote computer and vice versa.

Remote control is accomplished using special applications designed for this purpose. You run the remote control software on both the LAN-connected computer and the remote computer. The connection is established over a dial-up line or through the Internet.

Two types of remote control applications are available. The first runs on a single computer and supports a single remote computer at a time. pcAnywhere and GoToMyPC are examples of this type. Another type allows multiple sessions to run on a single computer, so you can allow more than one user making use of a single computer connected to the LAN. Windows NT Terminal Server, Windows Terminal Services, and Citrix XenServer are examples of this type. The multiuser solutions use the LAN computer's multitasking capabilities to construct multiple virtual PCs, windows, and desktops, sort of like a mainframe with multiple terminal sessions.

Any of the remote connection technologies can work with both remote node and remote control. You can connect to a remote control system through modems connected directly to the remote control computer, through ISDN lines, over the Internet, or even over a LAN or WAN link.

How do you know whether to choose remote node or remote control connections? Consider these points:

- When a remote user needs only LAN file access and e-mail access, a remote node connection can meet these needs and is often simpler to set up and maintain on both sides of the connection.

- If a remote user needs to run an application that is LAN-connected, choose remote control. A few applications might be able to run reasonably well over a remote node connection, provided the application itself is already installed on the remote computer and the application must access only relatively small amounts of data through the remote link. For example, accessing e-mail through Microsoft Outlook works fine over a remote node connection, provided the remote users already have Outlook installed on their local computer.

- Many applications are now web-enabled, so a remote user can use a web browser to access and use such applications. These types of applications run equally well—more or less—over a remote node or remote control connection. For example, Microsoft Exchange Server supports a number of connection types, including web access to mailboxes and calendars, through a feature called Outlook Web Access. Many client/server accounting systems are also starting to implement web access.

- If you need to maintain an application directly for the users, remote control might be the way to go, because it leaves the application on the LAN-connected machine, where you can easily access it to make configuration changes or perform other maintenance. The remote user runs only the remote control software and instantly benefits from any work you do on the LAN-connected machine. This capability can provide a real advantage if your network's users are not comfortable doing their own maintenance or troubleshooting on the software. With such a connection, you can more easily handle any problems that arise, without needing to travel to some remote location or requiring users to ship their computers to you for repair or maintenance.

Remote control is the best bet when the remote users need to access applications that don't work well over lower-bandwidth connections. And because most applications don't run well over slower connections, remote users will usually find that a LAN-connected application works better with remote control than with remote node.

Whether you choose remote node or remote control, you then must determine how the users will connect to the LAN. A variety of different ways exist to make this connection, as discussed in the following sections.

To Modem or Not To Modem, That Is the Question ...

Remote users can connect to your network in two ways: through devices connected to the network in some fashion, or by connecting to an ISP and then accessing the network over the LAN's Internet connection. For example, users can use a modem to dial in to a modem connected to the LAN that you maintain. Alternatively, users can use a modem to connect to a modem managed by an ISP and then make use of the LAN's connection to the Internet to get into the LAN.

For small networks, it can often be easiest to simply add a modem or two to a computer set up to accept remote connections, and then let the users use those modems to connect. You can set up the modems on individual PCs that run remote control software, on PCs that run remote node software (such as Windows Routing and Remote Access Service), or on special LAN-connected interfaces built for the purpose of providing remote node connections.

You can also build your own "modem farms" with tens or hundreds of modems, using special hardware that supports such uses. However, it can be a real hassle to manage your own modems—not only do you need to manage the modems themselves, but also the remote node software and hardware, the telephone lines used, and all the problems that can occur at any time.

If a LAN already has a high-speed link to the Internet, such as through a fractional or full T-1, it can be easier to let the remote users dial in to a local ISP and then connect to the LAN through the Internet. Such a setup has many advantages:

- **No need to support modems directly** You don't need to worry about managing the modems. If users can't connect, they can call the ISP for connection help. Larger ISPs have round-the-clock support staff in place to provide such help, which beats getting woken up at 2:00 A.M. because a user in Europe can't connect.

- **No long-distance tolls** The ISP connection is usually a local call, saving money on long-distance charges that may be incurred when dialing the LAN directly.

- **Minimal impact on LAN performance** Using the LAN's Internet connection usually doesn't affect the LAN users who also use that connection, for two reasons. First, many remote users connect to the LAN outside normal working hours when the Internet connection probably isn't being used much. Second, because the remote user is often connected to the ISP through a slower connection, the total impact to your high-speed Internet link is minimal, even during working hours.

- **High-speed connections** Your users can take advantage of whatever high-speed Internet links are available to them, and you don't need to worry about implementing matching technology on the LAN side. A user can use an *xDSL* line, a cable modem, or an ISDN line, and then connect to an ISP that supports that high-speed connection. On the LAN side, the high-speed connection (for example, a T-1) remains the same.

- **Better global access** Users traveling internationally will have better luck making connections to a local ISP than over an international telephone connection. Using a modem internationally is problematic at best—connection speeds are slow, the quality of the line is usually not good, and delays added by satellite connections (most international telephone traffic goes through a satellite) cause additional problems. And, of course, the cost can be prohibitive.

NOTE I once spent hundreds of dollars just checking e-mail from Singapore to the United States several times in one week. Singapore telephone rates are much higher than U.S. rates; originating calls from Singapore at the time cost $2 to $3 per minute (although even the standard U.S. rate of $0.75 per minute to Singapore would have been expensive). A far better solution would have been to dial in to a Singapore-located ISP modem (most large ISPs have a presence in several countries) and use the Internet to get to the U.S.-based LAN. Such a solution would have been cheaper, more reliable, and faster. (Unfortunately, at the time, those types of connections weren't possible.)

Modem connections are fairly slow, usually running at only up to 33.6 Kbps. However, modems are still the lowest common denominator for remote access, because standard plain old telephone service (POTS) connections are available virtually everywhere. Modems work reasonably well, all things considered.

NOTE Modems available these days are typically rated at up to 56 Kbps. There is an important caveat in this rating, however: It requires that the other end of the connection have a digital connection. Moreover, the 56 Kbps rating is a maximum available in the downstream direction; upstream never exceeds 33.6 Kbps, even when connected to an ISP that uses 56 Kbps-capable digital connections on its end. You can't achieve 56 Kbps over standard telephone lines, even if you have matched 56 Kbps modems at both ends; the maximum you will get is 33.6 Kbps in both directions over standard telephone lines with standard modems on each end.

In a nutshell, users who travel to different locations need to rely on modem connections. Currently, no type of standard high-bandwidth connection is ubiquitous enough to find in all locations. But the situation keeps improving; for example, most hotel rooms have high-speed Internet access ports.

For remote users who are at a single location, higher-speed connections become feasible. Home users in many areas can get high-speed DSL and cable modem connections to the Internet. And using a virtual private network, as discussed in the next section, they can benefit from these higher speeds when connecting to the corporate LAN. Even for users who don't have DSL or cable modems available in their area, ISDN is usually an option from the local telephone company. (ISDN and DSL technology are discussed in more detail in Chapter 7.)

Remote users using DSL or cable modems are "hard-wired" to a particular ISP for their connection, so they need to use a virtual private networking approach to connecting to the LAN. ISDN users, on the other hand, have the choice of either connecting to an ISDN-capable ISP or to ISDN "modems" hosted on the LAN. Through a process called *bonding*, ISDN users can achieve speeds up to 128 Kbps, although this consumes two B-channels. (and doubles the call charges!) Still, such speeds are better than the 33.6 Kbps that you can otherwise achieve through a modem.

Virtual Private Networks

A virtual private network (VPN) is a network link formed through the Internet between the remote user connected to an ISP and the company LAN. A VPN connection is carried over a shared or public network—which is almost always the Internet. VPNs use sophisticated packet encryption and other technologies, so the link from the user to the LAN is secure, even though it may be carried over a public network. VPN connections cost much less than dedicated connections, such as the WAN technologies discussed in Chapter 7, because they take advantage of the cost efficiencies of the Internet without compromising security.

VPN solutions range from simple ones that can be implemented on a Windows server essentially for free—using the Remote Access Service (RAS) included with Windows NT Server or the equivalent Routing and Remote Access Service (RRAS) in Windows 2000 Server or later—to stand-alone specialized VPN routers that can support hundreds of users. Figure 10-6 shows how a VPN connection works.

VPN connections are used in two important ways:

- To form WAN connections using VPN technology between two networks that might be thousands of miles apart but which each have some way of accessing the Internet
- To form remote access connections that enable remote users to access the LAN through the Internet

The emphasis in this chapter is on remote access, but it's important to know that VPNs support WAN connections in much the same way as they support a remote access connection. The main difference for a WAN VPN connection is that it connects two networks together, rather than a user and a network, and relies on different hardware (typically) than a remote access connection uses. A WAN VPN connection takes advantage of the existing Internet connection for both LANs and might run virtually 24 hours a day. A remote access connection, on the other hand, is usually formed when needed and uses less expensive hardware on the remote side, such as a dialup modem or perhaps a higher-speed Internet connection, such as *x*DSL, ISDN, or cable modem.

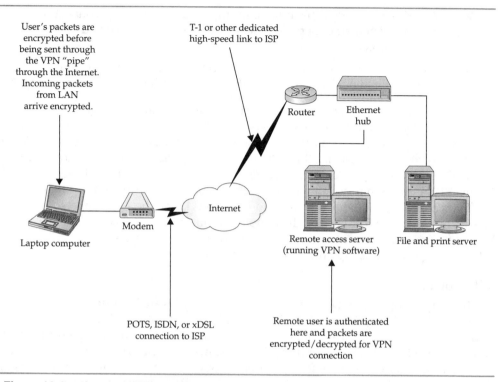

User's packets are encrypted before being sent through the VPN "pipe" through the Internet. Incoming packets from LAN arrive encrypted.

T-1 or other dedicated high-speed link to ISP

Router   Ethernet hub

Internet

Modem

Remote access server (running VPN software)   File and print server

Laptop computer

POTS, ISDN, or xDSL connection to ISP

Remote user is authenticated here and packets are encrypted/decrypted for VPN connection

Figure 10-6.   A typical VPN connection

TIP   In some circumstances, a VPN might even be an appropriate way to segregate users in a single location from other users, by using the company's intranet to host the VPN tunnel. Such a scheme might be appropriate, for example, if one group of users accesses data that is so sensitive that it must be separated from the rest of the company in some fashion. In such cases, the sensitive network can be separated from the corporate LAN, except for a firewall that allows VPN connections from the sensitive LAN to the corporate LAN, but not vice versa. This configuration would still allow users on the sensitive LAN to access general corporate network services.

A VPN connection has several requirements:

■   Both sides of the VPN connection must be connected to the Internet, usually using the Point-to-Point Protocol (PPP). (Other public or private networks can also carry VPNs, but this discussion will stick with the Internet because it's the most frequently used network for this purpose.)

■   Both sides must have a networking protocol in common. This protocol is usually TCP/IP, but can also be IPX, NetBEUI, or AppleTalk.

■ Both sides must establish a tunnel through their existing PPP connections, through which their data packets will pass. The tunnel is formed using a tunneling protocol.

■ Both sides must agree on an encryption technique to use with the data traversing the tunnel. A variety of different encryption techniques are available.

So, both sides of a VPN connection must be running compatible VPN software using compatible protocols. For a remote access VPN solution, the software you install depends on the VPN itself. Dedicated VPN solutions also sell client software that you can distribute to your users. Usually, this software carries a per-copy charge, typically around $25 to 50 per remote computer supported. (Some VPNs include unlimited client licenses, but the VPN is licensed to accept only a certain number of connections at a time.)

If you are using a Windows server and RRAS service on the server, and some version of Windows 95 or later on the remote computer, you can take advantage of the VPN software included for free with those network operating systems. However, this software must still be set up on each client computer.

VPN Protocols

The three most popular tunneling protocols used for VPNs are Point-to-Point Tunneling Protocol (PPTP), Layer 2 Tunneling Protocol (L2TP), and Internet Protocol Security (IPSec). PPTP is a Microsoft-designed protocol that can handle IP, IPX, NetBEUI, and AppleTalk packets. PPTP is included with Windows, starting with Windows 95, and is also supported by Windows RRAS (a free upgrade to RAS) and by later versions of Windows servers. For a Windows-oriented network, PPTP is the way to go.

L2TP is a newer protocol that is an Internet Engineering Task Force standard. It will probably become the most widely supported tunneling protocol because it operates at layer 2 of the OSI model, and thus can handle all layer 3 protocols, such as IP, IPX, and AppleTalk.

IPSec, while probably the most secure tunneling protocol, seems to be most popular for LAN-to-LAN VPNs and for UNIX-oriented VPNs, due to its reliance on IP. IPSec is a layer 3 protocol and is limited to handling only IP traffic.

TIP   While IPSec works only with IP packets, an L2TP VPN can also carry the resulting IPSec packets, because they can be handled like the other major layer 3 packets, such as IP, IPX, and AppleTalk packets.

Types of VPNs

Four major types of VPNs are in use today. One type uses a router with added VPN capabilities. VPN routers not only can handle normal routing duties, but they can also be configured to form VPNs over the Internet to other similar routers, located on remote networks. This method is used to create VPN WAN links over the Internet, usually between multiple company locations.

Another major type of VPN is one built into a firewall device. Most popular firewalls, such as Check Point's Firewall-1 or WatchGuard's Firebox, serve not only as firewall devices, but also as VPN hosts. Firewall VPNs can be used both to support remote users and also to provide WAN VPN links. The benefit of using a firewall-based VPN is that you can administer your network's security—including both standard firewall security and VPN security—entirely within the firewall. For example, you could configure the firewall to allow connections to the network only when they are made as part of a valid VPN connection.

The third major type of VPN includes those offered as part of a network operating system. The best example of this type is Windows RRAS, and Novell's BorderManager software. These VPNs are most often used to support remote access, and they are generally the least expensive to purchase and install.

The fourth major type is the SSL VPN, a relatively new category. This is actually my overall favorite for remote access support. An SSL VPN takes advantage of the Secure Sockets Layer (SSL) encryption technology built into most web browsers to offer VPN services through the web browser. SSL is the same technology used to encrypt information in web pages that use the http:// prefix, such as for shopping or online banking web sites.

SSL VPNs bring a number of attractive benefits to supporting remote access:

- No client software needs to be installed on the remote computer, except for usually an ActiveX or Java add-in that installs into the browser automatically.

- There is essentially no configuration or management required on the remote system. This is an important point, because most VPN client software is very difficult to support.

- Provided the users know the web address of the SSL VPN server and have the correct information to authenticate (log in) to the system, they can log in from almost any Internet-connected computer in the world and access a wide range of network services through simple web pages.

- Because many common functions, such as file management, can be performed using web pages, SSL VPNs work much better over lower-bandwidth connections than other VPN alternatives. HTML was designed to be stingy in its use of network bandwidth, so many tasks that are slow over a traditional VPN connection are much faster with an SSL VPN.

- Most SSL VPNs, in addition to their web-based access features, also allow the user to start a remote node connection on demand, and this remote node connection runs using automatically installing and configuring browser plug-ins.

SSL VPNs are typically offered as an appliance—a rack-mountable piece of equipment that contains all of the hardware and software needed to run the VPN.

This gives rise to the only real drawback to SSL VPNs: They are still fairly expensive for smaller companies, with the smallest configurations starting at $8,000 to $10,000 to support up to 100 simultaneous users. Still, even if you need to support only 20 to 30 remote users, you may find this to be a small price to pay to reduce the administrative burden of a traditional VPN, which is often considerable.

At the time of this writing, there are a number of SSL VPN vendors. The pioneer in this space is the NetScreen product family from Juniper Networks (which acquired a product originally launched by a company called Neoteris, which pioneered SSL VPNs). Another leader is the FirePass line of products from F5 Networks. AEP Networks, SonicWALL, and Nokia are some other firms that offer SSL VPNs. Since this product area is evolving rapidly, you should conduct a careful search for products that meet your needs.

To give you an idea of how an SSL VPN looks to a remote access user, some screens of a demo version of F5 Network's FirePass 4000 are shown in this section. Figure 10-7

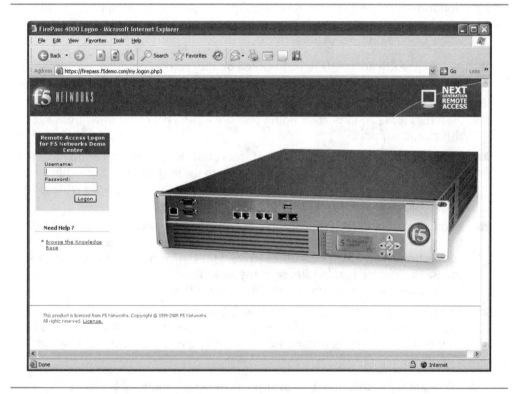

Figure 10-7.   An SSL VPN login screen

shows a typical login screen after browsing to the SSL VPN's URL. (If you deploy an SSL VPN, this screen would be customized with your own company's logo and other information.)

SSL VPNs can authenticate users using a variety of different techniques, including the following:

- Through user names and passwords defined in the SSL VPN for each user.

- Through integration with an existing authentication system, such as Windows Active Directory. Choosing this option lets remote users use their normal network user name and password, and the SSL VPN then integrates with the preexisting authentication system on the network.

- Through the integration of a two-factor authentication system. Two-factor authentication systems usually include a small device for each user that displays a number that changes every minute or so. Users log in by typing the number on the device at the time they are logging on, plus an additional number that is known only to them (sort of like an ATM PIN). Two-factor authentication systems are extremely secure, because the devices use a randomized sequence of numbers known only to a secure server installed in the network.

Once users log in to an SSL VPN, they are shown a home page that displays all of the connection options available to them, such as the example shown in Figure 10-8. The choices available to a remote user may include the following:

- Access to a remote node connection through the SSL VPN

- Access to other web servers on the company's network, such as a corporate intranet site, which are not normally accessible through the Internet

- Access to e-mail, either through an application like Web Outlook or through a web-enabled e-mail client provided by the SSL VPN

- The ability to perform web-based file management through the SSL VPN; files that are managed might be hosted on Windows- or UNIX-based servers

- Access to shared corporate applications that have been set up to work through the SSL VPN, such as an accounting system

- Access to Windows Terminal Services or Citrix sessions via the SSL VPN

- Access to mainframe terminal sessions

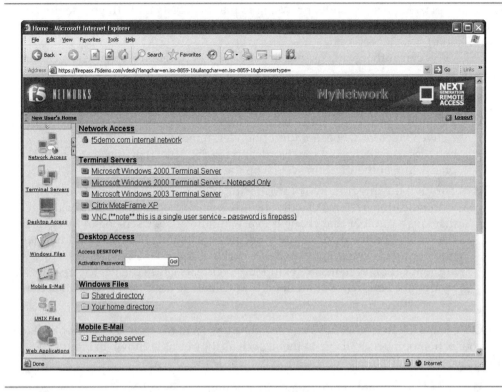

Figure 10-8.   A sample user's home page on the SSL VPN

While many of these choices are important for companies, the mainstay of remote access is letting remote users access e-mail and files stored on the network. SSL VPNs provide web-based access to many different types of e-mail servers. They also include the ability to manage files and directories through a web interface, such as the one shown in Figure 10-9. In this example, the user can select files in the left pane and can then choose to download, add to a download cart, view within the web browser, rename, or even delete files. The user can also manage folders and upload new files. All file access follows network permissions granted to the user that is logged in to the SSL VPN.

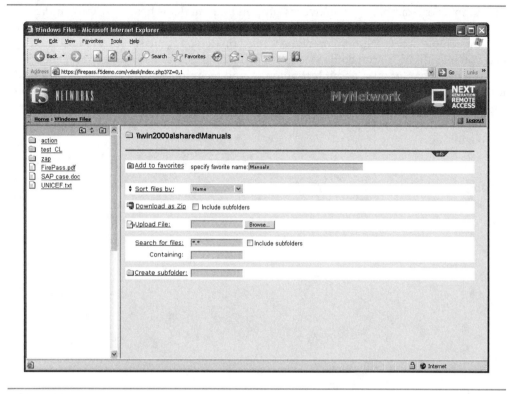

Figure 10-9.   A folder containing several files that can be managed

Chapter Summary

Most network administrators would agree that supporting remote access is one of the trickiest parts of managing any network. Many factors come together to make this so. You can support remote connections in a number of ways. Most remote connection speeds have lower bandwidth than remote users would like. Many remote users are often important people in the company, and various problems are introduced with any connection made over a distance. Still, remote access is an important network service, and its benefits to the company justify most levels of effort to make it reliable and work right.

Use the information you learned in this chapter to assess your own company's remote access requirements, to learn what your users actually need, and to start searching among different possible solutions for the ones that make the most sense for your situation. You should also consider whether you need to support more than one type of solution. For example, most networks support both modems hosted by the company and other types of connections that come in through a VPN link. Or you may support an existing remote access solution for a time while you deploy some sort of VPN solution, and you may decide to run both systems for some time to deal with your specific needs.

The next chapter talks about technologies and techniques that can keep a network's information safe and from falling into the wrong hands. Network security, when done right, shouldn't require much of your time to maintain. You need to spend enough time and effort when you set up a network to ensure the network's security is strong from the beginning.

Chapter 11

Securing Your Network

M ost networking tasks are relatively straightforward. Do you want a new file and print server? You install it and set it up, and it either works or it doesn't. If it doesn't work, you proceed to troubleshoot it, fix any issues, and ultimately complete the task. Network security, on the other hand, is a horse of a different color. You can *never* really finish the project of securing a network, and you can *never* be certain that a network is completely secure. How much money you invest in securing a network, how much time you devote to the job, and how much fancy security hardware and software you install doesn't matter—no network is ever completely secure. Having said that, network security is one of the most important jobs facing any network administrator. Good network security helps prevent the following:

- Company secrets, such as proprietary designs or processes, falling into the wrong hands (both internally and externally)
- Personal information about employees falling into the wrong hands
- Loss of important information and software
- Loss of use of the network itself or any part of the network
- Corruption or inappropriate modification of important data

These are just some of the more important losses that network security can prevent. If you spend any time thinking about all the information that is stored on and that flows through networks with which you work (and you *should* spend time thinking about this), you'll probably come up with additional dangers to avoid.

This chapter provides an overview of the subject of network security. Its aim is to familiarize you with important network security ideas and concepts, as well as various technologies involved in network security. If you are responsible for a network's security, you should pursue more detailed information, and you should also seriously consider hiring a specialist on this subject to help you secure your network. Even if you don't have primary responsibility to keep your network secure, the security of the network is everyone's job. If you're an IT professional, security is an even more important part of your job.

Understanding Internal Security

Internal security is the process of securing your network from internal threats, which are generally much more common than external threats. Examples of internal threats include the following:

- Internal users inappropriately accessing information such as payroll records, accounting records, or business development information.
- Internal users accessing other users' files to which they should not have access.
- Internal users impersonating other users and causing mischief, such as sending e-mail under another person's name.

- Internal users accessing systems to carry out criminal activities, such as embezzling funds.

- Internal users compromising the security of the network, such as by accidentally (or deliberately) introducing viruses to the network. (Viruses are discussed in their own section later in this chapter.)

- Internal users "sniffing" packets on the network to discover user accounts and passwords.

To deal with threats such as these, you need to manage the network's security diligently. You should assume that, in the population of internal users, at least some exist who have the requisite sophistication to explore security holes in the network and that at least a few of those might, at some point, try to do so.

NOTE   One of the more unpleasant parts of managing security is that you need to expect the worst of people, and then you must take steps to prevent those actions you expect. In other words, a certain amount of paranoia is required. It's not a pleasant mindset, but it is required to do a good job in the security arena. Remember, too, that you're likely to get better results if you hire an outside firm to help manage the network's security. Not only should the outside firm have a higher skill level in this area, but its workers will be used to thinking as security people, and they will have invaluable experience gained from solving security problems at other companies. Perhaps even more important, using an external firm doesn't put employees in the position of being in an adversarial relationship with other employees.

Account Security

Account security refers to the process of managing the user accounts enabled on the network. A number of tasks are required to manage user accounts properly, and the accounts should be periodically audited (preferably by a different person than the one who manages them daily) to ensure that no holes exist. Following are a number of general steps you should take to manage general account security:

- Most network operating systems start up with a user account called Guest. You should remove this account immediately, because it is the frequent target of crackers (a *hacker* is a person who likes to explore and understand systems, while a *cracker* is a person who breaks into systems with malicious intent). You should also avoid creating accounts that are obviously for testing purposes, such as Test, Generic, and so forth.

- Most network operating systems start up with a default name for the administrative account. Under Windows server operating systems, the account is called Administrator; under NetWare, it is called either Supervisor or Admin (depending on which version you are using). You should immediately rename this account to avoid directed attacks against the account. (Under NetWare 3.*x*, you cannot rename the Supervisor account.)

TIP   As a safety measure, also create a new account to be a backup of your administrative account. Call it whatever you like (although less obvious names are better), give the account security equivalence to the administrative account, and safely store the password. If something happens that locks you out of the real administrative account, you can use the backup account to regain access and correct the problem.

- You should know the steps required to remove access to network resources quickly from any user account and be sure to explore *all* network resources that might contain their own security systems. For example, accounts will be managed on the network operating system (and possibly on each server) and also in specific applications, such as database servers or accounting systems. Make sure that you find out how the system handles removed or deactivated accounts. If you delete a user account in order to remove access, some systems don't actually deny access to that user until they log out from the system.

- Work closely with the human resources (HR) department. Make sure that the HR staff is comfortable working with you on handling security issues related to employee departures, and develop a checklist to use for standard employment changes that affect IT. The HR department might not be able to give you much—if any—advance notice, but it needs to understand that you need to know about any terminations *immediately*, so you can take proper steps. Along the same lines, you should develop a set of procedures on how you handle accumulated e-mail, files, and other user access—both for friendly departures and terminations. Your relationship with the appropriate people in the HR department is crucial in being able to handle security well, so make sure that you establish and maintain mutual trust.

- Consider setting up a program whereby new users on the network have their assigned permissions reviewed and signed off by their supervisor. This way, you won't mistakenly give people access to things they shouldn't have.

- For publicly traded companies, the advent of the Sarbanes-Oxley Act of 2002 (discussed in Chapter 1) means you will likely need to set up a system to document how users of the network are added, modified, and removed from the system. This type of system usually involves a set of request forms initiated by the appropriate department (HR, accounting, and so on), signed by the individual's supervisor and any other parties that need to authorize access to certain systems, and then documents the IT staff's actions. These forms are then filed and will be examined by the company's auditors.

Password Security

Another important aspect of account security is account password security. Most network operating systems enable you to set policies related to password security. These policies control how often the system forces users to change their passwords, how long their passwords must be, the complexity of the password (alphanumeric, capital letters, or symbols), whether users can reuse previously used passwords, and so forth. At a minimum, consider these suggestions for password policies:

- Require users (through network password policy settings) to change their main network password every 90 to 180 days. (Actually, 30 days is a common recommendation, but this might be too frequent in most environments.)

- Set the reuse policy so that passwords cannot be reused for at least a year.

- Require passwords that are *at least* eight characters long. For case-insensitive passwords that do not allow special characters, this yields potentially 36^8 possible permutations, or almost 3 trillion possibilities. And if the network operating system uses case-sensitive passwords, the possibilities are much larger: 62^8 (218 trillion). For systems that allow special characters to be part of the password (characters like a space, comma, period, asterisk, and so forth), the number of possible combinations is even higher still.

NOTE Even 2 billion possible combinations for passwords is a lot. If crackers were able to try one password a second, they would need to spend 63 years to try that many permutations. Or, with an optimized program that can try 5 million possibilities a second, it would take about a year to crack an eight-character mixed-case password using brute force.

- Encourage users to create passwords that are not words in any language or, if they are words, that they have numbers and other nonalphanumeric characters inserted somewhere in the word, so a "dictionary attack" won't easily work. (Many password-cracking programs rely on dictionaries of common words and names to reduce dramatically the number of possibilities they need to try.) Also, for networks that support mixed-case passwords, encourage users to use mixed-case characters.

- Make sure that you turn on any policies that monitor for and deal with people entering in wrong passwords. Often called *intruder detection*, this type of policy watches for incorrect password attempts. If too many attempts occur within a set period of time, the system can lock out the user account, preventing further attempts. I usually set this type of feature to lock an account any time five incorrect passwords are entered within an hour, and then lock the account until it's reset by the administrator. This way, if users enter a large number of incorrect passwords, they will need to talk with the administrator to reopen the account. Usually, this occurs when users forgot their passwords, but someone else may be trying to guess passwords, so it deserves to be examined.

■ Novell NetWare and Windows servers enable you to establish limits on when and where a user can log in to the network. You can establish times of day that a user is allowed to log in, and you can also restrict a user account to particular network computers. Doing so for all users on the network is usually overkill, but you might want to consider restricting the administrative account to several different workstations so someone at a different workstation (or coming in through a WAN connection) cannot log in to the account, even if that person somehow knows the password.

There's an interesting catch-22 concerning network security policies: If you make them *too* strict, you can actually *reduce* the security of your network. For example, suppose that you set the network to require 12-character passwords, to force a password change once a week, and to disallow the reuse of passwords. Most users will be unable to remember from week to week what password they're using, and they will naturally resort to writing down their password somewhere in their office. Of course, a written password is much less secure than a remembered password. The trick with network security is to strike a balance between security and usability.

Are There Alternatives to Passwords?

There are a number of emerging alternatives to passwords that should make networks more secure, and also make network security easier on the users. The first alternative is something called *two-factor identification*. This is a system whereby the user carries around a small electronic device called a *fob*, which is about the size of a USB key. The fob displays a constantly changing set of numbers that are specific to that particular fob. The user remembers just a four-digit PIN. When users log in to the system, they enter in whatever number is currently displayed on the fob, plus their PIN. Because the network side of the system has a matching inventory of fobs and their sequence of numbers, and also has the user's PIN, the user can be very securely identified. If a fob is lost, it can be easily deactivated in the system and a new one issued. Two-factor identification is often used for remote access identification.

Another emerging alternative to passwords is the use of biometric data, such as fingerprint readers. Some notebook computers now come with integrated fingerprint readers that can quickly scan users' fingerprints and log them in to a system. Other companies sell similar stand-alone devices. However, the vendors specifically state that they are not intended for corporate use. So, although such devices are not yet suitable for corporate use, security is rapidly moving in this direction. I believe the day is not far off when computers will routinely come equipped with fingerprint readers, and users will only have to touch their thumb to the reader to securely identify themselves to their systems.

File and Directory Permissions

Another type of internal security that you need to maintain for information on your network involves the users' access to files and directories. These settings are actually a bit tougher to manage than user accounts, because you usually have at least 20 directories and several hundred files for every user on the network. The sheer volume of directories and files makes managing these settings a more difficult job. The solution is to establish regular procedures, follow them, and then periodically spot-audit parts of the directory tree, particularly areas that contain sensitive files. Also, structure the overall network directories so that you can, for the most part, simply assign permissions at the top levels. These permissions will "flow down" to subdirectories automatically, which makes it much easier to review who has access to which directories.

Network operating systems allow considerable flexibility in setting permissions on files and directories. Using the built-in permissions, you can enable users for different roles in any given directory. These *roles* control what the user can and cannot do within that directory. Examples of generic directory roles include the following:

- **Create only**   This type of role enables users to add a new file to a directory, but restricts them from seeing, editing, or deleting existing files, including any they've created. This type of role is suitable for allowing users to add new information to a directory to which they shouldn't otherwise have access. The directory becomes almost like a mailbox on a street corner: You can only put new things in it. Of course, at least one other user will have full access to the directory to retrieve and work with the files.

- **Read only**   This role enables users to see the files in a directory and even to pull up the files for viewing on their computer. However, the users cannot edit or change the stored files in any way. This type of role is suitable for allowing users to view information that they should not change. (Users with read privileges can copy a file from a read-only directory to another directory and then do whatever they like with the copy they made. They simply cannot change the copy stored in the read-only directory itself.)

- **Change**   This role lets users do whatever they like with the files in a directory, *except* give other users access to the directory.

- **Full control**   Usually reserved for the "owner" of a directory, this role enables the owners to do whatever they like with the files in a directory and to grant other users access to the directory.

These roles are created in different ways on different network operating systems. Chapter 17 provides more details on how Windows server operating systems handle directory permissions.

Just as you can set permissions for directories, you can also set security for specific files. File permissions work similarly to directory permissions. For specific files, you can control a user's ability to read, change, or delete a file. File permissions usually override directory permissions. For example, if users had change access to a directory, but you set their permission to access a particular file in that directory to read-only, they would have only read-only access to that file.

TIP   For a network of any size, I recommend avoiding the use of file-specific network permissions, except in very rare cases. It can quickly become an unmanageable mess to remember to which files each user has special permissions and to which files a new hire needs to be given specific permission.

Practices and User Education

The most insecure part of any network is the people using it. You need to establish good security practices and habits to help protect the network.

It's not enough to design and implement a great security scheme if you do not manage it well on a daily basis. To establish good practices, you need to document security-related procedures, and then set up some sort of process to make sure that the employees follow the procedures regularly. In fact, you're far better off having a simple security design that is followed to the letter than having an excellent but complicated security design that is poorly followed. For this reason, keep the overall network security design as simple as possible, while remaining consistent with the needs of the company.

You also need to make sure—to the maximum extent possible—that the users are following prudent procedures. You can easily enforce some procedures through settings on the network operating system, but you must handle others through education. The following are some tips to make this easier:

- Spell out for users what is expected of them in terms of security. Provide a document that describes the security of the network and what they need to do to preserve it. Examples of guidelines for the users include choosing secure passwords, not giving their passwords to anyone else, not leaving their computers unattended for long periods of time while they are logged in to the network, not installing software from outside the company, and so forth.

- When new employees join the company and are oriented on using the network, make sure that you discuss security issues with them.

- Depending on the culture of the company, consider having users sign a form acknowledging their understanding of important security procedures that the company expects them to follow.

- Periodically audit users' security actions. If the users have full-control access to directories, examine how they've assigned permissions to other users.

- Make sure that you review the security logs of the network operating system you use. Investigate and follow up on any problems reported.

TIP   It's a good idea to document any security-related issues you investigate. While most are benign, occasionally you might find one in which the user had inappropriate intent. In such cases, your documentation of what you find and what actions you take might become important.

While it's important to plan for the worst when designing and administering network security, you also need to realize that most of the time, security issues arise from ignorance or other innocent causes, rather from malicious intent.

Understanding External Threats

External security is the process of securing the network from external threats. Before the Internet, this process wasn't difficult. Most networks had only external modems for users to dial in to the network, and it was easy to keep those access points secure. However, now that nearly all networks are connected to the Internet, external security becomes much more important and also much more difficult.

At the beginning of this chapter, I said that no network is ever totally secure. This is especially true when dealing with external security for a network connected to the Internet. Almost daily, crackers discover new techniques that they can use to breach the security of a network through an Internet connection. Even if you were to find a book that discussed all the threats to a specific type of network, the book would be out of date soon after it was printed.

Three basic types of external security threats exist:

- **Front-door threats**   These threats arise when a person from outside the company somehow finds, guesses, or cracks a user password and then logs on to the network. The perpetrator could be someone who had an association with the company at some point or could be someone totally unrelated to the company.

- **Back-door threats**   These are threats where software or hardware bugs in the network's operating system and hardware enable outsiders to crack the network's security. After accomplishing this, the outsiders often find a way to log in to the administrative account and then can do anything they like. Back-door threats can also be deliberately programmed into software you run.

- **Denial of service (DoS)**   DoS attacks deny service to the network. Examples include committing specific actions that are known to crash different types of servers or flooding the company's Internet connection with useless traffic (such as a flood of ping requests).

NOTE   Another type of external threat exists: computer viruses, Trojan horses, worms, and other malicious software from outside the company. These threats are covered in their own section later in the chapter.

Fortunately, you can do a number of things to implement strong external security measures. They probably won't keep out a determined and extremely skilled cracker, but they can make it difficult enough that most crackers will give up and go elsewhere.

DEFINE-IT! Important Network Security Devices

Here are some important security devices you should be familiar with:

- A *firewall* is s system that enforces a security policy between two networks, such as between a local area network (LAN) and the Internet. Firewalls can use many different techniques to enforce security policies.

- A *proxy server* acts as a proxy (an anonymous intermediary), usually for users of a network. For example, it might stand in as a proxy for browsing web pages, so that the user's computer isn't connected to the remote system except through the proxy server. In the process of providing proxy access to web pages, a proxy server might also speed web access by caching web pages that are accessed so that other users can benefit from having them more quickly available from the local proxy server, and might also provide some firewall protection for the LAN.

- Usually built into a router or a firewall, a *packet filter* enables you to set criteria for allowed and disallowed packets, source and destination IP addresses, and IP ports.

Front-Door Threats

Front-door threats, in which someone from outside the company is able to gain access to a user account, are probably the most likely threats that you need to protect against. These threats can take many forms. Chief among them is the disgruntled or terminated employee who once had access to the network. Another example is someone guessing or finding out a password to a valid account on the network or somehow getting a valid password from the owner of the password.

Insiders, whether current or ex-employees, are potentially the most dangerous overall. Such people have many advantages that some random cracker won't have. They know the important user names on the network already, so they know what accounts to go after. They might know other users' passwords from when they were associated with the company. They also know the structure of the network, what the server names are, and other information that makes cracking the network's security easier.

Protecting against a front-door threat revolves around strong internal security protection because, in this case, internal and external security are closely linked. This is the type of threat where all the policies and practices discussed in the section on internal security can help to prevent problems.

An additional effective way to protect against front-door threats is to keep network resources that should be accessed from the LAN separate from resources that should be accessed from outside the LAN, whenever possible. For example, if you never need to provide external users access to the company's accounting server, you can make it nearly impossible to access that system from outside the LAN.

You can separate network resources through a number of measures. You can set up the firewall router to decline any access through the router to that server's IP or IPX address. If the server doesn't require IP, you can remove that protocol. You can set up the server to disallow access outside normal working hours. Depending on the network operating system running on the server, you can restrict access to Ethernet MAC addresses for machines on the LAN that should be able to access the server. You can also set the server to allow each user only one login to the server at a time. The specific steps that you can take depend on the server in question and its network operating system, but the principle holds true: Segregate internal resources from external resources whenever possible.

Here are some other steps you might take to stymie front-door threats:

- Control which users can access the LAN from outside the LAN. For example, you might be running VPN software for your traveling or home-based users to access the LAN remotely through the Internet. You should enable this access only for users who need it and not for everyone.

- Consider setting up remote access accounts for remote users who are separate from their normal accounts, and make these accounts more restrictive than their normal LAN accounts. This might not be practicable in all cases, but it's a strategy that can help, particularly for users who normally have broad LAN security clearances.

- For modems that users dial in to from a fixed location, such as from their homes, set up their accounts to use dial-back. *Dial-back* is a feature whereby you securely enter the phone number of the system from which users are calling (such as their home phone numbers). When the users want to connect, they dial the system, request access, and then the remote access system terminates the connection and dials the preprogrammed phone number to make the real connection. Their computer answers the call and then proceeds to connect them normally. Someone trying to access the system from another phone number won't be able to get in if you have dial-back enabled.

- If employees with broad access leave the company, review user accounts where they might have known the password. Consider forcing an immediate password change to such accounts once the employees are gone.

 NOTE   An important aspect of both internal and external security is physical security. Make sure that the room in which your servers are located is physically locked and secure.

People trying to access the network who have not been associated with the company at some point often try a technique euphemistically called *social engineering*, which is where they use nontechnological methods to learn user accounts and passwords inside the company. These techniques are most dangerous in larger companies, where not all the employees know each other. An example of a social engineering technique is calling an employee and posing as a network administrator who is trying to track down a problem and who needs the employee's password temporarily. Another example is to sort through a company's trash looking for records that might help the culprit crack a password. Make sure to instruct your company's employees carefully to never give out their password to anyone over the telephone and also that IT people usually never need to ask anyone's password.

Back-Door Threats

Back-door threats are often directed at problems in the network operating system itself or at some other point in the network infrastructure, such as its routers. The fact is that all network operating systems and most network components have security holes. The best thing you can do to prevent these problems is to stay current with your software and any security-related patches that are released. You should also periodically review new information about security holes discovered in the software you use.

TIP Don't rely on the vendor's web site for the best information about software security holes. A good web site to use to stay current on security holes is the one maintained by the Computer Emergency Response Team (CERT), located at http://www.cert.org. Aside from finding advisories on security holes, you can also discover much valuable security information on the site.

Web servers are a frequent target for crackers. Consider the following tips to help protect against threats to web servers:

- You're better off if you can host the company's web site on an external server, such as an Internet service provider's (ISP's) system, rather than on your own network. Not only is an ISP better able to provide the server service 24 hours a day, 7 days a week, but it also probably has better security. Also, you don't need to worry about allowing web server access to your LAN from outside the company, which can sometimes leave open other holes.

- Make sure that you implement a strong firewall router for your network. Firewall routers are discussed in more detail in Chapter 6. You should also have someone knowledgeable about the specific firewall and web server you implement test your configuration or help with the configuration. Remember that firewalls also need to have their software kept current.

- Make absolutely certain that you've carefully reviewed the security settings appropriate for your web server and have implemented all of them, and that you audit these settings occasionally.

- Consider placing a web server designed for people outside the company outside your firewall (in other words, between the firewall and the router that connects you to the Internet—this area is called a *demilitarized zone*). This way, even if crackers are able to break into the web server, they won't have an easy time getting to the rest of your network.

- Safely guard your e-mail traffic. E-mail is one of the most commonly used means to get viruses or Trojan horse programs into a company. Make sure you run virus-scanning software suitable for your e-mail server, and that the virus signatures are updated at least *daily*.

DoS Threats

DoS attacks are those that deny service to a network resource to legitimate users. These are often targeted at e-mail servers and web servers, but they can affect an entire network. DoS attacks usually take one of two forms: they either deny service by flooding the network with useless traffic or they take advantage of bugs in network software that can be used to crash servers. DoS attacks against an e-mail server usually flood the server with mail until the e-mail server either denies service to legitimate users or crashes under the load placed on it.

Here are few ways to help prevent DoS attacks:

- Make sure to keep your various network software current.

- Use settings on your firewall to disallow Internet Control Message Protocol (ICMP) traffic service (which handles ping requests) into the network.

- Deny access to servers from outside the LAN that do not need to be accessed from outside the LAN. For example, the company's accounting system server probably does not need to be accessed from outside the LAN. In such a case, you would configure the firewall or packet-filtering router to deny all outside traffic to or from that server's IP address.

DEFINE-IT! Demilitarized Zone

When you place computers between your firewall (on the other side of the firewall from your network) and your connection to an external network, such as the Internet, the area between those two devices is called the *demilitarized zone*, or DMZ for short. Usually, an organization will place its public web server in the DMZ, and that computer will not have any sort of confidential information on it. This way, if the security of that computer is broken, the attacker hasn't gained entry to the network itself.

Viruses and Other Malicious Software

Unfortunately, an increasing array of malicious software is circulating around the world. Many different types of this software exist, including the following:

- ■ **Viruses**   A computer *virus* is a program that spreads by infecting other files with a copy of itself. Files that can be infected by viruses include program files (COM, EXE, and DLL) and document files for applications that support macro languages sophisticated enough to allow virus behavior. (Microsoft Word and Excel are common targets of macro-based viruses.) Sometimes even data files like JPEG image files can be infected by sophisticated viruses.

- ■ **Worms**   A *worm* is a program that propagates by sending copies of itself to other computers, which run the worm and then send copies to other computers. Recently, worms have spread through e-mail systems like wildfire. One way they spread is by attaching to e-mail along with a message that entices the recipients to open the attachment. The attachment contains the worm, which then sends out copies of itself to other people defined in the user's e-mail address book, without the user knowing that this is happening. Those recipients then have the same thing happen to them. A worm like this can spread rapidly through the Internet in a matter of hours.

- ■ **Trojan horses**   A *Trojan horse* is a program that purports to do something interesting or useful and then performs malicious actions in the background while the user is interacting with the main program.

- ■ **Logic bombs**   *Logic bombs* are malicious pieces of programming code inserted into an otherwise normal program. They are often included by the program's original author or by someone else who participated in developing the source code. Logic bombs can be timed to execute at a certain time, erasing key files or performing other actions.

There are an enormous number of known viruses, with more being written and discovered daily. These viruses are a major threat to any network, and an important aspect of your network administration is protecting against them.

To protect a network from virus attacks, you need to implement some sort of antivirus software. Antivirus software runs on computers on the network and "watches" for known viruses or virus-like activity. The antivirus software then either removes the virus, leaving the original file intact, quarantines the file so it can be checked by an administrator, or locks access to the file in some other fashion.

Antivirus software can be run on most network computers, such as file servers, print servers, e-mail servers, desktop computers, and even computerized firewalls. Antivirus software is available from a number of different vendors, with three of the most notable being Symantec (Norton AntiVirus), Trend Micro (PC-cillin), and Network Associates (McAfee VirusScan).

Your best bet is to make sure you run antivirus software on all your servers and set up the software so that it is frequently updated (every few days, or better yet, daily).

(You can set up most server-based antivirus software to update its list of known viruses securely over an Internet connection automatically.) Also, because e-mail is the chief mechanism of transmission for computer viruses these days, make especially sure that you run antivirus software on your e-mail server. I recommend updating virus signatures on an e-mail server hourly, if possible. This is because new e-mail–borne viruses can spread throughout the world very rapidly—in a matter of hours. By having your antivirus software on your e-mail server update itself hourly, you're a little more likely to get a necessary update before the virus hits your network.

> **TIP**   Consider using antivirus software from different companies for differents parts of your network. For example, you might use one company's antivirus software for your e-mail server and some other company's software for your other computers. While rare, I have seen cases where one company's offerings do not detect certain viruses, while a different company's offering does. On a network that I manage, we run one company's antivirus software on all the desktop computers and a different company's antivirus software on the e-mail server. I've seen cases where one of those systems permits a virus that the other one catches.

You should also run antivirus software on your workstations, but you shouldn't rely on this software as your primary means of prevention. Consider desktop antivirus software as a supplement to your server-based software.

Chapter Summary

In this chapter, you learned about common security threats and read advice that can help you formulate and implement good security practices. You should seriously consider retaining an outside security consultant to help you set up your security plans and to review and audit them on a regular basis.

Even in an entire book devoted to the subject of network security, you can't learn all you need to know to make a network as secure as possible. New threats are discovered constantly, and the changing software landscape makes such information quickly obsolete. If you're responsible for network security, you should know it's a job that never sleeps, and you can never know enough about it. You need to spend time learning more of the ins and outs of network security, particularly for the operating systems that you use on your network. The following books can help further your network security education:

- *Network Security: A Beginner's Guide,* Second Edition, by Eric Maiwald (McGraw-Hill/Professional, 2003)

- *Hacking Exposed: Network Security Secrets and Solutions*, Sixth Edition, by Stuart McClure, Joel Scambray, and George Kurtz (McGraw-Hill/Professional, 2009)

- *Windows 2000 Security Handbook*, by Tom Sheldon and Phil Cox (McGraw-Hill/Professional, 2001)

You also might want to read *Internet Firewalls and Network Security*, Second Edition, by Chris Hare and Karanjit Sayan (New Riders Publishing, 1996). This is an older book, but has an excellent explanation of true "security" (that is, Department of Defense levels). The book also describes how to develop network security policies in a company and explains packet filtering and firewall technology.

Finally, *The Happy Hacker: A Guide to (Mostly) Harmless Computer Hacking*, Fourth Edition, by Carolyn P. Meinel (American Eagle Publishing, 2002), is an excellent introduction to hacking. The book applies a "how-to" approach and teaches both novices and moderately experienced network security persons what to look for on a daily basis.

Chapter 12

Network Disaster Recovery

Network servers contain vital resources for a company, in the form of information, knowledge, and invested work product of the company's employees. If they were suddenly and permanently deprived of these resources, most companies would not be able to continue their business uninterrupted and would face losing millions of dollars, both in the form of lost data and the effects of that loss. Therefore, establishing a network disaster recovery plan and formulating and implementing the network's backup strategy are the two most important jobs in network management.

In this chapter, you learn about the issues that you should address in a disaster recovery plan, and also about network backup strategies and systems. Before getting into these topics, however, you should read about the City of Seattle's disaster recovery experiences.

Notes from the Field: The City of Seattle

The technical editor of the first through third editions of this book, Tony Ryan, had a personal experience with network disaster recovery. Tony worked in the IT department for the City of Seattle. On February 28, 2001, Seattle experienced an earthquake that caused the city's disaster recovery plans to be tested. What follows is Tony's discussion about Seattle's disaster recovery operations and how it handled the problems that occurred in the wake of the earthquake. This is an excellent example of why you need a disaster recovery plan that encompasses all possible events that could occur during a disaster.

Notes on the Seattle 2001 Earthquake and Its Disaster Recovery

By Tony Ryan

Seattle has seen some very unusual and attention-grabbing events over the past few years. Notable among them were the World Trade Organization (WTO) conference of 1999 and the violent demonstrations that accompanied it, which were broadcast worldwide on television and the Internet. Also, riots broke out during Mardi Gras celebrations in 2000. However, nothing compared to the potential and realized damage wrought by the 6.8 magnitude earthquake that struck Wednesday, February 28, 2001.

The EOC Situation

The City of Seattle has an Emergency Operations Center, or EOC, which is activated during any event or crisis that has a potential impact on public safety, or that might otherwise affect any number of services provided by the city to its citizens. Sometimes that EOC can be activated ahead of time; for example, for the Y2K event and the anniversary of the WTO demonstrations. Looking at the preparation made for those events and comparing it to what happens during unplanned events such as the earthquake helps to illustrate some important principles about IT disaster recovery and disaster preparedness.

Never Assume

During the preparation for Y2K, members of my staff were asked to augment the staff normally assigned to support the EOC's desktop and laptop PCs, and printers. The staff members who normally support the EOC are from a different IT organization than ours, and as can be expected, their way of doing things differed from ours for a number of valid reasons. However, once my staff members had a chance to look at the EOC's environment, they were able to share some new perspectives and methods that were welcomed and adopted by EOC support staff, and all involved had a new idea of what would be expected to be the "standard" way of configuring EOC PCs. Examples ranged from hard-coding certain models of PC network interface cards (NICs) to run better on the switches in their wiring closet to developing and implementing a base image for all the laptops to be deployed in the building. The Y2K event, as a result, was lauded as an example of ideal cooperation between IT groups and excellent preparation overall. It was a very calm Saturday morning!

Change Management?

Between events, however, there was a great deal of time and opportunity for things to change. The facility might have been used for other business purposes; equipment such as laptops might have been loaned out, or customers could have come in and used the equipment; and other IT groups besides ours might have assisted the staff and performed alterations to the configurations that went undocumented or were not communicated to all involved.

The Results

Whatever it was that might have happened remains unknown. What we did discover following the earthquake was that when customers who normally use the EOC in emergency situations went to use the equipment, in some cases the machines did not work as expected. Software could not be loaded on this PC; that laptop would not connect to the network anymore; some PCs were not the same or had been swapped for less-powerful processors. Things had changed, and the result was that some of the emergency work IT professionals such as web support technicians, had to perform took more time than we had anticipated. Ironically, the Web played a crucial role in our overall communications "strategy." The impact of that equipment not immediately working was not yet evident; however, the following events illustrate how they might have been.

(Continued)

A few minutes after the earthquake struck, several of the downtown buildings in which Seattle employees worked were evacuated due to fear of structural damage. No one was injured, and amazingly only two keyboards were broken throughout all the buildings in which we provide support. But imagine a couple thousand very frightened and concerned people streaming onto the sidewalks and streets, flooding cellular telephone networks in frantic attempts to contact loved ones, and looking for any possible focus for communication—especially managers such as myself and other supervisory staff, all possessing varying levels of training in disaster preparedness.

Luckily, the mayor's office had sent representatives to the gathering sites indicated for staff to walk to in such events, and informed everyone in the core buildings that were directly affected that they were to go home. With that announcement, the CTO announced to all to "check the Web" for information, meaning the city's internal web site. But what if the EOC PC had been swapped out (let's say) for a Pentium 133 with 64MB RAM and that PC could not run Microsoft's FrontPage 2000? If that web site had to be updated with news and official information on a routine basis, the results could have been at best inconvenient and confusing.

Contingency and Costs

Because we are a publicly funded entity, we are very careful about how we spend our customers' money, as it is subject to great scrutiny (and rightfully so). Customers often do not have the funds to afford both modern PC equipment to run the latest version of Windows and a spare PC to sit in the closet, "just in case." After the earthquake, a couple of buildings were temporarily unavailable for occupancy until inspectors had a chance to examine the damage to see if the buildings were safe for employees. One of those buildings actually houses a lot of our IT staff, and as a result, not only were we trying to find "spare PCs" for our customers to use (while they looked for office space), but as IT support staff, we found ourselves doing the same thing. The direct impact was that we found it difficult in a few cases to support our customers as quickly as our service-level agreements (SLAs) required, especially since we could not immediately reenter our building to gather our PCs or other necessary equipment.

Lesson Learned: Keep Spares ... At Least a Few

So it seems that you either pay up front or pay later. It makes sense to keep a percentage of PCs available for these rainy-day events; 10 to 15 percent of replaceable inventory should work. Consider that businesses of any kind are obligated in such situations to perform a kind of "triage" as to which of their business functions are most critical and which can be postponed—until their entire stock of equipment can be reconnected or replaced—and 10 to 15 percent is justified.

Have a Plan for Communications and How You Will Communicate

Following the CTO's announcement, some asked, "What about those who don't have web access at home?" As IT staff, we asked, "What if the web servers themselves had all been destroyed?" (In fact, ceiling debris in the room in which they were housed fell very close to them, but the servers were not damaged and the service was never down.) Still others asked, "What about those who missed the message and don't know to check the Web? These questions, as well as "What to do in the event of …?" could be addressed with a clear, ever-ready communications plan. Ironically, such plans had been developed down to the last detail for other events, but in the case of a real "emergent" event, we as a department had not identified a plan to follow. A priority for our department now is to reexamine that situation and develop a plan, using communications plans developed for the Y2K event and the like as models.

Another point: As previously mentioned, our staff is not responsible for supporting the EOC on a routine basis. We are more than happy to be directed to assist in that support, and as evidenced, have done so on a few occasions. Almost immediately following the earthquake, I received a page indicating that I was to dispatch technicians to the EOC to support the city officials who report there during emergencies. While our team was under no agreement with the EOC to provide support even "on demand," I immediately asked two of my senior technicians, who had worked at the EOC in the past, to respond. They reported for duty there and supported the facility until the assigned staff arrived. There was never a doubt that we would pitch in whenever asked, but I made it a point to ask our divisional director if developing some clearer expectations, or even an SLA, between our staff and the EOC would be appropriate, and he agreed. I did find out that those in the EOC are granted power by legislation to use "all" city resources in the event of an emergency, but a clear agreement could also permit me to identify a rotating on-call staff person who could be proactive and call the EOC in such instances.

I must point out that none of these preparations can substitute for dedicated, intelligent people. The shining example is one of my technicians who supports programmers responsible for the city's payroll application. He had the presence of mind to come early to work the day after the quake, and he somehow persuaded the construction crew and inspectors to permit him access to the building. He walked up 13 flights of stairs, picked up a PC and peripherals, carried it back down the stairs and to another building, and configured it to work on the segment in the new building. This made it possible for the programmer to run the operations necessary for the city's payroll run that weekend, and employees received their checks on time, as expected. You cannot ask for more than that.

Disaster Recovery Plans

A *disaster recovery plan* is a document that explores how a network recovers from a disaster that either imperils its data or stops its functioning. A company's external financial auditors often require annual disaster recovery plans, because of the data's importance to the business and the effect that such a network failure would have on a company. Moreover, disaster recovery plans are also important because they force the manager of the network to think through all possible disaster scenarios. By taking these scenarios into account, the manager can make more effective plans to protect the network's data from loss and to restore full operations of the business as quickly as possible. As mentioned at the beginning of this chapter, planning for disaster recovery and managing the company's backup systems are a network manager's two most important jobs.

Most companies do not have extremely long disaster recovery plans. For a single network of up to several hundred nodes and 15 or so servers, such a plan usually consists of about 10 to 20 pages or fewer, although its length varies depending on the complexity of the company's network operations. Fortune 500 companies, for instance, may have disaster recovery plans that are several hundred pages long, when all sites are considered in aggregate.

One strategy to keep disaster recovery plans concise and to maximize their usefulness is to focus on problems that, while remote, are at least somewhat likely to occur. Alternatively, you can focus on disaster results—what happens—rather than trying to cover disaster causes—why it happened. Focusing your plan on disaster results means contemplating problems such as loss of a single server, loss of the entire server room, loss of all of the customer service workstation computers, and so forth, without worrying about the possible disasters that might cause those results.

The following sections discuss the minimum key issues that a disaster recovery plan should address. Depending on your own company, your plan may need to address additional issues.

Assessing Disaster Recovery Needs

Before drafting the actual plan, you should first assess the needs that the plan must meet. These needs will vary depending on who requires input into the disaster recovery planning process and what issues these people want the plan to address. Consider these types of needs:

- Formally planning for contingencies and ensuring that all possible disasters have been considered, and defining countermeasures in the plan

- Assuring the company's external accounting auditors that the company has considered and developed plans to handle disasters

- Informing the company's top management about the risks that exist for the network and its data in different situations, and how much time you expect to need to resolve any problems that occur

- Soliciting input from top management of the company as to recovery priorities and acceptable minimum requirements to reestablish services

- Formally planning with the key areas of your company's business (for example, manufacturing, customer service, and sales) considerations surrounding different types of computer-related disasters or serious problems

- Assuring customers of the firm that the firm's data operations are safe from disaster

Identifying these needs will not only give you a clear vision of what the plan must address, but also which other people from the different parts of the company should be involved in the planning process.

Considering Disaster Scenarios

You should start your planning process by considering different possible disaster scenarios. For example, consider the following disasters:

- A fire in your server room—or somewhere else in the building—destroys computers and tapes.

- Flooding destroys computers and backup batteries low enough to the server room floor to be affected. Remember that floods may be caused by something within the building itself, such as a bad water leak in a nearby room or a fire that activates the fire sprinklers.

- An electrical problem of some kind causes power to fail.

- Some problem causes total loss of connectivity to the outside world. For example, a critical wide area network (WAN) or Internet link may go down.

- A structural building failure of some kind affects the network or its servers.

- Any of the preceding problems affects computers elsewhere in the building that are critical to the company's operations. For example, such an event may happen in the manufacturing areas, in the customer service center, or in the telephone system closet or room.

While none of these events is very likely, it is still important to consider them all. The whole point of disaster recovery planning is to prevent or minimize serious losses, and the process is much less useful if you consider only those disasters that you think are the most likely.

After considering disasters such as those mentioned, you should next consider serious failures that could also affect the operations of the network. Here are some examples:

- The motherboard in your main server fails, and the vendor cannot get a replacement to you for three or more days.

- Disks in one of your servers fail in such a way that data is lost. If you are running some kind of redundant array of independent disks (RAID) scheme (discussed in Chapter 13), plan for failures that are worse than the RAID system can protect. For example, if you use RAID 1 mirrored drives, plan for both sides of the mirror to fail in the same time frame. If you are using RAID 5, plan for any two drives failing at the same time.

■   Your tape backup drive fails and cannot be repaired for one to two weeks. While this doesn't cause a loss of data in and of itself, it certainly increases your exposure to such an event.

You should plan how you would respond to these and any other possible failures. If the motherboard in your main server fails, you may want to move its drives to a compatible computer temporarily. To address disk failure, you should design a plan under which you can rebuild the disk array and restore data from your backups as rapidly as possible. Regarding your tape backup drive, you will likely want to find out how quickly you can acquire an equivalent drive or whether the maker of the tape drive can provide reconditioned replacement drives quickly in exchange for your failed drive.

For all of these failures, you will also want to consider the cost of keeping spare parts, or even entire backup servers, available so that you can restore operations as rapidly as possible. You should consider and investigate all of the following types of possible responses:

■   Should you carry a maintenance contract? If so, make sure you thoroughly understand its guarantees and procedures.

■   Should you stock certain types of parts on hand so that they are readily available in case of failure?

■   Are other computers available that might work as a short-term replacement for a key server? What about noncomputer components that are important, such as routers, hubs, and switches?

■   If you need to take temporary measures, are the affected employees trained to do their jobs with the replacement, or with no system at all, if necessary? For example, if a restaurant's electronic systems are down, can the restaurant (and the food servers, kitchen staff, cashiers, and so on) still operate the business manually until the system is repaired?

■   Should you maintain a cold or hot recovery site? A "cold" recovery site is a facility maintained by your company and near the protected data center. The cold site has all of the power, air conditioning, and other facility features needed to host your site should the data center experience some disaster. A "hot" site is the same as a cold site, except that it also has all of the necessary computer equipment and software to duplicate the processing of the data center. Hot sites usually synchronize their data on a real-time basis with the main processing center, so that they can literally take over the work of the main site in seconds. Companies with very sensitive, mission-critical data operations often maintain cold or hot recovery sites.

The process of considering possible problems, such as disasters or failures of key pieces of equipment, and then making plans for handling them is certainly the meat of disaster recovery planning. However, your written plan should also discuss or address other issues, which are covered in the following sections.

Handling Communications

An important part of any disaster recovery plan concerns how you will handle communications. Without effective communications, your attempts at handling the disaster will be hampered, and other people will not be able to do their jobs as well as they might otherwise.

Start by listing all of the different parties who may need to be notified of a problem, its progress toward resolution, and its final resolution. Your list might look something like this:

- The board of directors
- The chief executive officer or president
- The vice presidents of all areas
- The vice president or head of an affected area
- Your supervisor
- Employees affected by the problem

For each of these parties—and any others you may identify—you next need to consider what level of problem requires their notification. The board of directors, for example, might not need to know about a disaster unless it is likely that it will have a material effect on the company's performance. Your supervisor, on the other hand, probably wants to be notified about every problem, and certainly any affected employees need to be notified.

Once you have listed the parties to notify and what they need to be informed about, you should then decide *how* you will inform them. If you're the primary person resolving the disaster, it's best to delegate notification to someone else who is less directly involved so that you can focus on resolving the problem as quickly as possible. For example, the job of communicating with the appropriate people should be delegated to your supervisor or to an employee who works in your department and is free to handle this job. Whoever has this job should be clear on the communication procedures and should have access to the necessary contact information—such as home phone numbers, pager numbers, cell phone numbers, and so forth—for situations that require notification after working hours. You may also want to consider setting up a telephone tree for rapid notification. Finally, for your environment and for different types of disasters, you may need to specify the order in which people are notified, which may not match their order in the company's organization chart.

The written disaster recovery plan should include all of the preceding information.

Planning Off-Site Storage

Off-site storage is an important way of protecting some of your backup tapes in the event that a physical disaster, such as a fire, destroys all of your on-site copies. Because off-site storage is such an important aspect of disaster protection, it should be discussed in your disaster recovery plan.

NOTE   If you do not yet have an off-site storage procedure, you should seriously consider adopting one. While fireproof file cabinets can protect tape media from small fires, they are not necessarily invulnerable to very large or hot fires. Plus, tapes are more sensitive to smoke and heat than the papers that a fireproof file cabinet is designed to protect.

Companies that provide off-site storage of files often also offer standardized tape-storage practices. These usually work on a rotation basis, where a storage company employee comes to your office periodically—usually weekly—and drops off one set of tapes and picks up the next set of tapes. The companies typically use stainless steel boxes to hold the tapes, and the network administrator is responsible for keeping the boxes locked and safeguarding the keys. You need to decide which tapes you should keep on-site and which ones to send off-site. One rule of thumb is always to keep the two most recent complete backups on-site (so that they're available to restore deleted files for users) and send the older tapes off-site. This way, you keep on hand the tapes that you need on a regular basis, and you minimize your exposure to a disaster. After all, if a disaster destroys your server room and all of the tapes in it, you probably won't be too worried about losing just a week's worth of data.

NOTE   The amount of data that you can accept exposing to a disaster will vary widely depending on the nature of your company's business and the nature of the data. Some operations are so sensitive that the loss of even a few minutes' worth of data would be catastrophic. For example, a banking firm simply cannot lose any transactions. Businesses that need to protect supersensitive data sometimes enlist a third-party vendor to provide off-site online data storage. Such a vendor replicates a business's data onto the vendor's servers over a high-speed connection, such as a T-1 or T-3. These vendors usually also offer failover services, where their computers can pick up the jobs of your computers should your computers fail. Alternatively, if a business runs multiple sites, it might set up software and procedures that enable it to accomplish the same services using its own sites.

Describing Critical Components

Your plan should describe the computer equipment and software that will be required to resume operations if the entire building is lost. This list should roughly estimate the cost of the equipment and how it can be procured rapidly. By preparing such a list, you can reduce the time required to resume operations in a temporary facility. Also, if your company purchases insurance against business interruptions, you will need these estimates for that insurance policy.

Network Backup and Restore Procedures

A network disaster recovery plan is worthless without some way of recovering the data stored on the server. This is where network backup and restore procedures come in. If you're a network administrator, or aspire to become one, you should already know about the importance of good backups of the system and of important data. If you don't know this, then it's probably the most important lesson that you can take away from this book. Making regular backups is a requirement when using computers—period.

You don't need to work with computers for very long before you observe firsthand the importance of good backups. Computers can and do fail, and they sometimes fail in ways that render the data stored on them unrecoverable. Also, some turn of events may cause certain important files to be deleted or corrupted. In cases such as these, jobs are saved or lost based on the quality of the backups in place and the ability to restore that important data.

Assessing Backup Needs

Before designing network backup procedures, you must understand the company's backup and restoration needs. Questions such as the following may help in assessing the needs that you must meet:

- How dynamic is the data stored on the servers? How often does it change, and in what ways does it change?

- How much data needs to be backed up, and at what rate is the amount of data growing?

- How much time is available to make the backup? Make sure that you avoid situations where you need to back up terabytes of data using a system that can handle only megabytes per hour.

- If a partial or complete restoration from a backup is required, how quickly must it take place? As a rule of thumb, restoring data takes about twice as long as backing it up, although in some cases the times may be approximately equal. In other words, if it takes your backup system 10 hours overnight to back up the entire network, it will take 10 to 20 hours to restore that data—and this estimate doesn't include the time required to resolve whatever problem made it necessary to restore data in the first place.

- How coherent does the backed up data need to be? In other words, does a collection of data files need to be handled as a single unit? For example, a directory containing a bunch of word processing files isn't terribly coherent; you can restore one, many, or all of them without much concern about how those restorations will affect other files. On the other hand, a collection of database files for a high-end database is often useless unless you can restore *all* of the files in the set, from *exactly* the same point in time. (High-end databases—such as Oracle's—that require this kind of backup will have their own detailed instructions for how backups must be made.)

- What is the required trade-off between cost and recoverability? You can design backup systems that operate minute to minute so that if something fails, the systems will not lose any data, and management can place a high degree of confidence in this fact. (A bank, for instance, requires this kind of high-end backup system.) However, such backup systems cost a lot of money and require a lot of administration. Most companies would gladly trade that sort of extreme cost for some lower degree of recoverability, such as nightly backups of the system. What does your company need and what is it willing to pay for?

■ How many levels of redundancy does the company need in its backups? Most backups are made onto tapes and support servers that use RAID arrays, so the tapes are actually the *second* level of protection. In some cases, multiple tapes may be required, each with a separate copy of the backup. Or another way to proceed for maximum redundancy is to copy backups to an off-site storage company over some sort of network connection.

When making your assessment, it is important to involve the senior management of your company in the process. At a minimum, you should present your findings and seek management's agreement or input.

Acquiring Backup Media and Technologies

Once you have some idea of your backup needs, you can then proceed to acquire the necessary hardware and software to create and manage your backups.

If you need to purchase new backup hardware for a system, you can choose from a number of proven, good systems, depending on your actual needs. When choosing a backup technology, consider the following factors:

■ Reliability of the hardware and the media

■ Cost of the hardware and the media

■ Storage capacity

■ Likely frequency of restorations

■ The importance of fitting the entire backup onto a single piece of media

Table 12-1 reviews different types of backup technologies, their approximate costs, and the relative pros and cons of each. Note that the prices of drives, media, and costs per megabyte in Table 12-1 are approximations.

If your company can afford digital linear tape (DLT) or Linear Tape-Open (LTO) systems and can make use of their capacities, you should definitely look into purchasing this technology. DLT and LTO tapes are rock solid, can be used a rated million times, and are said to have a shelf life of 30 years. Moreover, the drives are fast for both backups and restorations. Finally, robotic autochangers are available for DLT and LTO drives, which means that there is plenty of head room if you outgrow the size of your drive. Also, the robotic systems are relatively inexpensive and range from small systems that can hold five tapes up to large libraries that can hold tens or hundreds of tapes.

Some newer backup technologies, such as Super DLT S4 (600GB per tape) and LTO-4 (800GB per tape), promise to up DLT's ante. For larger networks, these emerging technologies may make sense. Both DLT and LTO are reliable tape formats with a lot of support from various computer equipment vendors.

Type	Approximate Cost of Drive	Approximate Cost of Media	Media Capacity	Pros and Cons
CD-R/RW drives	$100 ($153/GB)	<$1 (<$1.53/GB)	650MB	+ Random access −Small capacity −Slow speed −CD-R media is not reusable
DVD-ROM/ RW drives	$200 ($40/GB)	$1 ($0.2/GB)	5GB	+ Random access + Large capacity −Slow speed
Digital linear tape (DLT V4)	$1,000 ($3/GB)	$60 ($0.19/GB)	320GB	+ Very reliable + Very fast + High per-tape capacities + Extremely low media cost/MB
Super DLT (SDLT 600)	$3,000 ($5/GB)	$50 ($0.08/GB)	600GB	+ Very reliable + Very fast + High per-tape capacities + Extremely low media cost/MB
Linear Tape-Open (LTO-2 to LTO-4)	$2–7,000 ($6–10/GB)	$30–40 ($0.05–0.15/GB)	200–800GB	+ Very reliable + Very fast + High per-tape capacities + Extremely low media cost/MB

Table 12-1.   Types of Backup Technologies

Choosing Backup Strategies

After acquiring all the necessary information, you can plan a backup rotation strategy, which addresses how backup media is rotated. Backup rotations are designed to accomplish the following goals:

■ Rebuild the system with the most recent data possible, in case of a catastrophic failure

■ Restore files from older tapes that may have been accidentally erased or damaged without anyone noticing the potential loss of data immediately

- Protect against backup media failure

- Protect the data from an environmental failure, such as a fire, that destroys the original system and data

Most network operating systems maintain special bits for each file on the system. One of these is called the *archive bit*, which indicates the backup status of the file. When a user modifies a file, its archive bit is set to on, indicating that the file should be backed up. When the backup is accomplished, the archive bit is cleared. Using this archive bit and your backup software, you can make the following types of backups:

- A *full backup*, where all selected directories and files are backed up, regardless of their archive bit state. Full backups clear the archive bit on all of the backed-up files when they are finished.

- An *incremental backup*, where only files with their archive bit set are backed up. This backs up all files changed since the last full or incremental backup. Incremental backups clear the archive bit of the backed-up files; those files will not be backed up during the next incremental backup unless they are modified again and their archive bits are reset to the on state. Incremental backups generally minimize the amount of time needed to perform each daily backup, but they take longer to restore and pose a greater risk of media failure.

- A *differential backup*, which is similar to the incremental backup in that it backs up only files with their archive bits set. The key difference in a differential backup is that the archive bits are left turned on. Subsequent differential backups will back up those same files again, plus any new ones that have been modified. Differential backups take longer to make, but reduce the time required to restore and reduce the risk of media failure.

In a perfect world, it would be nice always to perform full backups. If the system were to fail, then you would need only the most recent backup tape to restore the system fully. However, for a number of reasons, performing a full backup may not always be feasible. For one thing, perhaps there is inadequate time to perform a full backup each day. Another reason is to extend the life of your media and tape drive by reducing the amount of work that they do. You need to weigh these concerns against the increased time it takes to restore from a combination of full and incremental or differential backups, and the increased possibility of being unable to restore backups properly using a combination approach. (For example, if a full restoration required a full backup from the previous week, plus four incremental backups since then, you're counting on having all five tapes be perfectly good, and you're somewhat more exposed to a bad tape.)

One common way to mix these types of backups is to perform a full backup of the system once a week and perform only incremental or differential backups each day of the week. Examine the following examples:

■ **Full backup Friday nights and incremental backups on Monday–Thursday** If the system fails Monday morning before any data is entered, you need to restore only the full backup from the previous Friday night. If the system fails on Thursday morning, you need to restore four tapes sequentially in order to retrieve all of the data: the full backup from the previous Friday, then the incremental tapes from Monday, Tuesday, and Wednesday nights. Moreover, to guarantee the integrity of the data, you must be able to restore *all* of those tapes, and in their proper sequence. Otherwise, you run the risk of ending up with mismatched data files. In this scenario, you have four media-based points of failure, which might entail more risk than you care to take.

■ **Full backup Friday night and differential backups Monday–Thursday** In this scenario, if the system fails Monday morning, you just restore the tape from the previous Friday night. However, if the system fails on Thursday morning, you need to restore only two tapes: the last full backup from Friday night, plus the differential backup from Wednesday night. Because differential backups back up all changed files since the last full backup, you never need to restore more than two tapes, thereby reducing the number of possible points of media failure.

To determine the best backup scheme for your system, you need to balance the nature of the data and the amount of risk you're willing to take against the cost of each backup, the capacity of the tapes, and the amount of time it takes to make each regular backup.

The most common backup rotation scheme is called grandfather-father-son (GFS). A common way to implement this scheme is to use at least eight tapes. You label four of the tapes as "Monday" through "Thursday," and four others "Friday 1," "Friday 2," "Friday 3," and "Friday 4." Every Monday through Thursday, you use one of those labeled tapes, replacing the data stored the previous week. Each Friday tape corresponds to which Friday in the month you are on: for the first Friday, you use Friday 1, and so forth. Finally, on the last day of each month, you prepare a month-end tape, which you do not reuse, but instead keep off-site in case an environmental failure destroys the system and all locally stored tapes.

There are three main variations of the GFS scheme. In the first, you simply make a full backup of the system each time you perform a backup. This variation offers the greatest amount of media redundancy and the minimum amount of restoration time. In the second, you perform a full backup on each of the Friday tapes and the monthly tape, but perform only incremental backups during the week. In the third, you do much the same thing, but use differential backups instead of incremental backups.

TIP   If your data is extremely critical and not easily reconstructed, you can often perform full backups every night and also squeeze in a quick incremental backup midday. This way, you can't lose more than a half day's worth of data.

You can also choose rotation schemes that are simpler than GFS. For instance, you may use just two or three tapes and then rotate them in sequence, overwriting the old data each time you do so. This lets you restore any of the previous three days' data. The shortcoming of this scheme is that you may need to go back further in time to restore data that was erased or damaged without anyone immediately noticing. You can combat this problem by using several tapes that you rotate weekly or monthly.

One factor to keep in mind when considering different tape rotation schemes is the *granularity* of your backups. Generally, granularity refers to the flexibility that you retain to recover data from earlier tapes. In the standard GFS scheme, where full backups are made all the time, you could restore a file from any given day for a week's time, for any given end of the week (Friday) for a month's time, or for any given month for a year's time. You could not, however, restore a file that was created three months ago in the middle of the month and erased (or damaged) before the month was over, because a clean copy wouldn't exist on *any* of the backup tapes.

The best advice for choosing a rotation scheme for important data is that unless there are reasons to do otherwise (as already discussed), use the GFS scheme with full backups. This maximizes the safety of your data, maximizes your restoration flexibility, and minimizes the risk of media failure. If other factors force you to choose a different scheme, use the discussions in this chapter to arrive at the best compromise for your situation.

Granularity and Data Corruption: A Tricky Balance

One reason to consider granularity carefully is the possibility of data becoming corrupted and the situation not being noticed. For instance, I once worked with a database file that had been corrupted several weeks earlier, but had continued to function and seemed normal. After problems started to develop, however, the database vendor's technical support staff discovered that a portion of the database that wasn't regularly used had become lost and wasn't repairable. The problem was caused by a bad sector on the database's hard disk. The only way that the support people could recover the database and ensure that it was clean was to restore backups, going further and further back in time, until they found a copy of the database that didn't have the damage. They then reentered the data that had been added since the nondamaged copy was made. Because of the increasing time span between backups as the support people dug further and further back in time, the amount of data that we needed to reenter grew rapidly.

Chapter Summary

You can be the most proficient person at networking in the world, but if you don't create and carefully manage an appropriate disaster recovery program for your company, you're not doing your job. The importance of this area cannot be overstated. In addition to this chapter, you should also study material covering specific backup and restore instructions for your network operating systems and databases, as well as the documentation for your backup hardware device and the backup software you select.

The next chapter discusses key information that you should know about selecting, installing, and managing servers. Servers are the heart of any network, and selecting reliable, productive servers not only will eliminate potential trouble spots for your network, but can also help you avoid needing to actually use the disaster recovery plans and strategies that you have put in place.

Chapter 13

Network Servers: Everything You Wanted to Know but Were Afraid to Ask

Many different *types* of servers exist: file and print servers, application servers, web servers, communications servers, and more. What all servers have in common, though, is that multiple people rely on them and they are usually integral to some sort of network service. Because servers are used by tens or hundreds (or thousands!) of people, the computers you use for servers need to be a cut—or two—above just any old workstation. Servers need to be much more reliable and serviceable than workstations. Plus, they need to perform in different ways from workstations.

This chapter covers network server hardware. You learn about what distinguishes a server from a workstation, about different server hardware configurations, and about preparing a server for use in your network.

What Distinguishes a Server from a Workstation?

With high-performance desktop computers selling for $1,500 to $3,000, it can be hard to see how a computer with the same processor can cost in excess of $7,000 just because it's designed as a "server." Server computers truly are different from workstations, however, and they incorporate a number of features not found in desktop computers. These features are important to a server's job, which is to serve up data or services to a large number of users as reliably as possible.

Server Processors

Much of the performance of a server derives from its *central processing unit*, or CPU. While servers are also sensitive to the performance of other components (more so than a desktop computer), the processor is still important in determining how fast the server can operate.

Servers can run using one processor or many processors. How many processors you choose for a server depends on various factors. The first is the network operating system (NOS) you use. You need to carefully research how many processors are supported on your proposed NOS if you wish to use multiprocessing.

If you plan to use one of the Windows family of servers, you can use multiple processors, depending on which version and edition you plan to run. Windows 2000 Server can handle up to 4 processors, while Windows 2000 Advanced Server can handle up to 8 processors, and Windows 2000 Datacenter Server can handle up to 32 processors. For Windows Server 2003, both the Standard and Web editions support up to 2 processors, Enterprise edition supports up to 8, and Datacenter edition supports up to 32 (and up to 128 processors for the 64-bit variant). For Windows Server 2008, both the Standard and Web editions support up to 4 processors, while the Enterprise edition supports 8 processors, and the Datacenter edition supports 32 processors (up to 64 processors for the 64-bit variant).

NOTE These days, some processors have multiple processor cores on the same chip. The values given for the number of allowed Windows server processors are for the number of processor chips (in other words, the *sockets* on the motherboard).

If you plan to use UNIX, then it depends—some versions of UNIX support multiple processors; others do not.

Another factor to consider is the job that the server does and whether the server's tasks are presently bottlenecked by the processor. File and print servers may not need multiple processors. While they benefit from fast processors, the advantage is not as great as you might think. It's far more important for a file and a print server to have a lot of random access memory (RAM) and a fast disk subsystem. Database servers, on the other hand, are processor-hungry and definitely benefit from as many processors as possible running at the fastest possible speed. (It's also important for the database server software to be configured in such a way that it can make optimal use of multiple processors.) Web servers tend to be modest in their processor requirements—they rely on fast buses, fast network connections, a lot of RAM, fast disks, and that's about it. A fast processor (or multiple processors) is nice on most web servers, but it also might be overkill.

Managing multiple processors requires a lot of overhead work on the part of the operating system. Because of this, having twice as many processors in a computer doesn't double its processing capability; instead, doubling the processors might improve the computer's speed by only about 50 percent. Depending on your operating system, there is also a point of diminishing returns, past which additional processors won't give you much additional performance. Part of this has to do with how the operating system handles multiple processors. Another part has to do with the number of threads doing work in the operating system. (Threads cannot be shared between processors, so if only two main threads are doing all the work on the system, more than two processors won't improve your performance by any meaningful amount.)

DEFINE-IT! What's a Thread?

Operating systems that multitask often do so using a mechanism called a *thread*. In fact, all modern operating systems use threads, including Windows (from Windows 95 on up), NetWare, and some versions of UNIX. In operating systems that make use of threads, each running program runs as a *process*, which has its own memory resources and is kept separate from other processes in the computer. However, the process is divided into different units of work, called *threads*. These threads have access to all the resources of the process in which they run and are the actual "agents of work" within the process. For example, a word processor such as Microsoft Word might have a thread that accepts typed input from the user and displays it on the screen, another that handles any printing chores, and others that constantly check spelling and grammar in the background as the user works. In this example, the application Word is a single process with multiple threads. In a multithreaded operating system, every process always has at least one thread.

To determine the number of processors you should use for any given task, you should consult with the maker of both the NOS you plan to use and makers of the primary applications you plan to run on the server. You might also want to discuss these issues with other companies that are performing similar work with the proposed server application. For instance, for a database server for an accounting system that supports hundreds of users, you should talk to people at other sites that use the same software and have roughly the same number of users, to learn about their experiences and suggestions. It's vital to double-check your proposed server configurations in this way, because different uses of a server might require far more—or far fewer—hardware resources than you might estimate. If you can find another company doing about the same thing and with approximately the same load, you can drastically improve your confidence in a proposed server hardware configuration's ability to meet your needs.

The Intel Pentium Family

Intel's Pentium family has a variety of different processors, ranging from the basic Pentium all the way up to the Pentium Xeon processor. Current server-class computers are shipping with Intel Core Duo or Pentium Xeon processors. The Xeon series of processors are optimized for server-type duties and are more amenable to running in a multiprocessor system.

Pentium Xeon processors are currently available in speeds ranging up to 2.66 GHz with up to 6 cores on a single chip. The design of the Xeon processor allows for 8 to 32 processors in a Pentium Xeon system. For certain applications, having such a large number of processors can be an advantage. The Xeon processor family is packaged in a Single Edge Contact Cartridge, which is much larger than the packaging used for the Pentium non-Xeon processors. The Xeon processors also generate quite a bit more heat than their non-Xeon brethren, mostly due to the much larger cache memory and other features that boost Xeon processor performance in a server. (It's a good thing that most servers can monitor their in-case heat levels; sometimes these chips can heat up to more than 170° Fahrenheit.)

The next big jump in server processors from Intel is coming from its new Itanium processor family, previously known as the IA-64 architecture. The Itanium family is based on a 64-bit architecture that uses something Intel calls Explicitly Parallel Instruction Computing (EPIC). Itanium 2 processors are currently available in speeds ranging from 1.0 to 1.66 GHz. This architecture relies heavily on compiler techniques to arrange the byte-level code so that it can execute as efficiently as possible in parallel (meaning multiple processor instructions execute at the same time).

NOTE   You cannot generally compare the clock speed of processors from one processor family with the clock speeds of processors from another family to get an idea of their relative performance. Processors in different families and from different manufacturers work in very different ways from one another. What takes one processor family four to six instruction cycles to perform might take another processor family only one instruction cycle. Instead, use clock speeds to get an idea of the relative speed difference only among processors within a single processor family.

Intel Clones

Advanced Micro Devices (AMD) makes the Opteron line of processors, which competes primarily with Pentium III and Pentium 4 processors, and essentially emulates the functioning of the Intel family of processors. In the past couple of years, AMD has been successful in actually producing processors that emulate Intel's, and in many cases, they outperform them.

The problem with clone chips such as AMD's is that, despite claims to the contrary, they won't ever be 100 percent compatible with Intel's processors. Because software vendors *usually* certify their software against only Intel processors, such vendors are likely to be slow to respond to any problems that crop up with the clones. Because of this issue, clone chips are not typically used in server-class machines, where reliability and serviceability are of paramount importance.

> **TIP**   Before choosing any server hardware, ensure that the maker of the NOS you plan to use certifies the entire system, including the processor. It is also wise to make sure that the maker of any applications you plan to run on the server certifies the hardware you are choosing. (Most server application makers insist only that the hardware be certified for the operating system, but it's wise to double-check.)

PowerPC

Originally, Motorola, IBM, and Apple teamed up to design and use the PowerPC processor, a RISC-based processor that is actually manufactured by Motorola but based largely on IBM's design. The PowerPC was used in Apple Macintosh (Macs now use Intel processors) computers and some UNIX-based servers from IBM and Motorola.

Bus Capabilities

For most servers, the name of the game is moving data—usually, a *lot* of data. File and print servers might need to serve up hundreds of files simultaneously to hundreds of users, and to coordinate and handle the data needs of all those users. Database servers might manage databases that are many gigabytes or terabytes in size, and they must be able to retrieve large chunks of data from their databases and provide it to users within milliseconds. Application servers might perform both processor-intensive and disk-intensive operations while providing application services to users.

Just as networks often have fast backbone segments connecting many slower segments together, a computer relies on its bus to do the same sort of work. A *bus* is the data transfer "backbone" of a computer system, to which the processor, memory, and all installed devices connect.

At any given time, a server might be moving megabytes of data from its disks to the network cards, to the processor, to the system's memory, and back to the disks as it performs its tasks. All these components are connected together by the system's bus, so optimizing that portion of the computer as much as possible makes sense. The bus might handle about five times more data than any single component in the system, and it needs to do so quickly. While it's true that a modern PCI bus can handle 33 MHz at 32 bits, this just isn't enough in a high-end server. Many servers must handle multiple NICs (each running at speeds up to 100 Mbps or even 1 Gbps) and multiple disk controllers running at speeds up to 40 Mbps. If those devices are busy at the same time, even a PCI bus will quickly get saturated.

Thus, server manufacturers need to get around bus speed limitations. The manufacturers use several schemes to do so. One way is by using multiple buses in a single system. For example, some of HP's Netserver servers use three PCI buses that can all run at full speed simultaneously. Just by using a little planning in placing certain peripherals on the different buses, you can greatly increase the system's overall speed.

RAM

Another important part of any server is its installed memory. Servers cache data from the network and from the server's disks to achieve the best possible performance, and they rely heavily on their RAM to do this. For example, most NOSs cache the entire directory of files they store for quick access. They also keep requested files in the cache for an extended period of time, in case the data from the file is needed again. They also buffer writes to the system's disk through write caches in RAM and perform the actual disk writes asynchronously, so the disks are not as much of a bottleneck as they otherwise would be.

For most servers, 1GB of RAM should be considered a bare minimum. For heavy-duty database servers supporting hundreds of users, you almost certainly will want multiple gigabytes of RAM to achieve the best possible performance.

TIP How much RAM do you really need for your server? This is hard to say because a lot depends on how the server is used. The good news is that both the Windows family of servers and Novell NetWare provide statistics showing how the memory in the system is used. You can use this information to help determine when more memory would be beneficial. For the Windows family of server operating systems, use Performance Monitor to see how memory and the system swap file are being used. For Novell NetWare, use the cache statistics in the console's MONITOR program. Also, most high-end databases (like Oracle's) will provide memory use information to help you determine the amount of RAM that will help the database to perform best.

RAM comes in three varieties: nonparity, parity, and error checking and correcting (ECC). Parity RAM uses an extra bit for every byte to store a checksum of the byte's contents. If the checksum doesn't match when the memory is read, the system stops and reports a memory error. Nonparity memory eliminates the parity bit and therefore can't detect any memory errors. Inexpensive desktop computers sometimes use nonparity RAM as a cost-cutting technique, although you should avoid its use whenever possible, even on desktop computers.

Parity-based memory has two problems. First, the system can only detect memory errors; it can't correct them. Second, because only one bit is used to store the parity, it is possible to "fool" the parity mechanism with a more severe error. For instance, if two bits were to simultaneously changed polarities, the parity system wouldn't detect the problem. ECC memory is designed to address these problems. Systems using ECC memory can detect up to two bits of errors and can automatically correct one bit of error. Most current servers use ECC memory because of the added protection that it offers.

Disk Subsystems

The third crucial performance subsystem for a server is its disk drives. Hard disk drives are usually the slowest components of any system, and because most of the server's work involves the hard disks, they are the components most likely to bottleneck the system. Also, the data stored on a server is usually critically important to the company, so it's important to have the most reliable disk configuration you can afford.

Disk Interfaces: SCSI Versus SATA

Two types of disk interfaces are in widespread use today: Serial Advanced Technology Attachment (SATA) and Small Computer Systems Interface (SCSI). For a workstation using Windows XP, SATA performs on par with a SCSI-based disk system. For a server running Windows, Linux, or Novell NetWare, however, SCSI offers clear performance advantages. SCSI systems perform much better when they have simultaneous access to more than one hard disk and when they are used on an operating system—such as the Windows server family or UNIX/Linux—that can take proper advantage of SCSI's features.

NOTE   SCSI is pronounced "scuzzy." For a while, Macintosh users tried to adopt the pronunciation "sexy," but it never took hold. (SCSI first saw widespread use on the Macintosh, at least in the personal computing world.)

Many varieties of SCSI-based disk systems are available, as follows:

- **SCSI-1**   The basic SCSI specification can transfer data to and from the disks at approximately 5 MBps using an 8-bit transfer width. Advances in SCSI technology have made SCSI-1 obsolete, and it is not used on current systems. (This is good because most SCSI-1 implementations weren't compatible with one another.)

- **SCSI-2**   This is the basic SCSI interface in use today. It extends the SCSI specification and adds many features to SCSI, and it also allows for much faster SCSI connections. In addition, SCSI-2 greatly improved the SCSI compatibility between different SCSI device manufacturers.

- **Fast SCSI**   With Fast SCSI, the basic SCSI-2 specification is enhanced to increase the SCSI bus speed from 5 MHz to 10 MHz and the throughput from 5 MBps to 10 MBps. Fast SCSI is also called Fast Narrow SCSI.

- **Wide SCSI**   Also based on SCSI-2, Wide SCSI increases the SCSI-2 data path from 8 bits to either 16 or 32 bits. Using 16 bits, Wide SCSI can handle up to 20 MBps.

- ■ **Ultra SCSI**   Also called SCSI-3, this specification increases the SCSI bus speed even higher—to 20 MHz. Using a narrow, 8-bit bus, Ultra SCSI can handle 20 MBps. It can also run with a 16-bit bus, increasing the speed further to 40 MBps.

- ■ **Ultra2 SCSI**   Yet another enhancement of the SCSI standard, Ultra2 SCSI doubles (yet again) the performance of Ultra SCSI. Ultra2 SCSI subsystems can scale up to 80 MBps using a 16-bit bus.

- ■ **Ultra160 SCSI**   By now you should know the story: Ultra160 SCSI again doubles the performance available from Ultra2 SCSI. Ultra160 SCSI (previously called Ultra3 SCSI) is named for its throughput of 160 MBps.

- ■ **Ultra320 SCSI**   Ultra320 SCSI can move data at a rate of 320 MBps.

- ■ **Ultra640 SCSI**   Another doubling of the SCSI interface speed, Ultra640 SCSI was promulgated as a new standard in early 2003.

NOTE   A storage connection technology, called Fibre Channel, can use either fiber-optic or copper cable, is a much more flexible connection scheme than SCSI, and promises throughput many times faster than even that of Ultra640 SCSI. Based loosely on a network paradigm, Fibre Channel is initially expensive to implement, but large data centers will benefit greatly from its advances over SCSI.

As you can see from the preceding list, a dizzying array of SCSI choices is available on the market today. Because of all the different standards, it's a good idea to make sure you purchase matched components when building a SCSI disk subsystem or when purchasing one as part of a server. Make sure the controller card you plan to use is compatible with the drives you will use, that the card uses the appropriate cables, and that it is compatible with both the server computer and the NOS you will use. The good news is that once you get a SCSI disk subsystem up and running, it will run reliably and with excellent performance.

Disk Topologies: It's a RAID!

The acronym RAID stands for redundant array of independent disks. RAID is a technique of using many disks to do the work of one disk, and it offers many advantages compared to using fewer, larger disks.

The basic idea behind RAID is to spread a server's data across many disks, seamlessly. For example, a single file might have portions of itself spread across four or five disks. The RAID system manages all those parts so you never know they're actually spread across all the disks. You open the file, the RAID system accesses all the appropriate disks and "reassembles" the file, and provides the entire file to you.

The immediate benefit you get is that the multiple disks perform much more quickly than a single disk. This is because all the disks can independently work on finding their own data and sending it to the controller to be assembled. A single disk drive would be limited by a single disk head and would take much longer to gather the same amount of data. Amazingly, the performance of a RAID system *increases* as you add more disks, because of the benefit of having all those disk heads independently working toward retrieving the needed data.

If you think about a simple RAID array with data spread across many disks, you'll probably notice that, while it improves performance, it also increases the chance of a disk failure. Using five disks to do the work of one means that five times more chances exist for a disk failure. Because the data is spread among all the disks, if one fails, you might as well throw away all the data on all the remaining disks because it's useless if a big chunk is missing. Fortunately, different RAID schemes address this problem.

There are many different ways to use multiple disks together in some sort of RAID scheme and, accordingly, a number of *RAID levels* are defined, each of which describes a different technique, as follows:

- **RAID 0**   This scheme is a configuration whereby data is spread (*striped*) across multiple disks, although *with no redundancy*. Losing one drive in a RAID 0 array results in the loss of data on all the disks. RAID 0 is appropriate only for improving performance and should be used only with nonessential data. RAID 0 arrays can stripe data across two or more disks, as shown in Figure 13-1.

- **RAID 1**   This type of array doesn't stripe data across multiple disks. Instead, it defines a standard whereby data is mirrored between disks. Two disks are used instead of one, and the data is kept synchronized between the two disks. If one of the disks fails, the remaining disk continues working just fine, until the failed drive can be replaced. RAID 1 is often simply referred to as *mirroring*. An enhancement to RAID 1 is called *duplexing*; the data is still duplicated between two disks, but each disk has its own disk controller, adding another level of redundancy (because you can lose either a disk or a controller and still keep operating). Duplexing can also improve performance somewhat, compared to straight mirroring. Some RAID 1 implementations are also intelligent enough to read data from either disk in such a way that whichever disk has its drive head closest to the data performs the read request, while the other one sits idle. However, all writes must occur simultaneously for both disks. Figure 13-2 shows a typical RAID 1 array layout.

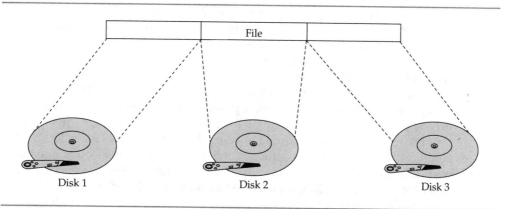

Disk 1   Disk 2   Disk 3

Figure 13-1.   A RAID 0 array stripes data across multiple disks

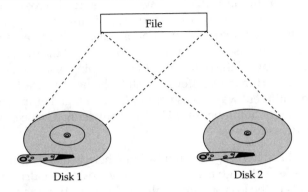

Figure 13-2.   A RAID 1 array mirrors data between two disks

TIP   You can combine RAID levels 0 and 1 to achieve the performance benefit of RAID 0 with the high level of redundancy of RAID 1. Imagine a series of RAID 1 arrays with two disks each. Combine each of these RAID 1 arrays so that data is striped across them, and you have what is called a RAID 10 array (with 10 referring to a combination of RAID 1 and RAID 0). This is sometimes also called RAID 0 + 1 or RAID 1 + 0.

- **RAID 2**   You probably won't see RAID 2 implemented in the real world. RAID 2 is a technical specification that stripes data across multiple disks and then uses a Hamming Code ECC that is written to a set of ECC disks. The ratio of ECC disks to data disks is quite high with RAID 2: There are three ECC disks for every four data disks. RAID 2 isn't used because of its inefficiencies.

- **RAID 3**   This is where RAID starts to get interesting. RAID 3 implementations used to be fairly common, although these days you see RAID 5 used much more often than RAID 3. RAID 3 stripes data across multiple data disks and then uses an exclusive OR (XOR) bit-wise operation against all the stored data on each data disk to come up with ECC data, which is written to a single ECC drive. So, for example, you can have four data drives and one ECC drive to back them up. Figure 13-3 shows a RAID 3 array. The XOR data has an interesting mathematical property. If you remove one of the data drives, you can take the remaining data, plus the data on the ECC drive, and reconstruct what is missing from the failed drive. RAID disk controllers do this automatically if a drive fails, although the drives operate at a slower rate than normal because of the overhead of having to reconstruct the data on the fly. A more useful technique is to replace the failed drive and then use the ECC data to rebuild the lost data.

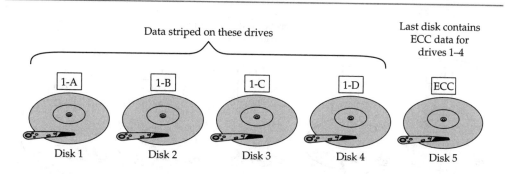

Figure 13-3.   A RAID-3 array stripes data across multiple disks, with an ECC disk to protect the data

NOTE   If more than one drive is lost from a RAID 3 or a RAID 5 array, all the array's data will be lost. Still, these arrays provide good protection at relatively low incremental cost.

■ **RAID 4**   This is another of the RAID standards that isn't used very much in the real world. RAID 4 is similar to RAID 3, except data is striped between the different data drives in much larger blocks than with RAID 3. RAID 4 still uses a single ECC disk for all the data drives.

■ **RAID 5**   RAID 5, depicted in Figure 13-4, is the current standard for RAID systems. (RAID 1 also remains a current standard, but it has different applications.) Recall how RAID 3 worked, with data striped to a set of data disks, and the ECC code written to a single ECC disk. RAID 5 improves on this scheme by interleaving the data and ECC information across all the disks. The big advantage of this approach over RAID 3 is that it doesn't rely on a single ECC drive for all write operations, which becomes a bottleneck on RAID 3 systems. Because all the drives share the ECC work, performance with RAID 5 is slightly better than with RAID 3. There is a small drawback to this, though, that most commentators miss. In RAID 3, if you lost a data drive, the system slowed down (usually dramatically) as the data was reconstructed on the fly. If you lost the ECC drive, however, the system would still run just as fast as if no drive were lost. With RAID 5, if you lose a drive, you're always losing part of your ECC drive (because its job is spread among all the disks), so you get a slowdown no matter what.

■ **RAID 6**   RAID 6 works the same as RAID 5, but stores parity data on two interleaving drives rather than the one of RAID 5. Also called *dual data guarding*, RAID 6 keeps your data safe while you are recovering from a single drive failure. (In RAID 5, if a drive failed while you were recovering from another drive's failure, you would lose the array's data.)

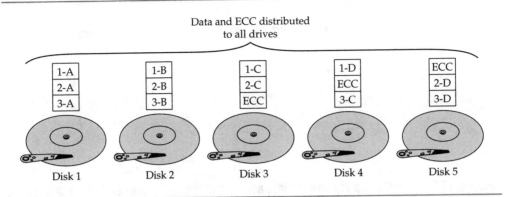

Figure 13-4. A RAID 5 array stripes data across multiple disks, and alternately uses all disks for ECC data

Which level of RAID should you use on your network server? Most network administrators favor RAID 5 because it requires only 20 to 25 percent of the total disk capacity for the redundancy function, yet it performs well and offers a measure of safety. However, RAID 3 and RAID 5 arrays do occasionally fail to recover data properly (although they very rarely lose data). For this reason, you usually should opt for either RAID 1 or a RAID 10 array for network servers that store vital data.

In general, the different RAID configurations offer different levels of reliability. Ranked from best to worst purely in terms of the system's likelihood of losing data would be RAID 1, RAID 10, RAID 6, RAID 5, and RAID 3. There are always trade-offs, though. A system with 20 disks using just RAID 1 would be unwieldy to manage, because you would have 10 logical drives to manage and use efficiently. However, if you configured those same 20 disks as two RAID 5 arrays, you would be able to manage more efficiently the two logical disks that would result.

You must make your own decision based on the importance of the data, the required levels of performance, the capabilities of the server, and the budget available to you. One thing you should *never* do, though, is trust that any RAID level replaces regular, tested, reliable tape backups of network data!

Server State Monitoring

An important feature of most servers is the capability to monitor its own internal components and to notify you if any problems develop or appear to be developing. Higher-end servers can typically monitor the following:

- Proper fan operation
- System voltage
- Memory errors, even if corrected by ECC memory
- Disk errors, even if corrected automatically

- In-case temperature
- Operating system hangs
- Computer case opening

Any of these errors might indicate a current or impending problem with the server. For example, a 1-bit memory error that is corrected by the system's ECC memory might not cause a problem for the server because it was corrected, but it might indicate that a RAM chip or bank of RAM is starting to experience trouble. Similarly, climbing temperatures in a case might not cause an immediate problem, but may indicate that a fan isn't operating properly, has a blocked intake, or is facing another problem, and ultimately temperatures higher than those allowed for in the server design will cause a failure.

Server state monitoring solutions can alert you to problems either via e-mail or through a pager. Some even operate if power is lost to the server or the server room (this is called "lights-out" capability). Many high-end servers also offer "prefailure" warranties that state that the manufacturer will replace any components reporting even minor errors, so you can replace them before serious trouble actually strikes. For those servers you depend on to be the most reliable possible, such monitoring and warranty features can be a real lifesaver.

Hot-Swap Components

Most modern servers include hot-swap components that you can replace while the system continues to operate. Usually, hot-swap components are limited to disks, power supplies, and fans, all of which are running in a redundant configuration. For example, a system might have two power supplies; if one fails, the system still operates normally and you can replace the failed power supply without needing to turn off the server. Similarly, most RAID disk configurations enable you to replace a failed drive without shutting down the server, provided the disks are installed in a hot-swap configuration.

 TIP   Many RAID disk systems enable you to install a standby disk, and the system itself uses that standby disk to replace any failed drive automatically. Of course, you would then replace the actual failed disk as soon as possible, and the replacement becomes the standby disk for the disk array.

Choosing Servers for Windows and NetWare

In this section, you learn about the basics of defining server needs, selecting a server, and purchasing a server.

Defining Server Needs

Before looking at different server models, you need to understand clearly the needs that the server has to meet. Otherwise, you risk either under- or over-purchasing hardware, both of which can cause problems and might lead you to spend more than you needed to spend. Under-purchasing leads to additional, unplanned purchases, which might include adding more disks or more memory, or even needing to replace the server much too soon. Over-purchasing means you spent more for a server than necessary, which might lead your company to deny your request for a particular server. Instead, you need to find the "sweet spot" for specifying just the right server for your needs; then you can defend your required configuration and its cost. You can't do any of this unless you have clearly defined your needs.

To specify the needs for a server clearly, you must be able to answer all the following questions:

- What is the useful life of the server? How long do you expect to use the server? Will you replace it in two, three, or four years? (Most servers are used for around three years before being replaced.) Everyone should agree on this time frame, because if you plan to replace the server in two years, you can get by with a smaller server than if you need one to last three or four years. If you specified a server capable of meeting two years' needs, however, you don't want to get to the end of two years and then find out that your company won't approve a replacement.

- What job will the server perform? Will it be a file and print server, a web server, a database server, or some other kind of server?

- How many users will the server support and what are the needs of those users? For example, with a file and print server, you must estimate the storage and bandwidth requirements needed to satisfy all the planned users' requests. For a database server, you must know how quickly the server needs to respond to various database operations.

- How reliable must the server be? What are the consequences (costs and impacts) if the server crashes for one or more hours, or for a day or two?

- Will you use clustering for the server? Clustering is a technique whereby multiple servers share the same essential job. If one fails, everything keeps working, albeit at a slower rate. Once the failed server is repaired, it can then be added back to the cluster.

- How safe must the data on the server be from loss? This is different from the preceding question because you might have cases in which a server must never lose data, even if it isn't a big deal if the server goes down for a few hours. In such a situation, you would use a RAID 1 or RAID 10 configuration, but you might not care too much about, say, redundant power supplies. You might also explore some kind of hierarchical storage scheme, where data is automatically copied to tape or optical disk in real time, or where you make several live incremental backups of files each day.

- If the server fails, what are your backup plans? Do you plan to keep a hot-spare server (one that's ready to be swapped in at a moment's notice for a failed server) available or do you plan simply to rely on the server manufacturer's service capabilities? Also, sometimes if a server fails, other existing servers might temporarily meet some of its needs. For example, in a Windows network, if a domain controller fails, you can have other domain controllers to provide this necessary functionality for the network as a whole. Or you might have redundant printer queues defined on another server, ready to be made available if the primary print server fails.

- How do you plan to back up the server? Do you plan to have a tape drive on the server itself, or do you plan to back it up over the network to some other server's backup device? Do you plan to make backups while the server is being used, or overnight when it's not being used? These are important questions to answer, because if you host the backup device on the server, you also need to have backup software on the server. If you plan to back up a server while it's being used, you need a fast backup system connected to a fast server bus to minimize the impact to the users during the day. If you plan to back up a server over a network connection, you need a network connection fast enough to handle the amount of data on the server. Think carefully about your backup plans when specifying a server.

- How could the demands placed on the server change over time? Is the company aggressively hiring more employees, so that the server might need to support twice as many users a year from now and four times as many users two years from now? Make sure you understand the company's overall plans and factor them into your assessment of server needs. Also, even in companies where the number of users is relatively static, the amount of storage required by each user will still grow rapidly. A rule of thumb is to estimate that current storage requirements double every 18 months, everything else being equal. If you have historical data for how much storage users consume, this data can help you estimate your system's requirements even more accurately. (And don't forget to anticipate any new network services that could more rapidly increase your storage needs!)

- Does the new server need to work with any existing hardware? If you need to reuse a network backup device, for instance, you should make sure that the new server can properly support it (and vice versa).

- How much physical room do you have available to house the server? Are you compelled by space requirements to go with the smallest server possible?

Once you answer these questions and any others that might crop up, you're ready to start looking at different servers that can meet the needs you defined.

Selecting the Server

Aside from choosing the types of equipment you need for a server, you must remember three basic prerequisites that all your server purchases should meet: compatibility, compatibility, and compatibility. If your NOS starts displaying error messages on a particular server, you'll need fast responses to these types of problems. If you built a server yourself by buying a motherboard, a disk controller, a video card, and so forth, you're not going to get effective support, either for the hardware or for any compatibility problems that crop up with the software. For both Novell and Microsoft NOSs, make sure that each part of the server—as well as the entire system collectively—is certified by Novell or Microsoft for its respective NOS.

For Microsoft operating systems, go to the following URL to look at Microsoft's Hardware Compatibility List (HCL) and make certain that the hardware you like is certified:

```
http://www.microsoft.com/whdc/hcl/default.mspx
```

When selecting servers, you often select a manufacturer first and then select the actual model you need. This is because, everything being equal, you're slightly better off if all your servers are from the same maker. Managing servers from one manufacturer is much easier than managing servers from many manufacturers. You can do a better job of stocking spare parts that might fit into all of your servers, and you can build a better relationship with the manufacturer or a particular dealer, which might hold additional benefits. For example, Dell lets companies certify their in-house technicians on Dell hardware (including servers), and then allows them order parts more directly, bypassing the first level of support (the first support people's job being mainly to intercept the easy questions that beginners ask), and also provides other benefits.

Be conservative in selecting servers and server brands. You should stick with the top names in the industry for many reasons, including these:

- They have much more established service organizations and practices
- They are likely to offer higher-quality support
- Because so many other networks are based on their equipment, their technical support databases probably already contain any problems you may encounter, and they probably have fixes available
- The NOS vendor is also more likely to have data on any problems concerning one of the top servers
- They have much better in-house engineering, and their servers are likely to perform better and to be more reliable

These are just the biggest reasons. You might remember a time when the mantra in management information systems (MIS) departments was, "Nobody ever got fired for buying IBM." A similar type of mindset makes sense when buying servers, not only because the purchase is more defensible, but because buying from major manufacturers actually makes better business sense, for the reasons cited in the preceding list.

Remember these general differences when you select a server for either NetWare or Windows networks: First, while any server is RAM-hungry, Windows servers work better with more RAM than an equivalent NetWare server. If everything else is equal, plan on giving a Windows server 50 to 100 percent more RAM than a NetWare server.

Also, database servers are RAM-hungry for databases of any appreciable size (10GB or larger), so plan on using at *least* 2GB of RAM. (4GB to 8GB of RAM isn't out of the question for the best possible performance).

Windows servers can operate with up to 8 or 32 processors. A Windows server will work very well with two or four processors. Also, remember that with a single processor, NetWare servers tend to perform better than Windows servers. Depending on the actual application, a NetWare server can outperform a Windows server by 15 to 30 percent, even if you've already added more RAM to the Windows server configuration.

Both Windows and NetWare server systems can implement certain RAID levels themselves. For the best performance, however, you should select a disk controller that can take this burden off the NOS. High-throughput disk controllers also often have a significant amount of RAM on them for caching disk data, and they usually have their own processor to help handle their chores. Moreover, I recommend you use a SCSI-based disk subsystems on a server. A workstation running Windows performs equally well with either SATA or SCSI, but a server can take advantage of SCSI's features to improve performance significantly over SATA disk interfaces. SCSI drives also have a tendency to be more reliable than SATA drives.

Choosing your actual disk configuration is relatively straightforward. You start by determining your current and planned space requirements, and then you consider your performance and reliability needs to choose a particular RAID level that makes sense. (See the "Disk Topologies: It's a RAID!" section earlier in this chapter for more information.) Once you know these requirements, you can choose the amount of disk space you need and ensure that the server you want can handle your current and planned disk space needs.

Remember this tip: You're better off knowing what your disk requirements will be over time and planning to purchase additional disk space as the need arises. This is because the capacity of disk drives increases at a rapid rate, while prices fall at a rapid rate. Buying a 1TB drive a year from now, for example, will be less expensive than purchasing the same drive today. Just make sure that the server you select can handle all the drives that you plan to purchase, and then install those drives as needed to save your company money. For NetWare servers, also remember that the optimal amount of RAM depends on the amount of disk space in the server, so you want to plan on purchasing more RAM when you add any significant amount of disk space. But, happily, the same rule of thumb for disks holds true for RAM: Prices tend to spiral downward, and tomorrow's RAM will almost certainly be much less expensive than today's RAM.

If you plan to purchase a server for Windows Server, you might also want to consider selecting a system that accepts additional processors. This way, if you find the system is becoming bottlenecked at the processor level, you can install more processors to reduce or remove that bottleneck.

Purchasing the System

Once you decide on the server you want, purchasing it is relatively straightforward. Shop around and get the best price on the system you want. Make sure that the suppliers you approach offer the level of support you need, both for presales selection assistance and for postsales support.

TIP Remember that it's not really "cricket" to rely on the expertise of a particular supplier to help you select a server and answer any presales questions you have, and then to purchase the server from some mail-order supplier with a slightly lower price. Try to be fair in your dealings. You should not abuse vendors with higher support capabilities in this fashion; if you do so, they might not be around to help you with after-sales issues that arise, or to help you with future purchases. This is not to say that you should pay a lot more for a piece of hardware from such vendors—just take into account the vendor's level of service when you evaluate different price quotes, and remember that price isn't everything.

Depending on your company's financial practices, you might want to consider leasing a server. Doing so brings you several benefits. First, leasing conserves your company's cash. Instead of shelling out $20,000 all at once, you can pay for the use of the server over time. Also, the annual impact of a lease is much lower than with a purchase, and leasing might make it easier to fit a particular server within your budget.

Leases also have a hidden benefit: They force you to consider whether to replace a server at the end of the lease term (usually three years). They also usually make it easy to return the server to the leasing company and then lease a new server with which you can move forward. In the end, you pay about as much for leasing as buying (all things considered), and leases can help discipline a company to keep its computer equipment relatively current. The only drawback to leasing is that you must have enough time to replace the server at the end of the lease, when you might prefer to do it several months before or after the lease is up. Still, in some companies, the benefits of leasing far outweigh the disadvantages. Discuss leasing with your financial department before ordering a server.

Installing Servers

The actual practice of setting up a server is mostly specific to the server itself and the NOS that you plan to use. In subsequent chapters, this book describes basic installations of Windows and Linux.

When you set up a new server, remember to plan on extensively testing its hardware prior to implementing it. While most servers are reliable right out of the box, the fact is that if some part of the server is going to fail, it almost always fails shortly after being set up and used. I prefer to test servers for at least a week, even before installing the NOS onto the server. Most servers come with diagnostic software that you can configure to operate continuously—testing the system's processor, video subsystem, disk surfaces, and RAM—and log any errors that crop up. Right after pulling a server from its box and installing any components that you need to install, plan on putting the server into a diagnostic loop using its diagnostic software and letting it run those tests for as long as possible. In no case should you test the server for less than several days (try to shoot for a week of testing).

TIP   It's important to start testing a server immediately after it arrives. Most vendors have different replacement versus repair policies depending on how long you've had a piece of hardware. For instance, many vendors will simply replace a server with an entirely new one if a failure is discovered in the first 30 days, but after that, they'll go through the normal repair process. If an error does appear during testing, you'll probably be more confident with a new server than going through a repair process. (Plus, the repair process will take more of your time for troubleshooting and such.)

After finishing the testing, you can install the NOS. During this phase, pay careful attention to any peculiarities of the server and to any error messages reported by the NOS or the server during the installation process.

You must resolve these errors fully prior to going live with the server. In particular, watch out for any intermittent messages, such as a message that there was a parity error in the system's RAM or an unexpected lockup of the server during installation. Even if those problems don't recur, consult with the maker of the server. (Be sure you carefully write down any messages or other things that you notice if this happens.) Servers have a tendency to fail at the most inopportune times, so make sure that you have complete confidence in the server before making it available to users. It might make sense also to let the server run its production software configuration for several days as an added test before putting it into use.

In particular, make sure to have all potential NetWare Loadable Modules (NLMs), Windows services and processes, or UNIX/Linux daemons running together as part of the testing. When you combine third-party software for these platforms, there are numerous opportunities for bugs or incompatibilities that the vendors did not anticipate (despite a NOS vendor's stamp of approval).

Most server manufacturers have made it easy to install their server and to install the NOS onto the server. Companies such as HP and Dell even ship their servers with special CD-ROMs that mostly automate the process of installing various NOSs onto the server and also install any needed support files that the NOS needs to work optimally with the server hardware. Prior to installing a NOS onto a server, make sure to read the server's documentation carefully and to take advantage of any automated tools provided by the server manufacturer.

TIP   The top-tier server makers (IBM, HP, and Dell, for example) maintain e-mail notification systems that let you know about any new patches they release or any serious problems they have with a particular model. These e-mail services are extremely useful, so you should plan on signing up for them immediately on receipt of any new server.

Here's something else to think about: Sometimes servers are built and then sit around in inventory for several months before being sold. Consequently, the server might not come with the most current software. Before installing the server, check the maker's web site for any updates that aren't in your package and consider whether to install those updates during your implementation process.

Maintaining and Troubleshooting Servers

To do the best job of maintaining and troubleshooting servers, you need to take steps to do two things: decrease the chance of failure and improve your chance of rapidly resolving any failures that do occur. Problems are inevitable, but you can greatly decrease your odds of having them, and you can also greatly improve your chances of resolving them quickly by taking steps *before* you actually have any problems.

To decrease the chance of failure, make sure to follow all the advice previously given: use reliable, tested servers and components. You should also take these additional steps:

- Whenever possible, try to reduce the number of jobs that a server must do. Although building a single server that will be a file and print server, a database server, an e-mail server, and a web server is certainly possible, you're much better off (from an overall reliability standpoint) segregating these duties onto smaller, separate servers.

- Set up a practice of frequently viewing the server's error logs. If the server NOS supports notification of errors (such as to a pager), consider implementing this feature. Many failures start with error messages that might precede the actual failure by a few hours, so getting an early heads-up might help you keep the server running or at least enable you to resolve the problem at the best possible time.

- If a server supports management software that monitors the server's condition, make sure to install the software.

- Most RAID arrays that support hot-swap of failed drives also require that the NOS have special software installed to support this feature fully. Make sure that you install this software before any failures occur.

- NOS software is among the most bug-free available, but it's still true that there is no such thing as completely bug-free software. Over time, any NOS will eventually fail. While many servers run for up to a year without requiring a restart, you're better off establishing a practice of periodically shutting down the server and bringing it back up again. This practice eliminates small transient errors that might be accumulating and could eventually lead to a server crash, such as memory leaks in the NOS. The best frequency for such restarts is monthly.

 CAUTION   Make sure that you do a backup before shutting down the server and restarting it. The greatest chance of hardware failure occurs when the system is powered back up again.

It's a good idea to make three good backups and test restorations prior to putting a server into use. It might seem redundant, but you never know when you might need to restore your data, and it's important to know that your backup and restoration practices will function properly.

You can also do some general things to improve your ability to resolve any server failures rapidly. The most important is to maintain for each server an extensive binder (or file box), which I call a "rebuild kit." This binder should contain the following:

- All purchase data for the server, including your purchase order and a copy of the supplier's invoice.

- A printout of the server's configuration. Most servers' setup programs can generate a detailed list with all components and their versions. HP's Insight Manager is great for this.

- All software needed to rebuild the server completely from scratch. This includes the setup software for the server, the NOS software, device driver disks, and any patch disks you need or have applied. Remember to add to the box any new drivers or patches that you get during the life of the server so that they will be available.

- Contact information for service on the server, including any extended warranty contract numbers or other information that you need to get service.

- Notepaper, for documenting all changes to the server's configuration and any error messages that appear. Write all the information clearly, noting the date, the time, and any other details that you (or someone else) might need to fix the server if it fails.

- A printout or document noting anything special about the server or how you configured the disk drives, including NOS settings. You need these settings if you have to rebuild from scratch. Knowing these settings might enable you to recover the data on the server's disks so that you don't need to restore the data from backup tape.

 CAUTION   You need a strong backup plan for any server, with appropriate tape rotations and regular tests of your ability to restore data from the tapes you make. The goal is to never need to use these tapes, but they give you an absolutely critical safety net if the server's disks crash and lose their stored data.

Even if you're the best computer troubleshooter in the world, you should plan on working with the service department of your server's manufacturer to troubleshoot any problems. Doing so can save you because the people in this department have extensive databases available to them of the problems others have experienced. They also are familiar with the steps needed to help prevent data loss as you work to troubleshoot the problem. Troubleshooting a server on your own, no matter how experienced and knowledgeable you are, is usually a mistake.

Chapter Summary

When building a network, the one component you should pay the most attention to is the server. While other parts of the network, like the wiring, network architecture, or workstations, are also significant, the server is the most likely component to experience trouble over time. The server is the single component you must spend the most time managing. Because of this, take extra care when selecting, implementing, and maintaining your servers. If you take care of your servers, your servers will take care of you.

The following chapter concerns network workstation computers and discusses the different requirements desktop computers have, how you should buy and manage them, and how to support them.

Chapter 14

Purchasing and Managing Client Computers

Desktop computers are really where the "rubber meets the road" when it comes to networks. These machines are the users' primary interface to the network and the resource on which users most rely to get their jobs done. In fact, the network is designed to support the desktop computers' work, rather than the other way around. Maintaining desktop computers is also the task on which you often spend the most time in managing a network, so their purchase, implementation, and management are important. You can have the best network in the world, but if your desktop computers aren't up to the task, the network's users won't be productive.

This chapter focuses on the management of desktop computers. Chances are that if you're reading this book, you already know about the bits and bytes that make up desktop computers and desktop operating systems. You're probably already a wizard with Windows or the Macintosh, and you're comfortable installing new computer hardware and repairing problems on desktop computers. If you don't know about these things yet, you can find many good books that cover the technologies in desktop computers in detail. In this chapter, the major concern is how desktop computers integrate with the network and how you can get the most out of them when you're managing or setting up a network.

Choosing Desktop Computers

Choosing desktop computers involves many considerations. Making good choices here will pay big dividends over time. When purchasing new desktop computers, you have the opportunity to select machines to reduce your support burden, improve end-user productivity, and—overall—conserve your company's cash. The following sections explore the different factors that go into selecting desktop computers.

Desktop Platforms

You need to know which desktop computer platform you will use. Generally, companies tend to gravitate toward either PC- or Macintosh-based desktop computers. (These days, it is increasingly rare to find companies that depend much on Macintoshes as a staple of their desktop computer diet.) In a few rare cases, companies might alternatively gravitate toward Linux- or UNIX-based desktop computers, but you'll usually choose between PCs and Macintoshes.

Advantages and disadvantages exist for each platform. Regardless of the specific pros and cons, you're *much* better off if you can keep the company standardized on a single desktop computer platform. Companies that have purchased their desktop computers in accordance with individual user preferences (users are free to choose a PC, a Macintosh, or something else) end up with real support headaches, which arise from many different sources. Supporting two desktop platforms is more than twice as difficult as supporting one platform. Why? Consider the following:

- You need to maintain expertise in two platforms, as well as expertise in their applications and platform-specific peculiarities. In a small company, you need more people to keep the requisite levels of expertise on both platforms than you would need if you had to support only one platform.

- You need to stock more spare parts and expansion hardware. Generally, components that work in a PC won't work in a Macintosh, and vice versa.

- You need to license and inventory more software titles (on average, twice as many).

- Problems that would never occur with one platform or another occur when you must support both, even in the network itself. Supporting two platforms is more complex than supporting one, so the servers must run additional software, must allow for the different ways that each platform works, and so forth. All this increases the complexity of the network, and increased complexity means less reliability for everyone.

- Interplatform incompatibilities cause problems for users who must work together. Even if they use the same application (such as Microsoft Word) on both PCs and Macintoshes, platform differences still exist. For example, Adobe fonts with the same name may look and paginate differently on Macs and PCs. Users might painstakingly format a document in Word, Excel, InDesign, or another application available on both platforms, only to find that the other platform doesn't present their work in exactly the same way. When users who frequently interact with one another have their files formatted for a variety of platforms, the incompatibilities become a real problem.

- In some cases, you might be unable to find software titles with matching versions available for both platforms. This usually means users who are using a particular application won't be able to interact with users who are using the other platform's functionally equivalent application. For example, Microsoft Access is available only for Windows.

- You will be limited in the programs you can develop for widespread use. For example, try developing a Microsoft Access-based application and then having Macintosh users use it. They can't, because Microsoft Access doesn't exist on the Macintosh, and there's no way to use the same database application on both platforms in such cases. You can probably exchange data, but not the program written in Access. The same situation exists for virtually all programming languages: They are almost universally platform-specific, despite the efforts of their makers to make them platform-neutral. Examples of this kind of problem are much more common than not. (One exception to this rule is a more advanced SQL-based application that makes use of something like an Oracle database server.)

These examples should convince you that you're better off running the *wrong* desktop platform than running *two* desktop platforms. If you're in a company where two desktop platforms are in use, you should work toward implementing a standard platform. This process is difficult and time-consuming, but is important both for increasing overall company productivity and keeping IT costs at a reasonable level.

NOTE If you move into PC management, you will probably be called on to perform cost analyses to determine which platform to choose or to justify why you chose the one you did. These exercises include costs of new hardware and software, dealing with legacy applications or systems to which the platform must connect, and maintaining and supporting the platform, as well as predicting the viability of the platform in one, two, five, and ten years. Remember that the chief technical officer (CTO) or chief information officer (CIO) usually reports to the chief financial officer (CFO), since IT has historically been considered a cost center rather than a profit center.

After deciding whether or not to standardize on a single platform, your next decision is which one to choose. Most often, a company has a history with a particular platform, so sticking with that platform is usually the easiest solution, unless a good reason exists for a change.

If you're lucky enough to be setting up a company network for the first time, then you get to help choose a platform. This choice should always be driven by what the users need to accomplish, which applications they need to run, and the platform that best supports those applications. You need to consider the full range of applications that the company is likely to need, but the users' needs should be the primary driver. For most companies, this means you'll strongly lean toward PCs as the standard. However, for some companies, Macs are still a good idea. Generally, Macs make sense in companies that have a strong artistic or graphic bent to their makeup, such as a web design firm, a graphic design house, and so forth.

NOTE As you have probably already noticed, many people want to make a platform decision based on the platform they like the best. Many people happily call themselves "PC fanatics" or "Mac fanatics." For some of these people, the issue rises almost to the same level of importance to them as a religion. Such fervent brand loyalty should never influence you in making a smart business decision. However, the presence of such strong opinions also means that you must tread carefully when discussing platform issues with the system's users!

If no need exists that strongly suggests a particular platform, then, for many reasons, you should lean toward PCs. They are the most price competitive, are in the widest use, attract the largest assortment of software and hardware developers, and have much more infrastructure to support them. Also, for certain important business application software categories, good solutions are available on the PC platform but not on the Mac platform.

NOTE   This book aims to be platform-neutral, but the fact is that more than 90 percent of networked desktop computers are PCs. While this book is just as applicable to Macs as PCs, the remainder of this chapter assumes a PC environment.

Reliability and Serviceability

The most important features to look for in any desktop computer are its reliability and serviceability. Studies have shown that the actual price of a desktop computer is a small percentage of its lifetime cost, which includes software costs, training costs, and support costs.

When assessing reliability, you need to look at the whole picture. Reliability comes from several sources:

- The computer uses tested, high-quality components.

- Those components are engineered to work well together. You can make a cake with the best ingredients available, but if your recipe isn't good, you still get a bad cake. Computers are no different. Even the best components don't always work well together. Top-tier manufacturers test all the components that go into their systems and ensure that they're compatible with one another.

- A reliable combination of software is used on the unit, and whenever possible, the software has been certified on the computer.

Serviceability is closely related to reliability. *Serviceability* simply means that working on or repairing a particular computer is relatively fast and easy. Features that enhance serviceability include cases that are easy to open (requiring no tools), quickly replaceable internal components (such as hard disks, memory, or video cards that require simple or no tools), and Basic Input Output System (BIOS) that is easy to update.

Serviceability is also strongly influenced by the services available from the computer's maker:

- Does the computer manufacturer stay current in offering updates to its computers?

- Does its web site offer a lookup that lets you determine the configuration of a computer based on its serial or service ID numbers?

- Is technical information about its systems readily available, or does the vendor tend to gloss over any discovered problems?

- How quickly can you get replacement parts?

- Does the manufacturer include on-site service for a period of time that reduces your support burden?

- What is the warranty on any given computer?

- Is the vendor sufficiently successful and stable that you can expect the company to be around for the entire useful life of the unit?

- What other value-added services are offered if problems occur?

Other factors that strongly influence serviceability are often overlooked. How many computers does the maker sell, and is the specific model that you are buying widely used? These factors are important because a widely used computer is more likely to be supported when new software or hardware comes out. Companies that make software and hardware know they must ensure that their products work properly with popular computer brands and models.

Suppose that you use computers from a small, local company (or, even worse, build the computers yourself), and some software package or operating system that comes out in a year or two fails to work properly on your machines. The maker of the software or hardware might say something like, "Well, we haven't tested on that computer, so we don't know why our product isn't working right." While the maker might act in good faith to resolve the issue, the problem might take much longer to fix on a widely used system, and it might never be resolved. On the other hand, if you're using a top-tier computer, such as one from Compaq, Dell, or HP (or other top-tier brands), the vendor of the new product probably knows how to resolve any problems that arise and has already done so before the product was shipped.

TIP If your company runs an application that is vital to its business but that is not widely used, it sometimes pays to find out which computers the application maker uses. If you know that the application maker has built the application using a particular make, you can reduce your risk of having trouble with that application by considering using the same brand in your organization.

Author's Note

I once joined a company that had been purchasing "no-name" clones for its desktop computers. In my first week, I set up five brand-new units right out of their boxes, only to find that three of them were dead on arrival (DOA). That same week, the company's CFO, who was working on an important financing activity, had his computer crash repeatedly (losing unsaved work each time), until I finally swapped his entire computer for one of the new ones that actually worked. Was the money saved on those computers (about $400 per unit) worth it? What was the cost to the company for all these mishaps? The answer is simple: far more than the company saved. I immediately changed the company's brand to a more reliable one (the CFO was sympathetic!) and got rid of the existing machines as quickly as possible. The lesson is that you shouldn't be penny-wise and pound-foolish when you purchase computers.

You can also improve serviceability if you standardize on a particular manufacturer because then you can focus your resources on supporting that line of computers. The people who support the desktop computers in the company will find it easier to stay up-to-date with the peculiarities of that manufacturer and will become more comfortable working with those computers. Also, your company's support staff will be able to solve a problem once and then apply the solution to many computers, rather than having to troubleshoot many different types of problems on many different types of computers. Finally, there might be service-quality benefits when you establish a strong, ongoing relationship with a computer manufacturer.

NOTE   If you support many computers, make sure that they are as consistent as possible. Not only do you want to ensure (as much as possible) that they are the same model and the same configuration, you also want to make sure the manufacturer uses the same components for all computers of a particular model. Some manufacturers are not careful about this; they will slip in different motherboards or network interface cards (NICs) without any notice. For someone buying a single computer, this isn't a problem. When you need to support 500 or 5,000 computers that are all supposed to be exactly the same but aren't, it becomes a huge problem, because then you also must keep track of different drivers and configuration information. Also, if you install and maintain computers through the use of disk images (such as those made by Norton Ghost), you will need to maintain different images for all of the different submodels of the computer.

Price and Performance

Once the preceding priorities are satisfied, you can then strike the appropriate balance between performance and price. You need to take into account the useful life that you plan for new computers and make certain to purchase systems that will be productive over that useful life. In determining this balance, don't look at how well a particular configuration can handle today's needs; look at how well it can handle tomorrow's needs.

Some people might disagree, but I firmly believe that price should be your *last* priority when you purchase computers. Although purchase price is important, you first need to determine your needs and then find the most reasonably priced computers that best fulfill those needs.

Different strategies exist for getting the best price. These strategies range from straightforward bargaining and competitive bids, to slightly under-purchasing on the performance side but planning to upgrade the existing computers when needed (at least in terms of RAM and hard disk space, both of which decrease pretty rapidly in price over time).

NOTE   Don't forget to estimate the cost involved to replace a computer or to upgrade a computer when you choose a system. It might be less expensive overall to purchase a more capable computer that you won't need to upgrade or replace as quickly, when you factor in the labor costs and user productivity impact from installing a replacement.

> **DEFINE-IT! Useful Life**
>
> The term *useful life* refers to the length of time a particular asset, such as a computer, will be able to perform useful work. The useful life of a computer will change depending on the computer, the software it needs to run, the user who uses it, and the budget available to upgrade or replace it. A programmer who needs the latest and greatest hardware and software all the time will get a relatively short useful life out of a computer, while a person who uses a computer only for word processing or e-mail and doesn't care about running the latest software will get a much longer useful life out of a computer. For most desktop computers, the useful life is around three to four years, although exceptions to this rule of thumb are easy to find.

As a rule of thumb, you can estimate that the demands placed on a desktop computer will double every 24 months or so, taking into account your planned useful life. Set your performance levels to meet that need. (People used to assume performance requirements doubled every 18 months, but this seems to be slowing a bit in recent years.)

For example, suppose that you've determined that today's user requires 40GB of disk space, 2GB of RAM, and a Pentium 2.8 GHz processor. In 24 months, your users are likely to be clamoring for 80GB of disk space, 4GB of RAM, and a Pentium quad-core 3 GHz processor. In another 24 months (about four years from purchase), these demands will double again, to 160GB of disk space, 8GB of RAM, and the equivalent of a Pentium 8-core processor. These projected demands might seem unlikely today, but when you look back at the needs of four years ago, such projections seem reasonable.

Using this way of estimating performance needs, you should be able to find a "sweet spot" between price, performance, and useful life that minimizes your costs and maximizes the benefits that your users will receive.

Understanding Network Workstation Requirements

Computers connected to a local area network (LAN) differ slightly from computers that stand alone. They have additional hardware installed in them, and they run additional network software. This section explores these differences.

Network Workstation Hardware

All network computers need an installed network interface to connect to the network. Generally, most desktop computers these days have an intergrated Ethernet network interface built-into them. And if a computer does not, then it can be added as a network interface card.

NICs are also usually specific to the cable media you have installed. For example, Ethernet NICs are available for 10Base-2, 10Base-T, 100Base-T, and 1000Base-T media.

Some NICs also support multiple media types, which can be a blessing if you're in the middle of migrating from one media type to another. For example, a single Ethernet NIC may support 10Base-2, 10Base-T, and 100Base-T. At the time of this edition's writing, most business computers come with integrated Ethernet ports capable of 100Base-T or 1000Base-T.

Network Workstation Software

Network workstations also need networking software to work with the network. This software consists of several components: a driver for the NIC, driver software for the protocols being used, and a network requestor (sometimes called a network *redirector*). Workstations acting in a peer-to-peer fashion also have peer software that provides network services to other workstations. Additionally, network service software might be needed, such as that required to use a particular network directory service (for example, Novell's eDirectory).

For Windows-based computers, you can choose to use software that is included with Windows to connect to both Novell networks and to Windows-based networks. You can also use Novell's network software for Novell-based networks. Both sets of network software work well, although differences exist.

For Novell-based networks, Microsoft's networking software consumes less memory than Novell's, but it doesn't offer as many features and doesn't integrate with the Novell servers quite as well. Still, it's reliable and performs well. Novell's client software (called Novell Client) works well and makes good use of the Novell server's features, and is also more secure than Microsoft's Novell network software.

When using the Microsoft software with NetWare 4.*x* or later servers, you must also run service software to access Novell's directory service. This software is included both with Windows and Novell Client.

Under Windows, you manage the network software through the network Properties dialog box for Network Neighborhood or through the Network object in the Control Panel (which also accesses the network Properties dialog box). Figure 14-1 shows an example of this dialog box.

The network Properties dialog box contains a number of entries, including the following main categories:

- **Client**   You might have client software installed for Novell networks or Microsoft networks. This client software interacts with the servers to request network services. In Figure 14-1, you can see that the Client for Microsoft Networks is an installed component.

- **Network interface**   This entry represents the driver software that is installed for any installed NICs or for "virtual NICs" used to connect to a network through a modem. In Figure 14-1, you can see the NVIDIA nForce driver listed.

- **Protocols**   This software adds support for any needed networking protocols, such as TCP/IP, IPX/SPX, or NetBEUI.

- **Services**   Any additional network service software, such as that used for Novell eDirectory, also appears in the network Properties dialog box.

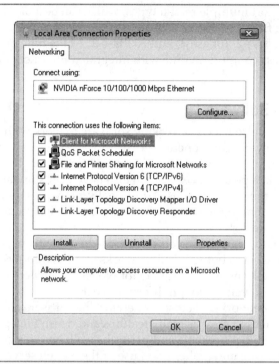

Figure 14-1. The network Properties dialog box in Windows Vista

NOTE For many networking components, you may need to have a the component available from the appropriate supplier.

Chapter Summary

Managing network workstation computers can be a daunting task. Many of them must be managed frequently, each user may have different needs, and because of how they are used, network workstation computers are the most likely to experience trouble. In this chapter, you learned general information about network client computers, along with how to select appropriate client computers for your network. You also learned about the components that network computers have in common, which separate them from stand-alone desktop computers.

In the next chapter, you learn about the basics of how you can design a network from the ground up. Generally, the process of network design is to first thoroughly understand the needs that the network must meet, factor in anticipated growth for the network, and then start to lay out how the network will be structured and which technologies will be needed.

Part II

Hands-on Knowledge

Chapter 15

Designing a Network

Networking professionals rarely have the opportunity to walk into a company and design a new network from the ground up, but those who do are certainly lucky. It's true that such an effort involves long hours, stress, deadlines, and the nagging worry that maybe you're forgetting something. But in return, you get to shape the computing environment of a large number of users, and—in many companies—set the tone for how efficiently the company itself can function in coming years. In some companies that rely heavily on information technology, a smoothly running network might even determine whether or not the company will be successful. It's an enormous responsibility, but also one of the most rewarding jobs you can have.

In practice, you usually start with some sort of network already in place. Networks start small and simply grow over time. Networks are almost like skin, where you're sure to replace each and every cell every few years, but only a few at a time. The process is usually evolutionary rather than revolutionary. Exceptions exist to this rule, though. For example, a company might move to a new building, decide to scrap the old network during the process, and install an entirely new one. Likewise, a well-funded startup company that goes from 5 to 500 employees in six months is likely to see the need for a new network.

Regardless of whether you're building a brand-new network from scratch or renovating an existing network, the tools you use are much the same, and the process of designing the network is also much the same. The concept is actually simple: You assess the needs that the network must meet and then you design to meet those needs. In practice, this process is much more involved, but the idea is straightforward. Even in an evolving network, using network planning to formulate a long-term plan to renovate the network makes sense.

This chapter describes how to design a network. It relies on all the information you learned in the preceding chapters. Think of this chapter as the one that brings together into a coherent whole all the information that you have already learned. Preceding chapters have focused on the bits and bytes of networks, while this chapter is the view from 30,000 feet where you start to see how everything works together.

The Network Design Process

Network design is not an exact science. Getting it *exactly* right the first time is nearly impossible, even with the best design tools and resources available. This is because every network has different demands placed on it, and these demands often interact in surprising ways. Moreover, predicting what new demands will be placed on the network over time, how users will use the network resources, and what other changes you might need to make is almost impossible. The entire situation is both fluid and chaotic. The trick is to do a good job of estimating needs, and then do the best job possible to create a design to meet those needs.

Having fallback plans is also important, in case some part of the network doesn't perform the way you intended. For instance, once the network is up and running, you might find that the distribution of bandwidth across segments is poor. You want to know in advance how you can measure and address these types of problems. You might also find storage requirements are much higher or lower than you expected. You need to know what to do if this happens. The point is that network design is a process, often an iterative one. Your job as a network designer is to get as close as possible to the needed design, and then fine-tune the design as needed.

A lot of the network design process is what you decide to make of it. There are simple network design processes, and there are horrendously complicated processes that involve dozens of people, complex statistical modeling, and even network simulation software to test a planned design and see if it holds together under load. In this chapter, you learn a relatively comprehensive process that is straightforward and simple. Using the information in this chapter, along with a good dose of experience, will yield a flexible network that should easily meet the needs of hundreds of users.

TIP You can't design a network of any size without plenty of experience running similar networks. You can manage the overall process by understanding the methodology, but you can't create a good design without hands-on experience. If you're new to networking and you are asked to design a network, make sure you get experienced people on the team—either as consultants or as part of a supplier-led team—and listen carefully to their advice. Listening well pays off with a design that will work, rather than one that might look good on paper but won't hold up to actual use.

Assessing Network Needs

"Measure twice and cut once" is a common adage that conveys the importance of planning. "Ready, fire, aim," is one that pokes fun at people who don't properly set goals. Assessing the needs that a network must meet corresponds to taking those measurements and aiming before you shoot.

Before you even think about any specifics—network topology; network operating system (NOS) platform; a structure for hubs, bridges, and routers; or the grade of wiring—you must first know what the network needs to accomplish. Doing a proper job can be tedious, but assessing needs is where you should place the most emphasis during a design process. Failing to do so almost certainly will result in a network that isn't productive for its users.

NOTE Many IT professionals are, at heart, technologists who love to play with the latest technologies. It's very tempting to design the network around the "hot" technologies, and then try to figure out how the needs fit into those technologies. However, this is not the way to go about designing a network. Instead, start with the needs, and then find out what technologies support those needs.

When assessing needs, you are trying to come up with detailed answers to the following questions:

- How much storage space is required?
- How much bandwidth is required?
- What network services are required?
- What is the budget for the project?

These basic questions are fairly easy to answer as a whole, but you need to break them down further to make sure no holes in the network design could lead to problems. For example, it might be easy to determine that the network must be able to support up to 100 Mbps of bandwidth, but you need to know how, when, and where that bandwidth is used. If the accounting department is using 90 percent of the bandwidth when communicating to the accounting server, for example, then naturally you want to put the accounting system's server and its users on their own network segment. You won't recognize such issues and how to address them unless your assessment leads you to determine with some degree of detail how the network resources will be used.

The following sections discuss what you should examine as you learn what a given network must be able to do. No particular order exists in which you should examine these issues, and you might find that you need to cycle through the list several times to get a complete picture. You also might find a particular company's needs require more or less analysis in each category. Common sense is required when you design a network. The following suggestions are guidelines to start you on the right path.

Applications

A good place to start with a network design is to list and understand the applications that will run on the network. Ultimately, a network is only as good as the work it helps people accomplish, and people do their work most directly through the application software they use. If the applications don't work right, then the users won't work right.

Most networks have both common applications and department- and user-specific applications. Most companies usually meet the common application needs through a suite of desktop applications, such as Microsoft Office or Lotus SmartSuite. The following is a list of applications that most companies install for all users, whether or not each user needs each one:

- Word processor
- Spreadsheet
- End-user database
- Presentation graphics
- E-mail
- Personal information manager (calendar, contact list, and so forth)
- Virus-scanning software

Your first order of business is to determine just how the common applications will be used. Determine whether all users need to have the entire suite installed, how often different users plan to use the different applications, how many files they will create and store, how large those files might be, and how those files will be shared among users.

For example, in a 1,000-user population, you might determine that 90 percent will use word processing to generate an average of ten documents a month, with each document averaging 100KB, and the users probably will want to keep two years' worth of documents on hand at any given time. Yes, these will be educated guesses, but it's important to come up with reasonable estimates. Experience with similar user populations and companies can pay off handsomely in determining these estimates. With this information alone, you know immediately that you need about 24MB of storage per user, or 21.6GB for the word processing population of 900 users, just for word processing documents. For applications where users frequently will share files, you might need to factor in that most users keep personal copies of some files that they also share with others.

TIP You can help reduce overall network storage requirements by establishing shared directories in which different groups of people can store and access shared files.

Then you come up with the same estimates for the other applications, taking into account their expected size, frequency of creation, and long-term storage requirements.

After determining the common applications, move on to department-specific applications. This step gets trickier for new networks in new companies, because you might not know which applications will be used. For existing companies, you have the advantage of already knowing which departmental applications you must support.

Different departmental applications can have wildly different impacts on the network. For example, an accounting system designed around shared database files needs a different network design than one using a client/server database design. The former relies more on file server performance and is more likely to be bandwidth-sensitive than an efficient client/server application that runs on a dedicated server. If a departmental application is not yet selected, talk with the managers of that department to get their best estimates and then proceed.

Following are common departmental applications you should consider:

- Accounting
- Distribution and inventory control
- Manufacturing/material requirements planning (MRP)
- Information technology
- Electronic commerce
- Human resources
- Payroll and stock administration

- Publishing
- Marketing support
- Legal
- Other line-of-business applications specific to the company's industry

For each of the departmental applications you identify, you need to ask several questions: How much storage will they consume? From where will the applications be run (from local computers with data on a server or completely centralized, where both the data and the application run on a central computer)? Will they have their own dedicated servers? How much network bandwidth will the application need? How will all these factors change as the company grows?

Finally, while you might not formally include them in your plan, consider user-specific applications that might be run. For example, you might estimate that the people in the company's research and development group are likely to run two or three unknown applications as part of their job. If you decide that user-specific applications will have a significant impact on the network, then you should estimate their needs, just as you have for the other types of applications. If you believe they will have minimal impact, then you might decide either to include a small allowance for them or none at all.

TIP Don't get bogged down in "analysis paralysis," worrying about whether you can scientifically prove that your estimates are accurate. Instead, make sure the estimates are reasonable to other network professionals. At a certain point, you need to justify the network design and cost and, to do this, having reasonable estimates is necessary. Just avoid overdoing it.

Users

Once you know the applications that the network must support, you can estimate how many users need to be supported and which applications each user will use. Estimating total users will likely be easier because the company should already have a business plan or long-range budget from which you can derive these estimates. Your user estimates should be reasonably granular; know the number of users in each department in the company as well as the company's total number of users.

You should estimate how many users will need to be supported immediately, in one year, in three years, and in five years. Even though five years is a distant horizon to use for an estimate, this information is important to know during the design process. Different growth rates suggest different network designs, even at the inception of the network. A company estimating that it will have 100 users immediately, 115 users in one year, 130 users in three years, and 150 users in five years needs a different network design than a company estimating 100 users immediately, 115 users in one year, 300 users in three years, and 1,000 users in five years. In the latter case, you must invest more in a design that is more quickly scalable, and you are likely to spend much more at inception to build the network, even though the network will have the same number of users in the first two years.

Knowing the number of users isn't enough, though. You need to know more about the users. At a minimum, consider the following questions to determine if any of the following will be important factors for the users generally or for subgroups of users:

- **Bandwidth requirements** Aside from the bandwidth required to save and retrieve files, send and receive e-mail, and perform an average amount of browsing on the Internet, do any users need significant amounts of bandwidth? For example, will scientists download a fresh copy of the human genome from the Internet once a week? Will groups of users need to exchange large quantities of data among different sites? Will any users be running videoconferencing software over your network connection? How much web browsing do you expect the network's users to do? Will people be sending large e-mail attachments frequently?

- **Storage requirements** Will any group of users need significantly more storage capacity than the overall average you already determined? For instance, will an electronic imaging group catalog millions of documents into image files on a server? If so, how many people need access to that data? Will the accounting group need to keep the previous ten years of financial information online? Will the company use or install an executive information system where all the managers have query capability into the company's accounting, distribution, and manufacturing systems, and, if so, how much additional bandwidth or server performance could that capability require?

- **Service requirements** Will any groups of users require additional network services not needed by most users? For example, does part of the company do work of such sensitivity that it should be separated from the rest of the local area network (LAN) by a network firewall? Will a subset of users need direct inward fax capability?

When examining user bandwidth requirements, remember to look at the timeliness of the bandwidth needs. If certain known activities require a lot of bandwidth and must be carried out during the normal workday, that high-bandwidth use might interfere with the performance of the rest of the network. Therefore, make sure to estimate both average and peak bandwidth needs.

Network Services

Next, you should look at the services that the network must provide. These can vary widely in different companies. A very basic network might need only file and print services, plus perhaps Internet connectivity. A more complex network will need many additional services. Consider which of the following types of services the network you are designing will need to provide, as well as any others that are specific to the company:

- File and print services
- Backup and restore services

- Internet web browsing
- FTP and Telnet
- Internet or external e-mail
- Internet security services
- Remote access to the LAN through a VPN or a modem pool
- Fax into the LAN (manually distributed or automatically distributed)
- Dynamic Host Configuration Protocol (DHCP) services
- Centralized virus-protection services
- Wide area network (WAN) services to other locations
- Streaming Internet radio and other media
- Voice over IP (VoIP)

For each service, you must answer a number of questions. First, you need to know the storage and bandwidth requirements for each service, and any other impacts they might have. For instance, a fax-in service might itself require a small amount of storage space, but all the fax bitmaps that users will end up storing could have a large impact on total storage needs.

Second, you need to know how the service is to be provided. Usually, this means that you need to know which server will host the service. Some services require such little overhead that you can easily host them on a server that does other jobs. A DHCP server, which requires minimal resources, is a good example of such a service. On the other hand, an e-mail system might require such high resources that you must plan to host it on its own dedicated server.

Third, you need to know what users or groups of users need which services. This is because, to minimize backbone traffic, you might need to break down the network into smaller segments and locate frequently used services for a particular user population on the same segment as the users use.

Security and Safety

The preceding considerations are all related to the bits and bytes required by different parts of the network. Security and safety concern the company's need to keep information secure—both inside and outside an organization—and to keep the company's data safe from loss. You need to know how important these two issues are before attempting to set down a network design on paper.

For both these considerations, a trade-off exists between cost and effectiveness. As mentioned in earlier chapters, no network is ever totally secure and no data is ever totally safe from loss. However, different companies and departments have different sensitivities to these issues, indicating that more or less money should be spent on these areas.

Some applications might be perfectly well suited to keeping their data on a striped RAID 0 array of disks, where the risk of loss is high (relative to other RAID levels), because the data might be static and easy to restore from tape if the disk array is lost. Other applications might require the highest level of data-loss safety possible, with failover servers each having mirrored RAID 1 or RAID 10 arrays and online tape backup systems updating a backup tape every hour or for every transaction. Similarly, some companies might work with data that is so sensitive that they must install the best firewalls, perhaps even two levels of firewalls, and hire full-time professionals dedicated to keeping the data secure. Other companies might be satisfied if they are only reasonably secure.

The point is that you must determine how important these issues are to the company for which you are designing the network. Then you can propose different solutions to address these needs and factor them into the rest of your design.

Growth and Capacity Planning

The final area to consider is the expected growth of the network, particularly if the company expects this growth to be substantial. As mentioned earlier in this chapter, a network designed for a rapidly growing company looks different from one for a slowly growing company, even if both companies start out at the same size. In the former case, you want a design that you can quickly and easily expand without needing to replace much of the existing hardware and software. In the latter case, you can get by with a simpler network design.

Consider the impact of growth on the different parts of the network that you've already examined (applications, users, and services), because linear growth does not always mean a matching linear impact to the network. Assuming linear growth, the impact to the network might be much lower or much higher than the curve.

For example, you saw in Chapter 4 how Ethernet uses a collision detection mechanism to manage network traffic. In that chapter, you also learned that Ethernet scales linearly, but only up to a point. Once the network starts to become saturated, performance begins to drop rapidly because of the chaotic nature of Ethernet's collision detection scheme. Consider a 10 Mbps Ethernet network transmitting 3 Mbps of traffic. This traffic probably flows smoothly, with few collisions and few retransmissions required. Push the network demand up to 4 or 5 Mbps, however, and its performance grinds to a halt as the network becomes saturated, and you end up with as many collisions and retransmissions as real data. In fact, the total amount of good data flowing over a saturated Ethernet network will be less than the amount flowing over a less-saturated network.

You can also find examples where an increase in demand doesn't cause a corresponding increase in network or server load. For example, the server load for a complex e-mail system might increase only by a small amount if you doubled the number of users, because the system's overhead generates most of the load. The storage requirements for an accounting system might not double just because you keep twice as much data in it to accommodate the overhead that might consume most of the existing space. Alternatively, that same accounting system might consume four times as much storage space if you double the data storage, because it might have a relatively inefficient indexing scheme. The point is that you need to know how different applications scale with increased use. The vendors of the main applications you will use should be able to provide useful data in this regard.

 TIP Be careful not only to consider how applications behave as they scale, but how they behave as they are scaled in your planned network environment. Different NOSs, network topologies, and client and server computers will all affect how well a particular application can support growth.

Meeting Network Needs

Once you complete your assessment (by this point, you're probably sick of the assessment process!), you can then start working on finding ways to meet all the needs you've identified. This process is largely holistic and is not worked through by following a series of steps and ending up with a single answer, like an equation. Instead, you should start by mapping out the various parts of the network, considering the three main topics discussed in this section, and "build a picture" of the network design. The design that you create will incorporate all you learned during the assessment process, taking into account your experience and the advice you have received to devise a concrete design that results in an equipment list, specifications, and a configuration.

Seeking criticism of your design from other network professionals, who might have valuable experience that you can then factor into your design, is important. No single networking professional has seen and had to cope with all possible design needs, so you want to combine the advice of as many seasoned people as you can.

Choosing a Network Type

You probably want to start the design by choosing a network type. This should be a relatively straightforward decision, based on the overall bandwidth requirements for the network. For most new networks, you almost certainly will decide to use one of the flavors of Ethernet. Ethernet is by far the most common type of network installed today, and it's an easy default choice.

You also need to decide what level of Ethernet you need. For wiring to the desktop, you should choose 100Base-T. It's reliable and provides plenty of capacity for most needs. For your network backbone, you can usually use a higher-bandwidth connection, such as 1000Base-T, without incurring too much additional cost.

Structuring the Network

Next, decide how you plan to structure the network. In other words, how will you arrange and wire the various hubs, switches, and routers that the network needs? This is probably the trickiest part to determine, because it's hard to predict how much data must flow from any given set of nodes to any other set of nodes. The estimates you have based on your assessment work will help. If you can identify expected heavy traffic patterns, you should also draw a network schematic with these patterns indicated to help you sort it out. Remember the following tips:

- Ethernet's CDMA/CD collision handling means that an Ethernet network will handle only about one-third of its rated speed. In other words, a 100Base-T segment, which is rated at 100 Mbps, will handle about 33 Mbps of actual data before starting to degrade.

- Whenever possible, use "home-run" wiring (in which each network cable runs from each workstation to a single location) for all nodes to a single wiring closet or server room. Doing so enables you to change the network structure more easily (for example, to break segments into smaller segments) as needs change.

- Except in the smallest networks, plan on installing a network backbone to which the hubs connect. An Ethernet switch rather than a nonswitching hub should handle the backbone, so each hub constitutes a single segment or collision domain. You still must plan to keep each segment's traffic below the Ethernet saturation point, but this structure will give you plenty of flexibility to meet this goal.

- The physical building might dictate how you structure your network. For example, a building larger than 200 meters (about 600 feet) in any dimension probably means you won't be able to employ a home-run wiring scheme for all your nodes. This is because twisted-pair Ethernet usually reaches only 100 meters (about 300 feet), which includes routing around building obstructions, patch cables, and other things that make the actual cable distance longer than you might measure on a map of the building.

- For multifloor buildings that are too big for a home-run wiring scheme, consider running the backbone vertically from floor to floor, and then have a wiring closet on each floor that contains the switches to service that floor's nodes. The wiring from the closet on each floor then fans out to each of the nodes on that floor.

- Consider running the backbone speed at ten times the hub/desktop network speed. If you're using 100Base-T hubs to connect to the desktop computers, plan on a 1000Base-T backbone.

- Most of the time, most nodes do the majority of their communication to one or two servers on the network. If you are planning department-specific servers or if you can identify similar patterns, make sure that each server is on the same segment as the nodes that it primarily serves.

- If your servers tend not to be assigned to support departments and instead support the entire company, make sure that the servers are directly connected to the backbone's Ethernet switch.

- If you have any high-bandwidth users, consider keeping them on a segment separate from the rest of the network (if appropriate) and also consider upgrading the speed of that segment to 100 Mbps or 1,000 Mbps if needed.

- As you start to implement the network, carefully watch the ratio of collision packets to data packets. If the number of collisions on any segment climbs 5 to 7 percent of the total number of packets, performance is starting to suffer, so you need to investigate the cause and find a way to decrease this ratio. You can usually do so by breaking the segment into smaller pieces or by configuring capable switches into what is called a virtual LAN (VLAN), unless you know of another way to reduce the amount of traffic.

Selecting Servers

When choosing servers for a network, start by determining which NOS you will use. For PC-centric networks, the decision is usually between Novell NetWare and Windows family of servers. As discussed in Chapter 13, whenever possible, avoid using both, because supporting two NOS systems makes managing the servers much more difficult. You're better off compromising on a single NOS platform.

Next, list the various network services that your servers must provide. You need to look for efficient ways to host these various services on your servers, balancing a number of factors:

- All else being equal, using more small servers to host fewer services each is more reliable than using fewer large servers to each host many services.

- Conversely, having more small servers increases your chance of having a server fail at any given time.

- Using more small servers is more expensive and requires more maintenance than using fewer large servers.

- If you plan to use more than one server, consider which services should be redundant on another server or how you plan to deal with the failure of any server.

Using your assessment information, you can easily determine how much storage capacity your servers will need. However, it's much harder to know how capable each server should be in terms of processor power, installed RAM, and other features, such as bus configuration. For these specifications, you need to rely on the advice of the NOS vendor and the manufacturer of the servers that you are considering. Fortunately, both Microsoft and Novell have published tests and recommendations for sizing servers given different service and user loads. Many first-tier server manufacturers also have such data to help you choose an actual server model and its specifications.

Chapter Summary

Designing an entire network can be extremely complex. If you are in the enviable position of designing a network, your best bet is to start with the framework described in this chapter and to use other resources to answer specific questions. Many resources are available to help you do this, ranging from books devoted to aspects of network design, server management, network performance tuning, and specific NOS management, to consultants experienced with similar networks and the various vendors you are working with on any planned purchases. In fact, so many resources exist to help you accomplish this job, you may have trouble deciding which advice to follow!

Always remember to leave some escape hatches in any network design, so you can respond quickly to new or changed requirements, many of which will occur while you're finalizing the design. The good news is that if you follow the advice in this chapter and the rest of the book, along with the other resources mentioned, it's a safe bet you'll end up with a solid, expandable, maintainable network design that meets the needs of the company and of which you can be proud.

Chapter 16

Installing and Setting Up Windows Server 2008

In this chapter, you learn how to install Windows Server 2008. Before you install Windows Server 2008, however, you first must conduct a variety of preinstallation checks that prepare the system for the process. Next, you perform the actual installation, providing information that the installation program needs. Finally, you test the installation by having a client computer log in to the server properly and perform some basic network duties. All these steps are described in detail in this chapter.

Understanding Windows Server 2008 Editions

Windows Server 2008 is an entire family of products, all built on essentially the same programming code, but with significant feature and tuning differences.

Standard Edition is the mainstream server version of Windows Server 2008. It includes all the power of Active Directory, as well as the following features:

- New management tools (compared with those provided with Windows Server 2003) based on the Microsoft Management Console (MMC)

- Windows Terminal Services, which allows Windows Server 2008 to host graphical applications, much like a mainframe hosts applications for dumb terminals

- Internet and web services, including Dynamic Host Configuration Protocol (DHCP), Domain Name System (DNS), Internet Information Services (IIS), and Index Server

- Remote access and VPN services

- Transaction and messaging services

- Support for up to four processors

- Support for up to 4GB of RAM (32-bit version) or 32GB of RAM (64-bit version)

- Support for the latest versions of the standard network protocols

Enterprise Edition is the mid-range offering of Windows Server 2008 products. It enhances the features of Windows Server 2008 by adding the following:

- Support for up to 64GB of installed RAM (32-bit version) or 2TB of RAM (64-bit version)

- Network load balancing (for example, Enterprise Edition can share a heavy TCP/IP load among a number of servers and balance their loads)

- Windows Server 2008 clustering

- Support for up to eight processors

- Support for 16-node clusters

Datacenter Edition is the most powerful version of Windows Server 2008. This version is used when extremely large databases need to be hosted for thousands of users or when other very heavy demands will placed on the server system. It includes all the features of the other versions, plus the following:

- Support for up to 64GB of installed RAM (32-bit version) or 2TB of RAM (64-bit version)
- Support for up to 32 processors (32-bit version) or 64 processors (64-bit version)
- Support for 16-node clusters

On the other end of the spectrum, Microsoft also sells *Windows Web Server 2008*. This is a more limited edition of Windows Server 2008 that is designed purely as a single-purpose web server. This edition is the most cost-effective for setting up a Windows-based web server. It supports up to four processors (32- and 64-bit versions) and up to 4GB of RAM (32-bit version) or 32GB of RAM (64-bit version).

Preparing for Installation

Before installing Windows Server 2008, you first must prepare the server computer that you will use and make important decisions about the installation. This preparation stage consists of a number of tasks, including the following:

- Make sure the server hardware is certified for use with Windows Server 2008.
- Make sure the server is properly configured to support Windows Server 2008.
- Carry out any needed preinstallation testing on the server hardware.
- Survey the hardware prior to performing the installation.
- Decide how you will install Windows Server 2008, after gathering all the configuration information you will need during the installation.
- Back up the system prior to an upgrade.

These tasks are discussed in the following sections.

Checking Hardware Compatibility

Microsoft maintains an extensive Hardware Compatibility List (HCL) that lists different hardware components and their testing status on various Microsoft products, such as Windows Server 2008. To avoid problems with your server, make sure that the server itself and any installed peripherals have been tested with Windows Server 2008 and work properly. The latest version of the HCL can be found at http://www.microsoft .com/whdc/hcl/default.mspx. You can also find a text-based copy on the Windows Server 2008 CD-ROM. Using the web HCL is preferred, however, because it might have more current data than the file included on the installation CD-ROM.

If a particular hardware component in your planned server isn't listed on the HCL, all is not lost. For one thing, the HCL might not have the most current data, and the hardware that you wish to use might be certified but not yet listed. It's best to check with the hardware's maker, because that company will know the current status of the hardware's certification.

> **NOTE**   Products not listed in the HCL might work fine with Windows Server 2008. If you are deploying a server for testing purposes or to support limited services, and you are comfortable doing so, you can still proceed to install Windows Server 2008 and begin working with it. You should not do this for production servers that many people will depend on, however. Not only might an undiscovered incompatibility cause serious problems with an uncertified server, but you will be unable to get the highest level of support from Microsoft for hardware that is not yet certified. For this reason, you should avoid deploying important servers that are not yet certified by Microsoft.

Checking the Hardware Configuration

Purchasing a computer for use as a server can be a complex task. You must contend with the myriad details of installed RAM, processor configuration, disk configuration, and so forth, as well as factor in your anticipated needs to come up with a reasonable server configuration. (Chapter 13 contains information about different server technologies and about specifying a server for general use.)

Windows Server 2008 requires the following *minimum* hardware configuration:

- One 1 GHz (x86 processor) or 1.4 GHz (x64 processor) or greater
- 512MB of RAM
- About 20GB (32-bit version) or 32GB (64-bit version) of free disk space
- A DVD-ROM or network connection from which to install Windows Server 2008

For any kind of server (even one that will support only a few users), you should consider using more capable hardware than that specified as the minimum by Microsoft. Here is some advice for configuring a server for Windows Server 2008:

- **Processor**   Start with at least an Intel Core 2 Duo processor running at 2.4 GHz or greater. Intel Xeon processors are a benefit in a server, and you should carefully consider the price of such systems relative to the expected performance improvement. (All else being equal, an Intel Xeon family processor will perform about 15 to 20 percent faster than an equivalent core 2 processor.) Also, consider using a system that has either two or more processors, or the capability to add processors later if your needs grow faster than expected.

- **RAM**   Windows Server 2008 runs best on systems that have plenty of RAM. For a server, make sure you have at least 1GB of RAM. If you plan on supporting all the different services available with Windows Server 2008 (such as Terminal Services, Routing and Remote Access Service, DHCP, DNS, and so forth), then 2GB to 3GB of RAM might be a better choice than 1GB of RAM.

- **Disk**   A fast SCSI-based disk subsystem is important, particularly for servers that will store a lot of data. (See Chapter 13 for more information about choosing SCSI systems, using different RAID levels, and other important disk information.)

Use the information in Chapter 13 to help you size your server, but remember this rule of thumb: Get the most capable server you can afford and make sure it is expandable to meet your future needs, through the addition of more RAM, more processors, and more disk space. Even with all of that, it is common for servers to be replaced three to four years from the date they were placed into service.

Testing the Server Hardware

You found all your server hardware in the Windows Server 2008 HCL, you made sure your server is adequately sized, you purchased it, and you have your shiny new Windows Server 2008 DVD-ROMs sitting there, all ready to be installed. Is it time to start the installation yet? Well, not quite. Before installing any network operating system (NOS), particularly on a server that will be used for production, make sure you carry out hardware testing (also called *burn-in)* on the server before installing Windows Server 2008.

Computer hardware tends to be most reliable after it has been running for a while. In other words, failures tend to happen when equipment is new, and the chance of hardware failure decreases rapidly after the hardware has been up and running for 30 to 90 days. Because of this, it's a good idea to test new servers for at least a week (testing for two weeks is even better) before proceeding to install the NOS. Doing this can help provoke any early failures in the equipment during a time when they're easy to fix and they won't affect any users or the network. Moreover, many servers have a 30-day return or exchange policy from their manufacturer, so if you discover problems, you'll have a chance to return the system and perhaps start over with a different model.

You test the hardware using diagnostic software that came with the server computer or is available from the maker of the server. Most such diagnostic software lets you to choose which components of the system are tested and enables you to test them in an endless loop, logging any discovered errors to a floppy disk, USB key, or the screen. You should focus the tests on the following components:

- Processor(s)
- System board components, such as interrupt controllers, direct memory access (DMA) controllers, and other motherboard support circuitry
- RAM
- Disk surfaces

TIP   Server-testing software often enables you to choose between nondestructive and destructive testing of the disks. (Destructive means any data on the disks is erased during the testing.) Destructive testing is best to discover any errors on the disks. This is one reason that you want to carry out this testing before you install your NOS.

If the diagnostic software allows you to do so, you can usually safely skip testing components such as the keyboard or the display. Your primary concern is that the unit continues running properly when it is under load for an extended period of time. You also want to make sure that the RAM is working properly and that no bad sectors show up on the disks during testing. It's also a good idea during testing to power the unit on and shut it down a number of times, since the impact to the unit of initially powering on often can provoke a failure in any marginal components, especially if the unit is allowed to cool down first.

Surveying the Server Prior to an In-Place Upgrade

The Windows Server 2008 family of products takes advantage of plug and play (PnP) hardware and can detect and automatically configure any PnP devices to work with Windows Server 2008 during the installation. PnP is not perfect, though. For one thing, you might have installed components that are not PnP devices, and Windows Server 2008 will not be able to configure those devices. Also, sometimes PnP devices can conflict with other devices, or the drivers for a specific device might not allow proper configuration for some reason. Because of these imperfections, it's important to survey the components installed in the server before installing Windows Server 2008 as an upgrade. Performing a survey is not really important when setting up a new server.

For the survey, write down all the installed devices, along with the resources that each one uses in the server. The resources include the IRQ channel, DMA channel, and memory I/O addresses used by each device. Then, if a device isn't working properly after you install Windows Server 2008, you might be able to configure the device manually to known settings that work.

NOTE   Some server computers come with utilities such as HP's SmartStart. Such utilities handle the server at a hardware level and keep the information in a space separate from the NOS. Server utilities such as HP's make life much easier when you are trying to troubleshoot a hardware problem with the server.

Making Preinstallation Decisions

After configuring, checking, preparing, and testing your hardware, you can actually begin installing Windows Server 2008. During this process, you first spend time making a number of important preinstallation decisions that you must be prepared to specify during the installation. The following sections discuss these choices.

NOTE   This chapter and the two following chapters provide an overall introduction to Windows Server 2008. Certain advanced installation scenarios and techniques are not described here. To learn about other features and choices available when installing, administering, or using Windows Server 2008, consult a book devoted to Windows Server 2008, such as *Microsoft Windows Server 2008: The Complete Reference* by Danielle Ruest and Nelson Ruest (McGraw-Hill/ Professional, 2008).

Upgrade or Install?

You can upgrade a server running Windows Server 2003 to Windows Server 2008 or perform a full installation, where you wipe out any existing NOS on the server. The main benefit to upgrading is that all your existing settings under Windows Server 2003 will be maintained and automatically carried forward into your Windows Server 2008 installation. These include networking details, such as TCP/IP configuration information, as well as security settings that you might have tediously set up over time. In fact, if the server can be upgraded, you should plan on doing so, unless you need to change something fundamental in the server, such as changing the disk format from FAT32 to NTFS.

NOTE   Different upgrade paths exist depending on which edition of Windows Server 2003 you were running. You can upgrade Windows Server 2003 Standard Edition to 2008 Standard or 2008 Enterprise. You can upgrade Windows Server 2003 Enterprise Edition to 2008 Enterprise or 2008 Datacenter Edition.

FAT or NTFS?

Windows Server 2008 supports hard disks formatted using either File Allocation Table (FAT16 and FAT32) or NT File System (NTFS). NTFS is required for any Windows Server 2008 servers that will function as domain controllers. NTFS also is the only file system that enables you to take full advantage of Windows Server 2008's security features. Moreover, NTFS is optimized for server performance and performs better than FAT under almost all circumstances.

Domain Controller, Member Server, or Stand-Alone Server?

Another choice you need to make is in which mode you will configure your server. To make this decision, you need to understand two important concepts: Windows Server 2008 domains and workgroups. A *domain* is a sophisticated administrative grouping of computers on a Windows network that makes it possible to administer the network's resources from a single point and to implement strong security. Domains enable you to manage multiple Windows Server 2008 or Windows 2003 servers more easily. A *workgroup* is a simple collection of computers on a network and is suited only to pure peer-to-peer networks.

You can configure Windows Server 2008 in one of three modes to support either domains or workgroups, as follows:

- *Domain controllers* hold the domain's Active Directory information and authenticate users and access to resources. Most Windows Server 2008 networks have at least one domain and therefore need at least one domain controller.

- *Member servers* are part of a domain, but do not hold a copy of the Active Directory information.

- *Stand-alone servers* do not participate in a domain, but instead participate in a workgroup.

Earlier versions of Windows servers (NT and 2000) needed to be designated as either primary domain controllers (PDCs) or backup domain controllers (BDCs). The PDC performed all administrative tasks, and the BDCs simply kept read-only copies of the domain information to continue authenticating security on the network in case the PDC failed.

Newer Windows servers, such as those running Windows Server 2008, simplify matters, so that all Windows Server 2008 domain controllers are just that—domain controllers. Each domain controller holds a copy of the Active Directory data and can perform all the functions of the other domain controllers. Windows Server 2008 uses the concept of *multimaster domain controllers*, which all seamlessly operate the same way as the other domain controllers.

 TIP Except in the smallest of networks, it's a very good idea to have two domain controllers. This way, all of your domain information is preserved and available to the network should one of the domain controllers crash. Domain information is automatically synchronized between the available domain controllers.

Per Seat or Per Server?

Yet another important choice to make when installing Windows Server 2008 is how the server will manage its Client Access Licenses (CALs). Windows Server 2008 supports two different ways of managing CALs:

- *Per-server licensing* assigns the CALs to the server, which will allow only as many connections from computers as there are installed CALs on that server.

- *Per-seat licensing* requires purchasing a CAL for each of your client computers, which gives them the right to access as many Windows servers as they wish; the servers will not monitor the number of connections.

Generally, Microsoft recommends that you use per-server licensing when running a single server and per-seat licensing when running multiple servers. If you are unsure of which mode to use, Microsoft recommends that you choose per server, because Microsoft lets you change to per-seat mode once at no cost (changing from per seat to per server has a price). Carefully review licensing options with your Windows Server 2008 reseller to determine the most economical way to license your network servers properly.

Wait! Back Up Before Upgrading!

If you are installing Windows Server 2008 as an upgrade to another NOS, such as Windows Server 2003, it's vital that you fully back up the server prior to installing Windows Server 2008. (It's a good idea to make two identical backups, just in case.) You should use whatever backup software you normally use for your existing NOS, making sure the software can properly restore the previous NOS in case you need to "unwind" the upgrade process and revert to your starting point.

Even when you are performing an upgrade and will not be reformatting any of the disks, making a preinstallation backup is good insurance in case of trouble.

Installing Windows Server 2008

To begin the installation of Windows Server 2008, you can either configure the server computer to boot from the Windows Server 2008 DVD-ROM or insert the Windows Server 2008 DVD-ROM while running Windows Server 2003. Most servers can boot from their DVD-ROM drives, which is the best way to start the installation.

Running the Windows Server 2008 Setup Program

The following steps outline the process of running the installation program for Windows Server 2008 and installing it onto a server. If you are learning about Windows Server 2008 and have a suitable computer to use, you should take the time to install Windows Server 2008 so that you understand how the process works. Or, if you like, you can read along through the following steps to familiarize yourself with the installation process. (I recommend actually performing an installation such as the one described here, and then playing with the resulting server as a way of more quickly and completely learning about Windows Server 2008.)

1. When you boot from the Windows Server 2008 DVD-ROM, the program first presents a screen that lets you choose the language to install, the formatting to use for time and currency displays, and the keyboard or input method (see Figure 16-1). Make the appropriate choices, and then click Next to continue.

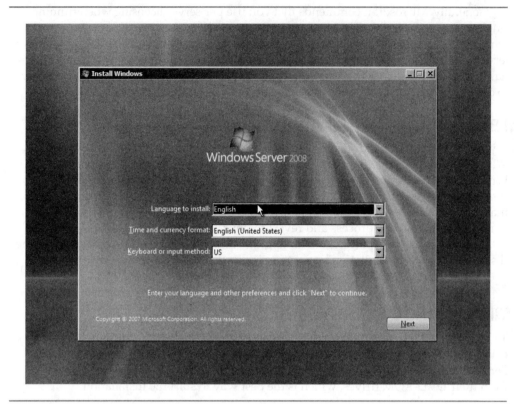

Figure 16-1.   Choosing the language and other preferences

2. You see the screen shown in Figure 16-2. If you booted your Windows Server 2008 DVD-ROM in order to try to repair an existing installation, you can choose Repair Your Computer. To start the installation, click Install Now to continue.

3. You are prompted to enter your Windows Server 2008 product key, as shown in Figure 16-3. Enter the appropriate key for the version you are installing. Alternatively, you can leave this field blank. If you do not enter a product key, Windows Server 2008 will install in a fully functional, but time-limited, trial mode. You can provide a key after the installation with no loss of data or functionality, but the key you provide must match the edition you installed and then click Next to continue.

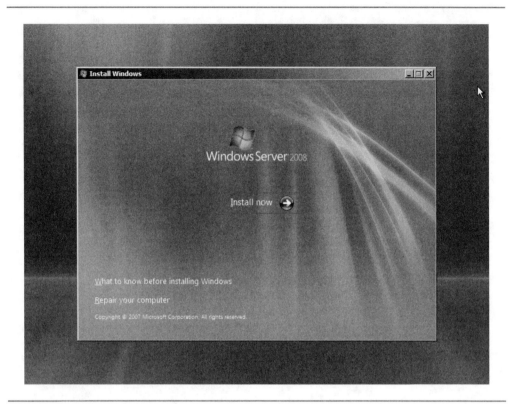

Figure 16-2.   Choosing to install the software

4. If you did not enter a product key, you are next prompted for the edition of Windows Server 2008 you are installing, as shown in Figure 16-4. (If you provided a key, the installation program can determine this automatically.)

5. Choose to accept the license terms, and then click Next to continue.

6. You are asked whether to perform an upgrade installation or a custom (clean) installation of Windows Server 2008, as shown in Figure 16-5. If you are installing on a computer that has an upgradable version, you can choose to upgrade. In this example, we are installing onto a fresh computer system, so performing a custom (clean) installation is the only selectable option.

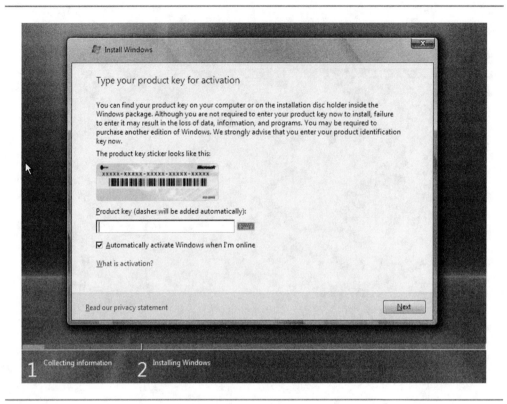

Figure 16-3. Entering the product key for installation

7. You next must choose where to install Windows Server 2008, as shown in Figure 16-6. If you are installing onto a computer with an empty hard disk that has never been used, as shown in Figure 16-6, you first need to partition the disk, and then you need to format the disk. To partition the disk, click the Drive Options (Advanced) link. This reveals some new options, as shown in Figure 16-7.

8. From the advanced drive options screen, click New to create a partition on the disk drive. Choose the size to use for the partition, and click Apply to create it. Next, with the partition selected, click the Format link to format it. When the format is complete (formatting usually takes just a few minutes), make sure the correct disk is selected, and then click Next to continue with the installation.

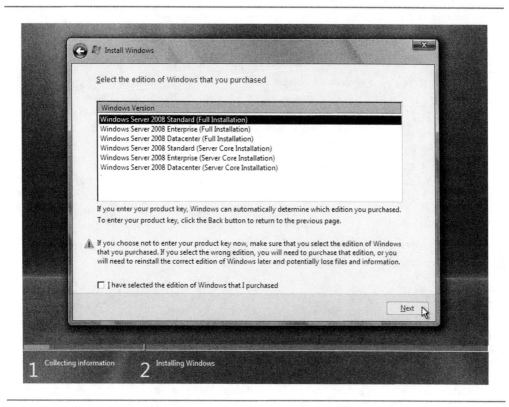

Figure 16-4.   No product key? Choose which edition you want to install in trial mode.

9. The installation will proceed, and you will see its status, as shown in Figure 16-8. This portion of the installation proceeds automatically and takes around 15 to 25 minutes, depending on the speed of the server.

10. After the installation completes, the server will restart, and you will see the screen shown in Figure 16-9, stating that you must change your password before you can log in. Click OK.

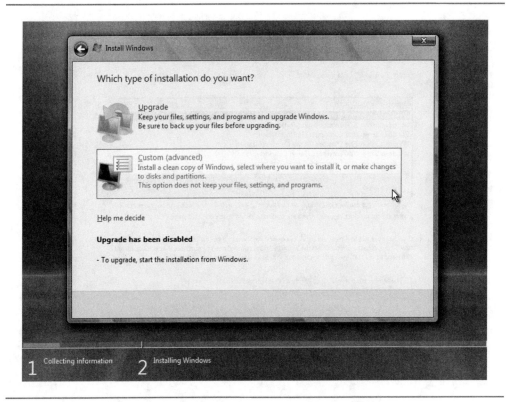

Figure 16-5.   Choosing to upgrade or perform a clean (custom) installation

11. You will be prompted to assign a new password for the administrator account on the server. Choose a good, strong password. Then click the right-arrow button on the screen to log in.

12. After you set your password and log in, you will soon see the new server's desktop, along with the Initial Configuration Tasks window (which appears automatically), as shown in Figure 16-10.

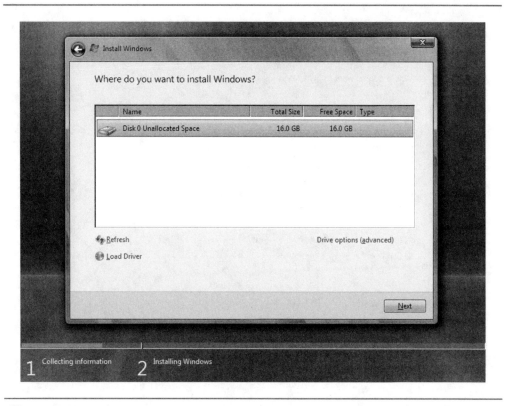

Figure 16-6.   Partitioning the installation disk drive

Performing the Initial Configuration

To complete the setup of Windows Server 2008, you use the Initial Configuration Tasks window and work through the numbered items shown in Figure 16-10.

Provide Computer Information

In the first section of the Initial Configuration Tasks window, first review the time zone for the computer's clock. Usually, the installation program correctly determines your time zone. However, if it's incorrect, click Set Time Zone and adjust it.

Figure 16-7. Advanced options for partitioning the installation disk drive

If you are installing Windows Server 2008 simply to learn more about it, and the network it's connected to already has a DHCP server, Windows will automatically obtain an IP address and access the network, so you do not need to change the network settings. However, in a production environment, most servers are assigned static IP addresses to use.

To assign a static IP address, click Configure Networking to display the Network Connections window. Find the active LAN connection in the window, right-click it, and choose Properties to open the Local Area Connection Properties dialog box. In this dialog

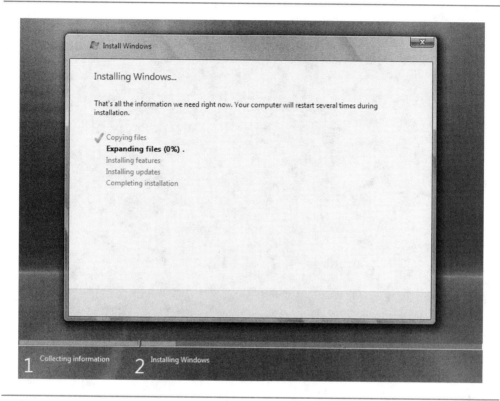

Figure 16-8.   Windows reports the status of the installation.

box, click the Internet Protocol Version 4 item in the list, as shown in Figure 16-11, and then click the Properties button. The Internet Protocol Version 4 (TCP/IPv4) Properties dialog box appears, as shown in Figure 16-12. Click the Use the Following IP Address button, and then provide a fixed IP address, subnet mask, and default gateway for your network. After entering this information, click OK to save your changes.

CAUTION   When assigning static IP addresses, it is important not to assign an address already in use on the network.

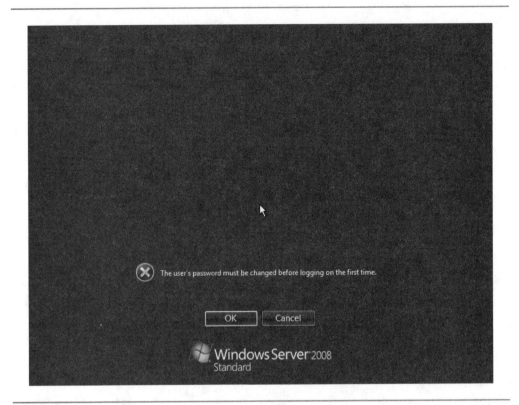

The user's password must be changed before logging on the first time.

OK   Cancel

Windows Server 2008
Standard

Figure 16-9. You need to change your password before logging in.

After configuring networking, you will also want to assign a computer name and, if there is an existing domain, connect this server to the domain. Click the Provide Computer Name and Domain link in the Initial Configuration Tasks window to display the System Properties dialog box, as shown in Figure 16-13.

Click the Change button, and you will see the Computer Name/Domain Changes dialog box, as shown in Figure 16-14. In this dialog box, enter an appropriate name for the new server. I usually recommend something relatively short and easy to remember and to type. If you want to connect this server to an existing Active Directory domain,

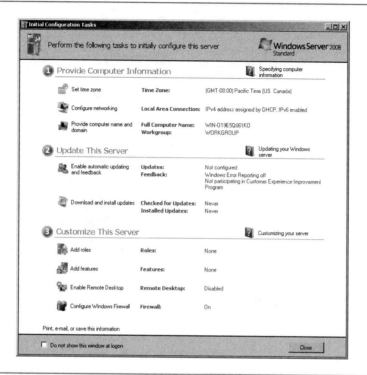

Figure 16-10.   The Initial Configuration Tasks window appears after installation

click the Domain option button and enter the correct domain name. (You will need an administrative account and password on a target domain in order to join this computer to it.) If you are just learning about Windows Server 2008 or you are going to create an Active Directory domain, you can leave the server in workgroup mode at this time. Click OK to save the new server name, which will require a restart of the server.

Update This Server

In the second section of the Initial Configuration Tasks window, choose to set the server to automatically download updates. Then go ahead and click the Download and Install Updates link to update the server with all of the released Windows Server 2008 patches.

Figure 16-11. Configuring networking

Customize This Server

The third section of the Initial Configuration Tasks window contains two simple options and two very powerful options. The two simple options are Enable Remote Desktop and Configure Windows Firewall. The two powerful options are Add Roles and Add Features.

The Windows firewall is turned on by default. I recommend also enabling Remote Desktop, which you can use to administer a Windows Server 2008 server over the network using Remote Desktop Connection.

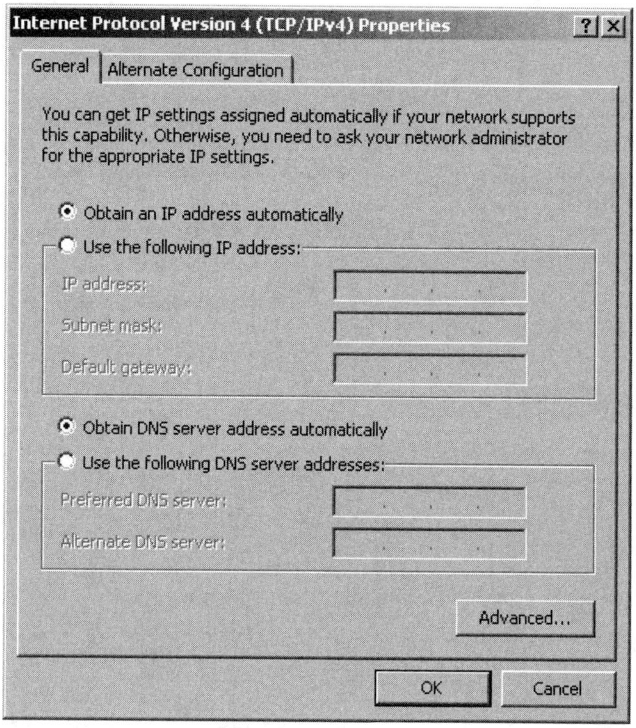

Figure 16-12. Configuring a TCP/IP address

Windows Server 2008 makes setting up the server to perform different roles a snap. Clicking the Add Roles link starts the Add Roles Wizard, as shown in Figure 16-15. If you are configuring the server as a file server, just check the File Services checkbox. To configure it as a web server using IIS, click the Web Server (IIS) checkbox. You can choose any combination of roles that you need, and the wizard will walk you through any necessary additional setup with a minimum of hassle. In this example, we are installing Windows Server 2008 as a stand-alone domain controller. Using the Add Roles Wizard, choose the Active Directory Domain Services role, and then click Next to install them. (You cannot install other roles at the same time as Active Directory Domain Services.)

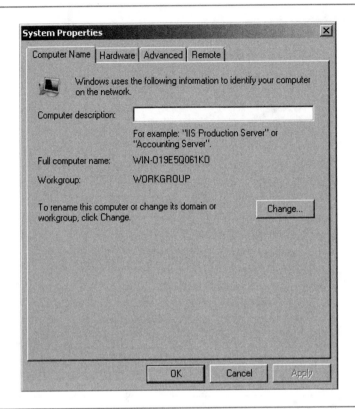

Figure 16-13.   Setting the server name and workgroup or domain

The Add Features option allows you to install particular Windows Server 2008 features. When you add roles, any required features are automatically installed. Accordingly, you will not often need to add specific features to a Windows Server 2008 installation. I do, however, recommend that you look through the list in the Add Features Wizard, as shown in Figure 16-16, so that you understand the types of features are available.

After the installation is complete (it usually does not take more than a few minutes), you need to run a program called DCPromo in order to create the new domain and complete the setup of the server.

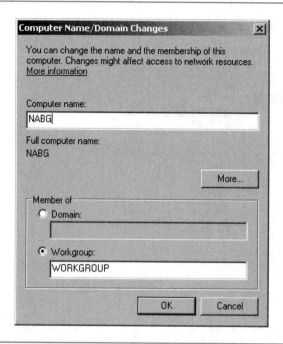

Figure 16-14.   Entering a new server name

Creating a New Domain

To install your new domain, follow these steps:

1. Open the Start menu, click Run, enter **DCPROMO**, and press ENTER. This starts the Active Directory Domain Services Installation Wizard, as shown in Figure 16-17. Click Next to continue.

2. The next wizard page lets you join an existing forest or create a new forest. For this example, we will create a new forest. Choose that option button and click Next to continue.

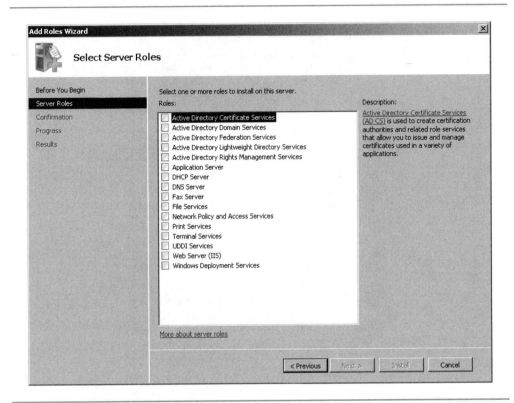

Figure 16-15. Using the Add Roles Wizard

CAUTION Join an existing forest only if you are the network administrator responsible for the existing Active Directory forest, and you are adding a new domain controller to that forest. If you are just evaluating and learning about Windows Server 2008, you should instead create a new forest.

3. You are prompted to enter the fully qualified domain name (FQDN) of the new forest root domain (nabg.com in this example), as shown in Figure 16-18.

4. You are prompted to enter a domain NetBIOS name. Usually, this will be the main portion of the domain name you entered for the FQDN of the forest root domain (for this example, the NetBIOS name NABG will be entered by default). If the default NetBIOS name is acceptable to you, click Next to continue.

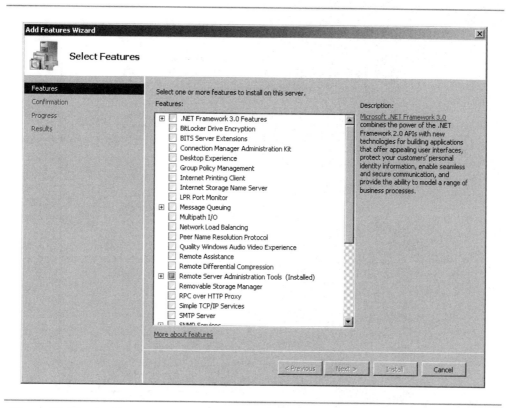

Figure 16-16. Looking over the features list offered by the Add Features Wizard

5. You now need to choose the functional level for the forest, as shown in Figure 16-19. Your choices are Windows Server 2000, Windows Server 2003, and Windows Server 2008. Choose Windows Server 2000 or 2003 functional levels if you wish the server to be compatible with domain controllers running those versions. For this example, choose the Windows Server 2008 functional level.

6. The wizard recommends that you add DNS services to the server. Accept this default and click Next to continue. (DNS services should run on each Active Directory domain controller.)

Figure 16-17.   Active Directory Domain Services Installation Wizard

7. You are prompted for the location for several critical Active Directory files and directories. Accept the defaults and click Next.

8. You are prompted for a directory services restore mode administrator password. This is an important password to set, and you need to keep it in a secure place. If the domain controller ever needs to be recovered, the password you specify here will be required in order to potentially recover the information in the domain.

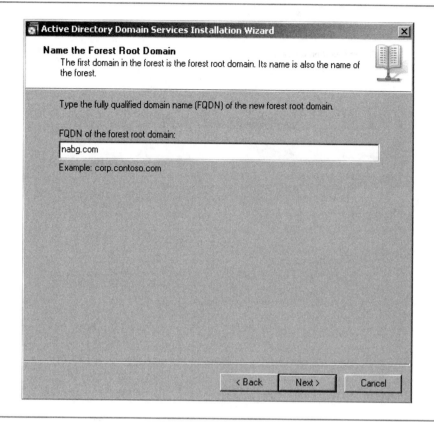

Figure 16-18. Naming a new forest

9. You see a final Summary screen. Review the configuration, and then click Next to complete the installation of Active Directory services. While this process can take up to a couple of hours for a very complex installation, for this stand-alone domain controller example, it is likely to finish within a few minutes. After it completes, you will be prompted to restart the server, which you should do immediately.

Congratulations! With the preceding steps, you have finished the installation and configuration of a Windows Server 2008 acting as a domain controller. You now have a server capable of serving the needs of many users and of performing a number of useful tasks.

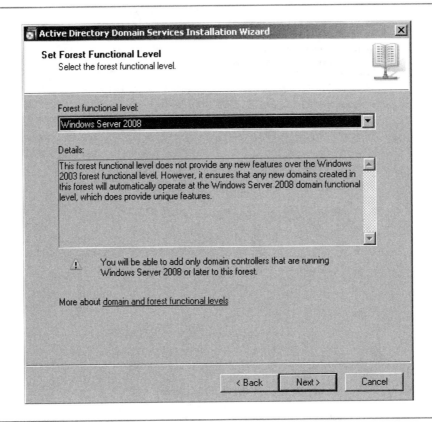

Figure 16-19.   Choosing a forest functional level

Chapter Summary

In this chapter, you learned how Windows Server 2008 is installed and set up, using basic installation choices that will be appropriate for many servers in small businesses. As you saw, installing Windows Server 2008 is really not much more difficult than installing Windows Vista.

This chapter did not cover all the myriad choices available to you during the installation of Windows Server 2008 or discuss more complex installation topics appropriate for larger networks. Instead, this chapter was intended to help beginners to networking understand the basic steps to install Windows Server 2008 and to provide enough information to get a basic server up and running with minimal problems.

If you will be installing Windows Server 2008 into a production environment—no matter how small—it's vital for you to learn much more about Windows Server 2008 than presented in this book. Fortunately, many fine training classes and books are available to teach you all you must do to set up and administer a Windows Server 2008-based network.

Installing the NOS is only a small part of the battle. Even more important is that you know how to administer the server and perform various administrative tasks for the NOS. These include managing user accounts, groups, printers, and other required maintenance tasks. Chapter 17 discusses the basics of Windows Server 2008 administration.

Chapter 17

Administering Windows Server 2008: The Basics

Installing and setting up Windows Server 2008 is only the tip of the iceberg. Far more important and time-consuming is the process of administering the server. This process includes regular and common duties such as adding new users, deleting old users, assigning permissions to users, performing backups, and so forth. These topics are covered in this chapter. Good administration habits will ensure that the network and the server remain productive and secure.

Thinking About Network Security

Before delving into the administrative activities discussed in this chapter, you should spend some time thinking about network security and how it relates to your specific company. Administering a server must be predicated on maintaining appropriate security for your network.

The key here is to remember that every network has an appropriate level of security. The security requirements for a Department of Defense (DoD) contractor that designs military equipment will be different from the security requirements for a company that operates restaurants.

Many beginning network administrators think they need to set up their networks to follow the strongest security measures available. The problem with this approach is that these measures almost always reduce the productivity of people using the network. You need to strike a balance between productivity and security in accordance with the needs of your company.

For example, Windows Server 2008 enables you to set various security policies that apply to users. These include forcing password changes at specified intervals, requiring that passwords be a certain minimum length, disallowing reuse of old passwords, and so on. For example, you could set up policies to require passwords that are at least 20 characters long and that must be changed weekly. In theory, these settings should be more secure than shorter, less-frequently changed passwords. A 20-character password is virtually impossible to crack using standard methods, and weekly password changes reduce the chance that someone else will discover a user's password and be free to use it for an extended period of time.

One problem with such strict policies is that users may resort to writing down their passwords so they can remember them from week to week. A written password is far less secure than one that is remembered, because someone else can find the written password and bypass security easily after doing so. Another problem is that users might frequently forget their passwords, which will lead to them being locked out of the system for periods of time. This means they will require a lot of help from the network administrator (you!) to clear up these problems each time they occur. For a DoD contractor, these trade-offs might be worthwhile. For the restaurant operator, however, they would be inappropriate and would end up hurting the company more than they help.

The primary reason you should pay attention to this subject before learning about administration is that you should determine the appropriate network security early, so that you can allow for it as you administer the network on a daily basis. Network security doesn't need to take up much of your time, provided you set up your administrative procedures so they presuppose the level of security you require. For example, if you know what your password policies will be on the network, it takes only a few seconds to ensure that new users have those policies set for their account. If you know that you maintain a paper-based log of changes to security groups in the network, then it takes only a second to follow this procedure as you change group membership occasionally. Failing to determine these security practices and policies early on will result in needing to undertake much larger projects as part of a security review or audit. Security is an area where you're much better off doing things right the first time!

Working with User Accounts

For anyone—including the administrator—to gain access to a server running Windows Server 2008, the user must have an account established on the server or in the domain. (A *domain* is essentially a collection of security information shared among Windows servers.) The account defines the *user name* (the name by which the user is known to the system) and the user's password, along with a host of other information specific to each user. Creating, maintaining, and deleting user accounts is easy with Windows Server 2008.

NOTE Every account created for a Windows Server 2008 domain is assigned a special number, called a security ID (SID). The server actually recognizes the user by this number. SIDs are said to be "unique across space and time." This means that no two users will ever have the same SID, even if they have the same user name and even the same password. This is because the SID is made up of a unique number assigned to the domain and then a sequential number assigned to each created account (with billions of unique user-specific numbers available). If you have a user called Frank, delete that account, and then create another account called Frank, the accounts will have different SIDs. This ensures that no user account will accidentally receive permissions originally assigned to another user of the same name.

To maintain user accounts, you use the Active Directory Users and Computers console. You can open this console by clicking the Start menu, choosing Programs, and then selecting Administrative Tools. To accomplish activities in the console, you first select either a container in the left pane or an object in the right pane, and then either right-click the container or object or open the Action pull-down menu and choose from the available options. Because the available options change based on the selected container or object, first selecting an object with which to work is important.

Adding a User

To add a user with the Active Directory Users and Computers console, start by selecting the Users container in the left pane (with the tree open to the domain you are administering), as shown in Figure 17-1. Then right-click the Users container, choose New from the pop-up menu, and choose User from the submenu. You see the New Object – User dialog box, as shown in Figure 17-2. Fill in the First Name, Last Name, and User Logon Name fields. Then click the Next button to move to the next dialog box.

TIP   You should establish standards by which you assign logon names on your network. Small networks (those with fewer than 50 users) often just use people's first names, followed by the first initial of their last names when conflicts arise. A more commonly used convention is to use the user's last name followed by the first initial of their first name. This latter standard allows far more combinations before conflicts arise, and you can then resolve any conflicts that arise by adding the person's middle initial, a number, or some other change so that all user names at any given time on the system are unique.

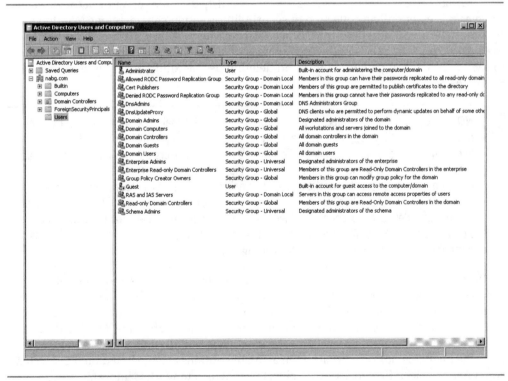

Figure 17-1.   The Active Directory Users and Computers console allows you to manage user accounts.

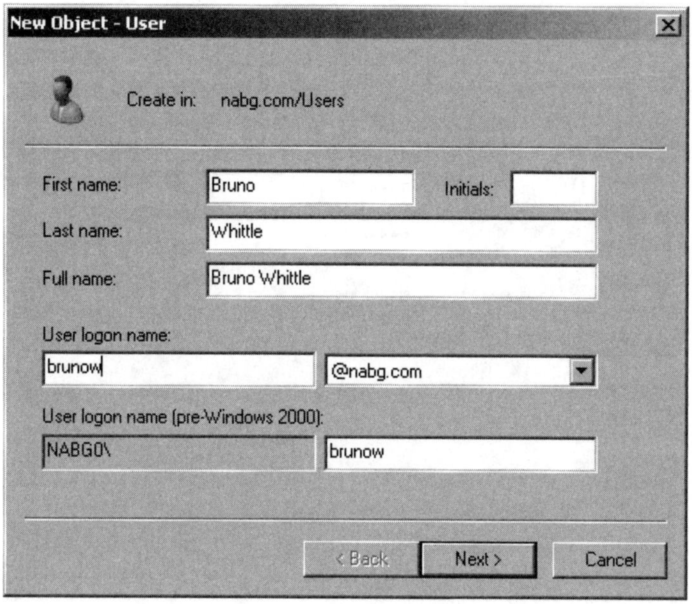

Figure 17-2.   Use the New Object – User dialog box to add a new user.

In the second dialog box, shown in Figure 17-3, you enter the initial password that the account will use. You also select several options that apply to the account, as follows:

- **User Must Change Password at Next Logon**   Selecting this checkbox forces users to choose their own password when they first log in to the system.

- **User Cannot Change Password**   You might select this option for resource accounts if you do not want to allow users to change their passwords. (For instance, you might have a specific user account established for a particular computer that performs a particular function that many people employ.) Generally, however, you should not select this option; most sites allow users to change their own passwords, and you want to permit them to do so if you've also set passwords to automatically expire.

- **Password Never Expires**   Choose this option to allow the password to remain viable for as long as the user chooses to use it. Activating this option for most users is generally considered a poor security practice.

- **Account Is Disabled**   Selecting this option disables the new account. The administrator can enable the account when needed by clearing the checkbox.

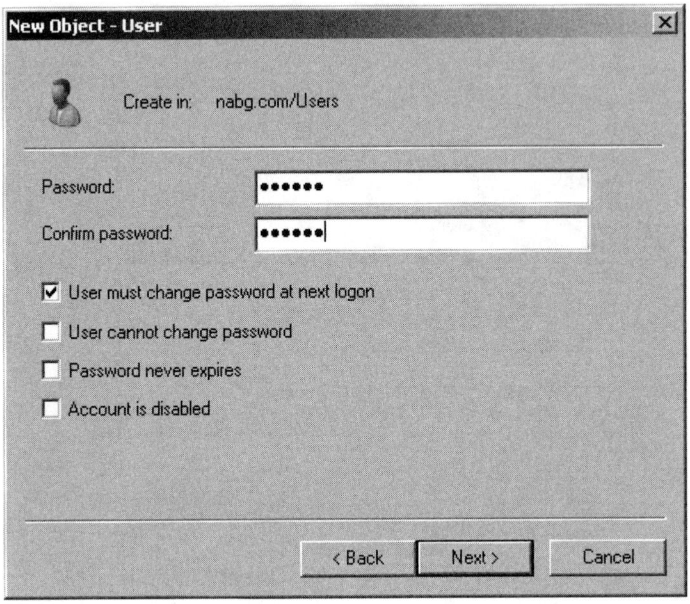

Figure 17-3.   Setting the user's password

After entering the password and selecting the options you want, click Next to continue. You will then see a confirmation screen. Click Next a final time to create the account, or click Back to return to either dialog box to make changes.

Modifying a User Account

The dialog box in which you modify the information about a user account contains many other fields than the ones to create the account. You can use these to document the account and to set some other security options.

To modify an existing user account, right-click the user object you wish to modify and choose Properties from the pop-up menu. You then see the tabbed dialog box shown in Figure 17-4.

In the first two tabs, General and Address, you can enter some additional information about the user, such as job title, mailing address, telephone number, e-mail account, and so forth. Because Active Directory also integrates with Exchange Server, this information might be important to enter for your network.

In the Account tab, shown in Figure 17-5, you can set some important user account options. At the top of the tab, you can see the user's logon name, as well as the Windows domain in which the user has primary membership. Below that is the user's Windows NT

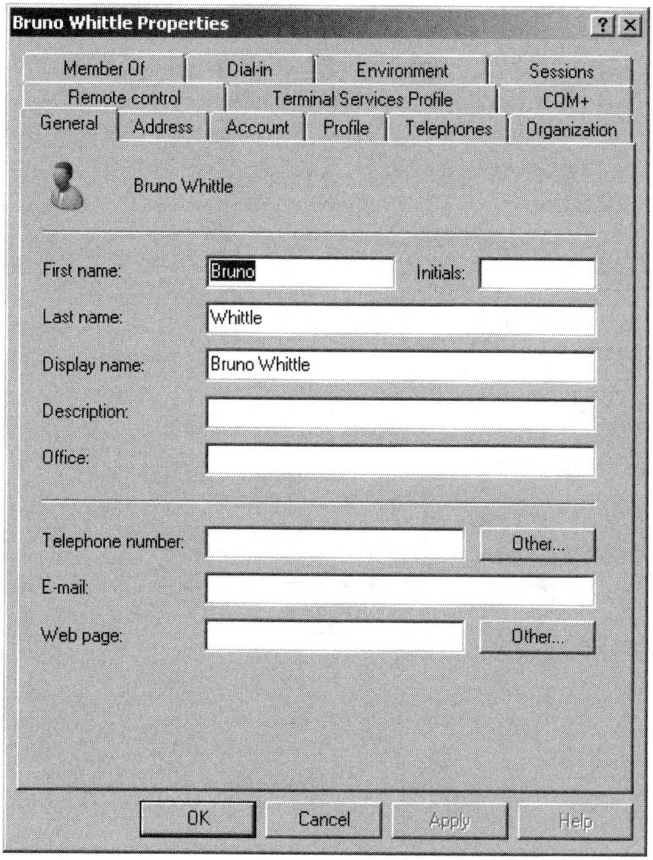

Figure 17-4. Setting properties for a user's account

logon name (called the pre-Windows 2000 logon name), which the user can optionally use to log in to the domain from a Windows NT computer or to use an application that doesn't yet support Active Directory logins. (Although you can set these two logon names to be different, doing so rarely is a good idea.)

Clicking the Logon Hours button displays the dialog box shown in Figure 17-6. In this dialog box, you select different blocks of time within a standard week, and then click the appropriate option button to permit or deny access to the network for that time period. In Figure 17-6, the settings permit logon times for a normal workday, with some cushion before and after those times to allow for slightly different work hours. By default, users are permitted to log on to the network at any time, any day of the week. For most networks, particularly smaller networks, permitting users to log on at any time is generally acceptable.

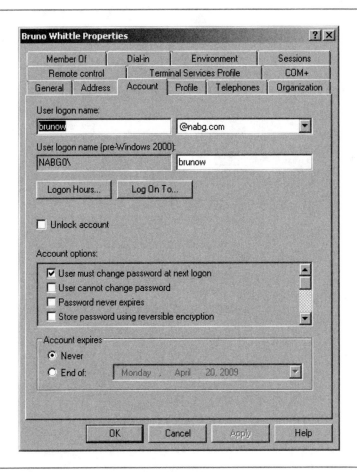

Figure 17-5. The Account tab of a user's Properties dialog box lets you set some important user account options.

Clicking the Log On To button on the Account tab opens the Logon Workstations dialog box, as shown in Figure 17-7. By default, users can log on to any workstation in the domain, and the domain authenticates them. In some cases, a system might require stricter security, where you specify the computers to which a user account can log on. For example, you might set up a network backup account that you use to back up the network, and then leave this account logged on all the time in your locked computer room. Because the backup account has access to all files on the network (necessary to do its job), a good idea is to limit that account to log on only to the computer designated for this purpose in the computer room. You use the Log On To feature to set up this type of

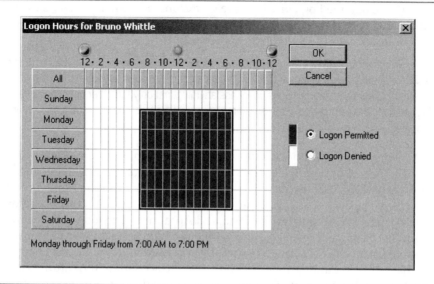

Figure 17-6.   Setting logon time restrictions for a user

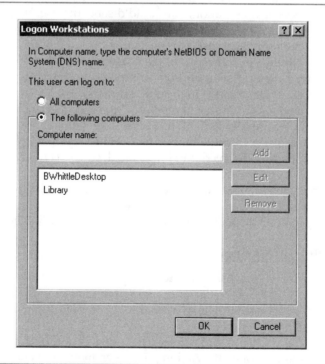

Figure 17-7.   Restricting the computers to which a user can log on

restriction. (Note that the Log On To feature works only if the network uses the NetBIOS or NetBEUI protocols; it will not work with TCP/IP-only networks unless the Windows Internet Naming Service is set up on the network.)

> **NOTE** Allowing a user to log on to another user's computer does not mean that user can log on with the other user's permissions or access anything that only the other user can access. This simply means the user can use the listed physical computer to log on to his own account from that computer.

The Account Options section of the Account tab enables you to select various binary (on/off) account options. Yet set some of the options, such as requiring a user to change the password at the next logon, as you add the account. Some options listed are unique to the user's Properties dialog box. The two most important of these additional options are Account Is Disabled and Account Is Trusted for Delegation.

Account Is Disabled, if selected, disables the user account while leaving it set up within Active Directory. This option is useful if you need to deny this user account access to the network, but might need to reenable the account in the future. (Account Is Disabled is handled as a high-priority change within the domain, and it takes effect immediately, even across large numbers of domain controllers.) Because deleting an account also deletes any permissions the user might have, you should always disable an account instead if you might need to grant access to the network again to that user. For example, if someone is on vacation, you could disable the user's account while she is gone, and then clear the Account Is Disabled checkbox when she returns.

You must select Account Is Trusted for Delegation option if you want to designate the user account to administer some part of the domain. Windows Server 2008 enables you to grant administrative rights to portions of the Active Directory tree without needing to give administrative rights to the entire domain.

The last option on the Account tab of the user Properties dialog box is the expiration date setting, Account Expires. By default, it is set to Never. If you wish to define an expiration date, you may do so in the End Of field. When the date indicated is reached, the account is automatically disabled (but not deleted, so you can reenable it if you wish).

Another tab that you will use often in the user's Properties dialog box is the Member Of tab, in which you define the security groups for a user, as shown in Figure 17-8. Security groups are discussed after the description of deleting or disabling a user account.

Deleting or Disabling a User Account

Deleting a user account is easy using the Active Directory Users and Groups console. In the left pane, select the Users folder, and then select the user in the right pane. Either right-click the user and choose Delete or open the Action pull-down menu and choose Delete.

Disabling an account is just as easy. Select the user account, right-click it, and choose Disable Account (or open the Action pull-down menu and choose Disable Account).

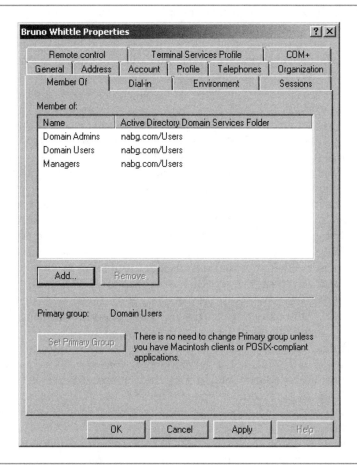

Figure 17-8. Controlling a user's membership in groups

TIP If you need to delete a large number of accounts, you can save time by selecting them all before choosing the Delete or Disable Account commands. Just be sure you haven't selected accounts that you don't want to delete or disable!

Working with Active Directory Security Groups

On any network, you usually need to administer permissions to many different folders and files. If you were able to grant access only by user account, you would quickly go crazy trying to keep track of all the necessary information.

For example, suppose that a group of people, such as an accounting department, has specific permissions to access 20 different folders on the server. When a new accountant is hired, do you need to remember or look up all those 20 folders so you can give the accountant the same permissions as the rest of the department? Or suppose that a user who has many different permissions changes departments. Do you need to find each permission so you can make sure he has only the appropriate permissions for his new department?

To address such problems, network operating systems support the concept of *security groups* (or just *groups*). You first create the group, and then assign all the appropriate users to it so you can administer their permissions more easily. When you grant permission to a folder on the server, you do so by giving the group the network permission. All the members of the group automatically *inherit* those permissions. This inheritance makes maintaining network permissions over time much easier. In fact, you shouldn't try to manage network permissions without using groups. Otherwise, you might quickly become overwhelmed trying to keep track of everything, and you're almost certain to make mistakes over time.

Not only can users be members of groups, but groups can be members of other groups. For instance, suppose that you define a group for each department in your company. Half those departments are part of a larger division called Research and Development (R&D) and half are part of Sales, General, and Administration (SG&A). On your network, some folders are specific to each department, some are specific to all of R&D or SG&A, and some can be accessed by every user on the network. In such a situation, you would first create the departmental groups, and then create the R&D and SG&A groups. Each departmental group would then become a member in either R&D or SG&A. Finally, you would use the built-in Domain Users group, or another one you created that represents everyone, and then assign R&D and SG&A to that top-level group for every user.

Once you've set up your groups, you can grant permissions in the most logical way. If a resource is just for a specific department, you assign that departmental group to the resource. If a resource is for R&D or SG&A, you assign those divisions to the resource; then all the individual departmental groups within that division will inherit permission to access the resource. If a resource is for everyone, you assign the master, top-level group to the resource.

Using such hierarchical group levels makes administering permissions even easier, and this approach is practically necessary for larger networks with hundreds of users.

Creating Groups

You create groups using the Active Directory Users and Computers console. Groups appear in two of the domain's containers: Builtin and Users.

The built-in groups, shown in Figure 17-9, are fixed. They cannot be deleted or made members of other groups. The built-in groups have certain important permissions already assigned to them, and other groups you create can be given membership in the built-in groups. Similarly, if you want to disable a particular built-in group, you would do so simply by removing all its member groups.

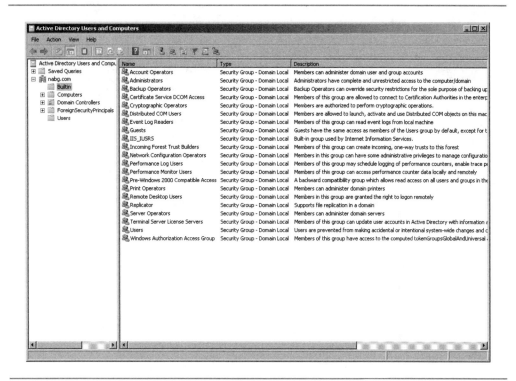

Figure 17-9. Viewing the list of built-in groups

 CAUTION Be careful changing the membership of the built-in groups. For most networks, while it's important to understand what these groups are and how they work, you generally want to leave them alone.

Generally, you work only with groups defined in the Users container. Figure 17-10 shows the default groups in the Users container, which you can distinguish from user accounts by both the two-person icon and the type designation.

To add a new group, select the Users container in the left pane. Then open the Action pull-down menu, choose New, and choose Group. You see the New Object – Group dialog box, as shown in Figure 17-10. Enter the name of the group in the first field. You'll see the name you enter echoed in the second field. This field enables you to specify a different group name for Windows NT (pre-Windows 2000) computers. However, using different group names is usually not a good idea, because it can quickly make your system confusing.

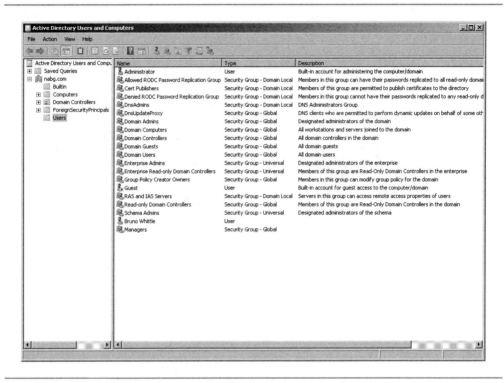

Figure 17-10. Creating a new group

After naming the group, you can select from the available option buttons in the lower half of the dialog box. The Group Scope section refers to how widely the group is populated throughout a domain:

- *Domain local* groups exist only within a single domain and can contain members only from that domain.

- *Global* groups can contain members only from the domain in which they exist. However, you can assign global group permissions to any domain within the network, even across multiple domains.

- *Universal* groups exist throughout an organization, even when the organization's network is made up of many individual domains. Universal groups can also contain members from any domain in an organization's network.

TIP Don't worry if you create a group with the wrong scope. You can easily change the group's scope, provided its membership doesn't violate the new scope's rules for membership. To change a domain scope, select the group and open its Properties dialog box (right-click and then choose Properties from the pop-up menu). If the group membership allows the change, you can select a different Group Scope option button.

After you set the group's scope, you can also select whether it will be a security group or a distribution group. Distribution groups are used only to maintain e-mail distribution lists for e-mail applications such as Microsoft Exchange Server. They have no security impact in Windows Server 2008.

Finally, click OK to create the group. Now you can add members to the group, as described in the next section.

Maintaining Group Membership

A new group starts out without any members. To set the membership for a group, follow these steps:

1. Select the group and open its Properties dialog box (by right-clicking it and choosing Properties from the pop-up menu). Then click the Members tab, as shown in Figure 17-11.

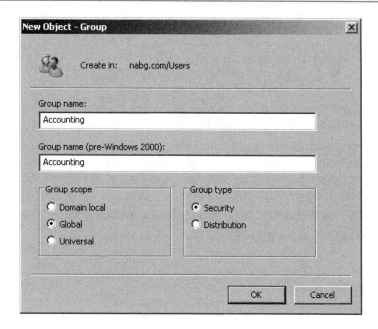

Figure 17-11. A brand-new group does not have any members.

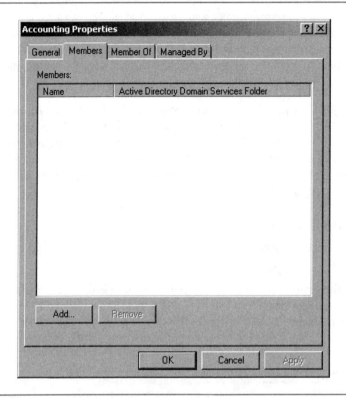

Figure 17-12.   Adding a member to a group

2. Click the Add button. You see the Select Users, Contacts, Computers, or Groups dialog box, as shown in Figure 17-12.

3. Type in enough of a user or another group's name to identify it, and then click the Check Names button. If you type in too few characters to uniquely identify the user or group, Windows will show you a list of the possible matches from which you can select the correct one.

4. Choose the member you want to add, and then click OK.

5. Repeat steps 3 and 4 to complete the group membership.

Working with Shares

Drives and folders under Windows Server 2008 are made available to users over the network as shared resources, simply called *shares* in Windows networking parlance. You select a drive or folder, enable it to be shared, and then set the permissions for the share.

Understanding Share Security

You can set both drives and folders as distinct shared resources, whether they are located on a FAT-formatted drive or on an NTFS-formatted drive. In the case of an NTFS-formatted drive (but not a FAT-formatted drive), you can also set permissions on folders and files within the share that are separate from the permissions on the share itself. Understanding how Windows Server 2008 handles security for shares, folders, and files on NTFS drives is important.

Suppose that you created a share called RESEARCH and you gave the R&D security group read-only access to the share. Within the share, you set the permissions on a folder called PROJECTS to allow full read and write access (called *change permission*) for the R&D security group. Will the R&D group have read-only permission to that folder or change permission? The group will have read-only permission. This is because when security permissions differ between folders within a share and the share itself, the most restrictive permissions apply.

A better way to set up share permissions is to allow everyone change permission to the share and then control the actual permissions by setting them on the folders within the share itself. This way, you can assign any combination of permissions you want; then the users will receive the permissions that you set on those folders, even though the share is set to change permission.

Also, remember that users receive permissions based on the groups of which they are members, and these permissions are cumulative. So, if you are a member of the Everyone group who has read-only permission for a particular file, but you're also a member of the Admins group who has full control permission for that file, you'll have full control permission in practice. This is an important rule: Permissions set on folders and files are always cumulative and take into account permissions set for the user individually as well as any security groups of which the user is a member.

Another important point is that you can set permissions within a share (sometimes called *NTFS permissions*) on both folders and files, and these permissions are also cumulative. So, for instance, you can set read-only permission on a folder for a user, but change permission for some specific files. The user then has the ability to read, modify, and even delete those files without having that ability with other files in the same folder.

There's a special permission called *no access*, which overrides all other permissions, no matter what. If you set no access permission for a user on a file or folder, then that's it—the user will not be able to access that file or folder. An extremely important corollary to this rule is that no access permission is also cumulative and overriding. So, if the Everyone security group has change permission for a file, but you set a particular user to no access for that file, that user will receive no access permission. If you set no access permission for the Everyone group, however, then all members of that group will also receive the no access permission, because it overrides any other permissions they have. Be careful about using no access with security groups!

To summarize, you can resolve most permission problems if you remember the rules discussed here:

■ When share permissions conflict compared to the file or folder permissions, the *most restrictive* one always wins.

■ Aside from the preceding rule, permissions are cumulative, taking into account permissions assigned to users and groups as well as files and folders.

■ When a permission conflict occurs, the no access permission always wins if it is set.

Creating Shares

As a network administrator, you will frequently create and manage the shares on the network. The following steps walk you through creating a new share.

1. Open either My Computer or Windows Explorer on the server.

2. Right-click the folder or drive you want to share, and then choose Share from the pop-up menu. You will see the File Sharing dialog box, as shown in Figure 17-13.

3. In the field provided, enter enough of a user's name to identify that person in the system, and then click Add.

4. Click the down arrow next to the user's name to set that user's permission level. The permission levels available are Owner, for full read and write access, plus the ability to grant permissions to other users; Contributor, for full read and write access; and Reader, for read-only access.

5. Click the Share button to create the share. You will see a confirmatory dialog box. Click OK, and the share will be created. By default, the share uses the folder's name as the share name.

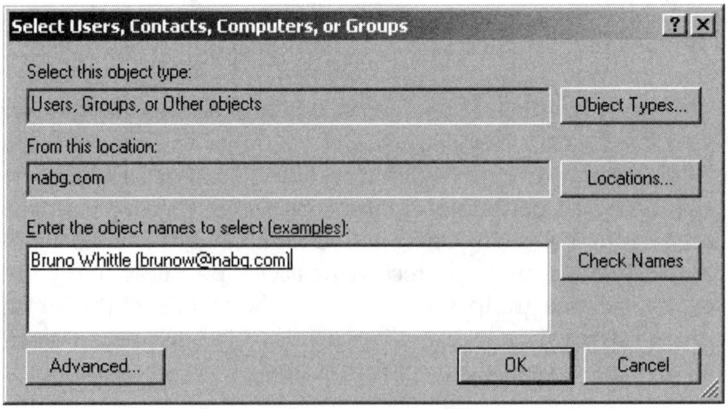

Figure 17-13. Creating a share

Once a share is created and the share information has propagated through the domain (usually within several minutes), users can browse it through Network Neighborhood (Windows 9*x* and NT), My Network Places (Windows 2000 and XP), or Network (Windows Vista). Double-clicking the share will open it (if allowed by the permissions).

Mapping Drives

You can use shares by opening them through Network Neighborhood, My Network Places, or Network, and they function just like the folders in My Computer. However, you might frequently want to simulate a connected hard disk on your computer with a share from the network. For example, many applications that store files on the network require that the network folders be accessible as normal drive letters. The process of simulating a disk drive with a network share is called *mapping*. You create a map (link) between the drive letter you want to use and the actual network share to remain attached to that drive letter.

You can create a drive mapping in many ways. The easiest way is to open Network from the client computer, locate the share you want to map, right-click it, and choose Map Network Drive. In the dialog box that appears, the name of the domain and share will already be filled in for you. Simply select an appropriate drive letter for the mapping and click OK. From then on, the share will appear to your computer as that drive letter, and users will see this share's letter in My Computer.

You can also map drives using a command-line utility called NET. The NET command takes a variety of forms and can fulfill many different needs, depending on the parameters you give it. To map a drive, you use the NET USE command. Typing NET USE by itself and pressing ENTER will list all currently mapped drives. (You can type NET HELP USE for more detailed help on the command.) To add a new drive mapping, you would type the following:

```
NET USE drive_letter: UNC_for_share
```

Most network resources in a Windows network use a naming system called the Universal Naming Convention (UNC). To supply a UNC, you start with two backslashes, then the name of the server, another backslash, and the name of the share. (Additional backslashes and names can refer to folders and files within the share.) For example, to map drive G: to a share called EMPLOYEES located on the server SERVER, use the following command:

```
NET USE G:\\SERVER\EMPLOYEES
```

TIP   You can use the NET command from any Windows client for any Windows network. Type NET by itself to list all of the different forms of the command. Type *NET command* HELP to see detailed help on the different NET commands.

Working with Printers

Before setting up and working with printers on a network, you need to understand the components involved in network printing and how they interact.

Understanding Network Printing

A *print job* is a set of binary data sent from a network workstation to a network printer. A print job is the same data that a computer would send to a locally connected printer—it's just redirected to the network for printing.

The network workstation that sends the print job to the print queue is responsible for formatting the print data properly for the printer. This is done through software installed on the workstation, called a *print driver*, which is specific to each type of printer. Printer drivers are also specific to each operating system that uses them. In other words, an HP LaserJet 5si driver for a Windows XP computer is different from a HP LaserJet 5si driver for a Windows 2000 workstation computer. More troublesome, different versions of the same operating system sometimes use different drivers, so a driver for a Windows XP computer might not work with a Windows Vista computer and vice versa.

Print jobs are often sent to the network through a captured printer port. The network client software redirects to the network one of the printer ports on a networked workstation, such as LPT1. The process of redirecting a printer port to a network printer is called *capturing*. Usually, captured ports are persistent and continue through multiple logins until they are turned off.

Print jobs sent to the network go to a place called a *print queue*. The print job sits in the queue until the network can service the print job and send it to the printer. Print queues can hold many jobs from many different users and typically are managed in a first-in, first-out fashion.

Print jobs are removed from print queues and sent to actual printers by *print servers*. After sending the complete job to the printer, the print server removes the job from the queue. You can accomplish print serving in many different ways. If the printer you are using is connected to a server or workstation on the network, that server or workstation handles the print server duty. If the printer is directly connected to the network (if it has its own network port), then the printer usually has a built-in print server as part of its network hardware. This built-in print server has the intelligence to log in to the network and to service a particular printer queue.

Print jobs start at the printing application, which sends its printer output to the local operating system. The local operating system uses the printer driver requested by the application to format the actual print job for the printer in question. The local operating system works with the installed network client software to send the formatted print job to the print queue, where the job sits until the printer is available. Then the print server sends the print job from the queue to the actual printer.

Many steps are involved, but once everything is set up, it works smoothly, as you will see in the next section. Figure 17-14 shows an overview of how network printing works.

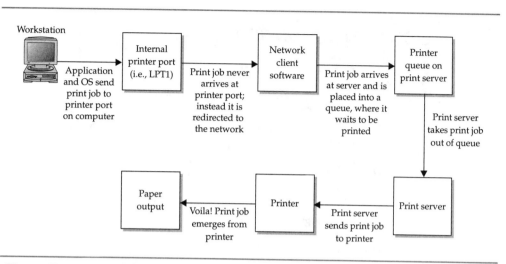

Figure 17-14. Overview of the network printing process

Setting Up a Network Printer

You can easily set up a printer connected to a server (or workstation) so other network users can access it. However, for networks with more than about 20 users, you're better off either buying printers with network interfaces and built-in print servers or using dedicated print server boxes that interface between a printer and the network. For most laser printers, adding a dedicated network interface and server increases the cost of the printer by about $150 to $300. This is money well spent, because sending a print job to a printer requires the print server to do a lot of processing. If that print server is also your main file server, its overall performance will decrease significantly while it is printing (and particularly while it services large print jobs).

Also, printers with built-in print servers are far easier to relocate on the network. They can go anywhere a network connection exists and where power is available. Once connected to the network at a new location, the printer logs in to the network and starts doing its work immediately.

If you want to share a printer connected directly to a Windows Server 2008 server, this is easy to do. First, open the server's Printers folder (from the Start menu, choose Control Panel, and then choose Printers), which lists all the installed printers. Right-click the one you want to share and choose Sharing from the pop-up menu. The Properties dialog box for the printer will appear, with the Sharing tab activated, as shown in Figure 17-15.

NOTE In this example, the printer and its Windows 2000 driver are already installed properly, as they would normally be during the installation of Windows Server 2008. If they are not properly installed, open the Printers folder and use the Add Printers icon to set up the printer on the server itself.

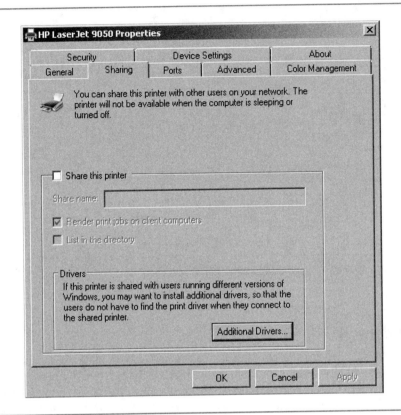

Figure 17-15.   Enabling printer sharing

On the Sharing tab, click the Share This Printer checkbox, and then assign the printer a share name, by which the client computers will recognize the printer. At this point, you can click the OK button because the default permissions for a shared printer are for the Everyone group to be able to print to it. Alternatively, if you want to set other permissions for a shared printer, use the Security tab of the printer's Properties dialog box.

The groups assigned in the Security tab are the default assignments for a shared printer, with the Administrators permissions shown. Three main permissions are assigned to each entity: Print, Manage Printers, and Manage Documents. The Everyone group has permission to print, but not to manage documents in the queue. However, a special group called Creator Owner has permission to manage documents. This means that the user who sent the print job automatically has permission to modify or delete his own print job, but not others waiting in the queue.

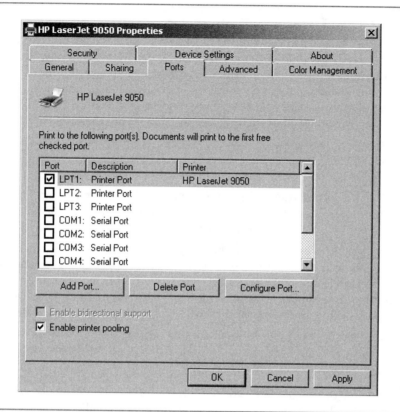

Figure 17-16.   Enabling printer pooling

For high-throughput requirements, you might want to use a feature called *printer pooling*, which enables you to set up a number of identical printers, all connected to a single printer queue, that appear to the network as one printer. Users print to the listed printer, and the first available real printer services the job. Using printer pooling, you could have a whole bank of printers appear as one printer to the users and dramatically increase the number of print requests you can handle. Keep in mind that pooled printers must be identical, because they will all use the same print driver. Figure 17-16 shows the tab on which printer pooling is enabled.

As you can see, setting up networked printers with Windows Server 2008 is a relatively straightforward process that gives you considerable flexibility in how you set up and manage your shared printers. Remember, too, that other printing models are also possible, such as network-connected printers. Consult the documentation that comes with such printers for details on setting them up on your network.

Chapter Summary

No single chapter can do justice to all the tools and knowledge needed to administer a Windows Server 2008 professionally. This chapter briefly covered how the most common and important tasks are handled. If you are or will be administering a Windows Server 2008 system, you should pursue more detailed knowledge about the topics discussed in this chapter and the many other subjects you will need to master.

In particular, start out by researching and learning about these important tools:

- Reliability and Performance Monitor for troubleshooting, performance tuning, and ongoing monitoring of important server statistics. Reliability and Performance Monitor can be configured to take certain actions when triggers that you set occur, such as beeping you or sending alert messages to other computers on the network. It is also an extremely useful tool for resolving any performance problems you encounter.

- Event Viewer is key to your ability to find and diagnose Windows Server 2008 problems. You should use Event Viewer on a regular basis (I recommend using it daily) to view new events and decide whether they need your immediate attention. You can use Event Viewer to save the event logs periodically, creating a long-term record of error and informational messages stored in its logs.

- Task Scheduler can be used to schedule recurring tasks you want to run frequently on your server, such as virus scans (with third-party virus software), disk defragmentation, and disk testing.

These are some of the core tools you should learn for basic Windows Server 2008 administration. In Chapter 19, you can also read about some other network services that are available on Windows Server 2008.

Chapter 18

Introducing Exchange Server 2010

Microsoft offers a number of specialized server systems, including the widely used Exchange Server application. Exchange Server is Microsoft's e-mail solution, and it is designed to be able to handle virtually any organization's e-mail needs.

This chapter introduces Exchange Server. You learn how to install it, perform basic configuration tasks, and access a mailbox using Exchange Server's Web Outlook functionality.

Exchange Server 2010 Features

Exchange Server is a comprehensive e-mail solution for organizations of all sizes, from small companies to large multinational conglomerates. It is highly reliable and scalable, and has been in very wide use for many years. Some of Exchange Server's features include the following:

- Numerous access methods for users to get to their e-mail, including from an e-mail client application such as Microsoft Outlook, a mobile device (like the BlackBerry or iPhone), a web browser, and even a voice-response system

- Unified Messaging, in which not only e-mail messages are delivered to users inboxes, but also voicemail messages and faxes

- Support for collaborative features such as calendaring, shared resource scheduling (such as conference rooms or equipment), meeting scheduling, and out-of-office notifications

- Support for user-defined rules that allow for the automation of routine e-mail tasks

TIP   Automating e-mail tasks can be very useful. For instance, you could set up an human resources department mailbox to which employment applicants send their resumes, and on receipt of each resume, the server responds to the sender with an immediate acknowledgment. It might also forward the resumes to appropriate personnel automatically.

- Close integration with Active Directory, which means that you can maintain user accounts, and their associated mailboxes, in one centralized place

- Some antispam and antivirus technologies, and easy addition of third-party add-on software for these tasks

Whether you need a basic internal e-mail system for a small organization or a sophisticated, powerful system to handle a company of hundreds of thousands of users, Exchange Server can meet those needs.

Installing Exchange Server 2010

If you are just learning about Exchange Server 2010 or evaluating it, you can download a fully functional copy from Microsoft that will operate for 120 days. Before installing it, however, review the following prerequisites:

- Windows Server 2008 (64-bit) Standard Edition or higher
- An Active Directory domain
- At least 2GB of RAM, plus recommended 2MB to 4MB of additional RAM per mailbox
- At least 1.2GB free disk space on the installation partition
- 200MB free space on the system partition
- For Unified Messaging features, 500MB free disk space for each Unified Messaging language pack
- All disk partitions formatted with NTFS

There are a number of other detailed requirements, but the Exchange Server installer will survey your system and will notify you of any additional requirements you must meet.

NOTE   This chapter was prepared with a late-stage beta version of Exchange Server 2010. It is possible that there may be minor differences between the screens and steps presented here and the final released version.

For this example installation, you can use the Windows Server 2008 installation that was discussed in Chapter 16. Before you begin, you should run Windows Update to ensure that you have all current system patches.

When you first start the Exchange Server installation program (see Figure 18-1), the installer will indicate any of the major prerequisites that may not yet be present on the system:

- .NET Framework 3.5
- Windows Remote Management 2.0
- Windows PowerShell version 2

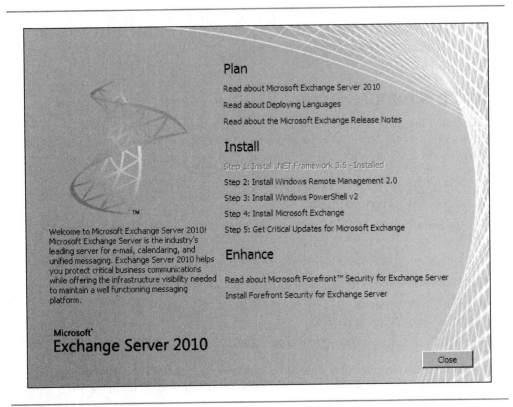

Plan

Read about Microsoft Exchange Server 2010

Read about Deploying Languages

Read about the Microsoft Exchange Release Notes

Install

Step 1: Install .NET Framework 3.5 - Installed

Step 2: Install Windows Remote Management 2.0

Step 3: Install Windows PowerShell v2

Step 4: Install Microsoft Exchange

Step 5: Get Critical Updates for Microsoft Exchange

Enhance

Read about Microsoft Forefront™ Security for Exchange Server

Install Forefront Security for Exchange Server

Welcome to Microsoft Exchange Server 2010! Microsoft Exchange Server is the industry's leading server for e-mail, calendaring, and unified messaging. Exchange Server 2010 helps you protect critical business communications while offering the infrastructure visibility needed to maintain a well functioning messaging platform.

Microsoft®
Exchange Server 2010

Close

Figure 18-1. Beginning the installation of Exchange Server

You can use the links provided for Steps 1 to 3 to install any of these missing components. Once each of these major prerequisites are installed, the links for Steps 1 to 3 will be unavailable. You can then install Exchange, as follows:

1. Click Step 4, Install Microsoft Exchange, to launch that option. The installer will initially ask you if you wish to install any additional language files, and you will then be prompted to accept the license agreement.

2. After you choose whether you want to send error reporting data to Microsoft, you see the setup screen, as shown in Figure 18-2. For this example, select Typical Exchange Server Installation.

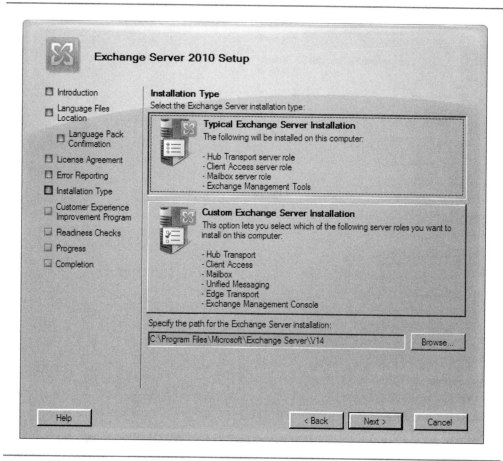

Figure 18-2.   Choosing the type of installation

NOTE   To install the Exchange Management Console on a client computer, choose Custom Exchange Server Installation, and then choose to install only the Management Console. You can then administer an Exchange Server from a client computer on your network.

3. You are prompted for the name of your organization, as shown in Figure 18-3. You can enter a name of up to 64 characters in length.

4. You are asked whether you will be supporting any client computers that use either Outlook 2003 or Entourage. Outlook 2003 and Entourage require a public folder database on the Exchange Server. As mentioned in the screen

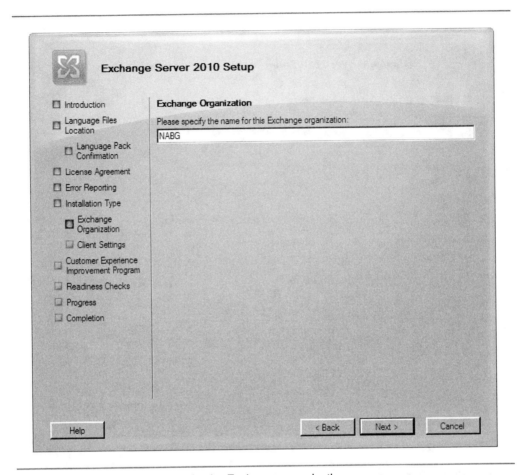

Figure 18-3. Entering a name for the Exchange organization

shown in Figure 18-4, if you choose No here, you can always add a public folder database to Exchange Server in the future in order to support these client applications.

5. You are asked whether you wish to join Microsoft's Customer Experience Improvement Program (see Figure 18-5). Choosing to do this will send to Microsoft statistical data about your organization's use of Exchange Server,

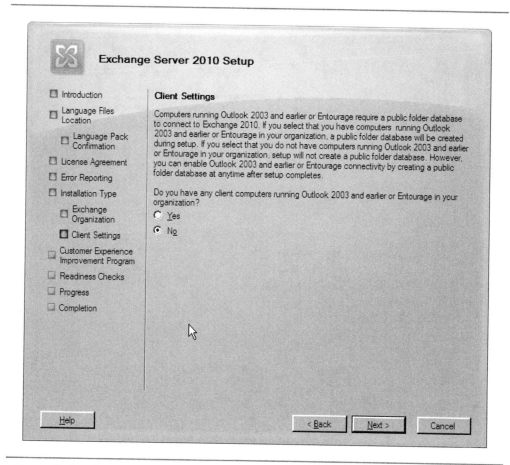

Figure 18-4. Support for Outlook 2003 or Entourage?

which Microsoft developers will use to help them understand how to best improve Exchange Server in the future. For this example, choose not to join the program at this time.

6. The Exchange Server 2010 setup program will perform a number of detailed checks of the server to ensure that all required software and patches are present on the system. It is typical for the program to find a number of items that need to be addressed, as demonstrated in Figure 18-6.

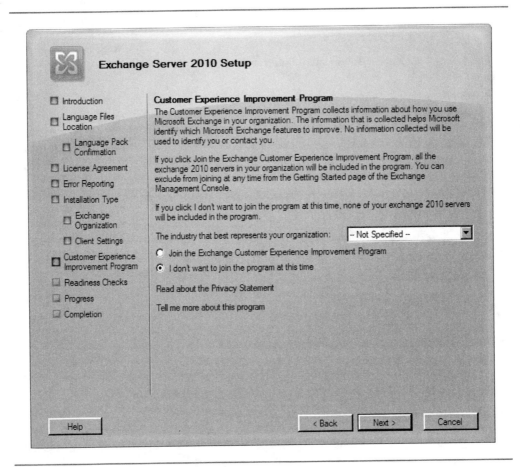

Figure 18-5.   Join the Exchange Customer Experience Program?

7. For each of the missing prerequisites, you can click the Recommended Action links to address each shortcoming. It may take a bit of time to work through them all, but it is fundamentally a straightforward process. After you have installed all of the required components in order for the Exchange Server Setup program to proceed, it's a good idea to first run Windows Update to ensure that you have the latest patches for all the added components, and then restart the system before proceeding with Exchange Server installation.

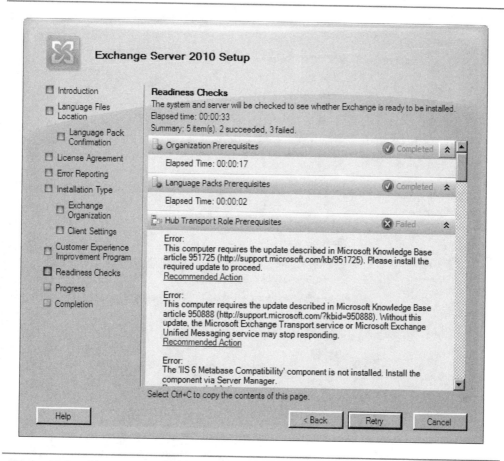

Figure 18-6.   More prerequisites!

TIP   One of the big prerequisites for most Exchange Server installations is Internet Information Services (IIS), which you will be prompted to add through the Server Manager. A large number of role services for IIS will also be required. As you progress through the Exchange Server prerequisites checks, periodically click the Retry button to have the system recheck the requirements.

8. Finally, you will see that you've completed all of the prerequisite role and feature installations, as shown in Figure 18-7. Click Install to complete the installation of Exchange Server.

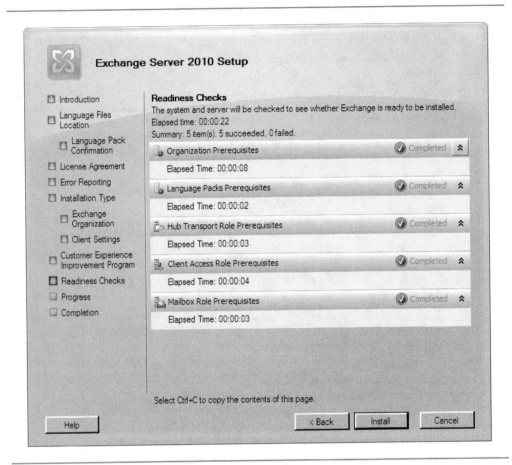

Figure 18-7.   Finally, ready to install Exchange Server

9. When the installation is complete (which will take around 15 to 30 minutes depending on the server hardware), you will see the completion screen shown in Figure 18-8. Make sure that the Finalize Installation Using the Exchange Management Console checkbox is selected before clicking Finish.

Setting Up Mailboxes

Once you get into the Exchange Management Console, you should first run a process to gather some information about your organization. To do this, click the second-to-top node in the Exchange Management Console, called Microsoft Exchange On-Premises.

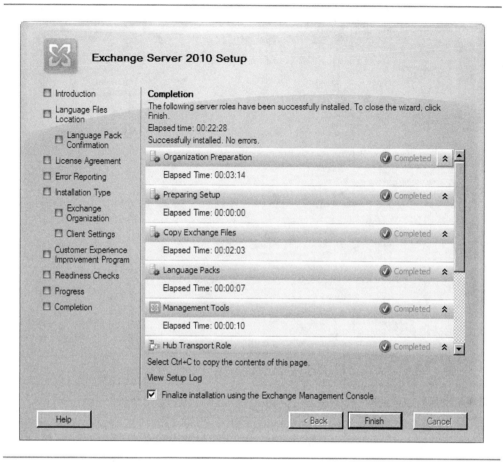

Figure 18-8.   Exchange Server is installed

In the Actions pane, you will see a link called Gather Organizational Information, as shown in Figure 18-9. Click this link to run the function. Doing so will allow you to see the default objects that have been created within the Exchange Management Console.

Creating a Mailbox

To create a mailbox in Exchange, follow these steps:

1. In the Exchange Management Console's left pane, navigate to Recipient Configuration, and then Mailbox. You will see the screen shown in Figure 18-10.

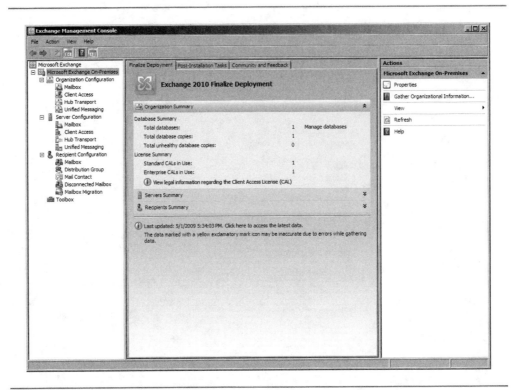

Figure 18-9.   First time in Exchange? Choose to gather organizational information.

2.   Click New Mailbox in the Actions pane. This starts the New Mailbox wizard, as shown in Figure 18-11. As you can see, along with user mailboxes, several other types of mailboxes can be created. Room and equipment mailboxes are assigned to a resource, rather than to a user account. They are used to allow users to easily schedule rooms and equipment when they set up meetings within Outlook. A linked mailbox is for larger organizations that have multiple Exchange Servers, and allows users from another Active Directory forest to establish a local, linked mailbox to their home mailbox.

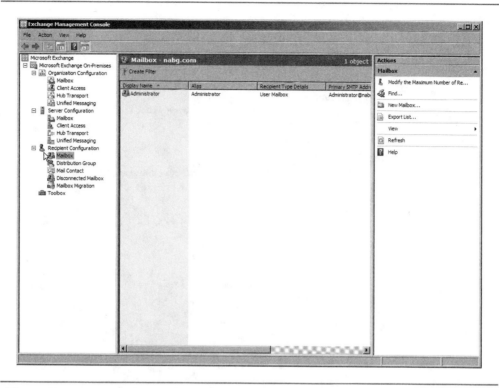

Figure 18-10.   Mailbox management in Exchange System Manager

3. For this example, ensure that User Mailbox is selected, and then click Next to continue. You will see the User Type screen, as shown in Figure 18-12. If you are creating a mailbox for a user account that you've already established, select Existing Users, and then click Add to locate the user account to which you want the new mailbox attached. Selecting New User will create the user in Active Directory and also create and attach a mailbox to the new user account.

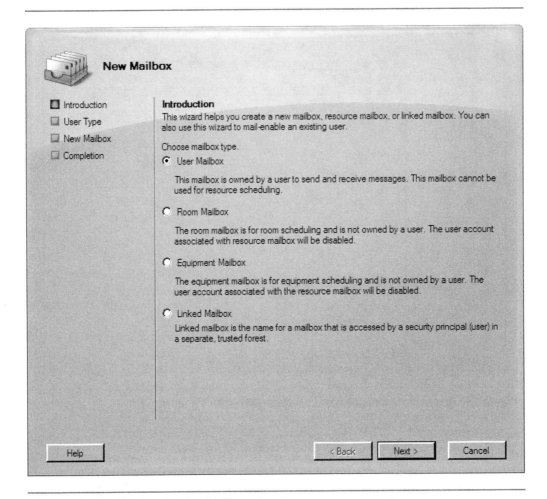

Figure 18-11.   Starting the New Mailbox wizard

4. For this example, select New User and click Next to continue. You now see the User Information screen, as shown in Figure 18-13. The example shows all the fields already complete for a test user. Go ahead and fill out the fields for a test user on your system, and then click Next to continue.

5. You are prompted for specific mailbox settings, as shown in Figure 18-14. Typically, the default settings are fine (especially for a test system), so go ahead and click Next to continue.

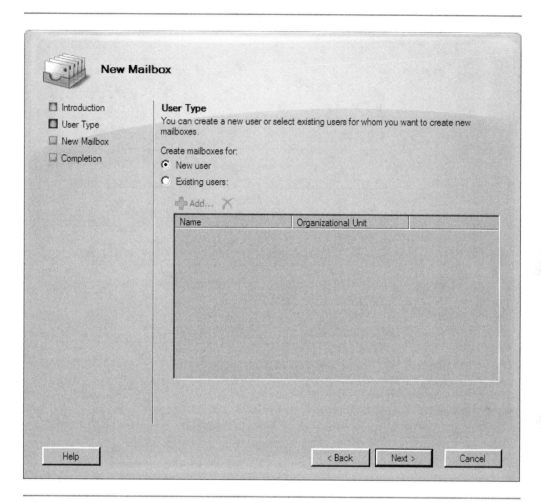

Figure 18-12.   Adding a user mailbox

6.   Finally, you will see a confirmation screen. Verify the information shown. If necessary, you can click Back to return to a screen and make changes. If it all looks good, click New and then Finish to complete the creation process.

Testing Your Mailbox

To enter the test mailbox that you just created, you'll use Outlook Web Access (OWA) on the server itself. Open Internet Explorer, and enter the URL https://*local_host_name*/owa/.

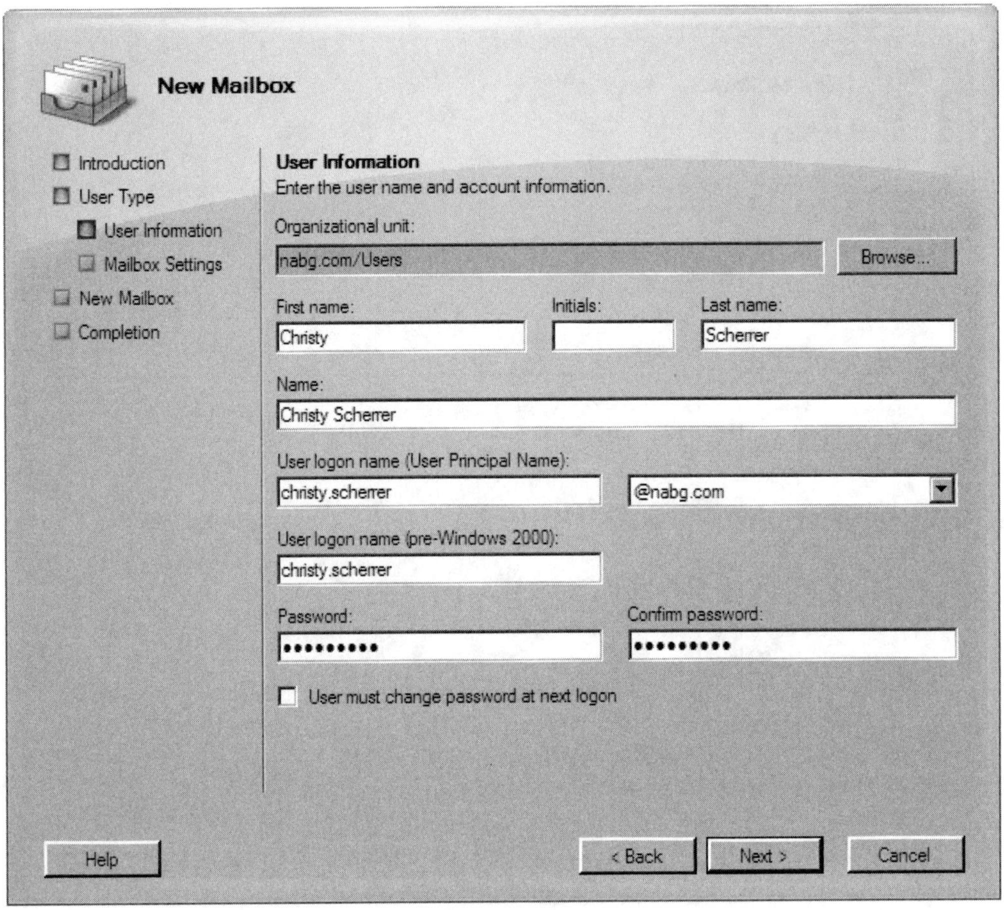

Figure 18-13.   Filling in user information for a new user with mailbox

You can use https://localhost/owa/ for testing, but Internet Explorer will likely complain that the certificate for localhost does not match the machine name. However, if you tell Internet Explorer to continue, it will work fine.

Figure 18-15 shows the login screen for the test user's mailbox. Complete the login fields as appropriate, and then click Log On to, well, log on.

You are next prompted to select your language and time zone. Choose the appropriate selections for your location (the defaults should be correct), and then click OK to complete the logon process.

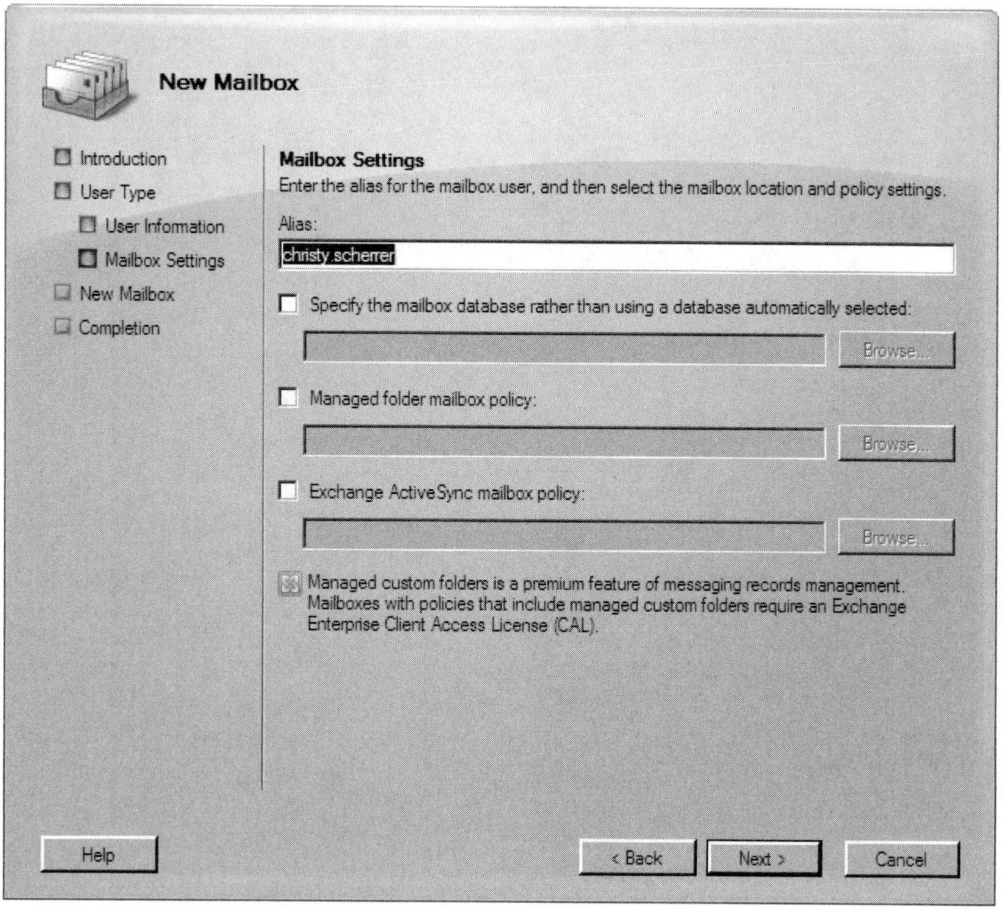

New Mailbox

- Introduction
- User Type
  - User Information
  - Mailbox Settings
- New Mailbox
- Completion

Mailbox Settings
Enter the alias for the mailbox user, and then select the mailbox location and policy settings.

Alias:

christy.scherrer

☐ Specify the mailbox database rather than using a database automatically selected:

[ ]   Browse...

☐ Managed folder mailbox policy:

[ ]   Browse...

☐ Exchange ActiveSync mailbox policy:

[ ]   Browse...

🔲 Managed custom folders is a premium feature of messaging records management. Mailboxes with policies that include managed custom folders require an Exchange Enterprise Client Access License (CAL).

Help   < Back   Next >   Cancel

Figure 18-14.   Specifying mailbox settings

You are now in OWA, as shown in Figure 18-16. For a web-based e-mail system, you'll find that it's very complete, and mimics regular Office Outlook to a large degree.

Spend some time exploring OWA. Although local users will typically use Microsoft Office Outlook to work with the Exchange Server, you'll find that OWA is an excellent remote-access solution to allow users to access e-mail, calendar information, and contacts stored on Exchange Server.

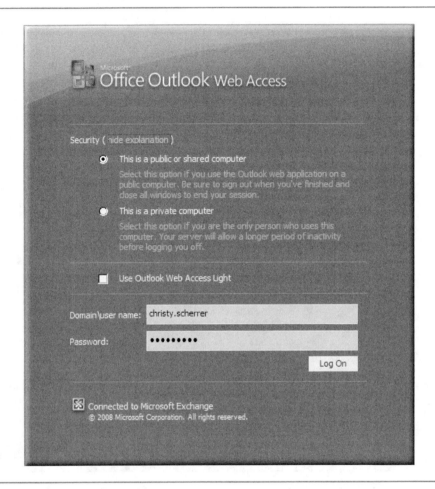

Figure 18-15.   Logging on to Outlook Web Access

Chapter Summary

In this chapter, you installed Exchange Server 2010 onto a Windows Server 2008 server with Active Directory. You also created a user account with an attached mailbox, and successfully accessed it using OWA. This demonstration showed that installing and using Exchange Server is not terribly difficult. However, if you will be working with a

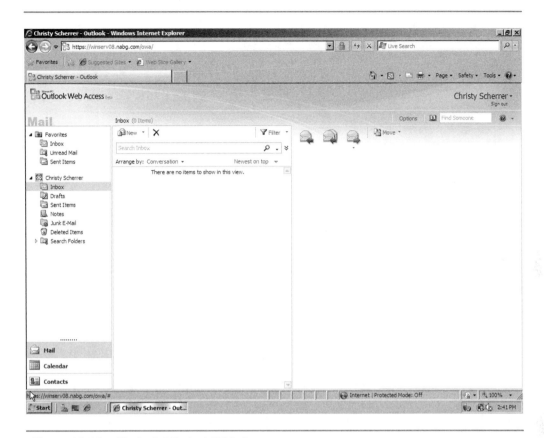

Figure 18-16.   You're in! Outlook Web Access

production system, you will definitely need much more information. One place to start is Microsoft's documentation, which you can find at http://technet.microsoft.com/exchange/.

While there are many applications and services available for Windows Server 2008, the services described in the next chapter are mainstays that are used in virtually every network. In Chapter 19 you learn about DHCP, DNS, remote access, Internet Information Services, and Windows Terminal Services, all of which are a part of Windows Server 2008.

Chapter 19

Understanding Other Windows Server 2008 Services

One of the strengths of Windows Server 2008 is that it can perform many functions and fill many roles. Not only is Windows Server 2008 a powerful and effective file server and print server, but it's also extremely capable of performing many other tasks right out of the box.

Chapters 16 and 17 explained how to set up Windows Server 2008 as a basic file server and print server, and how to administer Windows Server 2008 on a daily basis. To get the most out of Windows Server 2008, you need to know what additional services are available, how they work, and what they do. This chapter introduces some of the other services that come with Windows Server 2008. You can find detailed instructions for implementing these services in a book devoted to Windows Server 2008.

Exploring DHCP

If you've been involved with computers for long, you probably remember what it was like to manage TCP/IP addresses manually (and you might still do this now!). You needed to visit every computer on the network to set its TCP/IP address manually. You also had to keep track of which computers used which addresses, because you had a limited number of addresses with which to work. Plus, as you probably know, when two computers on a network try to use the same TCP/IP address, trouble quickly follows, and you must spend time sorting out these problems.

As discussed in Chapter 8, the Dynamic Host Configuration Protocol (DHCP) saves the day in such situations. A DHCP server is a computer on the network that keeps track of which TCP/IP addresses are available, and parcels them out to computers and other devices that boot up and request a TCP/IP address from the server. With a DHCP server, you don't need to worry about address conflicts or renumbering the addresses used on computers if your TCP/IP address range ever changes.

 NOTE   Because TCP/IP is the default protocol for Windows Server 2008-based networks and because Windows Server 2008 is designed to operate correctly over a TCP/IP-only network, DHCP services are installed with Windows Server 2008 by default. However, the DHCP services are not enabled by default, because you should not set up conflicting DHCP servers on a network.

To use DHCP, you must define a scope and other associated TCP/IP settings that the servers give to client computers. A *scope* is simply the range (or ranges) of TCP/IP addresses that the server is allowed to parcel out.

Among the associated TCP/IP settings that the server distributes are the addresses for Domain Name System (DNS) or Windows Internet Naming Service (WINS) servers also on the network. When a DHCP server assigns a TCP/IP address to a client computer, the address is said to be *leased*, and it remains assigned to that client computer for a set period of time. Leases are usually configured to last for two to seven days. (The default setting in Windows Server 2008 is eight days.) During this period, the assigned TCP/IP address is not given out to a different computer.

When a client computer boots up and joins the network, if it is configured to seek a DHCP server, the client computer does so while initializing its TCP/IP protocol stack. Any available DHCP servers respond to the client's request for an address with an available address from the DHCP server's address database. The client computer then uses this address for the duration of its lease.

The administrator can cancel and reassign TCP/IP information as necessary (usually, this is done after business hours, when the client computers are turned off). The administrator can then make changes to the DHCP scope information, which is then communicated to the clients when they reconnect to the network. In this way, you can easily make changes to information such as DNS server addresses or even TCP/IP address ranges without needing to visit all the computers.

Although DHCP is a great tool for managing TCP/IP addresses, you should use it only for client computers that do not host any TCP/IP services provided to other computers. For example, you would not want to set up a web server to use DHCP to get a dynamic TCP/IP address, because client computers wishing to connect to the web server would not be able to find the address when it changed. Instead, you should assign fixed addresses to computers that offer TCP/IP-enabled services either to the local network or through the Internet. You can assign these addresses in one of two ways:

- You can simply assign those computers fixed TCP/IP addresses locally and then set up *exclusion ranges* to the scope that the DHCP server manages, which prevents the DHCP server from using or offering those addresses to other computers.

- You can set up a *reservation* on the DHCP server, which forces the server always to assign the reserved address to a specific computer.

 TIP   It's a good idea to use static IP addresses for your network printers. Doing so makes troubleshooting printer connectivity problems easier.

Investigating DNS

As discussed in Chapter 8, DNS is a technology that allows easily remembered names to be mapped to TCP/IP addresses and ports. For instance, when you use a web browser and enter the address http://www.yahoo.com, you are using a DNS server to resolve the domain name www.yahoo.com to a particular TCP/IP address. Your web browser transparently uses the TCP/IP address to communicate with the server in question. The DNS system makes the Internet much easier to use than it otherwise would be. (Imagine how excited advertisers would be to say, "Visit our web site at http://65.193.55.38!")

Windows Server 2008 includes a full DNS server. In fact, a DNS server is required for Active Directory to function. If you install the first Active Directory server into a Windows Server 2008 domain, DNS services are automatically installed at the same time; otherwise, you must select them manually to add them.

A Windows Server 2008 running DNS services can manage your own domains and subdomains, and you can also set up multiple DNS servers that each manage a portion of the domain namespace. Of course, on small networks, it is possible—and probably desirable because of cost issues—to use only a single DNS server.

You manage the DNS services with the DNS Microsoft Management Console (MMC) plug-in, which you access by opening the Start menu and choosing Programs, Administrative Tools, then DNS. Figure 19-1 shows the DNS Manager window.

When you set up DNS for an organization, you first establish a root namespace (a virtual location in which domain names are stored), usually using the domain name you have registered for the Internet, such as omh.com. You can then create your own subdomains by prepending organizational or geographic units, such as italy.omh.com or accounting.omh.com.

Each DNS server is responsible for storing all the DNS names used for its managed namespace and for communicating any changes to other DNS servers. When you use multiple DNS servers to manage separate portions of your DNS namespace, each

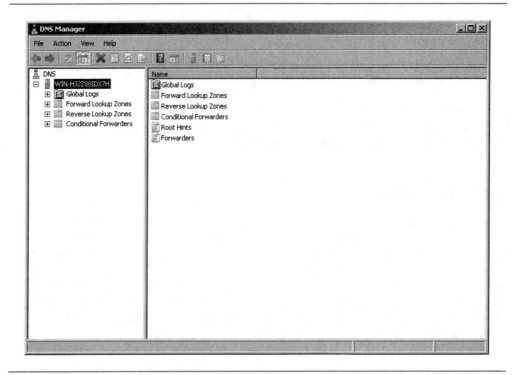

Figure 19-1.   Use the DNS Manager to manage DNS services.

DNS server manages a *zone*. Updates between different zones are called *zone transfers*. Windows Server 2008 DNS services support both full and incremental zone transfers. (Incremental zone transfers exchange only updated information, which cuts down on network traffic considerably on networks with large DNS namespaces.)

Because DNS is integral to Active Directory, it's important for you to establish redundancy for your DNS servers. Microsoft recommends that each domain controller also act as a DNS server, and you must have at least one primary and secondary DNS server for each managed zone.

Understanding RRAS

Routing and Remote Access Service (RRAS, pronounced "ar-razz") is a remote access technology. It includes routing capabilities that enable connections to the network over a public network, such as the Internet, using virtual private network (VPN) technology (discussed in Chapter 10). A VPN works by setting up a secure "tunnel" between a client and the RRAS server through which encrypted packets pass. The client computer dials up its normal Internet service provider (ISP), and then forms a secure VPN connection to the RRAS server over the Internet.

Remote access services under Windows Server 2008 are secure and offer considerable flexibility, so you can set them up to meet the requirements of your organization.

To administer RRAS, open the Start menu and choose Programs, Administrative Tools, then Routing and Remote Access to access the MMC plug-in. After the plug-in starts, right-click the server on which you want to enable remote access, and then choose Configure and Enable Routing and Remote Access. A wizard guides you through the process and enables you to choose whether to enable only remote access, only routing/ remote access, or both. Figure 19-2 shows the Routing and Remote Access MMC plug-in once RRAS has been enabled.

First, you must enable a user to access the network remotely, which you can do by editing the user's Properties dialog box (setting user properties is discussed in Chapter 17). Then you can configure RRAS to use a number of control features that enable you to keep remote access secure, including the following:

- Set times and days when remote access is operational.

- Set times and days when specific users or groups can use remote access.

- Limit access to only the RRAS server or to specific services on the network.

- Use callback features, where a remote client dials into the network and logs in. The network then disconnects the connection and dials the user back at a predefined phone number.

- Set access policies based on a remote client computer name or TCP/IP address.

Through the use of RRAS, you can easily set up Windows Server 2008 to provide important secure access services to remote users, both over dial-up connections and through the Internet.

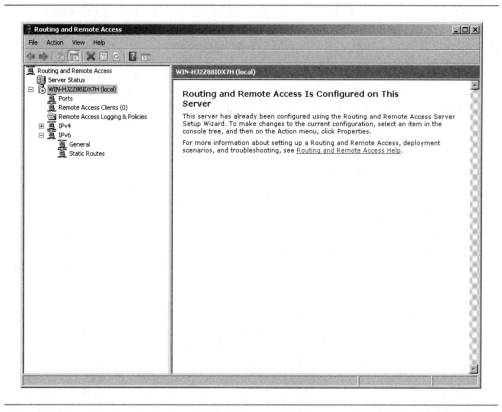

Figure 19-2. Use the Routing and Remote Access MMC plug-in to administer remote access.

Exploring IIS

Windows Server 2008 includes a set of Internet services that run as part of Internet Information Services (IIS). These include the following services:

- **Web**   IIS web services provide comprehensive web-hosting software. You can define multiple web sites with IIS, each one administered separately. For each site, you specify the directory in which the site's files can be found, as well as security settings for the site and performance parameters to optimize the performance of the web site.

- **File Transfer Protocol (FTP)**   IIS FTP services enable you to set up an FTP site on a Windows Server 2008 computer. You define the FTP directory, as well as whether directory listings will be shown in UNIX or MS-DOS style formats. You can also set security settings to allow or disallow different client computers or client networks access to the FTP server, and specify whether you will permit anonymous FTP logins.

■ **Network News Transfer Protocol (NNTP)**   The NNTP server in IIS enables you to set up your own Usenet-style site using the NNTP protocol. Clients can connect to your NNTP server using tools such as Outlook Express or other Usenet news readers.

■ **Simple Mail Transfer Protocol (SMTP)**   The SMTP server allows SMTP connections to be formed between the system running IIS and remote SMTP mail systems. SMTP is the standard protocol for exchanging e-mail over the Internet.

Each of these services can be started or stopped independently.

IIS is administered through the Internet Services Manager program found in the Administrative Tools program group. Figure 19-3 shows the Internet Information Services (IIS) Manager window.

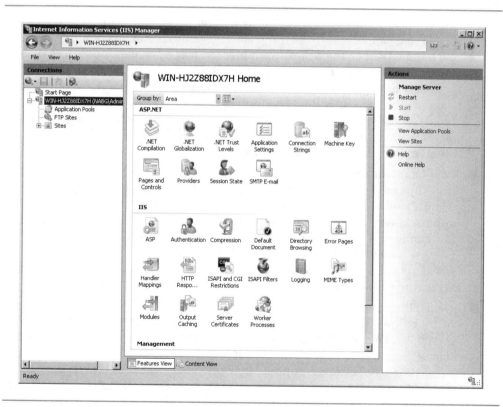

Figure 19-3.   The Internet Information Services Manager provides a single place to administer Internet services.

Understanding Windows Terminal Services

Windows Terminal Services is possibly one of the most powerful services discussed in this chapter. Using Terminal Services, you can set up a Windows Server 2008 almost as if it were a mainframe—where terminals can connect and all the work is performed on the central computer, which in this case would be a Windows Server 2008 computer.

A client computer connects to a terminal server using a TCP/IP connection—over a dial-up or a local area network (LAN) or wide area network (WAN) connection—and logs in. From then on, the client computer is responsible only for displaying screens and accepting keyboard and mouse input—all of the work is actually being done on the terminal server through the creation of a virtual Windows machine on the server. A terminal server can create many virtual Windows machines, each one carrying out its own tasks and running its own programs.

When would you use a Terminal Services connection to a network instead of a remote node connection, such as the remote node connections offered via RRAS? The answer depends on a number of factors, including the following:

- **Inadequate resources**   The remote computer doesn't have adequate resources to run some application or perform some task. By running its programs on the terminal server, the remote computer can take advantage of the terminal server's resources. For example, suppose that a particular application runs optimally only when it has 8GB of RAM with which to work. A Windows XP client with 1GB of RAM could connect to the terminal server (which has, say, 12GB of RAM) and run the application in question. Similarly, some applications might require many processors or direct access to large disk arrays or to some other centrally located resource to which the terminal server has access.

- **Low-bandwidth connections**   Over low-bandwidth connections, such as 33.6 Kbps modem connections, some applications work far more effectively using a remote control approach rather than a remote node approach (these approaches are explained in Chapter 10). Most remote access connections are low bandwidth, yet some applications need high bandwidth to work properly. Because a remote computer connected to a terminal server just needs to transfer display and input information, the application running on the terminal server can run much faster than it could over a remote node connection.

- **Demanding applications**   Some applications and tasks, such as administration of a Windows Server 2008, cannot be fully performed by another computer, even if it has a connection running at LAN speeds. Terminal Services allows a remote computer to run such applications if the computer has the appropriate permissions. For instance, suppose that your company has a remote network located somewhere in Asia, but the network is not large enough to justify a local administrator. Using Terminal Services, you could connect to that network over the company WAN and perform the necessary administrative tasks, such as configuring hard disks, shares, additional network protocols, and so forth.

Certain applications might require that you use Terminal Services. However, in any case, you might want to consider Terminal Services as an adjunct to your remote access services. If you have many remote users to support, you might find that some users have needs best served by remote node connections and some have needs best served by remote control connections. Running both services on your network will give you considerable flexibility in supporting remote users and solving any problems that they might encounter.

 CAUTION   If you implement Terminal Services, make sure that you carefully review Microsoft's license agreement and pricing models, which differ when you use Terminal Services.

Chapter Summary

The Windows family of servers, including Windows Server 2008, is perhaps the richest network operating system environment available today. While other products can perform all the tasks described in this chapter, none include all these capabilities out of the box; add-on purchases are required. Because of the richness with which Windows Server 2008 is packaged, you can more easily put together a server to meet nearly any need you may have. And because the various Windows Server 2008 services work so well together, you can easily implement nearly all these advanced services on just a single server!

This out-of-the-box flexibility and ease of administration are two of the reasons the Windows family of network operating systems has gained a leading share of the market, and why it's a safe bet Windows Server 2008 will continue this trend.

Although Windows servers probably run most servers in most companies, another popular choice is servers that run Linux. In the following three chapters you learn about installing and administering Fedora Linux, as well as installing an Apache web server under a Fedora Linux installation.

Chapter 20

Installing Linux

A key component of Linux's success has been the remarkable improvement in installation tools. What once was a mildly frightening process many years back has now become almost trivial.

Most default configurations in which Linux is installed are already capable of creating a server. This is, unfortunately, due to a slightly naïve design decision: A server serves everything, ranging from disk services to mail. Often, all of these services are turned on from the start (depending on the distribution you are using and whether it was installed as a workstation or a server). As you know, most servers are dedicated to performing one or two tasks, and any other installed services simply take up memory and slow performance.

This chapter discusses the installation process of Fedora Linux as it pertains to servers. This process has two objectives: to differentiate servers from client workstations and to streamline a server's operation based on its dedicated purpose.

You may be wondering why of all of the available Linux distributions, I chose to focus on Fedora. The answer is simple: Fedora is both popular and technically sound. It is friendly to a lot of different types of users and serves many uses. (That the entire distribution is available free from the Internet is also a plus!) As you become more experienced with Linux, you might find other distributions interesting and should look into them. After all, one of the war cries of Linux users everywhere is that freedom of choice is crucial. You should never feel locked into a proprietary system.

Configuring Computer Hardware for Linux

Before you get into the actual installation phase, you need to consider the hardware on which the system will run and how the server will best configured to provide the services you need from it. Let's start by examining hardware issues.

Hardware Compatibility

As with any operating system, determining which hardware configurations work before starting an installation process is prudent. Each commercial vendor publishes a list of compatible hardware and makes that list available on its web site. Be sure you obtain the latest versions of these lists so you are confident that the vendor fully supports the hardware you are using. In general, most popular Intel-based configurations work without difficulty. Red Hat's certified hardware compatibility list is at http://bugzilla .redhat.com/hwcert. For Novell's SUSE Linux. you can search compatibility at http:// developer.novell.com/yessearch/Search.jsp.

TIP   Some computer manufacturers sell computers with Linux preloaded on them. When you purchase a computer like this, you can usually be confident that the computer manufacturer has ensured that the hardware is fully compatible with the installed Linux version, and that the appropriate Linux drivers are loaded and work properly.

Because Fedora is a fast-moving distribution, and because development is occurring at a breakneck pace, there is no hardware list available for Fedora Linux. However, you can read more about hardware compatibility with Fedora at http://fedoraproject.org/wiki/HCL. Note also that, generally speaking, hardware that works with Red Hat Linux will typically work with Fedora.

A general suggestion that applies to all operating systems is to avoid bleeding-edge hardware and software configurations. Although these appear impressive, they have not undergone the maturing process that some of the slightly older hardware has experienced. For servers, the temptation to use a bleeding-edge configuration usually isn't an issue because a server has no need for the latest and greatest toys, such as fancy video cards. After all, the main goal is to provide a highly available server for the network's users, not to play the latest games.

Server Design

When a system becomes a server, its stability, availability, and performance are significant issues. These three issues are usually addressed through the purchase of more hardware, which is unfortunate. Paying thousands of dollars extra to get a system capable of achieving all three objectives when the desired level of performance could have been attained from existing hardware with a little tuning is a waste. With Linux, achieving these objectives without overspending is not hard. Even better, the gains are outstanding!

The most significant design decision that you must make when managing a server configuration is not technical, but administrative. You should design a server *not* to be friendly to casual users. This means without any cute multimedia tools, sound card support, or fancy web browsers (when possible). In fact, your organization should make a rule that casual use of a server is strictly prohibited. This rule should apply not only to site users, but to site administrators as well.

Another important aspect of designing a server is making sure that it has a good environment. As a systems administrator, you must ensure the physical safety of your servers by keeping them in a separate, physically secure room. The only access to the servers for nonadministrative personnel should be through the network. The server room itself should be well ventilated, cool, and locked. Failing to ensure such a physical environment is an accident waiting to happen. Systems that overheat and helpful users who "think" they know how to fix problems can be as great a danger (arguably an even greater danger) to server stability as bad software. Moreover, Linux is particularly vulnerable to hacking at its command prompt.

Once the system is well secured behind locked doors, installing battery backup is also crucial. This backup serves two key purposes. The first purpose is to keep the system running during a power failure so that it can gracefully shut down, thereby avoiding the loss of any files. The second is to ensure that voltage spikes, drops, and various noises don't interfere with the health of your system.

To improve your server situation, you can take the following specific actions:

■ Take advantage of the fact that the graphical user interface (GUI) is uncoupled from the core operating system and avoid starting X Window System unless someone needs to sit on the console and run an application. After all, X Window System, like any other application, requires memory and CPU time to work, both of which are better off going to the server processes instead.

■ Determine which functions you want the server to perform and disable all other functions. Not only are unused functions a waste of memory and CPU time, but they are also just another security issue that you need to address.

■ Linux, unlike some other operating systems, enables you to choose the features that you want in the kernel. The default kernel you get is already reasonably well tuned, so you shouldn't need to adjust it. If you do need to change a feature or upgrade a kernel, though, be picky about what you add and what you leave out. Make sure that you need a feature before including it.

Server Uptime

All this chatter about taking care of servers and making sure that silly things don't cause them to crash stems from a longstanding UNIX philosophy: *Uptime is good. More uptime is better.*

The **uptime** command tells the user how long the system has been running since its last boot, how many users are currently logged in, and how much load the system is experiencing. The latter two statistics are useful measures necessary for daily system health and long-term planning. For example, if server load has been staying consistently high, you should consider a more capable server.

But the all-important number is how long the server has been running since its last reboot. Long uptimes are a sign of proper care, maintenance, and, from a practical standpoint, system stability. You often find UNIX administrators boasting about their server's uptimes the way you hear car buffs boast about horsepower. This focus on uptime is also why you hear UNIX administrators cursing at Windows installations that require a reboot for every little change. In contrast, you'll be hard-pressed to find any changes to a UNIX system that require a reboot in order to take effect.

Dual-Booting Issues

If you are new to Linux, you might not be ready to commit the use of a complete system for the sake of "test driving." Because the people who built Linux understand that we live in a heterogeneous world, all distributions of Linux have been designed so that they can be installed on separate partitions of your hard disk, while leaving other partitions alone. Typically, this means that Microsoft Windows can coexist on a computer that also can run Linux. Additionally, many Linux distributions can be run from a bootable "live" CD-ROM, which lets you run a fully functional build of the Linux distribution, without affecting your computer's existing installed operating system. If you like the Linux distribution, there is usually a simple procedure you can run from within the live CD environment to install that distribution to the hard disk.

Because the focus of this chapter is server installations, this section will not cover the details of building a dual-boot system. Anyone with a little experience in creating partitions on a disk should be able to figure out how to build such a system. If you are having difficulty, you can refer to the installation guide that came with your distribution or one of the many beginners' guides to Linux.

To repartition a system that has already had Windows installed on it, without needing to reformat the disk and rebuild from scratch, you can use a commercial software program such as Norton's PartitionMagic.

Installing Fedora Linux

This section describes how to install Fedora Linux (version 10) on a stand-alone system. The section takes a liberal approach to the process, installing all the tools possibly relevant to server operations.

Before you begin the actual installation procedure, you need to decide how you will run the installation program.

Choosing an Installation Method

With the improved connectivity and speed of both local area networks and Internet connections, an increasingly popular option is to perform installations over the network, rather than using a local CD-ROM. Network installations can be a great convenience when installing a large number of hosts.

> **TIP** In UNIX (or Linux) parlance, a *host* is any computer on a network, regardless of whether the computer is functioning as a server or as a workstation.

Typically, server installations aren't well suited to being automated, because each server usually has a unique task and thus a slightly different configuration. For example, a server dedicated to handling logging information sent to it over the network will have especially large partitions set up for the appropriate logging directories. This is in contrast to a file server that performs no logging of its own.

Because servers are not usually set up using a "one-size-fits-all" approach, the focus in this section is exclusively on the technique for installing a system from a CD-ROM. After you have gone through the installation process from a CD-ROM once, you will find performing the network-based installations straightforward.

Starting the Installation

Usually, you will start the installation by downloading a copy of Fedora Linux and burning it onto a CD-ROM. Here are the steps for installing that copy:

1. To start the installation process, boot off the CD-ROM. This will boot Fedora Linux in its live mode, in which a fully operating system will start on the system, as shown in Figure 20-1. (If you like, you can explore Fedora's menus and basic applications at this point, before continuing with the installation.)

2. Double-click the Install to Hard Drive icon on the desktop. This launches the Fedora installation program.

3. You are prompted for the language to use when installing. By default, U.S. English is selected. Click Next to continue.

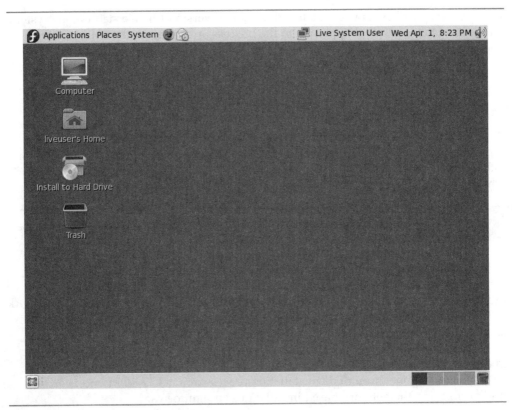

Figure 20-1.   Fedora Linux started in live mode

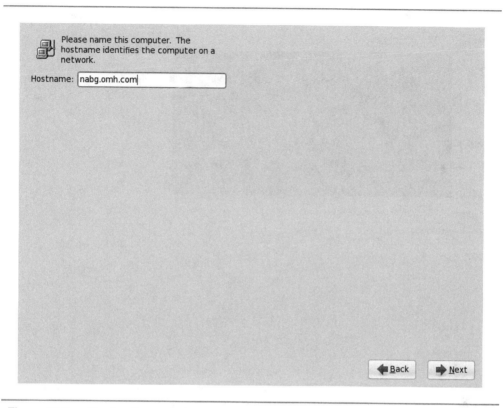

Please name this computer. The hostname identifies the computer on a network.

Hostname: nabg.omh.com

Back   Next

Figure 20-2. Naming the computer

4. You are prompted to name the computer, in the format *computer_name.domain*, as shown in Figure 20-2. Enter an appropriate name for your computer, and then click Next to continue.

5. Choose the time zone in which you are located, as shown in Figure 20-3. You can click the map until a city in the same time zone as you is located, or you can choose from the available options in the drop-down menu. Once you have selected the time zone, click Next to continue.

6. You are prompted to enter a password for the system's *root account*, which is a user named *root* that has full and complete access to change anything about the system. It is similar to the administrator password on a Windows server.

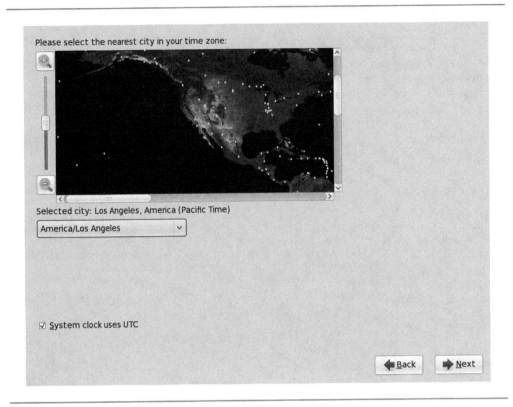

Please select the nearest city in your time zone:

Selected city: Los Angeles, America (Pacific Time)

America/Los Angeles

☑ System clock uses UTC

← Back   → Next

Figure 20-3. Choosing a time zone

Accordingly, you should choose a good, strong password for the root account. Enter your password where prompted, and also in the confirmation field. Click Next to continue.

7. You now need to partition the hard disk for the computer. This example assumes that you are installing Fedora on a system with a blank hard disk. You will be asked to confirm that anything existing on the hard disk will be erased by the partitioning process. When you continue, the default option is "Remove Linux Partitions on selected drives and create default layout." I recommend this option. If you would like to see what the default partitioning scheme looks like, select the Review and Modify Partitioning Layout checkbox before clicking Next to continue. Figure 20-4 shows an example of a default partitioning scheme on a 10GB disk.

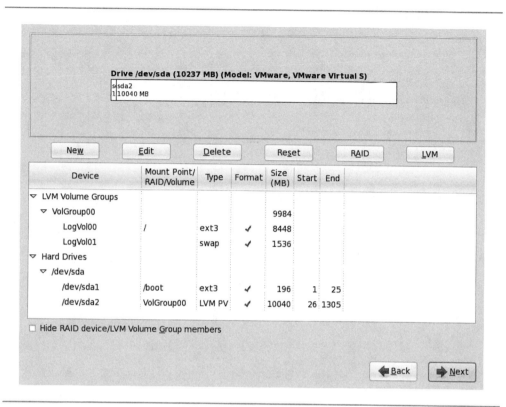

Figure 20-4.   Default partitioning scheme on a 10GB disk

NOTE   While the Fedora installer lets you customize the partitioning scheme in a variety of ways, for most uses, the default choices will work best. If you decide to install Linux for production use, you will want to explore other options in the partitioning, such as setting up RAID disk arrays.

8. After confirming the creation of the partitioning scheme you have selected, you will see the boot loader installation screen, as shown in Figure 20-5. Here, you can customize the boot loader to enable the booting of multiple operating systems from the system, or to set a password that must be entered before the system will boot. For this example, accept the default options and click Next to continue.

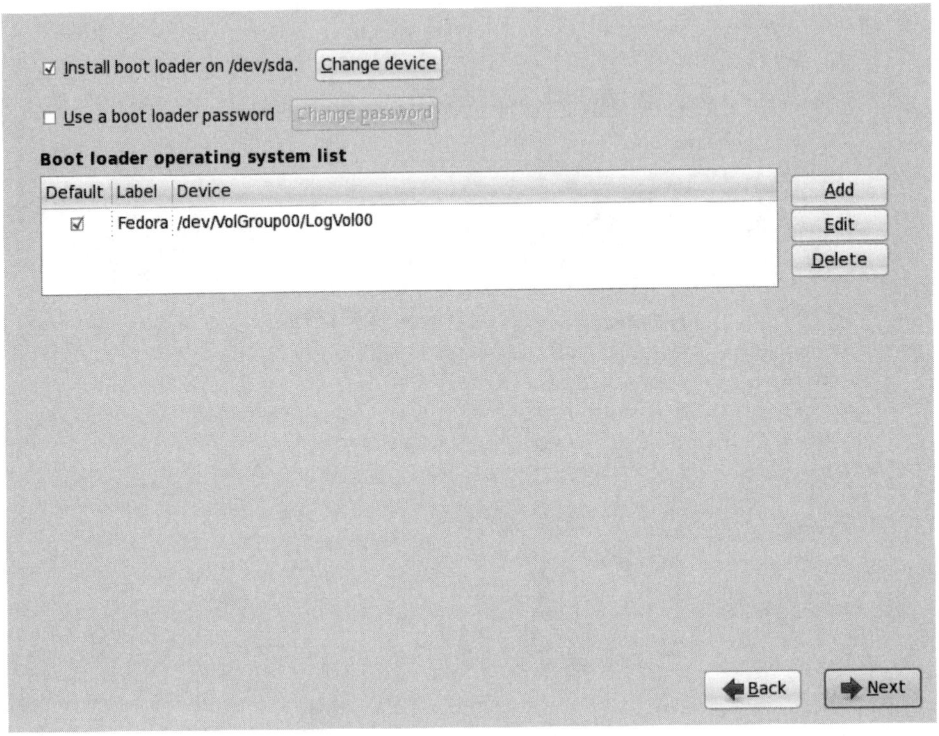

Figure 20-5.   Configuring the boot loader options

At this point, Fedora will be installed onto the hard disk. Typically, the process is fairly quick and should take around 5 to 10 minutes. When it's complete, you are prompted to restart the system. After the system restarts, you will need to do some initial configuration, as described in the next section.

Initially Configuring Fedora Linux

When your new Fedora Linux system boots for the very first time after the main installation, you are walked through various initial configuration options. Initially, you will see the screen shown in Figure 20-6. The left pane lists the basic configuration areas.

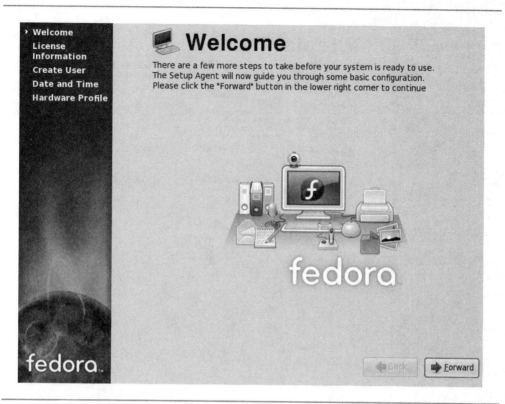

Figure 20-6.   Initially configuring Fedora Linux

Here is the procedure for completing the initial configuration of Fedora:

1. First, you are prompted to accept the software license. As you will read, there are no restrictions on using, copying, or modifying the Fedora Linux code. However, there are restrictions on redistribution of the code, use of the Fedora trademarks, and other matters. If you wish, you can read the full agreement at http://fedoraproject.org/wiki/Legal/Licenses/LicenseAgreement.

2. You are prompted to create a user account, as shown in Figure 20-7. It is important to avoid using the root account except for when you absolutely need it. Instead, create a user account for yourself to use, even if you are the only person using the system.

Figure 20-7.   Creating your nonadministrative user account

3. Check the time and date for the system, as shown in Figure 20-8. If this computer will not be connected to the Internet, update the time and date, if necessary. Otherwise, click the Network Time Protocol tab and then select the Enable Network Time Protocol checkbox.

4. Finally, you are prompted to submit a profile of the hardware on which you have installed Fedora Linux to the developers of the system. Doing so helps the developers understand the hardware that people are using for Fedora Linux, and allows them to focus their efforts on supporting the most popular hardware choices being made. Make whichever choice you prefer, and then click Finish to complete the configuration.

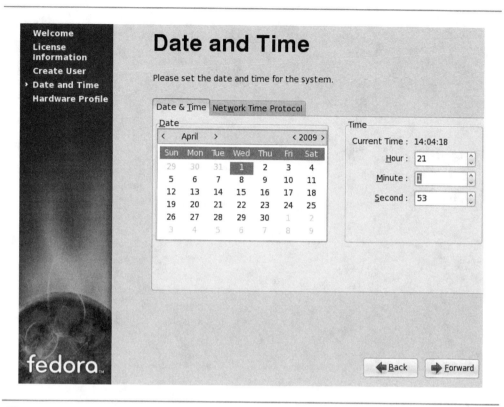

Figure 20-8.   Adjusting the system's date and time

Logging in to Fedora Linux

After completing the configuration, you will see the normal login screen for Fedora Linux, as shown in Figure 20-9. This screen will display all of the normal user accounts available on the system. If you followed the procedure outlined in this chapter, you will have only one user account (aside from the root account, which is not shown by default).

To choose an account to log in with, double-click the name in the login screen. You will be prompted for your password. After you've successfully logged in, you will see the Fedora desktop.

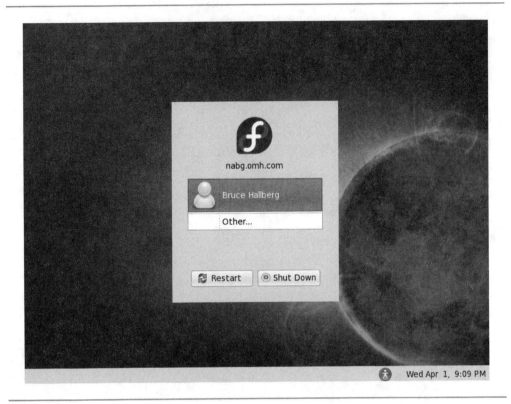

Figure 20-9.   Logging in to Fedora Linux

And You're Finished!

That's it! The installation process is over. I recommend you spend time exploring Fedora's menus and various functions.

Keep in mind that if you make a change that will be systemwide and is considered an administrative change to the system, you will be prompted for the root password you set up during the installation. This process of prompting you for the root password for important system changes is how most Linux distributions, such as Fedora, ensure that a valid system administrator is making the change, and not some random person who happened to connect to the computer remotely over a network.

If It Just Won't Work Right

You've gone through the installation procedure, maybe more than once. This book said it should work. The installation manual said it should work. The Linux guru with whom you spoke last week said it should work. But it's just not working.

In the immortal words of Douglas Adams, "Don't panic!" No operating system installs smoothly 100 percent of the time. (Yes, not even Mac OS X!) Hardware doesn't always work as advertised, combinations of hardware conflict with each other, or that CD-ROM that your friend burned for you has errors on it. (Remember that it is legal for your friend to burn you a copy of most Linux distributions!) Or, as much as you might hope that it does not, the software has a bug.

With Linux, you have several paths that you can take to get help. If you have purchased a Linux distribution, such as from Red Hat or Novell, you can always call the distribution's tech support lines and talk to a knowledgeable person who is dedicated to working through the problem with you. If you didn't purchase a box set, most Linux distributions have rich help available online. For Fedora, you can find a lot of helpful documents at http://fedoraproject.org.

Chapter Summary

In this chapter, you learned about the process of installing a popular and very capable Linux distribution. The steps to installing Fedora Linux are quite straightforward. If you ever witnessed the procedure for prior versions, you will be aware of how much easier the process has become, with fewer configuration choices to make to begin working with the operating system. What makes Linux wonderful is that, even though those options are no longer part of the installation process, you can still change them and tweak them to your heart's delight once you complete the installation and start the system.

The next chapter continues with the system as it was installed here, and shows you how to perform basic administrative tasks within Fedora Linux.

Chapter 21

Introduction to Linux
Systems Administration

When Linux first came out in 1991, you had to be either a systems administrator with a lot of time or a good hacker to be able to use the system effectively. While this was fine for folks who were willing to expend the effort, it wasn't great for the vast majority who saw potential for using Linux but shied away from the learning curve. Thankfully, many Linux distribution developers have realized this shortcoming and have gone to great lengths to make Linux not only easy to install, but relatively painless to administer.

This chapter provides an overview of some of the basic administrative chores necessary to keep a Linux server running smoothly. Although it is by no means a complete guide to systems administration, this chapter will get you started in the right direction.

This chapter assumes that you have Fedora Linux already installed and the graphical user interface (X Window System) configured. The chapter also assumes that you are logging in to the system and running all programs as the user root.

CAUTION   The root user is almighty under Linux. If you are familiar with Windows server, you can think of root as being somewhat equivalent to the administrator account. With root access, you have full control of the system, including the ability to break it. If you are new to Linux, you should definitely take some time to practice on a nonproduction system before trying things out on your system's users.

This chapter is divided into two main sections. The first section deals with configuring Fedora Linux with graphical tools for systems administration functions. The second part of the chapter deals with the command-line interface. While this section isn't about systems administration per se, the commands it covers are the foundation for basic systems administration tasks.

Managing Fedora Linux with Graphical Tools

The graphical tools are the basis for most of the administrative tasks you will need to do. They handle user administration, network administration, disk administration, and so on. What makes these tools especially helpful is that they provide a very consistent interface for Linux administrative tasks. The only downside is that, like other graphical user interfaces (GUIs), these tools have limitations. You might find that for more advanced tasks, you will need to use the command-line interface, as described later in this chapter.

Managing Users

To take advantage of the multiuser nature of Linux, you need to be able to add, edit, and remove users from the system. You can perform all of these actions through the User Manager program, as follows:

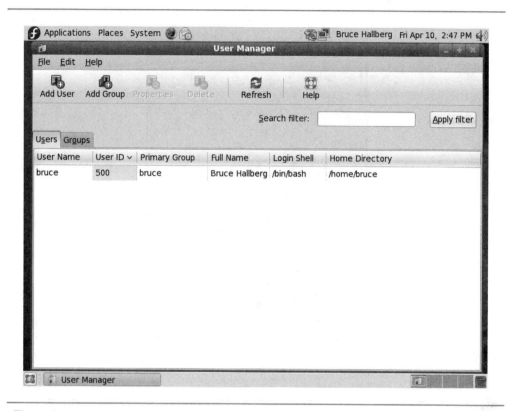

Figure 21-1. Use the User Manager program for user administration.

1. Open the System menu and choose Administration, then Users and Groups. After being prompted for the system's root password, you see the User Manager program window shown in Figure 21-1.

2. Click the Add User button in the toolbar at the top of the window to open the Create New User dialog box, as shown in Figure 21-2.

3. In the Create New User dialog box, you must, at a minimum, fill in the login name and a password for the user. The user's home directory and type of shell will be filled in automatically, and you can accept those default options. Click OK to create the user account.

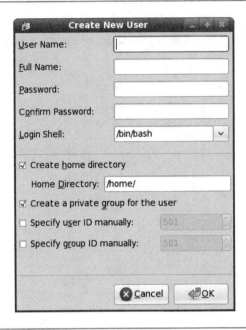

Figure 21-2.   Creating a new user

 TIP   As discussed in Chapter 11, picking a good password means not using a dictionary word (including foreign language words). One technique is to take the first letter of each word in a phrase. For example, "Snacking on Oatmeal Squares is good for you" translates into SoOSigfy. The phrase is easy to remember, and the resulting password is cryptic. Another strategy is to take a word of six letters or more and substitute two or more letters with numbers. For example, the password le11ers (with ones in the middle instead of the letter *l*) is not a bad password. But be warned that sophisticated password-cracking programs often will try these sorts of number substitutions within dictionary words.

Once the account is created, you can double-click it in the list of user accounts in order to set some additional properties for the account through the User Properties dialog box, as shown in Figure 21-3:

- The User Data tab lets you change the user's name, password, home directory, and login shell.

- The Account Info tab lets you set an account expiration date for the user, if you desire, and also to lock the user account if that becomes necessary for any reason.

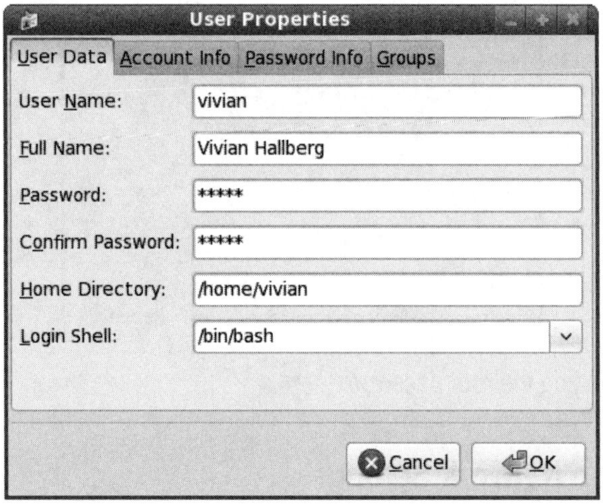

Figure 21-3.   Setting user properties

- The Password Info tab lets you set password expiration settings for the selected user account.
- The Groups tab lets you assign security group membership to the selected user account.

To remove a user, from the main User Manager window, select the user account to be deleted, and then click the Delete button in the toolbar.

Changing Root's Password

As mentioned in the previous chapters, the root user is a special user who has a lot of power on the system. Obviously, an account with this much power needs to be protected with a good password. If you think that someone might have gotten the *root* password, or that someone who had the *root* password should no longer have it (for example, a former employee), you should immediately change it.

To change the root password on a system, from the System menu, choose Administration, then Root Password. After being prompted for the current root password, you see the dialog box shown in Figure 21-4. Enter the new password to use for the root account in the two fields provided. The program will not let you change the root password if both entries do not match exactly. (Remember that Fedora Linux, like all UNIX operating systems, uses case-sensitive passwords.) Click OK to complete the change.

Figure 21-4. Changing the root password

Configuring Common Network Settings

Linux is very much at home in a networked environment. In fact, its design from the onset supports its use on a network. Networks are dynamic, and Linux makes it easy to change the network configuration to accommodate the changes in the network.

You manage network settings through the Network Configuration window, as shown in Figure 21-5. To access this window, open the System menu, choose Administration, and then choose Network.

Figure 21-5. Use the Network Configuration window to change the network configuration.

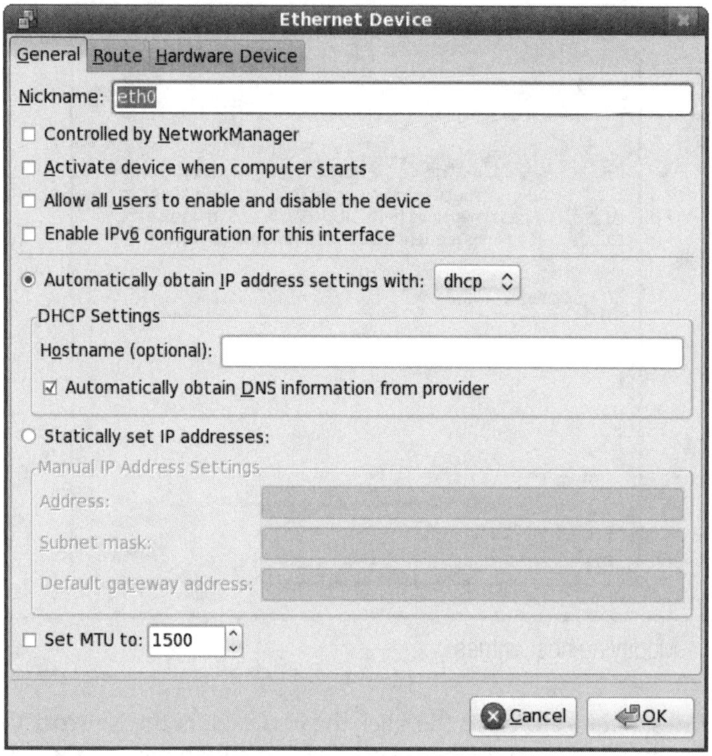

Figure 21-6.   Changing Ethernet device settings

Changing Your IP Address

In most cases, if a system is configured to use DHCP to acquire its IP address, you should not change the IP address setting. However, at times you will need to set a static IP address on a system. To change the IP address of your system, click the Edit button in the toolbar at the top of the Network Configuration window. This brings up the Ethernet Device dialog box, as shown in Figure 21-6.

Click the Statically Set IP Addresses option button. Then enter the appropriate IP address information in the Manual IP Address Settings fields. Once you have made all of your selections, click OK to accept the changes.

Adding Entries to the /etc/hosts File

The /etc/hosts file contains a list of hostname-to-IP mappings. Most systems use this list so that they can find other machines on the network if DNS ever becomes inaccessible. Typical entries include the host itself, servers for common services (such as the DNS server), and gateway entries.

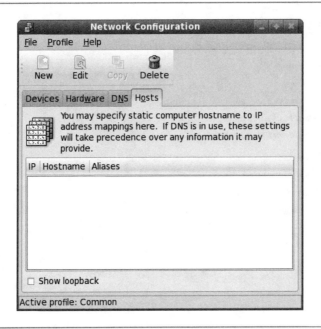

Figure 21-7.   Modifying host entries

To add entries to the /etc/hosts file, click the Hosts tab in the Network Configuration window, as shown in Figure 21-7. Then click the New button to open the Add/Edit Hosts Entry dialog box, as shown in Figure 21-8. Enter the appropriate information into the Address and Hostname fields, and if desired, the Aliases field. Then click OK to save your changes.

Changing the DNS Client Configuration

If your system needs to work with a larger network (such as the Internet), it is a good idea to configure your system to point to a DNS server so that it can resolve host names

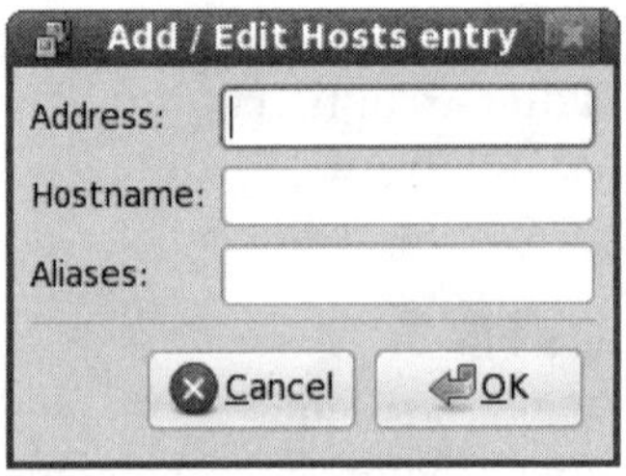

Figure 21-8.   Adding a new host to the hosts file

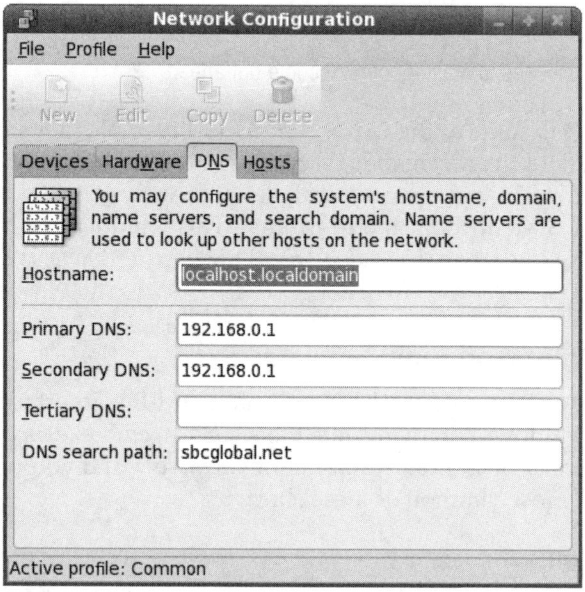

Figure 21-9.   Configuring a system's DNS settings

to IP addresses, and vice versa. Many times, the appropriate DNS servers to use are automatically assigned through the DHCP process, but if necessary, you can control these settings using the Network Configuration window.

Click the DNS tab in the Network Configuration window to see the DNS configuration of the computer, as shown in Figure 21-9. Enter the IP addresses for the DNS servers you want to use in the Primary DNS, Secondary DNS, and Tertiary DNS fields. Close the Network Configuration dialog box to commit these changes.

Mastering Linux Command-Line Basics

Historically, the aspect of UNIX that makes it so powerful and flexible has been the options available through the command line. Casual observers of UNIX gurus are often astounded at how a few carefully entered commands can result in powerful actions. Unfortunately, this power comes at the expense of ease of use. For this reason, GUIs have proliferated and have become the de facto standard for so many tools.

As you become more experienced, however, you will find that it is difficult for GUIs to present all of the available options to a user, because doing so would make the interface just as complicated as the command-line equivalent. Thus, the GUIs have remained overly simplified, and experienced users have needed to resort to the command line.

> **TIP** Before you get into a "which interface is better" holy war with someone, remember that both types of interfaces serve a purpose, with each having weaknesses as well as benefits. In the end, the person who chooses to master both will come out ahead.

This section covers some of the Linux command-line tools that are most crucial for day-to-day work. All of the commands discussed in this section are to be performed in a terminal window. You can open a terminal window by opening the Applications menu and choosing System Tools, then Terminal. This window displays a prompt that looks something like [root@*hostname* /root]#, where *hostname* is the name of your machine.

Working from the Command Line

One of the difficulties in moving to the Linus command-line interface, especially if you are used to using Windows command-line tools such as cmd.exe, is dealing with a shell that has a great number of shortcuts that might surprise you if you're not careful. This section reviews the most common of these shortcuts.

Filename Expansion

Under UNIX-based shells such as bash, you expand wildcards seen on the command line *before* passing them as a parameter to the application. This is in sharp contrast to the default mode of operation for DOS-based tools, which often need to perform their own wildcard expansion. This also means that you must be careful where you use the wildcard characters.

The wildcard characters themselves are identical to those in cmd.exe. The asterisk (*) matches against all filenames, and the question mark (?) matches against single characters. If you need to use these characters as part of another parameter, you can "escape" them by placing a backslash (\) in front of them. This character will cause the shell to interpret a wildcard as just another character.

Environment Variables as Parameters

You can use environment variables as parameters on the command line. This means that issuing the parameter $FOO will result in passing the value of the FOO environment variable instead of the string "$FOO."

Multiple Commands

Under the bash shell, it is possible to execute multiple commands on the same line by separating them with a semicolon (;). For example, suppose that you want to execute the following sequence of commands on a single line:

```
[root@ford /root]# ls -l
[root@ford /root]# cat /etc/hosts
```

You could instead type the following:

```
[root@ford /root]# ls -l ;cat /etc/hosts
```

Backticks

How's *this* for wild: you can make the output of one program the parameter of another program. Sound bizarre? Well, it's time to get used to it—this is one of the most creatively used features available in all UNIX shells.

A backtick (`) enables you to embed commands as parameters to other commands. A common instance of the use of this character is to pass a number sitting in a file as a parameter to the **kill** command. A typical instance of this occurs with the DNS server *named*. When this server starts, it writes its process identification number into the file /var/run/named.pid. Thus, the generic way of killing the *named* process is to look at the number in /var/run/named.pid using the **cat** command, and then issue the **kill** command with that value, as in the following example:

```
root@ford /root]# cat /var/run/named.pid
253
[root@ford /root]# kill 253
```

One problem with killing the *named* process this way is that you cannot automate the killing, so you are counting on the fact that a human will read the value in /var/ run/ named.pid and then kill the number. The second problem isn't so much a problem as it is a nuisance—it takes two steps to stop the DNS server.

Using backticks, however, you can combine the steps into one and do so in a way that you can automate. Here's the backticks version:

```
[root@ford # kill`cat /var/run/named.pid`
```

When the bash shell sees this command, it will first run **cat /var/run/named.pid** and store the result. It will then run the **kill** command and pass the stored result to it—all in one graceful step.

Environment Variables

The concept of environment variables is almost the same under Linux as it is under Windows. The only difference is in how you set, view, and remove the variables.

Printing Environment Variables

To list all of your environment variables, use the **printenv** command, as in the following example:

```
[root@ford /root]# printenv
```

To show a specific environment variable, specify the variable as a parameter to **printenv**. For example, to see the environment variable USER, type the following:

```
[root@ford /root]# printenv USER
```

Setting Environment Variables

To set an environment variable, use the following format:

```
[root@ford /root]# variable=value
```

where *variable* is the variable name, and *value* is the value that you want to assign the variable. For example, to set the environment variable FOO with the value BAR, type the following:

```
[root@ford /root]# FOO=BAR
```

After setting the value, use the **export** command to finalize it. The format of the **export** command is as follows:

```
[root@ford /root]# export variable
```

where *variable* is the name of the variable. In the example of setting FOO, type the following:

```
[root@ford /root]# export FOO
```

You can combine the steps of setting the environment variable with the **export** command, as follows:

```
[root@ford /root]# export FOO=BAR
```

If the value of the environment variable you want to set has spaces in it, you need to surround the variable with quotation marks. For example, to set FOO to "Welcome to the BAR of FOO," type the following:

```
[root@ford /root]# export FOO="Welcome to the BAR of FOO."
```

Clearing Environment Variables

To remove an environment variable, use the **unset** command:

```
[root@ford /root]# unset variable
```

where *variable* is the name of the variable you want to remove. For example, to remove the environment variable FOO, type the following:

```
[root@ford]# unset FOO
```

Documentation Tools

Linux comes with two tremendously useful tools for making documentation accessible: man and info. Currently, the two documentation systems have a great deal of overlap between them, as many applications are moving their documentation to the info format. Info is considered superior to man because it allows the documentation to be hyperlinked together in a web-like way, without actually being written in HTML format. The man format, on the other hand, has been around for decades. Thousands of utilities have only man pages as their source of documentation. Furthermore, many applications continue to release their documentation in man format since many other UNIX-like operating systems such as Sun Solaris default to the man format for their documentation. As a result, both of these documentation systems will be around for a long while to come. Becoming comfortable with both of them is highly advisable.

man: View Man Pages

Man (short for *manual*) pages are documents found online covering the usage of tools and their corresponding configuration files. The format of the **man** command is as follows:

```
[root@ford /root]# man program_name
```

where *program_name* is the name of the program for which you want to read the manual page. Here's an example:

```
[root@ford /root]# man ls
```

While reading about UNIX and UNIX-related sources for information (such as newsgroups), you might find references to commands followed by numbers in parentheses, as in ls(1). The number represents the *section* of the manual pages; each section covers various subject areas. The section numbers are handy for some tools, such as **printf**, that are commands in the C programming language as well as command-line commands. Thus, two entries would exist for such a command under two different sections.

To refer to a specific section, simply specify the section number as the first parameter and the command as the second parameter. For example, to get the C programmers' information on **printf** (assuming that the C programming man files are installed), enter the following:

```
[root@ford /root]# man 3 printf
```

To get the command-line information, enter the following:

```
[root@ford /root]# man 1 printf
```

By default, the manual page for the lowest section number is printed first. The section numbers' meanings are shown in Table 21-1.

Section Number	Meaning
1	User tools
2	System calls
3	C library calls
4	Device driver-related information
5	Configuration files
6	Games
7	Packages
8	System tools

Table 21-1.   Manual Page Section Numbers

A handy option to the **man** command is **-k**. With this option, **man** will search the summary information of all the man pages and list which pages have a match along with their section number. For example, the following command will find pages matching the search criteria "printf":

```
[root@ford /root]# man -k printf
```

info: View info Pages

In addition to man pages, info pages are another common form of documentation. Established as the GNU standard, info is a documentation system that more closely resembles the Web in the sense that documents can be hyperlinked together, whereas man pages are single, static documents. Thus, info pages tend to be easier to read and understand.

To read the info documents on a specific tool or application, simply invoke **info** with the parameter specifying the tool's name. For example, to read about emacs, simply type the following:

```
[root@ford /root]# info emacs
```

Usually, you will first want to check if there is a man page. This is because a great deal more information is still available in the man format than in info format. However, some man pages will explicitly state that the info pages are more authoritative and should be read instead.

Option	Description
-l	Long listing. In addition to the filename, show the file size, date/time, permissions, ownership, and group information.
-a	All files. Show all files in the directory, including those that are hidden. Hidden files begin with a period.
-1	Single column listing. List all files in a single column.
-R	Recursive. Recursively list all files and subdirectories.

Table 21-2. Common ls Command Options

File Listings, Ownerships, and Permissions

Managing files under Linux is different from managing files under Windows. This section discusses the tools necessary to perform basic file management.

ls: List Files

The **ls** command is used to list all of the files in a directory. The command has more than 26 options. The most common of these options are shown in Table 21-2. See the man page for the complete list of options.

You can use these options in any combination with one another. For example, to list all files in a directory with a long listing, type the following:

```
[root@ford /root]# ls -la
```

To list nonhidden files in a directory that start with *A*, type the following:

```
[root@ford /root]# ls A*
```

About Files and Directories

Under Linux (and UNIX in general), you will find that almost everything is abstracted to a file. Linux's developers originally did this to simplify the programmer's job. Thus, instead of having to communicate directly with device drivers, you use special files (which to the application appear as ordinary files) as a bridge instead. To accommodate all of these uses of files, different types of files exist:

- ■ **Normal files** Normal files are just that—normal. They contain data or executables, and the operating system makes no assumptions about their contents.

■ **Directories**   Directory files are a special instance of normal files in that their contents list the location of other files. Among the files to which directories point might be other directories. In your day-to-day work, it won't matter to you much that directories in Linux (and UNIX) are actually files, unless you happen to try to open and read the directory file yourself, rather than use existing applications to navigate directories.

■ **Hard links**   Each file in the Linux file system gets its own *i-node*. An i-node keeps track of a file's attributes and location on the disk. If you need to be able to refer to a single file using two separate filenames, you can create a *hard link*. The hard link will have the same i-node as the original file, so it will look and behave just like the original file. With every hard link that is created, a *reference count* is incremented. When a hard link is removed, the reference count is decremented. Until the reference count reaches zero, the file will remain on disk.

NOTE   A hard link cannot exist between two files that are on separate partitions. This is because the hard link refers to the original file by i-node. A file that is referred to by one i-node on one file system will refer to another file on another file system.

■ **Symbolic links**   Unlike a hard link, which points to a file by its i-node, a symbolic link points to another file by its name. Thus, *symbolic links* (often abbreviated as *symlinks*) can point to files located on other partitions or even on other network drives.

■ **Block devices**   Since all device drivers are accessed through the file system, files of type *block device* are used to interface with devices such as disks.

■ **Character devices**   Similar to block devices, character devices are special files that allow you to access devices through the file system. The obvious difference between block and character devices is that block devices communicate with the actual devices in large blocks, whereas character devices work one character at a time. A hard disk is a block device; a modem is a character device.

■ **Named pipes**   A named pipe is a special type of file that allows for interprocess communication. Using the **mknod** command (discussed later in the "File Management and Manipulation" section), you can create this special kind of file that one process can open for reading and another process can open for writing, thus allowing the two processes to communicate with one another. Named pipes work especially well when a package refuses to take input from a command-line pipe, you have another program that you need to feed data, and you don't have the disk space for a temporary file.

Block devices, character devices, and named pipes have certain characteristics that identify their file type.

The three identifying traits of a block device are that it has a major number, has a minor number, and when viewed using the **ls -l** command, shows the first character of the permissions to be a *b*. Here's an example:

```
[root@ford /root]# ls-l /dev/sda1
brw-rw----   1 root      disk      8,   1  2009-04-10  /dev/sda1
```

In this case, the *b* is at the beginning of the file's permissions, the 8 is the major number, and the 1 is the minor number. The significance of the major number is that it identifies which device driver the file represents. When the system accesses this file, the minor number is passed to the device driver as a parameter to tell the driver which device it is accessing. (For example, if there are two serial ports, they will share the same device driver and thus the same major number, but each serial port will have a unique minor number.)

The distinguishing characteristics of a character device are that its permissions start with a *c*, and the device has a major and minor number. Here's an example:

```
[root@ford /root]# ls -l /dev/ttyS0
crw-------   1 root      tty       4,  64  May  5   1988  /dev/ttySo
```

You can tell that a file is a named pipe by the fact that the first character of its file permissions is a *p*, as in the following example:

```
[root@ford /root]# ls-l mypipe
prw-r--r--   1 root      root          0  June  16  10:47  mypipe
```

chown: Change Ownership

The **chown** command allows you to change the ownership of a file to someone else. Only the root user can change this ownership. (Normal users may not "give away" or "steal" ownership of a file from another user.) The format of the command is as follows:

```
[root@ford /root]# chown [-R] username filename
```

where *username* is the user's login to which you want to change the ownership and *filename* is the name of the file that will have its ownership changed. The filename may be a directory as well.

The **-R** option applies when the specified filename is a directory name. It tells the command to descend recursively through the directory tree and apply the new ownership not only to the directory itself, but to all of the files and subdirectories within it.

chgrp: Change Group

chgrp is another command-line utility that allows you to change the group settings of a file. The command works in much the same way as **chown** does. The format of the command is as follows:

```
[root@ford /root]# chgrp [-R] groupname filename
```

where *groupname* is the name of the group to which you want to change *filename*. The filename may be a directory as well.

The **-R** option applies when the specified filename is a directory name. As with **chown**, the option tells the **chgrp** command to descend recursively through the directory tree and apply the new ownership not only to the directory itself, but to all of the files and subdirectories within it.

chmod: Change Mode

Permissions are broken into four parts. The first part is the first character of the permissions. If the file is a normal file, then it will have no value and be represented with a hyphen (-). If the file has a special attribute, it will be represented with a letter. The two special files that you are most interested in are directories that are represented with a *d* and symbolic links that are represented with an *l*.

The second, third, and fourth parts are represented in three-character chunks. The first part is the permissions for the owner of the file. The second part is the permissions for the group. Finally, the last part is the permissions for the world. In the context of UNIX, the world is simply all the users in the system, regardless of their group settings.

The letters used to represent permissions are *R* for read, *W* for write, and *X* for execute. Each permission has a corresponding value. The read attribute is equal to 4, the write attribute is equal to 2, and the execute attribute is equal to 1. When you combine attributes, you add their values. The reason that these attributes need values is to ensure that you can use the **chmod** command to set them. Although the **chmod** command does have more readable ways to set permissions, it is important that you understand the numbering scheme since it is used for programming. Plus, not everyone uses the naming scheme, and Linux users often assume that if you understand file permissions, you understand the numeric meanings as well.

The most common groups of three and their meanings are listed in Table 21-3.

Permission	Values	Meaning
---	0	No permissions
r--	4	Read only
rw-	6	Read and write
rwx	7	Read, write, and execute
r-x	5	Read and execute
--x	1	Execute only

Table 21-3.   Common Permission Combinations

Each of these three-letter chunks is then grouped together three at a time. The first chunk represents the permissions for the owner of the file, the second chunk represents the permissions for the group of the file, and the last chunk represents the permissions for all of the users on the system. Table 21-4 lists some common permission.

Permission	Numeric Equivalent	Meaning
-rw-------	600	The owner has read and write permissions. You want this setting for most of your files
-rw-r--r--	644	The owner has read and write permissions. The group and world have read-only permissions. Be sure that you want to let other people read this file.
-rw-rw-rw-	666	Everyone has read and write permissions on a file. This setting is bad. You don't want other people to be able to change your files.
-rwx------	700	The owner has read, write, and execute permissions. You want this setting for programs that you wish to run (such as the file that results from compiling a C or C++ program).
-rwxr-xr-x	755	The owner has read, write, and execute permissions. The rest of the world has read and execute permissions.
-rwxrwxrwx	777	Everyone has read, write, and execute privileges. Like the 666 setting, this is bad.
-rwx--x--x	711	The owner has read, write, and execute permissions. The rest of the world has execute-only permissions. This setting is useful for programs that you want to let others run but not copy.
drwx------	700	This is a directory created with the **mkdir** command. Only the owner can read and write to this directory. Note that all directories must have the executable bit set.
drwxr-xr-x	755	Only the owner can change this directory, but everyone else can view its contents.
drwx--x--x	711	A handy trick is to use this setting when you need to keep a directory world-readable, but you don't want people to be able to list the files by running the **ls** command. The setting enables users to read a directory only if they know the filename that they want to retrieve.

Table 21-4. Common File Permissions

File Management and Manipulation

This section provides an overview of the basic command-line tools for managing files and directories. Most of this overview should be familiar if you have used a command-line interface before. Basically, you use the same old functions, just with new commands.

cp: Copy Files

The **cp** command is used to copy files. By default, this command works silently, displaying status information only if there is an error condition. For example, to copy index.html to index-orig.html, type the following:

```
[root@ford /root]# cp index.html index-orig.html
```

The **cp** command has a large number of options, which are detailed on its man page. The most common options are **-f** to force copy (do not ask for verification) and **-1** for an interactive copy (ask for verification before copying). For example, to copy interactively all files ending in .html to the /tmp directory, type the following:

```
[root@ford /root]# cp -i *.html /tmp
```

mv: Move Files

Use the **mv** command to move files from one location to another. The command can move files across partitions as well; however, realize that when moving a file between partitions that you are actually copying the file to the other partition, and then erasing the original, so it can take longer than moving a file within a partition. Moving a file within a single partition just tells the system that the file is in a different directory; the file isn't copied or physically moved on the disk.

For example, to move a file from /usr/src/myprog/bin/* to /usr/bin, type the following:

```
[root@ford /root]# mv /usr/src/myprog/bin/* /usr/bin
```

The most common options are **-f** to force a move and **-1** to move interactively.

Although Linux has no explicit rename tool, you can use **mv** to accomplish this task. To rename /tmp/blah to /tmp/bleck, type the following:

```
[root@ford /root]# mv /tmp/bleck /tmp/blah
```

ln: Link Files

The **ln** command allows you to establish a hard link or a soft link. (See the "About Files and Directories" section earlier in this chapter for additional information.) The general format of this command is as follows:

```
[root@ford /root]# ln original_file new_file
```

The **ln** command has many options, most of which you'll never need to use. The most common option is **-s**, which creates a symbolic link instead of a hard link. For example, to create a symbolic link so that /usr/bin/myadduser points to /usr/ local/ bin/myadduser, type the following:

```
[root@ford /root]# ln -s /usr/local/bin/myadduser /usr/bin/myadduser
```

find: Find a File

The **find** command enables you to find files based on a number of criteria. The following is the command's general format:

```
[root@ford /root]# find start_dir [options]
```

where *start_dir* is the directory from which the search should start.

find, like the other commands that we have already discussed, has a large number of options that you can read about on its man page. Table 21-5 list the most common options used with **find**.

Option	Description
-mount	Do not search file systems other than the file system from which you started.
-atime *n*	Specify that the file was accessed at least *n**24 hours ago.
-ctime *n*	Look only for files changed at least *n**24 hours ago.
-inum *n*	Find a file that has i-node *n*.
-amin *n*	Specify that the file was accessed *n* minutes ago.
-cmin *n*	Look only for files that were changed *n* minutes ago.
-empty	Find empty files.
-mmin *n*	Specify that the file was modified *n* minutes ago.
-mtime *n*	Search only for files modified *n**24 hours ago.
-nouser	Find files whose UID does not correspond to a real user in /etc/passwd.
-nogroup	Look only for files whose GID does not correspond to a real group in /etc/group.
-perm *mode*	Specify that the file's permissions are exactly set to *mode*.
-size *n[bck]*	Search only for files at least *n* blocks/characters/kilobytes big. One block equals 512 bytes.
-print	Print the filenames found.
-exec *cmd*\;	On every file found, execute *cmd*. If you are using the bash shell, be sure to follow every *cmd* with a \; otherwise, the shell will become very confused.
-name *name*	Specify that the filename should be *name*. You can use regular expressions here.

Table 21-5.   Common find Command Options

For example, to find all files in /tmp that have not been accessed in at least seven days, type the following:

```
[root@ford /root]# find /tmp -atime 7 -print
```

To find all files in /usr/src whose names are *core* and then remove them, type the following:

```
[root@ford /root]# find /usr/src -name core -exec rm {} \;
```

To find all files in /home with the extension .jpg that are bigger than 100KB, type the following:

```
[root@ford /root]# find /home -name "*.jpg" -size 100k
```

dd: Convert and Copy a File

The **dd** command reads the contents of a file and sends them to another file. What makes **dd** different from **cp** is that **dd** can perform on-the-fly conversions on the file and can accept data from a device (such as a tape or floppy drive). When **dd** accesses a device, it does not assume anything about the file system and instead pulls the data in a raw format. Thus, you can use the data to generate images of disks, even if the disk is of foreign format. Table 21-6 lists the most common parameters for **dd**:

For example, to generate an image of a floppy disk (which is especially useful for foreign file formats), type the following:

```
[root@ford /root]# dd if=/dev/fd0 of=/tmp/floppy_image
```

Option	Description
if=*infile*	Specify the input file as *infile*.
of=*outfile*	Specify the output file as *outfile*.
count=*blocks*	Specify *blocks* as the number of blocks on which **dd** should operate before quitting.
ibs=*size*	Set the block size of the input device to be *size*.
obs=*size*	Set the block size of the output device to be *size*.
seek=*blocks*	Skip *blocks* number of blocks on the output.
skip=*blocks*	Skip *blocks* number of blocks on the input.
swab	Convert big endian input to little endian, or vice versa.

Table 21-6.   Common dd Command Options

gzip: Compress a File

In the original distributions of UNIX, a tool to compress a file was appropriately called **compress**. Unfortunately, an entrepreneur patented the algorithm, hoping to make a great deal of money. Instead of paying out, most sites sought and found **gzip**, a different compression tool with a patent-free algorithm. Even better, **gzip** consistently achieves better compression ratios than **compress** does. Note that **gzip** compresses the file "in place," meaning that after the compression takes place, the original file is removed, leaving only the compressed file.

> **TIP**   You can usually distinguish files compressed with **gzip** from those compressed by **compress** by checking their extensions. Files compressed with **gzip** typically end in .gz whereas files compressed with **compress** end in .Z.

Table 21-7 lists the most-used optional parameters to **gzip**. See the man page for a complete list.

For example, to compress a file and then decompress it, type the following:

```
[root@ford /root]# gzip myfile
[root@ford /root]# gzip -d myfile.gz
```

To compress all files ending in .html using the best compression possible, enter the following command:

```
[root@ford /root]# gzip -9 *.html
```

> **NOTE**   The **gzip** tool does not share file formats with either PkZip or WinZip. However, WinZip can decompress gzip files.

Option	Description
-c	Write compressed file to the standard output device (thereby allowing the output to be piped to another program).
-d	Decompress.
-r	Recursively find all files that should be compressed.
-9	Provide the best compression.
-1	Achieve the fastest compression.

Table 21-7.   Common gzip Command Options

mknod: Make Special Files

As discussed earlier, Linux accesses all of its devices through files. To create a file that the system understands as an interface to a device, you must specify that the file is of type block or character and has a major and minor number. To create this kind of file with the necessary values, you use the **mknod** command. In addition to creating interfaces to devices, you can use **mknod** to create named pipes.

The command's format is as follows:

```
[root@ford /root]# mknod name type [major] [minor]
```

where *name* is the name of the file; and *type* is the character *b* for block device, *c* for character device, or *p* for named pipe. If you choose to create a block or character device, you need to specify the *major* and *minor* number.

The only time you will need to create a block or character device is when installing some kind of device driver that requires it. The documentation that comes with your driver should tell you which values to use for the major and minor numbers.

For example, to create a named pipe called /tmp/mypipe, type the following:

```
[root@ford /root]# mknod /tmp/mypipe p
```

mkdir: Create a Home Directory

The **mkdir** command in Linux is identical to the one in other flavors of UNIX as well as in MS-DOS. For example, to create a directory called mydir, type the following:

```
[root@ford /root]# mkdir mydir
```

The only option available is **-p**, which creates a parent directory if none exists. For example, if you need to create /tmp/bigdir/subdir/mydir, and the only directory that exists is /tmp, using **-p** will automatically create bigdir and subdir along with mydir.

 NOTE   Under Linux, you cannot abbreviate the **mkdir** command as **md** as you can under DOS.

rmdir: Remove Directory

The **rmdir** command offers no surprises if you are familiar with the DOS version of the command. It simply removes an existing directory. For example, to remove a directory called mydir, type the following:

```
[root@ford /root]# rmdir mydir
```

One command-line parameter available for this command is **-p**, which removes parent directories as well. For example, if the directory /tmp/bigdir/subdir/mydir exists and you want to get rid of all of the directories from bigdir to mydir, issue the following command:

```
[root@ford /tmp]# rmdir -p bigdir/subdir/mydir
```

NOTE   Under Linux, you cannot abbreviate the **rmdir** command as **rd** as you can under DOS.

pwd: Print Working Directory

It is inevitable that eventually you will sit down in front of an already logged-in workstation and not know where you are located in the directory tree. To get this information, you need the **pwd** command. It has no parameters and its only task is to print the current working directory. The DOS equivalent is to type **cd** alone; however, under bash, typing **cd** simply takes you back to your home directory.

For example, to get the current working directory, enter the following command:

```
[root@ford src]# pwd
/usr/local/src
```

tar: Tape Archive

If you are familiar with the **pkzip** program, you are used to compression tools not only reducing file size, but also combining multiple files into a single large file. Linux separates this process into two tools. The compression tool is **gzip**, which was discussed earlier.

The **tar** program combines multiple files into a single large file. The reason for separating this program from the compression tool is that **tar** allows you to select which compression tool to use or whether you even want compression. Additionally, **tar** is able to read and write to devices in much the same way that **dd** can, thus making **tar** a good tool for backing up tape devices.

 NOTE   Although the name of the program includes the word *tape*, you do not need to read or write to a tape drive when creating archives. In fact, you will rarely use **tar** with a tape drive in your day-to-day work (aside from your backups).

The format of the **tar** command is as follows:

```
[root@ford /root]# tar [commands and options] filenames
```

Some of options available to **tar** are listed in Table 21-8. Refer to the man page for the complete list.

For example, to create an archive called apache.tar containing all the files from /usr/ src/apache, type the following:

```
[root@ford src]# tar -cf apache.tar /usr/src/apache
```

To create an archive called apache.tar containing all the files from /usr/ src/apache and see the list of files as they are added to the archive, type the following:

```
[root@ford src]# tar -cvf apache.tar /usr/src/apache
```

Options	Descriptions
-c	Create a new archive.
-t	View the contents of an archive.
-x	Extract the contents of an archive.
-f	Specify the name of the file (or device) in which the archive is located.
-v	Be verbose during operations.
-z	Assume that the file is already (or will be) compressed with gzip.

Table 21-8.   Common tar Command Options

To create a gzipped compressed archive called apache.tar.gz containing all the files from /usr/src/apache and list the files as they are being added to the archive, type the following:

```
[root@ford src]# tar -cvzf apache.tar.gz /usr/src/apache
```

To extract the contents of a gzipped tar archive called apache.tar.gz and list the files as they are being extracted, type the following:

```
[root@ford /root]# tar -xvzf apache.tar.gz
```

cat: Concatenate Files

The **cat** program serves a simple purpose: to display the contents of files. While you can do more creative things with it, you will almost always use the program simply to display the contents of text files, much like you would use the **type** command under DOS. Because you can specify multiple filenames on the command line, it is possible to concatenate files into a single large continuous file. Thus, **cat** differs from **tar** in that the resulting file has no control information to show the boundaries of different files.

For example, to display the /etc/passwd file, type the following:

```
[root@ford /root]# cat /etc/passwd
```

To display the /etc/passwd file and the /etc/group file, type the following:

```
[root@ford /root]# cat /etc/passwd /etc/group
```

To concatenate the /etc/passwd file with the /etc/group file into the /tmp/ complete file, type the following:

```
[root@ford /root]# cat /etc/passwd /etc/group > /tmp/complete
```

To concatenate the /etc/passwd file to an existing file called /tmp/orb, type the following:

```
[root@ford /root]# cat /etc/passwd >> /tmp/orb
```

more: Display a File One Screen at a Time

The **more** command works in much the same way as the DOS version of the program. It displays an input file one screen at a time. The input file can come from either **more**'s standard input or a command-line parameter. Additional command-line parameters exist for this command; however, they are rarely used. See the man page for additional information.

For example, to view the /etc/passwd file one screenful at a time, type the following:

```
[root@ford /root]# more /etc/passwd
```

To view the directory listing generated by the **ls** command one screenful at a time, type the following:

```
[root@ford /root]# ls | more
```

du: Disk Utilization

You will often need to determine where and by whom disk space is being consumed, especially when you're running low on it! The **du** command allows you to determine the disk utilization on a directory-by-directory basis. Table 21-9 lists some of the options for **du.**

For example, to display in a human-readable format the amount of space each directory in the /home directory is taking up, type the following:

```
[root@ford /root]# du -sh /home/*
```

which: Show the Directory in Which a File Is Located

The **which** command searches your entire path to find the name of the file specified on the command line. If it finds the filename, the tool displays the actual path of the requested file. The purpose of this command is to help you find fully qualified paths.

Options	Description
-c	Produce a grand total at the end of the run.
-h	Print sizes in human-readable format.
-k	Print sizes in kilobytes rather than block sizes. (Note that under Linux, one block is equal to 1KB. However, this is not true for all flavors of UNIX.)
-s	Summarize; print only one output for each argument.

Table 21-9. Common du Command Options

For example, to find out which directory the **ls** command is in, type the following:

```
[root@ford /root]# which ls
```

whereis: Locate the Binary, Source, and Manual Page for a Command

The **whereis** program not only searches your path and displays the name of the program and its absolute directory, but also finds the source file (if available) and the man page for the command (again, if available).

For example, to find the location of the binary, source, and manual page for the command **grep**, type the following:

```
[root@ford /root]# whereis grep
```

df: Determine the Amount of Free Space on a Disk

The **df** program displays the amount of free space on a partition-by-partition basis. The drives/partitions must be mounted for **df** to retrieve this information. You can also gather Network File System (NFS) information using this command.

Two options are commonly used with **df**: **-h** and **-l**. The **-h** option specifies to use a human-readable measurement, other than simply the number of free blocks, to indicate the amount of free space. The **-l** option lists only the mounted file systems that are local; do not display any information about network-mounted file systems. Additional command-line options are available; however, they are rarely used. You can read about them in the **df** man page.

For example, to show the free space for all locally mounted drivers, type the following:

```
[root@ford /root]# df -l
```

To show the free space in a human-readable format for the file system on which your current working directory is located, type the following (the trailing period is shorthand that means "current directory," just as it does under DOS):

```
[root@ford /root]# df -h .
```

To show the free space in a human-readable format for the file system on which /tmp is located, type the following:

```
[root@ford /root]# df -h /tmp
```

sync: Synchronize Disks

Like most other modern operating systems, Linux attempts to improve efficiency by maintaining a disk cache. This means, however, that at any given moment not everything you want written to disk has been written to disk.

To schedule the disk cache to be written out to the disk, use the **sync** command. If **sync** detects that writing the cache out to disk has already been scheduled, the tool causes the kernel to flush the cache immediately. For example, to ensure that the disk cache has been flushed, type the following:

```
[root@ford /root]# sync ; sync
```

The **sync** command does not have any command-line parameters.

Process Manipulation

Under Linux (and UNIX in general), each running program is composed of at least one process. From the operating system's standpoint, each process is independent of one another, and unless you specifically ask the processes to share resources with each other, they are confined to the memory and CPU allocation assigned to them. Processes that overstep their memory allocation (which could potentially corrupt another running program and make the system unstable) are immediately killed. This method of handing processes has been one of the key reasons that UNIX has been able to sustain its claims to system stability for so long—user applications cannot corrupt other user programs or the operating system.

This section discusses the tools used to list and manipulate processes. This information is very useful to systems administrators, since it's always important to keep an eye on what's going on.

ps: List Processes

The **ps** command lists all of the processes in a system, as well as their state, size, name, owner, CPU time, wall clock time, and much more. The command has many command-line parameters. Table 21-10 lists the ones that are most commonly used.

The most common parameter used with the **ps** command is **-auxww**, which shows all of the processes (regardless of whether or not they have a controlling terminal),

Option	Description
-a	Show all processes with a controlling terminal, not just the current user's.
-r	Show only running processes.
-x	Show processes that do not have a controlling terminal.
-u	Show the process owners.
-f	Show which processes are the parents to which other processes.
-l	Produce long format.
-w	Show the process's command-line parameters (up to half a line).
-ww	Show all of a process's command-line parameters, despite length.

Table 21-10.   Common ps Command Options

each process's owners, and all of the process's command-line parameters. Here is an example of the output of an invocation of **ps -auxww**:

USER	PID	%CPU	%MEM	VSZ	RSS	TTY	STAT	START	TIME	COMMAND
root	1	0.0	0.3	1096	476	?	S	Jun10	0:04	init
root	2	0.0	0.0	0	0	?	SW	Jun10	0:00	[kflushd]
root	3	0.0	0.0	0	0	?	SW	Jun10	0:00	[kpiod]
root	4	0.0	0.0	0	0	?	SW	Jun10	0:00	[kswapd]
root	5	0.0	0.0	0	0	?	SW<	Jun10	0:00	[mdrecoveryd]
root	102	0.0	0.2	1068	380	?	S	Jun10	0:00	/usr/sbin/apmd
-p 10 -w 5										
bin	253	0.0	0.2	1088	288	?	S	Jun10	0:00	portmap
root	300	0.0	0.4	1272	548	?	S	Jun10	0:00	syslogd -m 0
root	311	0.0	0.5	1376	668	?	S	Jun10	0:00	klogd
daemon	325	0.0	0.2	1112	284	?	S	Jun10	0:00	/usr/sbin/atd
root	339	0.0	0.4	1284	532	?	S	Jun10	0:00	crond
root	357	0.0	0.3	1232	508	?	S	Jun10	0:00	inetd
root	371	0.0	1.1	2528	1424	?	S	Jun10	0:00	named
root	385	0.0	0.4	1284	516	?	S	Jun10	0:00	lpd
root	399	0.0	0.8	2384	1116	?	S	Jun10	0:00	httpd
xfs	429	0.0	0.7	1988	908	?	S	Jun10	0:00	xfs
root	467	0.0	0.2	1060	384	tty2	S	Jun10	0:00	/sbin/mingetty tty2
root	468	0.0	0.2	1060	384	tty3	S	Jun10	0:00	/sbin/mingetty tty3
root	469	0.0	0.2	1060	384	tty4	S	Jun10	0:00	/sbin/mingetty tty4
root	470	0.0	0.2	1060	384	tty5	S	Jun10	0:00	/sbin/mingetty tty5
root	471	0.0	0.2	1060	384	tty6	S	Jun10	0:00	/sbin/mingetty tty6
root	473	0.0	0.0	1052	116	?	S	Jun10	0:01	update (bdflush)
root	853	0.0	0.7	1708	940	pts/1	S	Jun10	0:00	bash
root	1199	0.0	0.7	1940	1012	pts/2	S	Jun10	0:00	su
root	1203	0.0	0.7	1700	920	rpts/2	S	Jun10	0:00	bash
root	1726	0.0	1.3	2824	1760	?	S	Jun10	0:00	xterm
root	1728	0.0	0.7	1716	940	pts/8	S	Jun10	0:00	bash
root	1953	0.0	1.3	2832	1780	?	S	Jun11	0:05	xterm
root	1955	0.0	0.7	1724	972	pts/10	S	Jun11	0:00	bash
nobody	6436	0.0	0.7	2572	988	?	S	Jun13	0:00	httpd
nobody	6437	0.0	0.7	2560	972	?	S	Jun13	0:00	httpd
nobody	6438	0.0	0.7	2560	976	?	S	Jun13	0:00	httpd
nobody	6439	0.0	0.7	2560	976	?	S	Jun13	0:00	httpd
nobody	6440	0.0	0.7	2560	976	?	S	Jun13	0:00	httpd
nobody	6441	0.0	0.7	2560	976	?	S	Jun13	0:00	httpd
root	16673	0.0	0.6	1936	840	pts/10	S	Jun14	0:00	su -sshah
sshah	16675	0.0	0.8	1960	1112	pts/10	S	Jun14	0:00	-tcsh
root	18243	0.0	0.9	2144	1216	tty1	S	Jun14	0:00	login -- sshah
sshah	18244	0.0	0.8	1940	1080	tty1	S	Jun14	0:00	-tcsh

The very first line of the output is the header indicating the meaning of each column, as listed in Table 21-11.

Heading	Description
USER	The user name of the owner for each process.
PID	The process identification number.
%CPU	The percentage of the CPU taken up by a process. Remember that for a system with multiple processors, this column will add up to greater than 100 percent!
%MEM	The percentage of memory taken up by a process.
VSZ	The amount of virtual memory that a process is taking.
RSS	The amount of actual (resident) memory that a process is taking.
TTY	The controlling terminal for a process. A question mark (?) means that the process is no longer connected to a controlling terminal.
STAT	The process's state. S is sleeping. (Remember that all processes that are ready to run—that is, those that are being multitasked while the CPU is momentarily focused on another process—will be asleep). R means that the process is actually on the CPU. D is an uninterruptible sleep (usually I/O-related). T means that a process is being traced by a debugger or has been stopped. Z means that the process has gone zombie. Each process state can have a modifier suffixed to it: W, $<$, N, or L. W means that the process has no resident pages in memory (it has been completely swapped out). $<$ indicates a high-priority process. N indicates a low-priority task. L indicates that some pages are locked into memory (which usually signifies the need for real-time functionality).
START	The date that the process was started.
TIME	The amount of time the process has spent on the CPU.
COMMAND	The name of the process and its command-line parameters.

Table 21-11.   ps Command Output

DEFINE-IT! Going Zombie

Going zombie means one of two things: either the parent process has not acknowledged the death of its child process using the wait system call or the parent was improperly killed and thus the init process cannot reap the child until the parent is completely killed. A zombied process usually indicates poorly written software.

top: Show an Interactive List of Processes

The **top** command is an interactive version of **ps**. Instead of giving a static view of what is going on, this tool refreshes the screen with a list of processes every two or three seconds (the user can adjust the interval). From this list, you can reprioritize or kill processes.

The key problem with the **top** program is that it is a CPU hog. On a congested system, this program tends to make memory problems worse as users start running **top** to see what is going on, only to find several other people are running it as well. Collectively, they have made the system even slower than before!

By default, **top** installs with permissions granted to all users. You might find it prudent, depending on your environment, to allow only root to be able to run it. To do this, change the permissions for the **top** program with the following command:

```
[root@ford /root]# chmod 0700 /usr/bin/top
```

kill: Send a Signal to a Process

For some reason, the **kill** program was horribly named. The program doesn't really kill processes! What it does is send *signals* to running processes. By default, the operating system supplies each process a standard set of *signal handlers* to deal with incoming signals. From a systems administrator's standpoint, the most important handler is for signal numbers 9 and 15: kill process and terminate process. (Okay, maybe using *kill* as a name wasn't so inappropriate after all.)

When **kill** is invoked, it requires at least one parameter: the process identification number (PID) as derived from the **ps** command. When passed only the PID number, by default, **kill** will send signal 15, terminate process. Sending the terminate process signal is a lot like politely asking a process to stop what it's doing and shut down. Some programs intercept this signal and perform a number of actions so that they can cleanly shut down; others just stop in their tracks. Either way, sending the signal isn't a guaranteed method for making a process stop.

The optional parameter is a number prefixed by a dash (-), where the number represents a signal number. The two signals that systems administrators are most interested in are 9 and 1: kill and hang up. The kill signal is the impolite way of making a process stop. Instead of asking a process to stop, the operating system takes it upon itself to kill the process. The only time this signal will fail is when the process is in the middle of a system call (such as a request to open a file), in which case the process will die once it returns from the system call.

The hangup signal is a bit of a throwback to when most users of UNIX connected to the system via VT100-style terminals. When a user's connection would drop in the middle of a session, all of that user's running processes would receive a hangup signal (often called a SIGHUP, or HUP for short). This signal gave the processes an opportunity to perform a clean shutdown or, in the case of some programs designed to keep running in the background, to safely ignore the signal. These days, the hangup (HUP) signal is used to tell certain server applications to reread their configuration files. Most applications otherwise ignore the signal.

For example, to terminate process number 2059, type the following:

```
[root@ford /root]# kill 2059
```

To kill process number 593 in an almost guaranteed way, type the following:

```
[root@ford /root]# kill -9 593
```

To send the init program (which is always process ID 1) the HUP signal, type the following:

```
[root@ford /root]# kill -1 1
```

CAUTION   The capability to terminate a process is obviously a very powerful one. The developers of the **kill** command realized this and made sure that security precautions existed so that users can kill only those processes they have permission to kill. For example, nonroot users can send signals only to their own processes. If a nonroot user attempts to send signals to processes that she does not own, the system returns error messages. On the other hand, the root user may send signals to all processes in the system. This means that when using the **kill** command, the root user needs to exercise great care to avoid accidentally killing the wrong process!

Miscellaneous Tools

If this book were devoted to the commands available in your Linux system, the tools discussed in this section would each fit into specific categories. But since this overview is focused on only the most important tools for day-to-day administrative chores, the following tools are lumped together under "miscellaneous." However, even though this section declines to classify them under their own specific categories, that doesn't mean the tools are not important!

uname: Show the System Name

The **uname** program allows you to learn some details about a system. This tool is often helpful when you've managed to log in remotely to a dozen different computers and have lost track of where you are. This tool is also helpful for script writers since it allows them to change the path of a script based on the system information. The command-line parameters for **uname** are listed in Table 21-12.

Option	Description
-m	Print the machine hardware type (for example, i686 for Pentium Pro and better architectures).
-n	Print the machine's hostname.
-r	Print the operating system's release name.
-s	Print the operating system's name.
-v	Print the operating system's version.
-a	Print all of the preceding information.

Table 21-12.   Common uname Command Options

For example, to get the operating system's name and release type, enter the following:

```
[root@ford /root]# uname -s -r
```

It might appear odd that **uname** prints such things as the operating system name when the user obviously will know that the name is Linux. However, such information is actually quite useful because you can find **uname** across almost all UNIX-like operating systems. Thus, if you are at an SGI workstation and enter **uname -s**, the tool will return IRIX; if you enter the command at a Sun workstation, it would return SunOS; and so on. People who work in heterogeneous environments often find it useful to write their scripts such that they behave differently depending on the operating system type, and **uname** provides a wonderfully consistent way to determine that information.

who: Find Out Who Is Logged In

When administering systems that allow people to log in to other people's machines or set up servers, you will want to know who is logged in. To generate a report listing the users currently logged in, use the **who** command, as follows:

```
[root@ford]# who
```

This command will generate a report similar to the following:

```
Sshah      tty1      Jun 14 18:22
root       pts/9     Jun 14 18:29      (:0)
root       pts/11    Jun 14 21:12      (:0)
root       pts/12    Jun 14 23:38      (:0)
```

su: Switch Users

Once you have logged in to the system as one user, you do not need to log back out and then log in again to assume another identity (for example, if you logged in as yourself and want to become the root user). Simply use the **su** command to switch to another user. This command has only two command-line parameters, both of which are optional.

By default, running **su** without any parameters results in an attempt to become the root user. For example, if you are logged in as yourself and want to switch to the root user, type the following:

```
[sshah@ford ~]$ su
```

Linux will prompt you for the root password; if you enter the password correctly, Linux then drops down to a root shell.

If you are the root user and want to take the identity of another user, you do not need to enter that user's password. For example, if you are logged in as root and want to switch over to user sshah, type the following:

```
[root@ford /root]# su sshah
```

You can use the dash (-) as an optional parameter. This character tells **su** not only to switch identities, but to run the login scripts for that user as well. For example, if you are logged in as root and want to switch to user sshah with all of his login and shell configurations, type the following:

```
[root@ford /root]# su - sshah
```

Chapter Summary

In this chapter, you first learned about setting some of the key server settings using the built-in graphical tools in Fedora Linux. Then you learned about the Linux command line and how to control the system using it.

Of course, this chapter didn't cover everything you need to know about Linux system administration. But given what you learned here, you should be able to perform basic administrative duties and find your way through the operating system.

The easiest way to gain more information is to spend time playing with both the command-line tools and the various System Tools programs. The graphical tools are capable of so much more than was shown here. In fact, for simple servers it is possible to perform system maintenance using the graphical tools alone! The command line, on the other hand, is the core of Linux's flexibility.

If you want to learn more about systems administration for Linux, be sure to check out *Linux Administration: A Beginner's Guide*, Third Edition, by Steven Graham (McGraw-Hill/Professional, 2002).

Now that you've learned about installing Linux and about administering a Linux system, in the next chapter you learn about installing one of the most common network services that are run under Linux; an Apache web server.

Chapter 22

Setting Up a Linux Web Server with Apache

One of the most popular web server applications is the Apache web server, a free program that runs under a variety of operating systems, including Linux, Windows, Mac OS X, Solaris, and NetWare. The Apache web server is a robust, proven platform on which to host a web site. The fact that it is open source and available for free, running on the UNIX-like operating system Linux, which is also often available for free, is a huge plus, and no doubt helps drive its continuing popularity.

This chapter introduces the Apache web server. You learn the basics that you need to install it, find web-based resources to support it, and set up a basic web site on a Fedora Linux system.

Overview of Apache Web Server

The Apache web server started out as a small development at the National Center for Supercomputing Applications (NCSA) in the early 1990s. Beginning as a very simple UNIX *daemon* (pronounced the same as "demon"), it was initially programmed by Rob McCool. McCool left NCSA in 1994, and the project began to be extended by a number of different programmers, some of whom added packages (modules) to the core program to enable it to support new web technologies. In those days, the web server was referred to as "patchy," because it kept getting new patches to correct problems or extend functionality. Eventually, it came to be called the Apache web server.

Version 1.0 of the Apache web server was released to the public at the end of 1995, and by 1996 was the most popular web server on the Internet. The latest statistics at the time this chapter was written (available from http://news.netcraft.com/archives/web_server_survey.html) reveal that Apache is being used to host approximately 50 percent (more than 113 million web sites) of the active web sites on the Internet. Microsoft's IIS is in second place, with around 25 percent (about 56 million web sites).

The Apache HTTP Server project is presently coordinated through the Apache Software Foundation (http://www.apache.org), a nonprofit corporation formed in 1999.

Apache is unlike most other server applications in that it is not a graphical program (despite the fact that its main purpose is to serve up graphical web pages) and has no graphical installation routine. Instead, Apache runs as a background process, or daemon, on the operating system, which is typically called httpd (Hypertext Transfer Protocol daemon). The management of an Apache web server is handled by editing its text-based configuration files, and by stopping and starting the daemon to cause any changes to those configuration files to take effect.

The fact that Apache is text-based and is administered through a command-line interface should not daunt you. It is straightforward to install and administer an Apache web server, and you should have no trouble doing so. In fact, if you followed the Fedora Linux installation instructions in Chapter 20, you already have Apache installed on that computer, and you just need to activate it (it is not turned on by default in a Fedora installation), as described in the next section.

Activating Apache Web Server Under Fedora

The simplest way to install Apache web server under Fedora Linux is to perform a default installation using the Fedora Linux installation routine, as described in Chapter 20. After Fedora is installed, you can start and test Apache with the following steps:

1. Open a terminal emulation window.

2. Change to the superuser (root):

   ```
   su
   ```

3. Provide the root password when prompted.

4. Type the following command to start Apache:

   ```
   apachectl start
   ```

5. Create a simple HTML file in the location /var/www/html/ and save the file as index.html. (Note that, by default, you must be the root user to create or modify files in /var/www/html.)

6. Open a web browser and navigate to the address http://localhost/. The file you saved as index.html should appear in the web browser, showing that Apache is up and running.

Downloading and Installing Apache Web Server

If you did not install Apache under Linux (for example, if you are using a distribution of Linux that does not come with Apache), you can download the latest version and install it manually.

To download the latest version of Apache, use a web browser to go to http://www.apache.org/dist/httpd/. Open the Binaries folder, open the folder representing the operating system you are using (Linux or RPM, for Red Hat Package Manager), and then choose the appropriate package from the list that appears. The packages are organized by the Apache version (which is also shown as part of the filenames), the processor, and the operating system. For example, you might download a file called httpd-2.2.3-i386.rpm (representing version 2.2.3 of Apache for 32-bit Intel-based systems running Linux and that use the RPM installation format) into a temporary directory on your Linux system.

After you've downloaded the package, you can install the Apache web server and start it, as follows:

1. Open a terminal emulation window.

2. Type the following to change to the directory that contains the downloaded Apache binary file:

   ```
   cd / directory
   ```

3. Unzip the gz file using the following command (substitute the actual filename of the file you downloaded):

```
gunzip filename.tar.gz
```

4. Untar the resulting .tar file with the following command (substituting the actual filename found in the directory after performing step 3; you can use the **ls** command to see its name):

```
tar -xvf filename.tar
```

5. The **tar** command in step 4 creates a directory that has the same name as the name and version portion of the tar file. Change to that directory, as follows (change the command to match your downloaded version):

```
cd /httpd-2.2.3
```

6. Run the Apache configuration script by entering the following command (it will take only a few seconds to run):

```
./configure
```

7. Now you need to prepare the binaries by compiling them. This takes two commands, each of which might take several minutes to complete:

```
Make
make install
```

8. At this point, Apache is installed but not yet running. To start Apache, execute the following command from any directory:

```
/usr/local/apache/bin/apachectl start
```

To test your Apache installation, you can use the **ps** command to verify that the daemons are running:

```
ps -e |more
```

The **ps** command will display all running processes. Because the preceding command pipes the output of **ps -e** through the **more** command, you might need to press the spacebar a number of times to see all of the running processes. In the output, you should see one or more copies of a process called httpd, which is the Apache daemon. You might see many of these processes, because Apache usually starts a number of them, depending on the computer on which you have installed Apache, but this is perfectly normal.

After you've verified that Apache has started, you can also test it using a web browser. Enter either of the following web addresses:

```
http://127.0.0.1
http://localhost
```

Both of these commands access any running web server on the computer on which they are used. (Remember that the address 127.0.0.1 is always shorthand for the local computer, as is the name *localhost*.)

You should also be able to access the page from another computer. Assuming that the computer on which you installed Apache has an IP address of 209.200.155.49, the following web address should bring up the page:

```
http://209.200.155.49
```

If you cannot access the page from a remote computer, but can on the local computer, you should check basic IP connectivity using the PING command and typical network troubleshooting techniques. It's also possible that you have a firewall running on the machine with Apache on it, and the firewall is preventing access.

Administering Apache Web Server

You will need to perform a number of basic administrative tasks on an Apache server, not the least of which is publishing a web site onto your newly installed Apache web server. This section briefly describes basic administrative tasks.

Stopping and Starting Apache

You use a script file called apachectl to start and stop the server. For a default Fedora installation, the apachectl file is located in the /usr/sbin directory and takes three main parameters: start, stop, and restart. For example, the following command will restart the server:

```
/usr/sbin/apachectl restart
```

Changing the Apache Configuration

As mentioned earlier in this chapter, Apache is essentially controlled through text-based configuration files, the main one of which is called httpd.conf. The httpd.conf file is located in the /etc/httpd/conf/ directory.

The httpd.conf file works through the use of plain-text directives contained in the file, along with the associated settings. For example, the following directive defines where Apache is installed:

```
ServerRoot "/etc/httpd"
```

If you wanted to move the Apache installation to a different directory on your Linux computer, you could certainly do so, but you would want to be careful to change the ServerRoot setting before attempting to restart Apache in its new location.

NOTE For any changes to the httpd.conf file to take effect, you must restart Apache using the **apachectl restart** command.

The httpd.conf file is divided into three main sections:

- Global environment
- Main server configuration
- Virtual hosts

Each of these sections contains a large number of directives that control how Apache works.

When learning about Apache, you should spend some time studying the contents of the httpd.conf file and reading the extensive comments included in the file. You should also look up the various directives in the online Apache documentation (http://httpd.apache.org/docs/), to get more information than provided by the comments in the httpd.conf file.

Publishing Web Pages

By default (for Apache version 2), the main web site published by Apache is located in the /var/www/html directory, and this directory is blank.

Once you are ready to publish a complete web site, you can place the files into /var/www/html with the home page stored as index.html. The easiest way to do this is to connect to the computer running Apache by using the FTP program, and then upload the web site's files, either directly to the /var/www/html directory or to a temporary directory on the server's hard disk. Once in the temporary directory, you can move them to the correct location on the server itself using the **mv** or **cp** commands (these, among a number of other useful Linux/UNIX commands, are covered in Chapter 21).

Chapter Summary

Most networking professionals will need to set up and maintain a web server in the course of their work. All server platforms have web servers available for them. An excellent web server that is available for just about all platforms is the Apache web server. As you saw in this chapter, Apache is easy to install, administer, and get up and running. If you have followed the instructions in the previous chapters and have set up Fedora Linux on a test system, I recommend that you also follow the steps in this chapter and set up and run Apache. Then add some files for a simple web site to it and browse the web server first from the computer on which it's running, and then from another computer on the network.

This chapter was intended to get you started with the Apache web server. If this is an area in which you wish to gain greater expertise, you will find more details in resources devoted to Apache server. Two books in this area that might interest you are *Apache Server 2.0: A Beginner's Guide,* by Kate Wrightson (McGraw-Hill/Professional, 2001) and *Apache Server 2.0: The Complete Reference,* by Ryan Bloom (McGraw-Hill/Professional, 2002).

Chapter 23

Introduction
to Virtualization

One of the most exciting areas to develop in networking over the past several years is *virtualization*, which is a method of creating multiple *virtual machines* on a single computer. These virtual machines operate as if they were running on their own computer, and the computer's actual resources—its processor, hard disk space, network connection, and other hardware—are virtualized so that they can be shared among the various virtual machines.

This chapter introduces virtualization. It discusses some of the main benefits of virtualization, and then provides of an overview of Microsoft's and VMware's virtualization offerings. To get you started, the chapter walks you through a VMware Server installation, along with the setup of an Ubuntu Linux virtual machine.

Benefits of Virtualization

The ability to virtualize computers can pay rich dividends. The following are some of the chief benefits of virtualization:

- **More efficient use of server resources** As noted in previous chapters, dedicating one server application per computer is the most reliable way to provide the services, and it's more maintainable as well. However, you often will have server applications that don't use that many server resources. For instance, you may have a web server that is used by 30 to 40 people within your organization on an occasional basis. With virtualization, however, you can run multiple virtual machines—all completely independent from one another—on a single server and more efficiently utilize the server's resources.

- **Ability to run multiple operating systems on a single computer** With virtualization, there is a *host operating system*, which is the operating system installed on the computer itself, and *guest operating systems*, which are the operating systems installed within each virtual machine. So you can, for instance, have a Windows Server 2008 host operating system installed on a computer, and then run operating systems like Windows XP, Ubuntu Linux, Windows Vista, or Sun Solaris within the virtual machines themselves. Or you can have Linux installed on a computer, and then have a variety of Linux and Windows operating systems running within virtual machines. You can even have no host operating system, and instead install what is called a *hypervisor*, which is a bare-bones operating system that just supports virtual machines.

- **Ease of moving virtual machines** You can easily move virtual machines from one virtual server to another, in order to better manage and balance resources like disk space, RAM, and processor utilization.

- **Reduced power requirements** You can reduce the energy required to run your IT infrastructure. By consolidating servers, your power requirements are reduced.

■   **Simplified maintenance**   When you put a lot of applications on a single server operating system, it becomes difficult to maintain each individual application without affecting the others. For example, if you upgrade an application and need to restart the server, you must restart the *whole* server, affecting all of the other jobs it may be doing. With a virtual machine setup, you can easily restart individual virtual machines without affecting how the other machines operate, and without interrupting their services.

Introducing Windows Server 2008 Hyper-V

Microsoft now offers Hyper-V technology within Windows Server 2008 64-bit edition, at no additional charge. Hyper-V is a full-featured hypervisor that runs within the Windows Server 2008 environment, and allows you to create and manage virtual machines within Windows Server 2008. This provides an easy way for a Windows 2008 Server-based organization to easily start using virtualization.

Microsoft's Hyper-V supports a single host operating system, of course: Windows Server 2008 64-bit. It supports the following guest operating systems:

■   Windows Server 2008 (64- and 32-bit)

■   Windows Server 2003 (64- and 32-bit)

■   Windows Server 2000

■   SUSE Linux Enterprise Server (64- and 32-bit)

■   Windows Vista (64- and 32-bit)

■   Windows XP Professional (64- and 32-bit)

These are the *supported* operating systems. Note that variants, such as other distributions of Linux, may—and often do—work perfectly fine.

Microsoft is dramatically expanding its virtualization efforts, but as of the publication of this book, they are not as mature as VMware offerings, which are described next.

Using VMware Virtualization Products

Currently, VMware has the most mature virtualization infrastructure available. VMware has a wide variety of products designed to help companies of any size manage virtual machines. And two powerful virtualization products are offered for free:

■   VMware Server, which is a full virtualization product designed to install onto a wide variety of host operating systems

■   VMware ESXi, which is a small (32MB) hypervisor that is installed directly onto a bare-metal computer, and can efficiently host guest operating systems

One of the nice features of VMware Server is that it is supported on a wide variety of host operating systems, including many that are designed as client operating systems. This means that you can install VMware Server onto, say, Windows Vista, and then install the full range of guest operating systems within virtual machines. This allows IT professionals to run a wide variety of operating systems, or to test various operating system and application combinations, without even starting with a server operating system.

VMware Server and ESXi require that they be installed on a computer that has a processor capable of supporting virtualization. Fortunately, virtually every Intel or AMD processor available these days supports virtualization. VMware Server can also be installed onto either 32-bit or 64-bit processors. However, keep in mind that if you want to install a 64-bit guest operating system in a virtual machine, the host operating system must also be 64 bits.

VMware Server supports the following host operating systems:

- Windows Server 2008 (64- and 32-bit)
- Windows Server 2003 (64- and 32-bit, including Small Business Server)
- Windows 2000 Server
- Various 64- and 32-bit versions of Red Hat, SUSE, Ubuntu, Mandrake, and Mandriva Linux operating systems (the detailed list of supported versions changes, so consult VMware documentation for the version you wish to install)

VMware Server supports the following guest operating systems:

- Windows Server 2008 (64- and 32-bit)
- Windows Server 2003 (64- and 32-bit, including Small Business Server)
- Windows 2000 Server
- Windows Vista (64- and 32-bit)
- Windows XP Professional (64- and 32-bit)
- Mandrake, Mandriva, Red Hat, SUSE, openSUSE, Open Enterprise Server, and Ubuntu Linux
- Sun Solaris
- Novell NetWare

As with the Hyper-V list, these are the *supported* operating systems. Variants, such as other distributions of Linux, may work. For example, while writing this book, I had no problems installing and extensively using VMware Server on Windows Vista 64-bit as a host operating system.

Downloading and Installing VMware Server

To download VMware Server, go to http://www.vmware.com/products/server/. You will need to register on VMware's site during the download process, and you will then be given a serial number to install both VMware for Windows and VMware for Linux. You can download whichever version matches your host operating system.

 NOTE   The example in this chapter uses VMware Server 2.0.1 installed onto Windows Vista 64-bit. Windows Vista is not an officially supported host operating system; however, for experimental/ learning purposes it should work fine. For production purposes, you should use a supported host operating system.

The installation of VMware Server 2 is actually very straightforward. You're prompted for where you wish to install it, and also for the machine name and the IP ports to use for remote access to the VMware management console. For all of these settings, you can accept the default choices provided.

Once the installation of VMware Server completes, you will need to restart the system.

Accessing the VMware Server Management Console

VMware Server's management console is accessed through Internet Explorer. Once VMware Server is installed, a copy of the Tomcat web server is also installed onto the local machine, and it is Tomcat that serves up the VMware web pages to Internet Explorer.

 NOTE   If you install VMware Server 2 onto Windows Vista as the host operating system, you need to create an administrator-class account named Admin on the machine in order to log in to the VMware Server management console. You do this through the standard Windows Vista Control Panel tools for managing local machine user accounts.

You can find the URL for the management console in the system's Start menu, under /Programs/VMware/VMware Server/VMware Server Home Page. You can also enter the URL into Internet Explorer, and then bookmark it into Internet Explorer as an alternate way of accessing it. Enter the following URL:

```
https://<local machine name>:8333/ui/
```

The login page for VMware Server will appear, as shown in Figure 23-1.

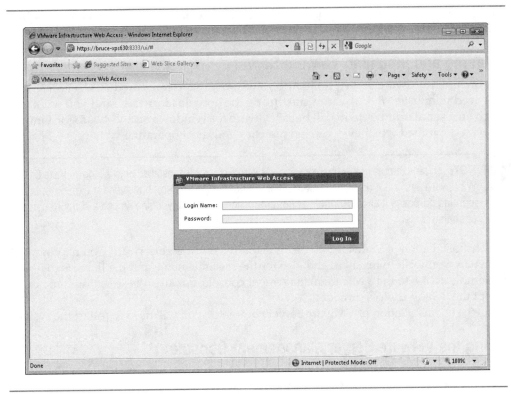

Figure 23-1.   Logging in to VMware Server

Figure 23-2 shows the main management console, which appears after you've logged in to VMware Server using an administrative account.

Creating a Virtual Machine for Ubuntu Linux

In this example, you will see how easy it is to create a virtual machine running Ubuntu Linux as a guest operating system. You will install Ubuntu from a CD image file (an ISO file). You can download the current version of Ubuntu Linux from http://www .ubuntu.com. I recommend downloading the desktop version of Ubuntu Linux, rather than the server version (the server version uses only a text-based console).

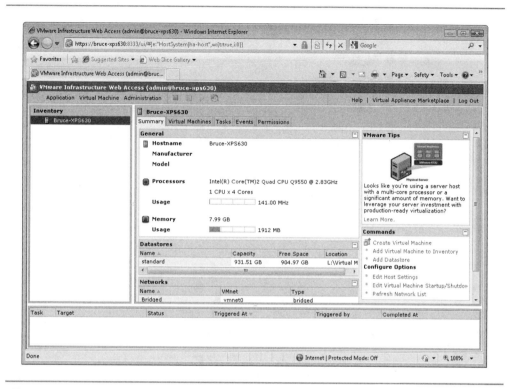

Figure 23-2.   Use the VMware Server management console to manage your virtual environment.

Before beginning, you will need to place a copy of the Ubuntu ISO file into the VMware datastore. The datastore is where the virtual machines you create with VMware Server will be stored. The location of the VMware datastore appears on the VMware Server management console, listed in the Datastores pane on the Summary tab. If the location that VMware's installation chose for the storage of your virtual machine is not to your liking, you can create a new datastore, and then remove the default standard datastore (or simply not use it). Figure 23-3 shows the Add Datastore dialog box.

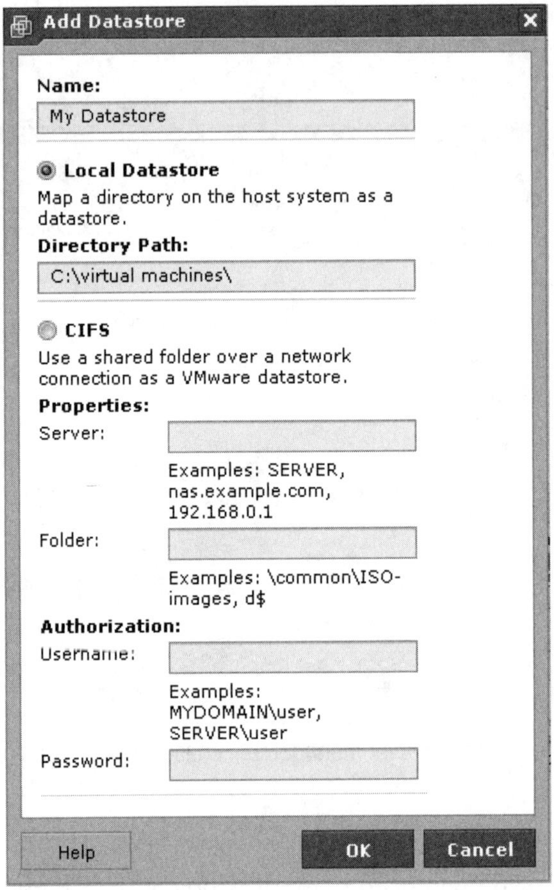

Figure 23-3. Creating a new VMware datastore

Virtual machines are created using a wizard-like process that walks you through making all the appropriate choices. Here are the steps:

1. Click the Create Virtual Machine link in the VMware Server console's Command pane. You see the Create Virtual Machine screen, as shown in Figure 23-4.

2. On the Name and Location page, name the virtual machine you will create. In this example, I've named it Ubuntu 9.0.3. You should also verify that the correct datastore has been selected (if you have more than one). Click Next to continue.

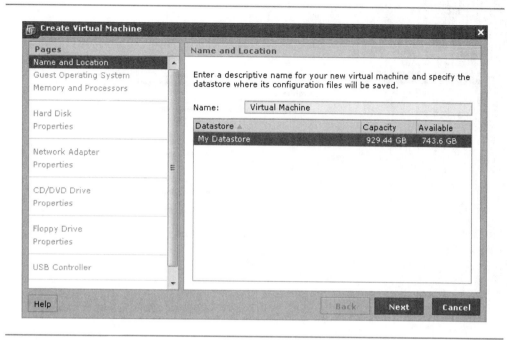

Figure 23-4.   Starting to create a virtual machine

3. On the Guest Operating System page, shown in Figure 23-5, first select the appropriate type of guest operating system that will run in the virtual machine. In the Version drop-down list, you will see that a wide variety of supported guest Linux versions are available, including some choices for generic Linux distributions. Select the version that is closest to that of your guest operating system. Then click Next to continue.

4. On the Memory and Processors page, shown in Figure 23-6, based on the guest operating system you chose in the preceding step, VMware will propose a suggested value for the amount of RAM to give it. You can accept this amount or change it. Note that you can increase this amount later if necessary.

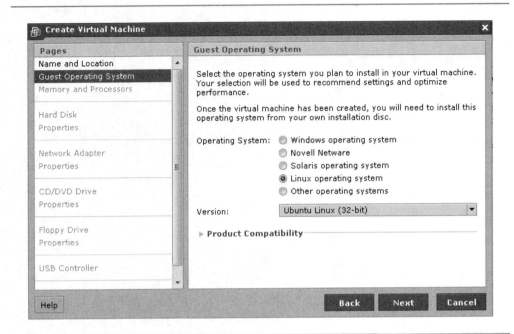

Figure 23-5. Choosing the guest operating system

 NOTE   The amount of RAM you allocate to the virtual machine will come from the host computer's available RAM and, while the virtual machine is running, will not be available for the host operating system. Therefore, you do not want to allocate all of the computer's installed RAM to the virtual machine, as then the host operating system would not have enough RAM to do its work, and it would likely thrash its virtual memory file and become unusable. On the other hand, you don't want to allocate too little RAM to the virtual machine, particularly if you know you'll be performing memory-intensive actions within the virtual machine, as then the virtual machine wouldl run poorly. As a general rule, unless you're limited in the amount of installed RAM on the computer, or if you're planning on running many parallel virtual machines at the same time, I recommend increasing the amount of RAM allocated by 50 to 100 percent of the default suggested by VMware.

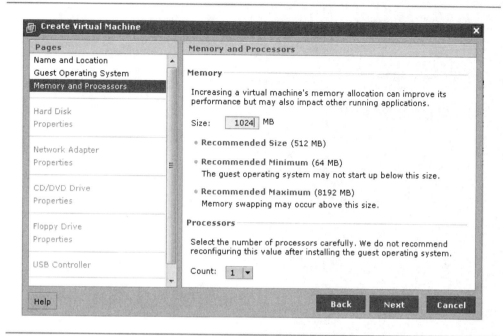

Figure 23-6.   Setting the amount of RAM for the guest operating system

5. If you're using a multicore or multiprocessor computer, you can select how many processors the virtual machine can monopolize while it's running. Unlike the amount of RAM, which can be easily changed later, the choice you make for the number of processors to allocate should not be changed without re-creating the virtual machine from scratch. This is because when you install a guest operating system, the guest operating system installation will often be installed to support the number of processors it originally detects. If you increase or decrease the number of processors allocated to the virtual machine, the guest operating system may no longer start or operate properly. After making your RAM and processor choices, click Next.

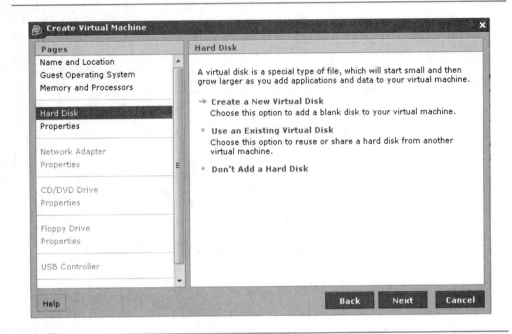

Figure 23-7. Choosing your virtual disk

6. From the Hard Disk page, shown in Figure 23-7, you can choose to create a new virtual disk or use an existing one. The hard disk for a virtual machine is actually a file stored on the real hard disk of the host operating system. All of the guest operating system's files will be stored in that virtual hard disk file. From the perspective of the virtual machine, it has a hard disk installed with a size that you specify. From the perspective of the host operating system, it's just a single file stored in the VMware datastore location. For almost all virtual machines, you will need to create a virtual hard disk, and this example is no exception. Click Create a New Disk.

7. On the Properties page for the hard disk, shown in Figure 23-8, you can set a number of properties for creating a virtual hard disk. Choose from the following choices, and then click Next.

   ■ **Size of the virtual hard disk**   VMware will, based on the operating system you've selected, propose a size for the virtual hard disk. While it is possible to increase this later, it can be difficult to do so. Accordingly, I recommend that you set the size to be larger than you think you need.

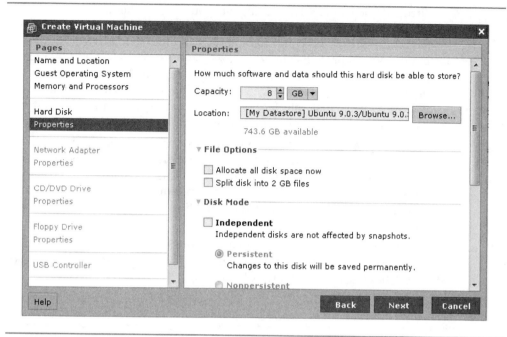

Figure 23-8.   Setting virtual hard disk properties

- **File options**   If you select the checkbox Allocate All Disk Space Now, VMware will create a virtual hard disk file that is the size you selected. Otherwise, VMware will automatically expand the virtual hard disk file's size as the space is used. The trade-off is that if you choose to allocate the space immediately, the virtual hard disk may consume much more space on the host system's hard disk than it is actually using. On the other hand, if the space is allocated immediately, then the performance of creating files or writing new blocks to the disk will be much faster, because the space is already allocated. I recommend leaving this checkbox unchecked, but choosing a size that is comfortably larger than you think you need. This way, you efficiently use actual hard disk space, and the automatic expansion process is generally not a huge price to pay for most uses.

- **Independent disk mode**   This option allows you to configure a virtual hard disk as independent of any snapshots you make of the virtual machine. Note that you can have multiple virtual hard disks in each virtual machine, and for some applications, you may want the one or more of the virtual hard disks to not be part of the VMware snapshot process. Generally, you will leave this option unselected.

- **Virtual device node**   This setting lets you choose whether VMware will emulate a SCSI or IDE controller for the virtual hard disk you are creating, and which virtualized controller interface number will be used. Realize that the type of hard disk interface used on the host computer does not matter here; VMware can run a virtual SCSI hard disk on a host computer that has only IDE drives or vice versa. For this setting, VMware will propose a virtual disk interface type based on the guest operating system you chose, and you should generally accept the default choice.

- **Write caching**   You can set the virtual hard disk to optimize write caching to optimize for data safety or for performance. In a production environment, where the data stored on the virtual machine is important, you should choose Safety. If you're just experimenting with an operating system and wouldn't mind if you lost the files stored on it, you can choose Performance.

8. On the Network Adapter page, shown in Figure 23-9, you can choose to create a virtual network adapter for the virtual machine. In most cases, you will need to do this. Click Create a Network Adapter.

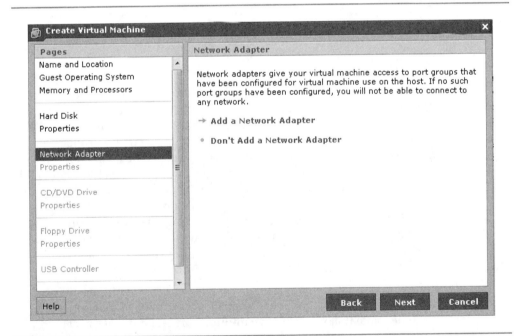

Figure 23-9.   Choosing whether or not to add a network adapter

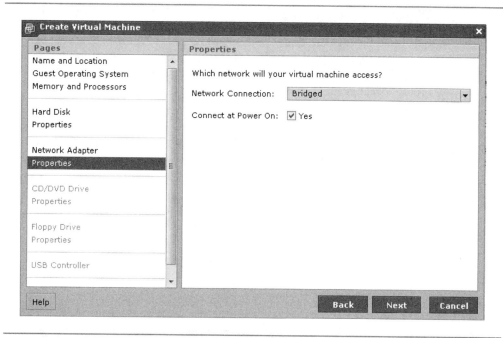

Figure 23-10.   Setting network adapter properties

9. On the Properties page for the network adapter, shown in Figure 23-10, you can choose to create three types of network adapters. Select from the following choices, and then click Next.

   ■ **Bridged**   This is the default choice and is best for most applications. A bridged virtual network adapter makes use of the host computer's network adapter, but it obtains its own IP address from the appropriate DHCP server, or it can have an IP address manually assigned to it. The main thing to keep in mind is that if you run many virtual machines simultaneously, each one with a bridged virtual network adapter will use one of the available IP addresses on your network.

   ■ **Network Address Translation (NAT)**   When you choose a NAT virtual network adapter, the virtual machine makes use of the IP and MAC addresses of the host computer when it communicates on the network. If you are running various servers as virtual machines, a NAT configuration can be difficult to set up, as you would need to configure port forwarding so that the packets are properly routed to the appropriate virtual machine.

For instance, if you have a web server running in a virtual machine that is using a NAT virtual network interface, you would need to configure the host operating system to forward incoming port 80 (and maybe port 443) packets to that virtual machine. If the virtual machine is running only client-type systems, however, then NAT would help conserve IP addresses on the local network.

■ **HostOnly** Choosing HostOnly creates a virtual network on the host computer. Virtual machines that use this type of virtual network adapter can communicate over the network, but only to other running virtual machines on the host computer or to the host computer itself.

10. On the CD/DVD Drive page, shown in Figure 23-11, choose how to access the CD/DVD drive. VMware Server can either share access to the host computer's CD/DVD drive or it can emulate a CD or DVD drive by connecting to an image file (ISO) stored on the host computer, within the VMware datastore. If the guest operating system download already exists on the host computer as an image file, then choosing this option is very convenient, and means you don't need

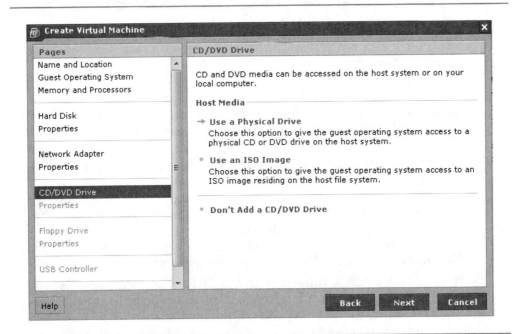

Figure 23-11. Setting CD/DVD drive access

to burn the image file to a piece of optical media. If you are installing a guest operating system that you have on a CD or DVD, then you should create a new virtual CD or DVD drive by choosing Use a Physical Disk. For this example, since you're probably installing Ubuntu Linux from a downloaded image file, you should choose Use an ISO Image. Once Ubuntu is fully installed, you can change this to give the virtual machine access to the host computer's CD or DVD drives, if you wish.

11. When you choose Use an ISO Image, you see the Properties page for the CD/DVD drive, as shown in Figure 23-12. Click Browse, and select the ISO file that you placed in the VMware datastore. Make sure that the Connect at Power On option is selected, so that the new virtual machine will be able to boot from the image file, which it will need to do to install the guest operating system. Click Next to continue.

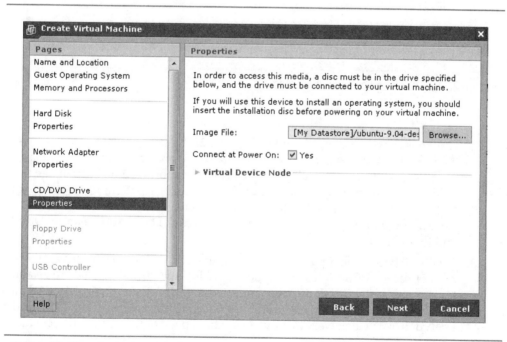

Figure 23-12. Setting the CD/DVD drive properties

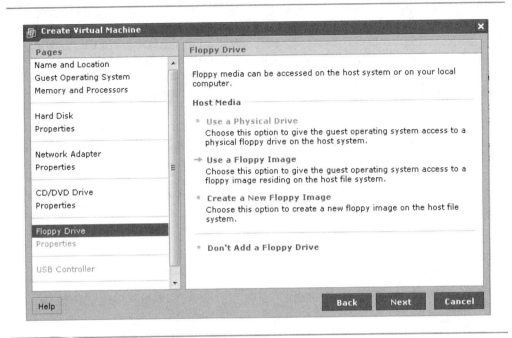

Figure 23-13. Setting floppy drive access

12. On the Floppy Drive page, shown in Figure 23-13, you can choose how to access the floppy drive. If you need to run a legacy program that needs to make use of a diskette drive installed on the host system or use a diskette image file (.FLP), you can create a virtual floppy drive (the process is similar to creating a CD/DVD drive). Since diskette drives are increasingly rare and are unlikely to be needed for this virtual machine, you can click Don't Add a Floppy Drive and then Next to continue.

13. On the USB Controller page, shown in Figure 23-14, you can choose whether or not to add a USB controller. If you would like the virtual machine to be able to read and write to USB devices connected to the host computer, select Add a USB Controller. There are no further options to configure if you choose to add a USB controller. Click Next to move to the final page of the virtual disk creation process.

14. You will see the confirmatory page shown in Figure 23-15. If any choices need to be changed, you can click Back and revise your answers. Otherwise, click Finish to create the virtual machine. Provided that you did not choose to allocate all disk space immediately, the virtual machine should be created within a minute or so, and you will return to the VMware Server management console.

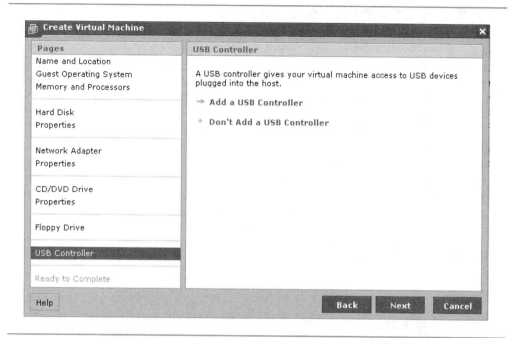

Figure 23-14.   Choosing whether or not to add a USB controller

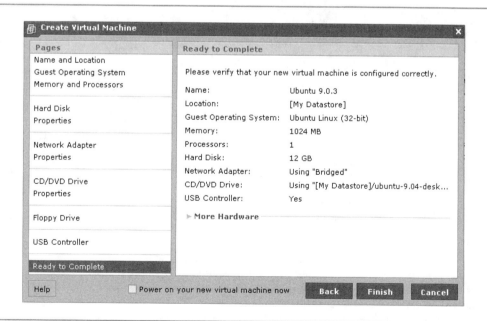

Figure 23-15.   Completing the virtual machine creation

Running Ubuntu Linux in the Virtual Machine

Now that you've created the Ubuntu virtual machine, from the main VMware management console, click the virtual machine in the Inventory pane, which will then display the details of the virtual machine, as shown in Figure 23-16.

If you made any mistakes, you can change the virtual machine parameters in the Hardware pane by clicking the various drop-down boxes. Otherwise, all you need to do is power on the virtual machine by clicking the Power On link in the Commands pane. Doing this starts the virtual machine, but you will not automatically see what is happening in the virtual machine. To do that, click the Console tab, and then click within the Console pane to open the console window.

Since the virtual machine's virtual hard disk is blank, and since you've connected the Ubuntu image file to the virtual machine, the virtual machine will boot from that image file, just as any computer would under those circumstances (bootable CD or DVD inserted, and blank hard disk). The Ubuntu image file is what is known as a *live CD*. It boots up a functional copy of Ubuntu, which you will see in the VMware console window, as shown in Figure 23-17.

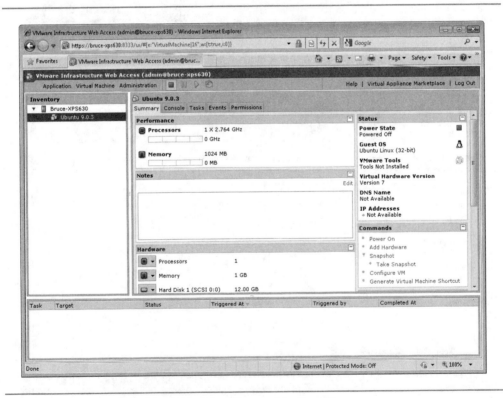

Figure 23-16. Viewing the details of the Ubuntu virtual machine

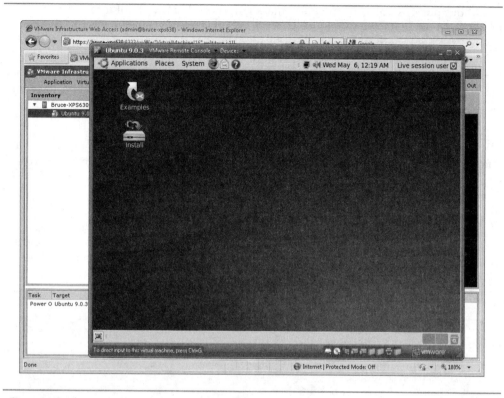

Figure 23-17. The Ubuntu live CD running in a virtual machine

Ubuntu is not yet "installed" into the virtual machine. The live CD version is instead running purely from the virtual CD-ROM. Accordingly, any files you create, applications you install, or changes you make to Ubuntu will not be saved. In order to make the virtual machine contain a fully functioning copy of Ubuntu, you need to run the Ubuntu installation process. On the live CD desktop is a shortcut called Install. Double-clicking it will begin the Ubuntu installation procedure. The detailed Ubuntu installation procedure is not covered here, but it is similar to the installation of Fedora Linux, which was discussed in Chapter 20.

NOTE   When you install a guest operating system into a virtual machine, it's just like installing it onto a bare-metal computer. You will need to partition and format the hard disk for the virtual machine during its installation, because the virtual hard disk starts out completely blank. The first time you install a guest operating system into a virtual machine, you might be concerned that all of the typical warnings about deleting the hard disk's contents might possibly affect the host computer. However, as long as you're running in the virtual machine, only the virtual hard disk can be partitioned and formatted by the guest operating system; your host system is completely insulated from the virtual machine.

At this point, there are some particulars you should know about interacting with the VMware virtual machine console. When you click in the console, the console "owns" the host computer's mouse and keyboard. To release the mouse and keyboard so that you can interact with the host system, press CTRL+ALT. When you want to return to the console, just click in it again. Also, rather than press CTRL+ALT+DELETE for a virtual machine, you press CTRL+ALT+INSERT. CTRL+ALT+DELETE is always interpreted by VMware as being intended for the host operating system.

Installing VMware Tools

After creating a virtual machine and installing the guest operating system into it, one of the first things you should do is to install VMware Tools into the virtual machine. The VMware Tools set helps make the virtual machines operate much more efficiently (especially for graphics operations).

The VMware Tools package is part of VMware Server, and installing it is fairly easy. To do so, when the virtual machine is running, navigate to the virtual machine's Summary tab, as shown in Figure 23-18. In the Status pane, you will see a link labeled

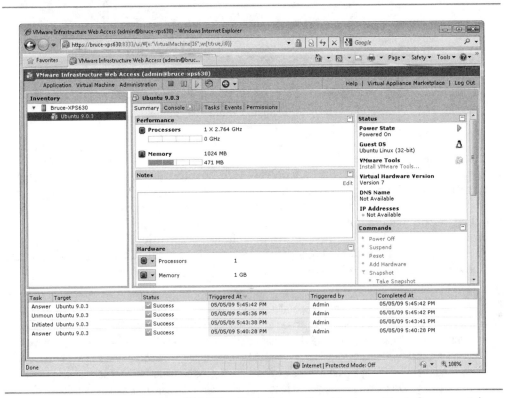

Figure 23-18. Choose the Install VMware Tools link on the virtual machine's Summary tab.

Install VMware Tools. Selecting this link immediately mounts a virtual CD-ROM into the virtual machine, which contains the software that you need to install.

The VMware Tools virtual CD contains versions for Windows and Linux guest operating systems, both of which typically will automatically display the virtual CD's contents. For example, Figure 23-19 shows the result in the Ubuntu virtual machine of selecting the Install VMware Tools option from the VMware management console.

TIP   When you install VMware Tools, you no longer need to press CTRL+ALT to release your mouse and keyboard from the virtual machine console. Instead, you can interact with the console and the guest operating system as if it were another window on the host computer's desktop.

Figure 23-19.   VMware Tools in the Ubuntu virtual machine

Backing Up Virtual Machine Data

In a production environment, you need to consider how you intend to back up the data on your virtual machines. There are several approaches:

- You can shut down or suspend the virtual machines, and copy the entire virtual machine file from its location in your datastore to some sort of backup media. If the virtual machine contains a number of installed applications but little changing data, then this can be a good backup strategy. (Note also that virtual machines can be moved between computers, so to recover a virtual machine, all you need to do is move it to a computer running a compatible version of VMware Server, and then import the virtual machine file and start it up.)

- From within the virtual machine, you can set up a process to copy its data files to another location on your network, which in turn might be backed up onto a tape drive or other backup media.

- Most of the higher-end backup software solutions sell add-on products that let you back up files from within VMware virtual machines.

Chapter Summary

In this chapter, you learned the essentials of virtualization, and the benefits it can bring to networks. You learned about inexpensive virtualization solutions from Microsoft and VMware, and you learned how to set up a virtual machine in VMware Server running Ubuntu Linux.

Virtualization has become very important in business networking, because ultimately it helps companies do more with less (a common corporate mantra). Accordingly, it is important that people working in the networking field understand virtualization, the benefits it can bring, and how to work with it. If you didn't actually set up a VMware Server system as outlined in this chapter, I strongly recommend that you do so at some point. There's no substitute for actually experiencing how powerful and useful virtual machines can be.

Appendix

Understanding the Sarbanes-Oxley Act

During 2001 and 2002, a number of large accounting scandals—involving companies like Enron, WorldCom, Global Crossing, and Tyco—rocked the business world. These various scandals, which substantially reduced investor confidence in the U.S. equity markets, resulted in Congress passing a law called the Sarbanes-Oxley Act of 2002. The Sarbanes-Oxley Act of 2002, also known as SarbOx or SOX, establishes a framework that governs the accuracy and fairness of financial reporting for publicly traded companies in the United States, and implements a number of rules to help reduce the potential for accounting fraud.

Because information technology (IT) systems and processes play an important role in a company's accounting and reporting duties, the IT department is a critical part of a company achieving SOX compliance. Almost all of the impact from SOX that affects IT departments comes from a single section of SOX, called Section 404. However, before exploring the effects of Section 404 on IT departments, it is helpful for you to understand the basic contents of SOX.

This appendix begins with a summary of SOX, and then covers key procedures for an IT internal control system, including compliance testing. The final section presents some examples of IT standard operating procedures (SOPs).

Sarbanes-Oxley Act Summary

SOX is divided into 11 main parts called *titles*, each further broken down into a number of *sections*. Each title contains between one and nine sections.

NOTE You can download the entire text of the Sarbanes-Oxley Act of 2002 from the Public Company Accounting Oversight Board web site (http://www.pcaobus.org). On the home page is a link to a PDF containing the full text of SOX. You can also use a search engine to look for "Sarbanes-Oxley Act of 2002," which should provide some alternative links from which you can download SOX.

Title I: Public Company Accounting Oversight Board

Title I mandates that a Public Company Accounting Oversight Board (PCAOB) be established. The PCAOB oversees the auditing of public companies. This includes setting up rules that control the auditing, quality control, ethics, independence, and other standards relating to audit reports.

Under Title I, all public accounting firms must register with the PCAOB. Each accounting firm must provide the PCAOB with details on which public companies it audits, the fees it earns, and any complaints or adverse actions against the public accounting firm. Title I also includes a number of administrative details about the PCAOB, such as the composition of the board, how long the members serve, and so forth.

Title II: Auditor Independence

Title II specifies rules that are designed to increase the independence of public accounting firms and help ensure that their audit opinions are not clouded by other business dealings they may have with the company being audited. It includes the following rules:

- The accounting firm may not provide, at the same time as its audit, any bookkeeping, computer system design or implementation, valuation services, actuarial services, or other nonaudit services for the company being audited.

- The accounting firm may provide some nonaudit services that are not specifically prohibited for the company being audited, provided the company's audit committee expressly approves such engagements.

- The accounting firm's partner that is engaged with the company being audited must be rotated to another partner every five years.

- The key financial executives (CEO, CFO, and Controller) of the company being audited cannot have worked for the accounting firm for a one-year period prior to the audit.

Title III: Corporate Responsibility

Title III of SOX sets a number of rules regarding corporate responsibility. These rules, if they are not followed, can result in a public company's stock being removed from the relevant stock exchange (such as NYSE or NASDAQ).

Section 301 covers public company audit committees, as follows:

- Audit committees are directly responsible for the appointment, compensation, and oversight of the accounting firm providing audit services, and for resolving any differences in opinion between the audit firm and the management of the company regarding accounting treatments and interpretations.

- Accounting firms that are providing audit services to a company must report directly to the audit committee of the board of directors.

- Members of an audit committee cannot accept any nonboard fees from the company for which they serve on the board of directors, and they cannot be "an affiliated person" of the company or any of its subsidiaries.

- The audit committee must set up procedures for the receipt, retention, and treatment of complaints received by the company regarding accounting, internal accounting controls, or auditing matters. This is sometimes called a "whistleblower" system.

NOTE   An audit committee is a subset of a company's board of directors. This committee is charged with ensuring the accuracy of the company's financial reports and for reviewing key accounting and financial policies.

Section 302 mandates that the principal executive officer (usually the CEO) and the principal financial officer (usually the CFO) certify each annual or quarterly report that is filed with the U.S. Securities and Exchange Commission (SEC). These certifications must state the following:

- The certifying officer has reviewed the report.

- Based on the officer's knowledge, the report does not contain any untrue statement of material facts, and does not fail to state any material facts that could result in the report being misleading.

- The officer has evaluated the effectiveness of the company's internal controls within 90 days of the report's date.

- The officers have presented in the periodic report their conclusions about the effectiveness of the internal controls of the company.

- The officers have disclosed to the audit committee and to the auditors all significant deficiencies regarding the operation of the company's internal controls, which could adversely affect the company's ability to record, process, summarize, and report financial data, and that they have disclosed any fraud, material or not, that involves management or employees who have a significant role in the company's internal controls.

- The officers have disclosed any significant changes to the system of internal controls used by the company, including any corrective actions that were taken to address any weaknesses.

NOTE   For public companies, a *periodic report* is their annual report on SEC form 10-K and their quarterly reports on SEC form 10-Q.

Section 303 makes illegal any improper influence on the conduct of audits. Specifically, it applies to any officer or director of the company, *or any other person acting under the direction of an officer or director,* to take any action that fraudulently influences, coerces, manipulates, or misleads the firm performing the audit of the company. I've emphasized the words in the preceding sentence because this rule applies to anyone who works with or provides information to the auditors, including IT personnel who are involved in the company's internal controls.

Section 304 states that the CEO and CFO must reimburse the company for any bonus they have received, including equity-based compensation, if the company is required to restate its financial reports as a result of any misconduct. (You can now see why CEOs and CFOs take SOX compliance very seriously!)

Section 305 modifies the Securities Exchange Act of 1934 to decrease the level of unfitness of an officer or director that could bar that individual from serving as an officer or director of a public company.

Section 306 bars directors and officers of a company from trading in the company's stock or stock options during times when a pension fund blackout is in effect.

Section 307 sets forth some professional obligations for any attorneys who represent a company with the SEC. For example, they are required to report to the company's chief legal counsel or the CEO any evidence of a material violation of securities law or breach of fiduciary duty. If those two individuals do not appropriately respond to the evidence, then the attorney is required to report to the board of directors.

Section 308 discusses that any civil penalties that are obtained from a person be added to any disgorgement of profits in a fund that is for the benefit of the victims of the underlying violation.

Title IV: Enhanced Financial Disclosures

Title IV covers disclosures in periodic reports, and it includes the famous Section 404, which impacts IT departments to a large extent.

Section 401 requires that financial statements include any material correcting adjustments, that all material off-balance-sheet transactions be disclosed (Enron had a number of very material off-balance-sheet transactions that were not disclosed), and that any *pro forma* financial tables be presented in a way that is not misleading.

Section 402 prohibits public companies from making personal loans that are not a routine part of the company's business to any director or executive officer of a public company. A bank, for instance, can make normal credit card, home, or auto loans to its executives, provided that the terms are the same as it makes available to the general public.

Section 403 requires that all directors, officers, and principal stockholders report any transactions in the company's stock promptly.

Section 404, despite it being one of the shorter sections of SOX, has caused a lot of headaches for accounting and IT departments. Because of its importance in these areas, following is the entirety of Section 404.

SEC. 404. MANAGEMENT ASSESSMENT OF INTERNAL CONTROLS.

(a) *RULES REQUIRED.—The Commission shall prescribe rules requiring each annual report required by section 13(a) or 15(d) of the Securities Exchange Act of 1934 (15 U.S.C. 78m or 78o(d)) to contain an internal control report, which shall—*

    (1) *state the responsibility of management for establishing and maintaining an adequate internal control structure and procedures for financial reporting; and*

    (2) *contain an assessment, as of the end of the most recent fiscal year of the issuer, of the effectiveness of the internal control structure and procedures of the issuer for financial reporting.*

(b) *INTERNAL CONTROL EVALUATION AND REPORTING.—With respect to the internal control assessment required by subsection (a), each registered public accounting firm that prepares or issues the audit report for the issuer shall attest to, and report on, the assessment made by the management of the issuer. An attestation made under this subsection shall be made in accordance with standards for attestation engagements issued or adopted by the Board.*

Any such attestation shall not be the subject of a separate engagement.

In a nutshell, two items are mandated by Section 404:

■ The management of a company must set up an adequate system of internal controls and regularly report its assessment of the effectiveness of the internal controls in the company's annual report.

■ The company's auditors must examine the system of internal controls and attest to their adequacy.

Later in this appendix, you'll learn more about what Section 404 means in practice. Section 405 exempts registered investment companies from Sections 401, 402, and 404.

Section 406 requires that a code of ethics be established for senior financial officers of a company, and enumerates several items that must be part of the code of ethics.

Section 407 requires that each audit committee have at least one member who qualifies as a "financial expert."

Section 408 requires the SEC to review the disclosures made by public companies and their financial statements.

Finally, Section 409 requires that any material financial changes be disclosed to the public on a rapid and current basis, in plain English.

Titles V, VI, and VII

Titles V, VI, and VII are not applicable to most public companies. Title V, "Analyst Conflicts of Interest," concerns conflicts of interest for stock analysts. You may recall that during the stock market bubble, stock analysts often spoke favorably about offerings that were being handled by their firm, and in some cases received bonuses based on how they moved the stock price. This, of course, is illegal besides being unethical.

Title VI, "Commission Resources and Authority," discusses how the PCAOB is funded.

Title VII, "Studies and Reports," calls for a number of studies and reports of various federal agencies, including the following:

■ The U.S. Government Accounting Office (GAO) must conduct a study examining the consolidation of public accounting firms.

■ The PCAOB must conduct a study regarding the role of credit rating agencies and how they affect the stock market.

■ The PCAOB must study violations and violators of federal securities laws from January 1, 1998, to December 31, 2001.

■ The PCAOB must study all SEC enforcement actions involving reporting violations.

■ The GAO must conduct a study of investment banks and financial advisors, and whether those parties helped companies manipulate their earnings and hide their true financial condition.

Titles VIII, IX, X, and XI

The final titles of SOX do concern most companies, but probably won't concern IT personnel directly. Title VIII, "Corporate and Criminal Fraud Accountability Act of 2002," discusses audit document retention and penalties for destroying or altering important documents. It also enhances federal sentencing guidelines for fraud and obstruction of justice sentences. Finally, it protects "whistleblowers" of potential violations of securities laws.

Title IX, "White-Collar Crime Penalty Enhancements," does exactly as its name suggests: increases penalties for a number of white-collar crimes.

Title X, "Corporate Tax Returns," states that company tax returns should be signed by the company's CEO.

Title XI, "Corporate Fraud Accountability," increases some other criminal penalties, and allows the SEC to ban anyone found to have violated the securities laws from serving as a director or officer of a public company, for as long as it determines.

About Internal Controls

Section 404 of SOX requires that public companies establish and evaluate a system of internal controls. Internal controls consist of procedures the company uses to help ensure the accuracy of financial reporting and minimize the chance of undetected fraud.

Most companies start with an existing framework of internal controls and then modify it to better suit their particular needs and business. The most commonly used framework for SOX compliance, and the one the SEC recommends, is one provided by COSO, which stands for Committee of Sponsoring Organizations of the Treadway Commission (http://www.coso.org).

COSO defines internal controls as a process, driven by a company's board of directors, management, and other professionals. The internal control process provides reasonable assurance that the operation is efficient and effective, that financial reporting is reliable, and that the company is complying with all applicable laws and regulations. It's important to note that any internal control process can provide only *reasonable assurances*, not absolute assurances.

The team setting up a system of internal controls will examine all of the different business process areas, such as the accounts payable (AP) process, the general ledger process, or the IT process. Each of the processes will be analyzed to determine what risks to inaccurate financial reporting exist, including the probability and impact of each risk. From these risks will be generated a set of control objectives, which are designed to avoid or prevent the risks, or to detect when a risk has occurred and reduce its impact. For example, an AP process might have some of the following control objectives:

- Invoices cannot be entered when they exceed 110 percent of the amount entered by the purchasing department, without controller approval.
- All invoices are charged to valid account numbers in the general ledger.

- An AP operator cannot release checks to vendors that have a "hold" status on their account.

- Uninvoiced receipts are reconciled every month.

- Only authorized AP operators can access the AP functions in the accounting system.

The complexity of the business and the analysis by the people implementing the internal control system will determine how many control objectives are put in place for each process area. Even for a small public company, there may be 20 to 50 control objectives for each business process. For a large enterprise, many more controls might be in place.

NOTE Internal controls affect nearly every area of a business. Effective internal controls are the responsibility of the managers of each process area ("process owners"), not the accounting or internal audit department. A company's CEO and CFO are ultimately responsible for the adequacy of the systems.

Key Procedures for an IT Internal Control System

An IT department's internal control system should minimally consist of various controls that support, either directly or indirectly, the controls of the areas involved in financial reporting. Accordingly, once the control objectives are known for the other areas of the business, the IT department can, with the assistance of the accounting or internal audit function, design these supporting controls. An IT department can also implement internal controls that help the IT department to function more effectively, and these can be included in the IT department's system of internal controls.

IT Department Narrative

One of the first documents that an IT department should write is a narrative that overviews the IT department's operations. This document is updated periodically, and it is used by the external and internal auditors to quickly understand the overall structure and operations of the IT department.

The narrative should contain enough information to allow the readers to quickly familiarize themselves with the IT department and to understand its overall system of controls. Suggested contents include the following:

- IT organization chart, including a breakdown of key responsibilities of the personnel

- How duties are segregated

- A description of the computer systems in place, including servers, type of network installed, and network operating systems used

- A diagram of the network showing key equipment and the overall connection scheme, and in particular, all routes into or out of the network such as primary and backup Internet connections or private wide area network (WAN) links

- How the network authenticates users, how permissions are managed, and how users are created and terminated from the system

- An overview of the disaster recovery capabilities of the IT department and any business continuity plans

- A description of the systems that are within the scope of the audit, such as the accounting system, any payroll system, stock administration system, and so forth

- Any custom software or modifications to in-scope systems

- The logical access path from a user to the in-scope systems

- A description of the change management process, including how changes are authorized, documented, and tested

Disaster Recovery Plan

While not technically part of the system of internal controls, a disaster recovery plan (also called a business continuity plan) is a document that a public company's external auditors will want to evaluate. They will be primarily concerned with details of how the company's critical business information is protected and how it could be accessed in the event of a disaster. Accordingly, a disaster recovery plan should describe the company's backup systems in detail, including the following:

- What sort of backup system is in use, in detail

- If tapes are used, how they are rotated internally on a daily basis

- What type of off-site secure storage is used, how tapes are rotated off-site, and how rotations are documented

- If a colocation scheme is in place, how it operates and how data is replicated to the other location(s)

- How the backup system is periodically tested to ensure that it is working as designed, that it can restore data, and how the testing is documented

- If backups are performed differently for in-scope systems, how they operate for the in-scope systems (for example, general network backups are typically not kept for extended periods of time, but backups of an enterprise resource planning system might periodically make permanent tapes that are kept indefinitely)

In addition to details of the backup and recovery systems, a disaster recovery plan should also address more general factors, such as these:

- What hardware and software would be needed to restore operations at a temporary site in the event of a total loss

- What the worst-case information loss would be if, for instance, the building burned to the ground

- How replacement software is obtained, and how much time and what skills would be needed to restore computing operations

- Any important software licenses or license keys that are needed and how they would be accessed in case of a total loss

- How communications are handled in the event of a disaster

- How a detailed remediation plan is generated and implemented once the exact details of the disaster are known

Access Management

An important procedure to carefully document is how the company manages access to its various systems. This document should describe the properties of the access management system and how the various steps are performed. One section should describe how users are authenticated to the network generally, and to any in-scope systems in particular, as follows:

- The password policies in place, both for the network and any in-scope systems

- How frequently passwords are to be changed, and whether this is enforced by the system

- How complex passwords must be, and whether this is enforced by the system

- How users are instructed about the nonsystem aspects of the password policy for which they are responsible (for example, that new users acknowledge that they must not share their password with any other individual, what they should do if they think their password has been compromised, and so on)

- How the intruder lockout system functions when an incorrect password is tried repeatedly

You also need to show how permissions to the various parts of the network are approved and documented. One way to do this is to develop a form for the creation of new users or modifications in permissions for existing users. This form should specify which parts of the network and in-scope systems a user has access to, and it should be approved by the person's manager. For any access to in-scope systems, usually the system is designed so that the corporate controller approves those permissions (or formally delegates the approval to another person). Once a new user account is created based on the form, the IT department files it and makes it available to auditors on request.

Similarly, you will need to document employee terminations. Of particular concern to the auditors is account termination for people who had access to financial systems, and assurance that their access to financial systems was terminated at the same time as their employment was terminated.

System Maintenance

Regular system maintenance of the in-scope systems should be defined and documented. The actual maintenance activities that are performed should be spelled out in a procedural document. For example, a Windows-based server might have the following maintenance activities defined:

- Examine event logs and note any serious problems.
- Save the event log.
- Apply any pending Microsoft patches through Windows Update.
- Examine disk space to ensure that adequate free space is available.
- Examine the backup system logs to ensure that backups are being performed properly and that there are no unresolved errors.
- Restart the system and ensure proper functioning after it restarts.

The performance of these tasks should be documented whenever they are done. Depending on the preferences of the company's auditors, this can be electronic or through the use of a paper form developed for this purpose.

Change Control

A critical procedure to develop is one that governs how changes to any in-scope systems are managed. This includes both changes to the in-scope software, such as applying an update or upgrade to the application or modifying a program used by the system, as well as changes to the operating system and hardware in a server that hosts in-scope systems.

All changes to in-scope systems need to be documented, and where approvals are required, they also need to be documented.

A general procedure for a routine change might be a request from a person in the accounting department to modify a financial report to make it more useful, or to develop a new report that will help the employees do their job better. In such a case, the requestor might complete a form describing the desired change, which is submitted to the IT department. The IT department then assesses the change to determine how it can be accomplished and what resources (time and money) are required to make the change. The IT department should also propose a way to test the change to ensure it is working as designed. The IT department then forwards the request, along with this assessment, to either the company's controller or CFO, who must approve the change. After the approval is granted, the IT department effects the change, performs the testing, and usually has the original requestor also accept the result.

Some routine changes may be initiated by the IT department. For instance, say the IT department notices that the server hosting the company's accounting system is getting low on disk space. The IT department would recommend that additional disk drives be installed in the server, the costs of doing so, and how any risks will be managed. The controller or CFO then approves the change before it is effected.

The company should consider whether or not to allow emergency changes to the in-scope systems. An emergency change would typically be a hardware failure that can be quickly resolved, such as a failed disk drive in a RAID 5 array or a video card that simply needs to be replaced. The change control procedure may allow the IT department to make defined emergency changes to the system, and then document them immediately after the fact. However, this would need to be negotiated and agreed upon by the IT department and the finance or accounting department.

SOX Compliance Testing

Once a company's system of internal controls is built and implemented, the job is far from over. For one thing, most organizations find that they need to adjust their internal controls after they have run them for a while. Perhaps the company decides to add some new controls in response to an event that highlights a previously unrealized risk, or maybe the company overdid its initial SOX compliance by implementing too many controls and needs to slacken them a bit. However, the real work in maintaining a system of internal controls is in auditing the controls.

Auditing Internal Controls

To show dilligence, companies must demonstrate that their controls are effective and that they are being followed by their employees. This means that the controls need to be tested on a periodic basis.

For each control in a system of internal controls, the company should develop a test that verifies that the control is working. For example, say your company has a control that mandates that users of the accounting system cannot access the AP functions unless they are an AP operator or manager. A test for such a control might have two aspects:

- A listing of the permissions in the accounting system should show which users have which permissions, and an examination of this list should show that no one who is not an AP employee has access to the AP system. The listing would become part of the testing evidence file, and a manager in an appropriate position in accounting or IT (or both) would review it and sign it to document that he reviewed it and found no inappropriate permissions.

- An auditor may ask one or two employees who do not work in AP to try to get into the AP system. Most systems will produce some kind of error message if an unauthorized access is attempted. The auditor would take a screenshot of the "access denied" message, initial and date it, and include it within the test file.

The frequency of the tests will vary depending on what is being tested. For example, a test for a control that requires the IT department to follow the written backup procedure regularly may be tested only annually, but a test that general ledger accruals are being done properly might be conducted quarterly. It's usually up to the company's controller and internal audit staff, perhaps with feedback from the external auditors, to devise a schedule that makes the most sense.

Sometimes testing is done on all cases of a particular procedure, and sometimes only a subset is tested. If there were only three changes to an accounting system over the year, and the change control process is being tested, it would make sense to examine each change control document. On the other hand, if a control applied to every purchase order the company generated, and the company generates 10,000 purchase orders every year, then a subset would be tested. A testing subset may be a random selection, or it may be only the most expensive orders. The auditors will determine what sort of testing should be done.

Deviations from Internal Controls

Since we're all human, and since the designers of internal controls cannot anticipate all possible events that may impact a particular control, it is certain that occasionally there will be deviations between written procedures and what was actually done. Perhaps a key employee was sick, and her replacement didn't realize that some particular task needed to be performed, or perhaps an employee wasn't properly trained on a procedure.

I like to say "there are only two kinds of people in a regulated company: those who have deviated, and those who will deviate." Deviations from management systems such as internal controls should be expected. What is important is that the deviations are detected (perhaps by a downstream control or from an audit), and that some form of cause and risk analysis is performed, and that corrective action was taken and documented.

The point is that a good system of internal controls should have as one of its components a procedure for handling deviations and corrective actions.

Sample SOPs

Following are some examples of IT procedures that come from a small public company that stood up to repeated testing by both large and small audit firms. Certainly, your company's procedures will and should be different, but the following examples should give you a sense of effective IT procedures.

Disaster Recovery Plan

GENERIC COMPANY, INC.

IT Documentation

TITLE: Disaster Recovery Plan

Document #:	IT-002 v3	Effective Date:	12/1/09
Issued by:	IT Department	Page Number:	1 of 4

Approvals:

IT Department: Date

Controller or CFO: Date

1) **PURPOSE**

    a) This document describes the actions, resources, and priorities to pursue to restore key IT services when a disaster causes the company's computing resources to become unavailable. The plan is intended to minimize further losses and business impacts in the event of a disaster.

    b) The objectives of the plan include:

        i) Assist in maintaining business continuity during a disaster

        ii) Protect data integrity and ensure system survivability

        iii) Restore the data processing function as quickly as possible

        iv) Satisfy audit and legal requirements

2) **SCOPE**

    a) This Disaster Recovery Plan was written specifically for recovering the IT infrastructure for which IT has primary responsibility, located at the Generic Company headquarters building. It does not cover the recovery of data processing infrastructure located at any other company location(s).

    b) The plan covers the restoration of the software and historical data for applications resident on servers for which IT has primary responsibility. This does not include the business continuity or contingency plans for which the business units are responsible. While IT is not responsible for the development or implementation of these business continuity plans or contingency plans, IT will assist with the implementation of these plans as required.

3) **RESPONSIBILITIES**

    a) The IT department is responsible for issuing this document, reviewing it annually, and issuing new versions as appropriate.

    b) The Controller or CFO is responsible for reviewing and approving any new versions of this document.

4) DEFINITIONS

   a) Disaster: An event, whether man-made or natural, that unexpectedly inhibits the company's ability to operate or deprives the company of access to its key business systems.

   b) Major disaster: An event that substantially destroys computing and data infrastructure that the company requires to operate. Examples include a fire in the server room, a large earthquake, a major structural failure of the company's building, flooding of interior spaces in the building that impact IT resources, and so forth.

   c) Minor disaster: A short-term disruption of the company's ability to access its key business systems. Examples include the loss of a critical data file (whether through systems failure or accident), a power outage, or a temporary operating problem in the computing chain of a key business system.

   d) Remediation plan: A plan developed to remediate the key effects of a given major disaster. The remediation plan includes necessary objectives, timelines, cost estimates, and acceptance criteria.

5) PROCEDURES

   a) Pre-disaster planning:

      i) The IT department will maintain a list of hardware resources on which key business resources reside and their necessary configurations. This list will be reviewed annually and updated as necessary, and is attached to this document as Attachment IT-002-A.

      ii) The IT department will maintain a list of software resources on which key or important business processes rely, including vendor contact data, account numbers, and any related serial or product ID numbers. This list will be reviewed annually and updated as necessary, and is attached to this document as Attachment IT-002-B.

      iii) The IT department will set up a backup and off-site storage plan that minimizes the risk of loss of data in the event of a disaster. The details of the backup and off-site storage plan will be reviewed annually and updated as necessary, and is attached to this document as Attachment IT-002-C.

   b) Testing:

      i) The IT department will annually test the ability of all backup systems to successfully restore data. The general procedure is as follows:

         (1) Select a recently created piece of backup media.

         (2) Using the backup software with which the media was created, haphazardly select several files that are normally unchanging

(such as program binary files) and restore those files to a test directory on the system's hard disk.

    (a) If the backup software is unable to restore the selected files, this constitutes a failure of this test.

(3) At the command prompt, use the FC.EXE program (file compare), or any other program that can perform bitwise comparisons of files, to compare the restored files to the on-disk live versions.

    (a) Any bitwise errors encountered constitute a failure of this test.

(4) If any failures are encountered:

    (a) The IT department will notify the relevant parties for the affected server and backup system (for example, the Controller and CFO if the error is on the server that holds the accounting system).

    (b) The IT department will develop and implement a plan to repair the error. This repair will be treated as an emergency and resolved as quickly as possible. The IT department will work with the server vendor, the maker of the tape drive, and/or the provider of the backup software to assess and resolve the error, as appropriate.

(5) The annual test and its outcome will be documented in each system's server log book.

c) Major disaster remediation:

  i) In the event of a major disaster, the head of IT will be notified immediately.

  ii) The head of IT will assess the scope and extent of the major disaster as it pertains to the company's key business systems and other important computing resources.

  iii) The head of IT will notify the following personnel of the initial IT assessment, as appropriate:

    (1) CEO

    (2) CFO

    (3) Controller

    (4) Head of Research

    (5) Head of Human Resources

    (6) Head of Development

  iv) The head of IT will develop a detailed remediation plan to address the specific disaster conditions.

(1) The remediation plan will prioritize recovery efforts in the following order:

    (a) Accounting system and data

    (b) Payroll system and data

    (c) Stock administration system and data

    (d) Systems to support regulatory and development activities

    (e) Systems to support research activities

    (f) Systems to support corporate and general computing needs

(2) The remediation plan will include estimated timelines and costs.

(3) Each affected department will determine testing procedures and acceptance criteria for the recovered operations, and is responsible for testing recovered operations and accepting or rejecting them.

d) The CEO is responsible for approving the remediation plan and ensuring that appropriate resources are made available for carrying it out.

e) The head of IT will update the CEO and affected departments of the status of the remediation efforts on a regular basis until the remediation is complete.

6) ATTACHMENTS

a) Attachment IT-002-A: Hardware list and configurations

b) Attachment IT-002-B: Software license list

c) Attachment IT-002-C: Backup and off-site tape storage

Server Maintenance

GENERIC COMPANY, INC.

IT Documentation

TITLE: Network Server Maintenance

Procedure #:	IT-003 V3	Effective Date:	12/1/09
Issued by:	IT Department	Page Number:	1 of 2

1) PURPOSE

a) To define Generic's procedure for performing regular maintenance on all network servers and to document any problems or observations that may arise in between regular maintenance visits.

2) **SCOPE**

    a) This procedure applies to the Generic network system server's hardware and software.

3) **REFERENCES**

    a) IT-001, IT Organization and Systems

    b) IT-FR-003, Generic Network Server Maintenance Electronic Log form

4) **RESPONSIBILITIES**

    a) Generic's IT department is responsible for preparation of this SOP.

    b) Generic's IT department is responsible for the execution of the server maintenance plan.

    c) Generic's IT department is responsible for reviewing the server logs as part of the regular maintenance.

    d) Generic's IT management is responsible for the approval of this plan and annual review of the server log books.

5) **DEFINITIONS**

    a) Network server: Computer and its software serving as a file or print server, or various other roles in the network, as documented in document IT-001. Examples include mail server, database server, DHCP server, accounting system server, etc.

6) **PROCEDURES**

    a) Each month as soon as practicable on a weekend following the second Tuesday of each month, maintenance tasks will be performed on each of the network servers and the administration workstation.

    b) The maintenance tasks will be documented on the electronic form IT-FR-003 as they are performed. This form is saved to the IT group folder on the company network.

    c) The following describes additional details used in the performance of the tasks listed on form IT-FR-003.

        i) Windows Update will be run on all servers and then the servers are restarted to test functionality.

        ii) All server event logs are reviewed for the prior month. Any errors that indicate a problem that requires remediation are noted on form IT-FR-003.

        iii) Each server (except server GCX) is configured to perform a disk defragmentation automatically on its main disk drive once a month. GCX is manually defragmented as part of the monthly maintenance.

    d) Any significant hardware or software errors will be documented on the IT-FR-003 form and in the server's log book. "Significant error" is nontransient and is one that represents a problem that needs correcting.

e) Each server will have a log book that will be used to document any reported problems or adverse

f) event observations made during visits to the server room by any IT staff member or system administrator. The log books are used to document errors that are discovered outside routine monthly maintenance, and for any configuration changes to each server or its key applications.

g) The server log books will be reviewed annually by IT management.

7) ATTACHMENT

a) Attachment IT-FR-003: "Generic Network Server Maintenance Electronic Log Form"

System Account Management

GENERIC COMPANY, INC.

IT Documentation

TITLE: SYSTEM ACCOUNT MANAGEMENT

Document #:	IT-005 V4	Effective Date:	12/1/09
Issued by:	IT Department	Page Number:	1 of 5

1) PURPOSE

a) To define Generic's procedures regarding user account management for the Generic network.

2) SCOPE

a) This procedure applies to the Generic computer system and administrative and user accounts for use on that system.

3) RESPONSIBILITIES

a) Generic's IT department is responsible for preparation of this SOP.

b) Generic's IT department is responsible for administering the accounts for the Generic computer system (i.e., system administrator).

c) Generic's IT management is responsible for approving this procedure.

d) The relevant department manager is responsible for approval of access and denial of access privileges, as indicated on the Employee Information Profile form and the Employee Departure form.

e) The Controller or CFO is responsible for annually reviewing user access within the accounting system.

4) **REFERENCES**

   a) Employee Information Profile form

   b) Employee Departure form

5) **DEFINITIONS**

   a) User account: An account on a computer or network server that authenticates a user to access certain resources on the computer or network server.

   b) Administrative account: An account on a computer or network server, similar to a user account, that authenticates the system's administrator(s) and gives them system permissions necessary to administer the system.

   c) Username: The plain-text readable name of the account being used.

   d) Password: A sequence of letters and/or numbers, determined by the user and known only to that user, that is used to confirm the user's identity to the system.

   e) Log in: The act of providing a username and password to an authenticating computer system for the purpose of receiving system permission to access resources.

   f) Security groups: Collections of users grouped together to make the task of administering the system's security easier and more logical.

   g) Secured resource: A resource located on a computer, such as a directory, file, or printer, which can be accessed or used only by accounts or groups authorized by the system administrator.

   h) Nonobvious password: A password that cannot be readily guessed by others. Common password components to avoid include the user's name or any portion thereof; family member, friend, or pet names or any portion thereof; and any word, date, or number associated with the user and potentially known to others.

   i) Home directory: A private folder created for each user with a drive letter designation of H:. This folder is for use by the system to hold system settings for that user, as well as for the user to store documents that are accessible only by that employee or the system administrators.

6) **PROCEDURES**

   a) Every individual who accesses the Generic computer system will be given a private account with which to access the system.

   b) When a new account is needed for access to the system (either by a new employee or any other party that needs to access the Generic computer system), an Employee Profile form will be generated for that account.

   c) The completed form is signed by the responsible manager and submitted to the IT department.

d) Significant changes in privileges (such as when an employee moves to a different job within the company) must be initiated by the completion of a new Employee Information Profile form and signed by the responsible manager.

   i) After the account is created, the Employee Information Profile form is signed by the IT staff member who performed the changes.

   ii) Completed Employee Information Profile forms will be maintained by the IT department.

e) Accounts are created and maintained using standard administrative tools on the system for which they are created. For example, creating a Windows network account uses the standard programs and procedures specified by Microsoft, creating an accounting system account follows the procedures outlined by its vendor, and so forth.

f) Accounting system annual review

   i) Once a year, the Controller or CFO will review all user accounts and their access to accounting functions by reviewing a current printout of user account information and menu security assignments prepared by the IT department.

   ii) The Controller or CFO will note any changes needed to user group assignment or menu security and will forward a list of changes to the IT department.

   iii) The IT department will make the security changes in the accounting system as indicated by the Controller or CFO.

   iv) If no changes are necessary, the printout of the user accounts and their access to the accounting system menu functions will be signed and dated by the Controller or CFO and retained as internal control documentation.

7) **POLICY**

a) The password policy for Generic is as follows:

   i) For the Generic network:

   (1) Must be no less than eight characters long.

   (2) Passwords must conform to the Microsoft Windows Network password "complexity rules." The complexity rules state that a password must include at least one character from three of the four following groups:

   (i) Uppercase alpha (A–Z)

   (ii) Lowercase alpha (a–z)

   (iii) Numeric (0–9)

   (iv) Special characters (!@#$, etc.)

(3) The system will force a password change once per year automatically. Users may change their passwords more frequently if required or desired.

(4) The system maintains a password history and will not allow users to use the same password for five changes.

(5) The system maintains an "account lockout policy" which will lock any account after eight invalid attempts within any 30-minute period. The account can be unlocked only by an IT system administrator.

(6) Special logins and passwords are set for certain computers in the building. These logins are restricted to be usable only from those computers, and are used for specific purposes (such as using a computer connected to a laboratory instrument, or using one of the presentation computers). These accounts are further secured with limited access to the network. These accounts are not subject to the normal password policy settings, but instead use a password assigned by the IT department, and those passwords are known to a number of employees and are not required to be changed.

ii) For the accounting system:

(1) Accounting system accounts are secured with an accounting system-specific username and password.

(2) The accounting system will force a password change every 90 days on all of its accounts. Users will be instructed to choose nonobvious passwords, although the accounting system has no facility to ensure the length or complexity of passwords.

b) User responsibilities:

i) All users must not share their passwords or security codes with anyone, including with administrators of the system and their management.

ii) All users will make reasonable efforts to conceal their passwords or security codes.

iii) All users will not ask others for the use of their password or security code.

iv) If users lose or forget their password, the administrator will assign a new, temporary password for them, and will set their account so that they are prompted to select a new private password at their first login.

v) Each user is responsible for logging off, shutting down or locking his or her computer at the end of each business day.

c) When a user leaves the company:

i) Human Resources and the appropriate supervisor will complete the Employee Departure form, indicating date of departure and any special considerations as specified in the form.

ii) In the case of a standard departure, Human Resources and will give the completed Employee Departure form to the IT department. The IT department will disable all appropriate accounts and handle any special considerations, as specified on the form, at the close of business on the last day of employment for that employee.

iii) In the case of a priority termination, all accounts held by the affected user will be disabled immediately.

iv) Upon completion of the termination and prior to the deletion of accounts or data, the Special Considerations section of the form will be reviewed to see if prior approval of deletions is required.

v) Completed Employee Departure forms will be maintained by the IT department

---

Change Control

GENERIC COMPANY, INC.

IT Documentation

TITLE: Accounting System Change Control

Document #: IT-006 v3	Effective Date: 12/1/09
Issued by: IT Department	Page Number: 1 of 3

1) **PURPOSE**

   a) Sets forth policies relating to program or direct database changes to the accounting system, its server, or its backup software used at Generic.

   b) Sets forth procedures to follow to request, review, approve, and test changes to the accounting system, its server, or its backup software at Generic.

2) **SCOPE**

   a) This document applies to the accounting system installed at Generic's headquarters.

3) **RESPONSIBILITIES**

   a) The IT department is responsible for generation and annual review and update of this document.

   b) The Controller or CFO is responsible for approving this document and any subsequent changes.

   c) Each requestor of a change is responsible for completing a change request form and submitting it to the IT department.

d) The IT department member responsible for maintenance of the accounting system is responsible for reviewing change request forms, investigating methods of making changes, estimating effort hours or direct costs involved in making the proposed change, and proposing a test plan for the changes. The IT department member will then forward the request with the completed information to the Controller or CFO.

e) The Controller or CFO is responsible for reviewing each change request form and approving it. The approved change request is then submitted to the IT project manager for the change.

f) The IT project manager for the change informs the Controller or CFO and the requestor once the change and any associated testing are complete.

g) The IT department is responsible for storing completed change request forms and making them available as appropriate to auditors.

4) **DEFINITIONS**

a) Program change: A change in a program that makes up the system. Program changes can be vendor-supplied updates or fixes, or changes to programs developed and maintained by Generic.

b) Emergency change: A change required to remediate a processing or reporting error within any part of the system, or to remediate an error that makes the system unavailable to users.

c) Direct database change: A programmatic change to the data within the accounting system database. Direct database changes bypass controls within the accounting system.

d) Server change: A change to the server computer's hardware, operating system software, or backup software.

5) **POLICIES**

a) All changes to any of the programs that make up the accounting system will be performed only within this document's procedures.

b) Direct database changes must be performed within this document's procedures.

c) Server changes must be performed within this document's procedures, except for routine maintenance changes. Routine maintenance changes include application of patches for the operating system, review and saving of server operating system log files, performance of routine changes using the system's built-in tools (such as adding a user or adjusting user permissions), and so forth. Routine changes and activities are described in IT-003.

d) Emergency changes can be performed prior to documentation; however, emergency changes must be documented afterwards using the Accounting System Change Control form and signed off and stored. Documentation of emergency changes must be completed within 30 days of the emergency change.

6) PROCEDURES

a) A user of the accounting system who desires a change to the system will complete a copy of form IT-FR-006. This form should be submitted electronically. (The IT department can also initiate change requests as appropriate.)

    i) The user should clearly describe the change desired. When appropriate, he or she should include mock-ups of the desired change. For example, when requesting a new report, the requestor should mock up how the report should look when done.

    ii) The requestor then forwards the IT-FR-006 form to the IT department member responsible for maintaining the accounting system.

b) An IT department Project Manager will be designated. Typically, this will be the individual responsible for maintaining the accounting system.

c) The IT Project Manager will review the change request and any attached examples or illustrations, and will analyze the requested change, including:

    i) Viability

    ii) Sources of appropriate existing data in the system

    iii) Capability of in-house personnel to perform the change or availability of external personnel to carry out the change

    iv) Impacts to integrity of system data or other system programs

    v) Impacts to system security

    vi) Impacts to disaster recovery procedures

    vii) Testing and acceptance procedure(s), including pseudocode when testing will be primarily programmatic

    viii) Estimating effort hours and/or direct costs to perform the change and testing

    ix) Estimating available schedule

d) The IT Project Manager will then print the form and associated information, sign it, and forward to the Controller or CFO.

e) The Controller or CFO is responsible for reviewing each change request form and approving it. The approved change request is returned to the IT Project Manager.

f) The IT Project Manager will then initiate the change and will oversee the change through to completion, which includes testing and acceptance of the change as described in the IT-FR-006 form. The IT-FR-006 change form is then stored by the IT department along with any associated documentation.

Index

Q

R